WOMEN
AND POLITICS

PATHS TO POWER AND POLITICAL INFLUENCE

FOURTH EDITION

JULIE DOLAN
MACALESTER COLLEGE

MELISSA DECKMAN
WASHINGTON COLLEGE

MICHELE L. SWERS
GEORGETOWN UNIVERSITY

ROWMAN & LITTLEFIELD
Lanham • Boulder • New York • London

Executive Editor: Traci Crowell
Editorial Assistant: Deni Remsberg
Executive Marketing Manager: Amy Whitaker
Interior Designer: Rosanne Schloss
Cover Designer: Sarah Marizan

Credits and acknowledgments for material borrowed from other sources, and reproduced with permission, appear on the appropriate page within the text.

Published by Rowman & Littlefield
An imprint of The Rowman & Littlefield Publishing Group, Inc.
4501 Forbes Boulevard, Suite 200, Lanham, Maryland 20706
www.rowman.com

6 Tinworth Street, London SE11 5AL, United Kingdom

British Library Cataloguing in Publication Information Available

Library of Congress Cataloging-in-Publication Data
Names: Dolan, Julie, author. | Deckman, Melissa M. (Melissa Marie), 1971– author. | Swers, Michele L., author.
Title: Woman and politics : paths to power and political influence / Julie Dolan, Macalester College, Melissa M. Deckman, Washington College, Michele L. Swers, Georgetown University.
Description: Fourth edition. | Lanham : Rowman & Littlefield, [2020] | Includes bibliographical references and index.
Identifiers: LCCN 2019017377 (print) | LCCN 2019020843 (ebook) | ISBN 9781538122310 (electronic) | ISBN 9781538122297 (cloth : alk. paper) | ISBN 9781538122303 (pbk. : alk. paper)
Subjects: LCSH: Women—Political activity—United States.
Classification: LCC HQ1236.5.U6 (ebook) | LCC HQ1236.5.U6 D635 2020 (print) | DDC 320.082/0973—dc23
LC record available at https://lccn.loc.gov/2019017377

♾™ The paper used in this publication meets the minimum requirements of American National Standard for Information Sciences—Permanence of Paper for Printed Library Materials, ANSI/NISO Z39.48-1992.

Brief Contents

Contents

Figures and Tables

FIGURES

TABLES

Preface

◆ ◆ ◆

AS GRADUATE STUDENTS IN THE MID-1990s, all three of us began studying women and politics. At that point, there was much excellent scholarship to guide us but certainly a manageable and seemingly finite amount. What we could not have known then is just how tremendously the field would grow in a relatively short period of time. In the past two and a half decades, the field has witnessed a virtual explosion of scholarship. One of our primary aims in writing this book is to synthesize and make accessible to a wider audience the vast amount of scholarly research on women as political actors and especially as political elites in the United States.

NEW TO THE 4TH EDITION

In our 4th edition of *Women & Politics: Paths to Power and Political Influence*, readers will see some significant changes, although we kept much material that we believe is essential to an understanding of women's role in American politics. As this edition goes to press, record numbers of women were successful in the 2018 midterm elections—Nancy Pelosi serves as Speaker of the House, and multiple women are running to secure the Democratic nomination for the 2020 presidential race.

These successes for women in politics, however, come after the high profile 2016 defeat of the first woman to be nominated for president by one of the major political parties, Hillary Clinton, to political newcomer and reality-star businessman, Donald J. Trump. The 2016 presidential campaign itself served as a reminder of how gendered our politics can be, with Trump, in particular, running what some called a campaign rife with toxic masculinity. His election spawned a massive political resistance movement. Indeed, the day after his inauguration, women across the United

States and in multiple countries across the globe staged one of the largest protests for women's rights in American history. Our cover shot, in fact, shows a diverse range of women of all ages flooding the streets during one of those marches in Washington, D.C. In the two years that have followed the Women's March, women continue to actively engage in politics as voters, political activists, and increasingly as elected officials with more women than ever running for and winning political office at all levels.

The ascendance of women in American politics in recent years has spawned much research in the area of gender and politics, with scholars expanding the field of women and political campaign research more generally, incorporating experimental research and assessing women's political candidacies in the twenty-first century as a new crop of women candidates—candidates that are more ethnically and ideologically diverse than ever before—seek political office. Yet, even with the recent electoral success, women remain drastically underrepresented across the nation's governing bodies. In this 4th edition of our book, we delve more deeply into the question of why women remain so underrepresented in political office—while also examining the factors that led a record number of women to seek office in 2018. We include two separate chapters about women as political candidates: one that focuses on why women are still far less likely than men to run for political office and another that considers women's experiences on the campaign trail, including new research about Hillary Clinton's failed presidential bid. We highlight a growing body of scholarship that digs deeper into the voting decisions of women voters, paying particular attention to differences in voting behavior among women based on race, ethnicity, and class. We examine how President Trump's explicit appeals to masculinity and his gendered attacks on Hillary Clinton impacted voting behavior in a way that differed from previous presidential contests and will reverberate in future elections. Some studies suggest, for example, that Trump was successful in stoking sexist and racial resentment among some women voters, particularly among the white working class. Other analyses show that Democratic candidates continue to appeal increasingly to younger, and more racially and ethnically diverse voters—particularly women.

In addition to the fascinating new work on women running for office and women as voters, our textbook considers the new scholarly work being done on women in legislatures, both in Congress and at the state level. We also consider newer works on women in state legislative bodies and summarize several excellent new studies on women in city politics and in other local governments as well. Since our last edition came out, President Trump nominated two men to the Supreme Court, in the wake of the late Justice Antonin Scalia's passing and Justice Anthony Kennedy's retirement in 2018. In both cases, Trump nominated conservative, white men. As we detail in this book, his nomination of US appellate judge Brett Kavanaugh to the Supreme Court, in particular, drew national attention because of sexual misconduct charges that emerged against him during the confirmation process. Another big story for women's representation that has been underreported, however, is that the Trump administration stands to appoint far fewer women to the federal bench than any of his predecessors. As the American population grows more racially and ethnically diverse, we examine the increasing presence of women of color in elected office, the bureaucracy, and in the judiciary. We devote special attention to the intersection of gender and race in our analysis, building on scholarship that argues for simultaneously examining the ways in which multiple facets of women's identities shape their political behavior.

We take stock of all of these developments and more as we continue to consider women's representation as an overriding theme. Each chapter investigates how questions of representation have shaped our understanding of women's paths to power, their contributions to politics and governance, and their influence. In the beginning of each chapter we present a recent narrative involving women and politics, such as Supreme Court Justice Sonia Sotomayor's controversial comments that a "wise Latina" would make a better judge than a white male, or the decision by Ashley Bennett, an African American health-care worker, millennial, and first-time candidate, to challenge her county official in New Jersey after he mocked the women who participated in the Women's March on his Facebook page by joking that he hoped they would be back home to cook dinner. Each of these narrative vignettes is designed to give the reader a sense of some of the key questions for discussion and debate to be raised in the chapter.

Chapter 1 introduces our theoretical framework, with a focus on political representation—a concept that is central to the study of American politics. By reviewing some classic works on representation, we consider how women fit into this narrative, as our notion of representation and whose interests should be included in politics have changed over time. We also consider how women's diversity in terms of race, ethnicity, sexual orientation and ideology raises questions as to *which* women best represent women's interests. How these themes played out in the 2018 midterm elections is also given special attention.

In chapter 2, we build on our rich history of women's involvement in social movements, including the suffrage movement that resulted in securing women's right to vote and the fight to pass an Equal Rights Amendment to the Constitution. We detail women's renewed engagement in women's rights activism since 2016, including the Women's March and the #MeToo movement. We devote additional attention to the particular role played by African American women in the suffrage and civil rights movements as well as the second wave of the feminist movement. This edition also includes greater discussion of intersectionality and the challenges faced by women of color in the feminist movement of the 1960s and 1970s as well as within the contemporary Women's March and the #MeToo movement.

Chapter 3 updates students about the gender gap in American politics, incorporating data from the 2016 presidential and 2018 midterm elections on women's voting patterns, while examining various issues that explain voting differences between men and women. Although female voters on the whole preferred Hillary Clinton to Donald Trump in 2016, white women were the least supportive of all racial groups. This edition examines the factors that contributed to Clinton's loss, including the role of "hostile sexism" among women and men. We also consider how the two major political parties court the women's vote in elections, including attempts by Democrats to characterize Republicans as engaged in a "war on women" with their stances on women's rights, and the GOP's response to such claims. We also consider whether the gender gap brings women political power.

Chapter 4 analyzes the factors that shape women's decisions to run—or not run—for elected office. Building on the three most common explanations for why women run less for office less often than men and noting the historic surge in female candidates, this updated chapter draws on interviews with more than 50 female congressional candidates running in 2018 to determine what changed to inspire so many to run. We also pay greater attention to the diversity of women's experiences, including new discussion of women's intersecting identities and how those shape their decisions to run.

We turn our attention to women's experiences on the campaign trail in chapter 5, updating our discussion to emphasize how race and gender intersect to shape these experiences, including the raced and gendered stereotypes voters apply to their candidacies and the ways in which female candidates are framed in media stories. The chapter also discusses the ways in which female candidates may have benefited from the political climate in 2018 and used the climate to highlight their gender. Finally, the chapter covers Carly Fiorina and Hillary Clinton's 2016 presidential campaigns, examining the ways in which both women navigated gender on the campaign trail.

Given that women are more likely to serve in local office than others, chapter 6 examines women's involvement in local government and grassroots politics. We examine women in local elected office, both as elected executives and as part of local legislatures such as city councils and school boards, and consider whether service in such local offices serve as political stepping-stones for higher office for women. We also consider whether women pursue different policies or govern differently at this level of government compared with men, incorporating new scholarship on women in city politics. Finally, we profile young women making a difference in their communities, whether fighting against police brutality in the Black Lives Matter movement, climate change in local environmental organizations, and gun violence as part of the Never Again Movement, first begun by the survivors of the mass shooting at Marjory Stoneman Douglas High School.

Chapter 7 provides an overview of the most recent political research on women's roles as legislators in Congress and the fifty states. We examine what it means for representation of group interests when women are consistently underrepresented in these bodies. We highlight changes in the type of women serving in Congress and the state legislatures including the expanding racial, ethnic, and ideological diversity among female legislators. The chapter analyzes the policy impact of women in office, paying special attention to how women's priorities are shaped by their party affiliation, ideology, racial and ethnic identity, and constituent opinion. As Congress and the state legislatures become more polarized, we look at the role women play within their parties, including how Democratic and Republican women utilize their gender to help their parties court the women's vote. Special attention is given to the new class of women legislators elected to Congress, who represent the most racially, religiously, and ethnically diverse group yet.

Turning to the executive branch, chapter 8 examines the challenges that women face in governing while serving in what scholars often describe as the most masculine of the three branches of government, particularly in certain departments such as the Department of Defense. With respect to the military, we focus on how the issue of sexual assault—an issue of particular importance to women—is being addressed and how women are helping to frame this debate. We pay particular attention to the appointment of women to presidential administrations and their impact on policy and governance. We also provide updated numbers about women serving in federal, state, and local government administrative positions, demonstrating that women's access to these positions is often shaped by glass ceiling and glass walls: women are least well represented at the highest rungs of these organizations and tend to have the greatest career success in agencies and departments that deal in feminine issue areas. In addition to the bureaucracy, we consider women's success as governors in American history. Despite making gains in the 2018 elections, only nine women serve as governors. In addition, nearly half of the states have never elected a woman to the governor's mansion, suggesting our masculine notions of leadership are particularly persistent at the executive level.

Finally, we consider women's role in the judiciary in chapter 9, providing readers with the most recent data concerning the appointment of women in both federal and state courts. We discuss scholarship that examines the gendered dimensions to Supreme Court appointments in an age in which race and gender now permeate the debate over nominees—and we discuss the controversy over Donald Trump's second nominee to the Supreme Court, Brett Kavanaugh. We provide an overview of the latest research by political scientists that evaluate the factors that explain why women are better represented as judges in some courts than others, with special attention given to research that considers how intersectionality impacts judicial behavior. We conclude with an assessment of why having more women on the bench matters in terms of democratic legitimacy.

Acknowledgments

◆ ◆ ◆

WE HAVE MANY PEOPLE TO THANK for their support and assistance. We owe a tremendous debt of gratitude to the extraordinary community of women and politics scholars. In fact, the idea for this book was born over the period of a few years at the Midwest Political Science Association's annual conference, where, for many years, the women and politics panels have been both inspiring and excellent. Without the incredible community of women and politics scholars presenting papers at the Midwest and other political science conferences or writing books and articles, and otherwise advancing the state of knowledge in the field, this book simply would not have been possible. The study of women and politics has grown terrifically in the last two decades and we are grateful to be part of the discussion.

Further, there are a number of individuals who have gone above and beyond to help us along the way. We would especially like to thank three senior scholars and pioneers in the field: Peggy Conway, Karen O'Connor, and Marian Lief Palley. All three of these women have written extensively about women and politics, and each of us has used their texts in preparing and teaching our own women and politics courses. We admire them as scholars, mentors, and teachers. We have all benefited from their guidance, advice, support, and friendship along the way. In fact, we owe special thanks to Karen O'Connor for bringing the three of us together and for introducing us to Peggy and Marian. We cannot express how grateful we are to be able to work with such extraordinary women.

New to this edition, we add our most heartfelt thanks to more than 50 female congressional candidates who graciously agreed to be interviewed about their stories, experiences, and perspectives about running for office in 2018. Each and every one of them had a remarkable and inspiring story to share, and we hope to see their continued engagement in public life moving forward. We are also tremendously grateful to fellow political scientist Paru Shah, who proved an ideal collaborator in conducting these interviews. Not only is she a first-rate political scientist, but a wonderfully insightful and supportive friend and colleague. We also thank Barbara Palmer for sharing her cutting-edge research, advice, and sense of humor with us over the years and Alana Jeydel, who provided much appreciated advice at the start of the project. The authors are also grateful to the principal coinvestigators of the American Municipal Officeholder Survey, Adam Dynes, Daniel Butler, Hans Hassell and Michelle Torres, for sharing their data to be used in this 4th edition of the book. We thank Mirya Holman and Emily Farris for sharing their data on women sheriffs. We also thank Irin Carmon and Shana Knizhnik for allowing us to reprint the fabulous cover of their book on Ruth Bader Ginsburg, *Notorious RBG*. Berna Oztekin-Gunaydin, Senior Analyst at the International City/County Management Association, graciously provided us updated data on the number of women serving in local councils, which we feature in chapter 6.

The three of us would also like to thank the students in our women and politics courses, who have served as our inspiration and sounding board for years. In particular, Julie Dolan would like to thank her Spring 2015 Women and Politics students at Macalester College, including Annie Gurvis, Eleanor Fuqua, Darwin Forsyth, Jake Greenberg, Gabriella Gillespie, Isabella Soparkar, and Mariah Sitler. Several individuals also served as excellent research assistants over the last few years including Roxanne Fisher, Rose Allen, Patrick Blomgren, Isabella Soparkar, Lucas Smith, and Ashley Dunn from Macalester College, Kelli Baker from Georgetown, and Caitlin Steele, Victoria Venable, and Kelley Gardner from Washington College. In previous editions, we benefited from the assistance of a number of highly talented, dedicated, and capable research assistants, including Alix Heard, Kate Henningsen, Laura Dziorny, Erin O'Connor, Waffiyah Mian, Michele Parvinsky, Carin Larson, and Shauna Shames at Georgetown University; Jonathan Kropf, Elizabeth Durney, Kara Bovee, Kellan Anfinson, Egle Tamosaityte, Andy Haug, Patrick McGarrity, and Ben Garnett at Macalester College; and Christy Rowan, Tracey Stewart, Becky Binns, and Martin Dunphy at Washington College. Melissa Deckman also wishes to thank her son, Mason, for help in updating figures in chapters 6 and 9 and Julie Dolan thanks her son, Oliver, for his assistance in navigating social media to track down female candidates from 2018.

Each of us would also like to extend the warmest thanks to a number of people at our respective institutions. We would like to thank our colleagues in the Departments of Political Science at Macalester College and Washington College and in the Department of Government at Georgetown University. We are very grateful for the supportive and collegial environments they provide. We continue to be excited to work with Rowman & Littlefield on this 4th edition and have found the enthusiasm and support for the project from Traci Crowell, our editor, and Mary Malley, assistant editor, to be remarkable. We would also like to thank the reviewers who provided comments and gave us feedback on the third edition of the textbook and helped to guide our revisions in this current edition: Allison D. Rank (SUNY Oswego), Catherine Connolly (University of Wyoming), Jaclyn J. Kettler (Boise State University), Jennie Sweet-Cushman (Chatham University), Judithanne Scourfield McLauchlan (University of South Florida, St. Petersburg), Natasha Nurse (Nassau Community College), Rebecca Evans (Ursinus College), and Rina Williams (University of Cincinnati).

Finally, we all three have amazing families to thank for their love and support. Each one of us is blessed with a wonderful husband (Bill Lee, Sean Fallon, and Andrew Todd Swers) and two amazing children (Oliver, Easton, Mason, Gavin, Alexander, and Lisa), and we cannot thank them enough for the constant joy and meaning they bring to our lives. Likewise, our extended families have provided years of support and love and we want to let them know how much we appreciate all they do for us: Glenys and Scott Dolan, Mildred Beltre, Sara and Phil Sanchez, TC, Lily and Ruby Lee, Lucy Wang, Jeff and Cathy Winter, Jack and Rose Cavanaugh, Lloyd and Diann Deckman, Andrew and Lesley Fallon, Fatma Jenkins, Theodore and Belle Probst, Arlene and Marvin Birnbaum, Ronald Swers, Jeffrey and Amy Swers, and forever in our hearts, Gwen and Shana Swers and Dennis Dolan.

About the Authors

JULIE DOLAN is Professor of Political Science at Macalester College. Her scholarly interests include American government and politics, women and politics, and bureaucratic politics. Her scholarship focuses especially on women in the public bureaucracies and in executive positions. Her scholarship appears in numerous journals, including *PS: Political Science and Politics*, *Public Administration Review*, the *Journal of Public Administration Research and Theory*, *Women & Politics*, and the *Harvard International Journal of Press/Politics*. She has received numerous grants and awards for her scholarship, including a National Science Foundation grant, the Erika Fairchild Award from the Southern Political Science Association, the Rita Mae Kelly Distinguished Research Award from the American Society for Public Administration, and a best dissertation award from the National Association of School of Public Affairs and Administration.

MELISSA DECKMAN is the Louis L. Goldstein Professor of Public Affairs and chair of the Political Science Department at Washington College. She also chairs the board and is an Affiliated Scholar of the Public Religion Research Institute (PRRI). Prof. Deckman's areas of specialty include gender, religion, and political behavior. She is the author of *Tea Party Women: Mama Grizzlies, Grassroots Leaders, and the Changing Face of the American Right* (NYU Press, 2016) in addition to several other books and more than a dozen scholarly articles. Her commentary on women, religion, and politics in American politics has appeared in the *Washington Post*, *Five Thirty Eight*, *Vox*, *Ms. Magazine* and the Brookings Fix-Gov blog, among other outlets. She was an expert contributor to the Center for American Women and Politics' Gender Watch Project at Rutgers University, which analyzed gender dynamics in American elections in 2018.

MICHELE L. SWERS is Professor of American Government at Georgetown University. Her research and teaching interests encompass Congress,

Congressional elections, and Women and Politics. She is the author of two books examining women's representation in Congress and their influence on policymaking, including *The Difference Women Make: The Policy Impact of Women in Congress* and *Women in the Club: Gender and Policy Making in the Senate*. Dr. Swers has written numerous articles and book chapters on women in Congress and women in elections as candidates and voters. Dr. Swers has provided expertise on Congressional policymaking and elections and the role of women in politics to media outlets, including *The News Hour*, *Washington Post*, *Vox*, *Roll Call*, *Politico*, and numerous national and state media outlets.

1

Introduction and
Theoretical Framework

◆ ◆ ◆

IN JULY 2016, HILLARY CLINTON MADE HISTORY by becoming the first woman ever to be nominated by a major party for the presidency. Yet less than four months later, Clinton conceded defeat to Donald Trump, dashing the hopes of many Americans who had dreamed of seeing the nation elect its first female president. The outlook for women in American politics at that point was downright grim for some. After seeing steady gains of women's representation in elected and appointed office at the state and federal level through the 1990s and the first decade of the 2000s, women's success in politics had stalled. For instance, women's representation as elected state legislators remained flat from 2009 to 2016, hovering at just around 24 percent (Center for American Women in Politics 2018). After the 2016 election, men still held roughly four out of five seats in Congress—a figure that had barely budged in several election cycles.

Yet, the day following Trump's inauguration on January 21, 2017, an outpouring of women's rights activists flooded the streets in Washington, DC and in sister marches held around the world to protest Trump's election, his misogynistic rhetoric, and his views about women's rights. By some estimates, more than 3 million Americans participated in these historic Women's Marches worldwide, making them among the most highly attended protests in American history (Silver 2017). Young women were a vital part of those marches and more recent analyses suggest that Trump's presidency has inspired a renewed effort by women of all ages to become involved in the political process, many for the first time. Women have become an important part of organized efforts to defeat Trump's supporters and policies at the federal and state level, taking a page from the Tea Party movement's earlier success in counteracting the Obama administration by forming grassroots organizations such as Indivisible (Deckman 2017). As Lara Putnam and Theda Skocpol (2018) document, college-educated, suburban women are largely responsible for leading many

1

of these efforts locally and, in doing so, are rebuilding America's social fabric and reinvigorating democracy.

Young women are defying historic trends by becoming more engaged in all sorts of political activism compared to young men—especially young women of color—with much of the activism being driven by their passion about gender equality (Deckman 2018a; Deckman and Shames 2018). The #MeToo movement, inspired by the early work of black civil rights activist Tarana Burke who initially coined the term in 2006, propelled millions of women and men who had been survivors of sexual harassment and assault to share their stories on social media in the wake of the downfall of many prominent men including Harvey Weinstein, Matt Lauer, Kevin Spacey, and Bill Cosby (Ohlheiser 2017). Its reach has also extended to politics, as dozens of legislators in Congress either stepped down or decided not to seek reelection in wake of sexual misconduct allegations in 2018 (Godfrey, Felton, and Hosking 2018).

Women have also made their mark as political candidates in reaction to the Trump era, with 2018 seeing a record number of women running for and winning elections nationally, as we detail more closely in chapter 4. For instance, in the US House of Representatives, the previous record of 298 female-filed candidacies was shattered in 2018, as 476 women sought a seat to Congress (Dittmar 2018a); similar jumps in the number of women running for state legislature also occurred and more women than ever ran for governor (Dittmar 2018b). While not all of these women were successful, the 2018 midterms resulted in women winning more seats in Congress and in state legislatures than ever before (Zhou 2018).

This election also saw several notable milestones for women in Congress, including the election of the nation's first Native American women (Deb Haaland and Sharice Davids), first Muslim women (Rashida Tlaib and Ilhan Omar), and the body's youngest women to ever serve (Alexandria Ocasio-Cortez and Abby Finknauer) (ibid.). Indeed, the diversity of women's candidacies in terms of race, ethnicity, and LGBTQ status is another remarkable story about 2018. The Reflective Democracy Campaign reports that the number of women of color in congressional general elections almost doubled from 4 percent of all candidates in 2016 to 7 percent in 2018; moreover, there has been a 75 percent increase in the number of women of color running in general elections since 2012 compared to a 36 percent increase of white women candidates during the same time period (Reflective Democracy Campaign 2018). Eight openly LGBTQ candidates were elected to Congress in 2018 as well, including Kyrsten Sinema, of Arizona, who became the first openly bisexual US senator (Victory Fund 2018). Additionally, a record number of female veterans began serving in Congress in 2019 (Mitchell 2018).

Another remarkable feature of this new crop of women candidates was the extent to which many of them embraced their status as women in their campaign messaging, which is far different from earlier eras, in which women candidates are often coached to downplay their more feminine traits or their status as women (Dittmar 2015). Dana Nessel, the new attorney general of the state of Michigan, won national attention for her first television ad, which ran right after the emergence of the #MeToo movement. Looking directly at the camera, Nessel told viewers that "we need more women in power," asking them, "Who can you trust most not to show you their penis in a professional setting? Is it the candidate who doesn't have a penis? I'd say so (quoted in Lessenberry 2017)." Other candidates shared their personal stories of overcoming sexual assault or facing sexual harassment in their professional lives, while not one, but two, gubernatorial candidates—Krish Vignarajah of Maryland and Kelda Roy of Wisconsin—even breastfeed their babies on camera in their political ads. Kelly Dittmar, a scholar with the Center for American Women and Politics at Rutgers, explains that such ads are important to start "disrupting the male, particularly white male, masculine norm of what it means to be in a campaign. I think that's what you're seeing in these ads, and I think it is really valuable" (Caygle 2018).

Democratic Michigan attorney general candidate Dana Nessel, who is openly gay, garnered national attention for her ad that raised awareness about sexual harassment in the midst of the #MeToo movement. Her ad ended with the tagline: "Yes, I'm a woman, That's not a liability, That's an asset." Nessel later won her race in November 2018. *Source*: Mandi Wright/TNS/Newscom.

In many ways, voters were more receptive to the idea of electing more women to office than ever before. Melissa Deckman (2018b), surveying voters in the summer of 2018, found that across a wide variety of issues, voters see women in elected office as either equally qualified as men or better able to handle the demands of political office—even on traditionally "masculine" issues such as law enforcement and foreign affairs, which is a contrast to surveys from previous eras. On gender issues, in particular, female political leaders had substantial advantages. For instance, 57 percent of respondents said women in elected office handle reproductive rights better, compared with 6 percent who said that men do. The divide was similar on sexual harassment, with 52 percent saying female politicians handle the issue better and just 11 percent favoring men. Deckman also found that respondents give female leaders the edge over men when it came to job performance. For instance, voters were five times as likely to say that women behaved more civilly in office than to say the same about men. Other polling by Public Religion Research Institute found that six in ten voters in September 2018 said the country would be better off if we had more women in office (Vandermass-Peeker et al. 2018). The desire to see more women elected to office was particularly pronounced among young women aged 18 to 44, who were more likely to say that electing more women to political office was critically important to them (61 percent) compared with just under half of older women in polling conducted by CBS News (Cox and Deckman 2018). By contrast, less than 40 percent of men of any age in the same poll said that having more women in elected office would make things better; most said instead that electing more women would not make much of a difference (ibid.).

Female voters also played a significant role in 2018, producing an historic gender gap in voting and leading many analysts to conclude that women's strong preference for Democrats helped the party take back a ruling majority in the US House of Representatives (Valencia 2018). As we discuss in far more detail in chapter 3, women have historically been more likely to vote for Democratic candidates than men. Exit polls from the 2018 midterms showed that this gender gap was alive and well, with women being more likely to vote for Democrats compared with men by 23 percentage points—the highest gender gap in congressional voting since 1992 (Valencia 2018). Analysis by the blog FiveThirtyEight shows that 59 percent of women voted for Democrats and 40 percent voted for Republicans in House elections, which was nearly the double the same margin in 2016 (ibid.). Women voters based their choices, in part, in response to Trump's presidency (Zhou 2018). Thus, a survey conducted by American University's Women and Politics Institute survey after the midterms found that two-thirds of women voters "said that Trump influenced their voting decision in November" (WeLead Survey 2018).

Of course, not all women vote the same. Party, race, and education are important caveats to women's choices at the ballot box. Women of color have consistently represented the largest voting blocs for Democratic candidates, which was once again the case in the 2018 midterms, with 92 percent of black women and 73 percent of Latinas indicating they voted for Democratic candidates for Congress (CNN 2018). Democratic candidates did especially well with white women voters with college degrees, who voted for Democratic candidates over Republican candidates by 20 percentage points, 59 percent and 39 percent, respectively (Valencia 2018). At the same time, white women voters without a college degree remained fairly loyal to the GOP, with 56 percent indicating that they voted for a Republican candidate for the House (Tyson 2018). Overall, however, white women's vote was split evenly (49 to 49 percent) between the two parties and is part of a trend in which Democratic House candidates have been gaining a larger percent of the white women's vote over the past three election cycles (Valencia 2018). In contrast, Democrats running in House races only secured 42 percent of the white women's vote in 2014 and 43 percent in 2016 (ibid.). Such findings remind us that women of color historically have driven the gender gap among American voters.

Whether white women are starting to abandon the Republican Party two years into Trump's presidency (North 2018) remains an open question; however, it is remarkable that the large surge in women's activism and candidacies in wake of Trump's presidency was largely located on the political left. Women's success at the ballot box in 2018 was largely a *Democratic* success story. In the House, a record number of Democratic women—89—were elected by voters, with women making up more than 60 percent of the House seats that Democrats flipped from red to blue in 2018 (Edmonson and Lee 2018); moreover, many of these newly elected House members—12 percent—are women of color and/or representatives from other marginalized communities such as LGBTQ groups or religious minorities (ibid.) At the state legislative level, Democratic women saw their numbers increase from 1,148 to 1,410 state legislators overall (National Council of State Legislatures 2018).

While there were a few notable bright spots for Republican women in 2018—for instance, Kristi Noem was elected the first woman governor of South Dakota and Marsha Blackburn became the first woman elected to the US Senate from the state of Tennessee—women's overall fortunes in the GOP were not great. At both the state and national level, Republican women suffered major losses. Republican women serving in suburban districts, such as Mimi Walters (CA) and Barbara Comstock (VA), were swept out in the Democratic wave; overall, Democrats took over almost half of the seats previously held by GOP women in the House of Representatives (Chappell 2018). Some of these incumbent women also vacated their House seats to seek higher office. In addition to Kristi Noem, Diane Black was also a candidate for governor in Tennessee, but lost her bid. Others, such as Ileana Ros-Lehtinen, the first Latina elected to Congress, retired. The diminution of Republican women nationally in elected office has prompted some prominent GOP women to call for efforts to recruit more conservative women to run for office including Representative Elise Stefanik (Cottle 2018) and Sabrina Schaeffer, chair of the Independent Women's Forum's Leadership Circle, a libertarian-leaning women's organization. Writing in the *Federalist*, Schaeffer argues that since Republicans have "hit rock bottom" with female voters, they should "begin to take the issue of electing more women more seriously. It's time to make a real effort at identifying, training, and advancing women in the party" (Schaeffer 2018). Given that the Republican Party historically rejects "identity politics," or the idea of promoting minority or women candidates within their ranks, such appeals have not gained much traction in recent political history (Bacon 2018).

While women saw historic political gains in 2018, the simple truth is that the vast majority of elected officials in the United States at all levels of government remain men. As we discuss in chapter 8, with Trump's

In January 2019, New York Rep. Elise Stefanik, the youngest Republican woman in Congress, launched a new fundraising effort called E_PAC to recruit and elect GOP women to Congress, warning her fellow Republicans that the gender gap has hit a "crisis level." *Source*: Michael Brochstein/Sipa USA/Newscom.

ascension to the presidency, the number of women serving as appointed members in his cabinet shrank compared with the two prior presidential administrations. President Trump is also set to appoint far fewer women to the federal bench, which we consider in chapter 9. For instance, as of the summer of 2018, women made up just 29 percent of all the Trump administration's nominees to Article III judgeships, who enjoy lifetime appointments. By contrast, 42 percent of President Obama's confirmed judges to the federal court were women, including two women to the Supreme Court (Stern and Wurthern 2018). As of January 2019, Trump had the opportunity to appoint two justices to the Supreme Court, and he chose two white men, Neil Gorsuch and Brett Kavanaugh. As discussed in closer detail in chapter 9, Kavanaugh's appointment, especially, was mired in controversy, amidst allegations of past sexual assault by Stanford professor Christine Blasey Ford, who knew Kavanaugh when they were both teenagers. Ultimately, Kavanaugh was confirmed largely along partisan lines after a riveting Senate Judiciary hearing that transfixed the nation. While President Donald Trump had initially been conciliatory toward Christine Blasey Ford shortly before she was set to appear before the Senate, Trump later mocked her at a campaign rally in Mississippi and cast doubt on her assertions (Malloy, Sullivan, and Zeleny 2018).

Trump's behavior toward Christine Blasey Ford is part of a larger pattern of Trump's misogynistic statements toward women, before and during his political career, that are almost too numerous to count (Lange 2018). But his comments toward Blasey Ford serve as a reminder of how gender in politics can also involve masculinity, or in Trump's case, what some deem "toxic" masculinity (Katz 2018). For instance, Trump has brushed aside the severity of sexual harassment complaints lodged by women as part of the #MeToo movement, saying that women are doing great and that the movement actually victimizes men more than women, telling reporters, "It's a very scary time for young men in America, where you can be guilty of something you may not be guilty of" (Diamond 2018). Other conservative male candidates in the 2018 midterm elections also double downed on masculine tropes, including frequent use of guns and hunting as themes in their campaign ads. In one ad, for example, Georgia gubernatorial candidate Brian Kemp sits down, with shotgun in hand, intimidating a potential suitor of his daughter. He would later go on to defeat Democrat Stacey Abrams in a close election that garnered national media attention as Abrams was the first African American woman nominee for governor. Such ads are a reminder, as Kelly Dittmar (2018) argues, that male candidates often "make strategic choices that are equally capable of maintaining or disrupting the status quo in campaigns that have favored masculinity and men."

So, what does the political future hold with respect to women, gender, and politics? While women made big gains in politics in 2018, gender parity remains far from reality. At the same time, in the two years since Hillary Clinton's close defeat for the presidency, a renewed effort of political engagement by women has emerged. Our updated fourth edition considers all of these recent trends and places them in historic context while addressing the following primary questions.

First, what do we already know about women's participation and impact in politics? Scholars have spent years detailing and describing the nature of women's contributions throughout the polity and we share the wealth of that accumulated knowledge.

Second, has women's historical exclusion from politics shaped the nature, extent, and efficacy of women's contemporary participation? After sitting on the sidelines for over 200 years, can women enter the political arena and expect to find it responsive to their concerns? Some feminist scholars argue that the very masculine nature of politics not only turns off many women but also creates an atmosphere that makes it more difficult for women to succeed once they decide to try their hand at politics (King 1995; Hawkesworth 2003). For example, MaryAnne Borrelli (2002) argues that "gender role traditions systematically privilege masculinity and deprecate femininity" such that women are routinely placed in less powerful political positions and have fewer opportunities to access the levers of power even when they hold virtually the same positions as do men in politics and government. Does women's status as relative newcomers and outsiders constrain their actions or necessitate that they play the game of politics in slightly different ways than their male colleagues?

Third, given that social scientists and feminists have long recognized that there is a difference between one's biological sex, which concerns biological differences between men and women, and gender, which is socially constructed and often relies on long-held stereotypes rooted in gender roles that men and women have held historically, how might such concepts shape the political behavior of ordinary Americans? A burgeoning body of scholarly literature has begun to consider how politicians and political activists "do gender," from a feminine or masculine perspective. Others are considering how individuals' gendered personality traits impact their political choices. For instance, Monica McDermott's work finds that citizens with higher levels of masculine traits are more likely to identify with the Republican Party and vote for Republican candidates while citizens with higher levels of femininity increase their propensity to identify with and vote for Democrats (2016). She also finds that masculinity is positively related to political engagement in terms of both interest in politics and propensity to discuss politics. Other nascent research finds that self-ratings of masculinity and femininity shape a range of public policy issue attitudes apart from sex (Bittner and Goodyear-Grant 2018). In particular, as younger Americans become comfortable in supporting or expressing gender fluidity (PRRI 2018), how gender shapes politics is increasingly important to consider.

Finally, does it matter if women participate in politics and political life more broadly? Does their presence signal that politics and government are legitimate and open to women, and ultimately encourage other women to become involved? When women are at the helm, do they prioritize, champion, and act on issues that matter to women? Do they change the representational process to ensure that a greater range of voices and perspectives are heard? Will the first female president behave differently than Donald Trump and his male predecessors on policy questions involving gender? Does it matter if she is a Democrat or a Republican? How might partisanship or ideology circumscribe or shape a female president's ability to speak on behalf of women more generally?

To begin tackling these questions, this chapter outlines our theoretical framework for the remainder of the book. The concept of political representation is central to the study of American politics, and we draw on classic as well as emerging discussions of political representation to explore and investigate how women participate in and influence American democracy. We begin with a discussion of women's interests and how scholars have understood them over time before delving more deeply into the multifaceted nature of political representation. Each chapter to follow investigates how questions of representation have shaped our understanding of women's paths to power, their contributions to politics and governance, and their influence. Most chapters begin with a short narrative that highlights contemporary issues and policy debates and gives the reader a sense of some of the key questions for discussion and debate raised in the chapters; most also take a deeper dive into the issue of gender as a social construct, both in terms of femininity and masculinity, and how such an understanding informs our politics.

HISTORY AND WOMEN'S POLITICAL INTERESTS

In a representative democracy, we expect that those who govern are responsive and accountable to the citizenry. Yet, before American women secured the right to vote in 1920, most individuals gave little thought to women as a distinct part of the citizenry needing their own representation. As political scientist Virginia Sapiro (1981) explains, "In the beginning there was no problem of political representation of women. The reason was not that everyone agreed that women should not be represented; rather, the argument was that women *were* represented" (701; emphasis in original). Most people assumed that women were already represented by the men in their families—their fathers, husbands, and brothers. The concept of separate spheres is instructive. Historically, men and women occupied different spheres in society. Men's primary contributions to society were in the public sphere, where they worked outside the home to provide for the family. Women's contributions were centered within the private sphere, where they were responsible for running the household, raising and educating children, and attending to the religious and moral health of the family. Of course, these "separate spheres" often applied disproportionately to white women of privilege, as slaves, free women of color, and working-class women were often forced to work outside of the home to provide for themselves and their families.

As a unit, men and women could cover both spheres. But when it came to politics or policy matters, the domain was reserved for men who were presumed to be looking out for the best interests of the family and society. As one US senator explained during a congressional debate on female suffrage, "The women of America vote by faithful and true representatives, their husbands, their brothers, their sons; and no true man will go to the polls and deposit his ballot without remembering the true and loving constituency he has at home" (Langley and Fox 1994, 140). As such, there was no reason for women to engage in the public sphere: not only would their contributions be superfluous, but would detract from their responsibilities and obligations in the private sphere.

In addition, most women and men agreed that such a division of labor was proper and naturally ordained. In fact, it was fairly common in the nineteenth and early twentieth centuries to exclude women from the public sphere based on assumptions about their different "natures." One accomplished paleontologist from the nineteenth century was opposed to female suffrage for the reason that "woman is physically incapable of carrying into execution any law she may enact. . . . [As such] the sexes cannot take an equal share of governmental responsibilities even if they should desire to do so" (Cope 1888). Besides natural differences in physical strength, he also drew distinctions between what he perceived to be natural differences in the mental capacities of the sexes: "We find in man a greater *capacity* for rational processes. . . . In women we find that the deficiency of endurance of the rational faculty is associated with a general incapacity for mental strain, and, as her emotional nature is stronger, that strain is more severe than it is in man under similar circumstances" (emphasis in original, Cope 1888). The US Supreme Court employed a similar type of reasoning in 1908 in the case of *Muller v. Oregon*, arguing that women's special role in the family, combined with their dependence on men, provided a societal justification for limiting their role in the workplace. As the opinion stated:

> that women's physical structure and the performance of maternal functions place her at a disadvantage in the struggle for subsistence is obvious . . . her physical structure and a proper discharge of her maternal functions—having in view not merely her own health, but the well-being of the race—justify legislation to protect her from the greed as well as the passion of man. (*Muller v. Oregon*, 208 U.S. 421)

At issue was an Oregon state law that prohibited businesses from allowing women to work shifts greater than 10 hours long. Just three years earlier, the Supreme Court had invalidated a New York state law that placed similar limitations on men's working hours (*Lochner v. New York*, 198 U.S. 45). Whether women wanted such restrictions on their labor or not, the nine male members of the Supreme Court unanimously declared that women's interests in negotiating the terms of their employment were less important than their family and societal responsibilities.

But our notions of representation and whose interests should be included in public deliberations have changed over time. Many social movements, such as the Black Lives Matter movement, the #MeToo movement, and the Women's March following Trump's inauguration, have successfully challenged and expanded our notions of whose interests matter and should be included in public discourse. These social movements have persuasively demonstrated that the status quo has been unresponsive to their interests and argued that extending greater political rights to women, people of

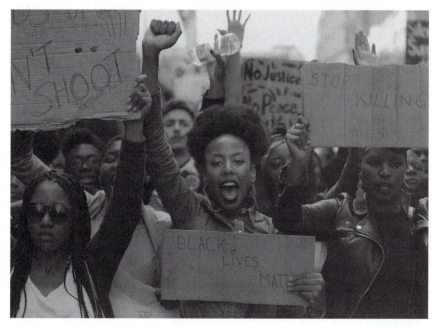

Black Lives Matters, formed by three women of color, Alicia Garza, Patrisse Cullors, and Opal Tometi, in 2013 to protest police violence against the black community, is among the most well-known social movements active in American politics today. Black Lives Matter often encourages peaceful, mass protests as a way to raise awareness about this important issue. *Source*: DANIEL LEAL-OLIVAS/AFP/Getty Images.

color, and lesbian, gay, bisexual, transgender, and queer (LGBTQ) individuals is a necessary change.

Social movements' successes in bringing new issues to the fore, however, may inadvertently signal that all group members share the same interests. But as we know, there is great diversity of perspectives and priorities among different members of the same group. Since the suffrage movement, women have repeatedly lined up on different sides of the aisle, fighting for their own conception of the ideal world. Yet, much research on women and men in politics highlights the ways in which women differ from men, suggesting that political women have more in common with one another than they do with political men. Although the temptation is to think of women as a monolithic bloc, the reality is much more complex.

We pay special attention to the diversity of women's experiences and interests in the chapters that follow. Much of the existing scholarship assumes that heterosexual white women's experiences are the norm and in doing so marginalizes the voices and experiences of women of color as well as LGBTQ women (hooks 1981; Strolovitch 2007). To return to an earlier example, when the Supreme Court handed down its ruling in *Muller v. Oregon*, not all working women were covered by protective labor legislation. Women's occupational choices were relatively limited at the turn of the century, even more so for women of color. Many African American women living in the post-Civil War south continued to toil greater than 10 hours a day, working in the fields by day and serving as house servants or domestics in the evenings (Jones 1986). Sojourner Truth's famous "Ain't I a Woman?" speech pointed out the hypocrisy of treating some women as too delicate to work long hours while black women like herself were expected to demonstrate strength over and over again. Assembled before the 1851 Women's Convention in Ohio, Truth called on her sisters to recognize her as a woman, too:

> That man over there says that women need to be helped into carriages, and lifted over ditches, and to have the best place everywhere. Nobody ever helps me into carriages, or over mud-puddles, or gives me any best place! And ain't I a woman? Look at me! Look at my arm! I have ploughed and planted, and gathered into barns, and no man could head me! And ain't I a woman? I could work as much and eat as much as a man—when I could get it—and bear the lash as well! And ain't I a woman?

Over 100 years later, many contemporary feminist scholars argue that women of color and LGBTQ women continue to be marginalized outsiders, doubly or triply disadvantaged by their gender, race, and sexuality in a political system that was created by and for white, heterosexual men (hooks 1981; Hawkesworth 2003). Many of these authors draw on the concept of intersectionality to better understand and reflect the totality of women's perspectives, highlighting that where one stands on any particular issue is related to the various identities she embodies: race, sexual orientation, class, and religion, for example (Hardy-Fanta et al. 2006; Smooth 2011; Strolovitch 2007). While the common experience of being excluded from the polity may create a shared interest in greater gender equality, as Sojourner Truth's comments above suggest, any single woman's orientation to politics and the way in which she articulates her own interests is likely shaped by her multiple identities and the interactions among these identities. Again reflecting Truth's experience, Patricia Hill Collins (2008) argues that because white women have long been dominant, they have set the standard for femininity such that women of color are never recognized as fully feminine beings worthy of the same protections and privileges as white women.

As we demonstrate throughout the remainder of this book, "women's interests" are no longer entirely relegated to the private sphere and are rarely monolithic. But whether or not women share some of the same interests and perspectives is immaterial if nobody is listening to their voices and attempting to translate their diverse desires and policy preferences into action. We turn next to a discussion of the various types of representation to provide a backdrop for interpreting women's actions and participation in American politics today.

WOMEN'S REPRESENTATION

Before the passage of the Nineteenth Amendment guaranteed women the right to vote in 1921, some women could legitimately resurrect the colonial cry of "no taxation without representation." Unmarried women owned property in many states and paid property taxes. With one foot placed in both the public and private spheres, the claim that their male brethren were looking out for their best interests rang hollow. Without the capacity to vote in their own interests, women had little recourse to change laws that governed their lives.

As we discuss in greater detail in chapter 2, many women began coming together in annual assemblies to discuss how best to improve their political, economic, and social status. The most well known of these meetings was held in Seneca Falls, New York, in 1848, where 100 attendees, mostly women, signed a "Declaration of Rights and Sentiments," modeled after the Declaration of Independence penned by colonists some 72 years earlier. The Declaration of Rights and Sentiments listed a number of women's grievances and produced a set of resolutions aimed at improving women's status in society. One, in particular, focused on women's limited political rights and lack of representation: "Having deprived her of this first right of a citizen, the elective franchise, thereby leaving her without representation in the halls of legislation, he has oppressed her on all sides" ("Declaration of Rights and Sentiments"; see appendix A). Seventy-three years later, women finally secured the right to vote.

But winning the right to vote did not make female citizens political equals in all respects. Many states and localities banned women from jury service until the Supreme Court ruled such laws unconstitutional in 1975 (*Taylor v. Louisiana*, 419 U.S. 522). The contemporary women's movement challenged many blatantly discriminatory policies that relegated women to second-class citizens, such as pay disparities in the workplace, unequal access to financial credit, and sex-segregated want ads for job postings. Such examples illuminate a central question for this text: Can we thus assume that women will advocate on behalf of other women, or does suggesting as much relegate women to a category of homogenized "special interests" rather than full-bodied citizens with a multitude of perspectives, experiences, and preferences, only some of which can be traced back to their gender? Can any one woman speak for all women any more than any one man can speak for all men?

To help consider these debates, scholars turn to theories of representation. As scholars have long agreed, representation can take on many different forms. In her classic treatise *The Concept of Representation*, Hanna Pitkin (1967) identifies four primary types of representation: formalistic, descriptive, symbolic, and substantive. A formal representative is someone who has simply been given the authority to act on behalf of others. Pitkin further clarifies that this type of representation gives a political actor "a right to act which he did not have before, while the represented has become responsible for the consequences of that action as if he had done it himself" (39). For example, members of Congress are formal representatives for their constituents because the Constitution provides formal authority to act on their behalf.

Descriptive representation, the second type of representation, is the act of standing in for those who are otherwise absent, with the emphasis on what the representative looks like rather than whatever actions she or he takes. According to Pitkin, descriptive representation "depends on the representative's characteristics, on what he or she *is* or is *like*, on being something rather than doing something" (61, emphasis in original). Proponents of descriptive representation argue that it is important to have elected or appointed government bodies that reflect the make-up of its citizenry. For instance, men are not descriptive representatives for women, whites are not descriptive representatives for people of color, and heterosexuals are not descriptive representatives for LGBTQ individuals: they do not share the relevant attributes or characteristics and, as a result, make poor descriptive reflections of those for whom they stand.

As mentioned earlier, women's descriptive representation has not yet come close to approaching parity as women are still vastly outnumbered in American politics today. For high-ranking political offices, such as the US Congress and state governorships, the vast majority of candidates are still male, despite the historic number of women who ran for and were elected to public office in 2018. While much attention was paid to the historic number of women candidates seeking congressional seats, for instance, less notice was made of the surge in male candidates for Congress compared with 2016, especially among Democrats (Kurtzleben 2018). Further, although women continue to make inroads into political office across all three branches of government, men still outnumber women by large margins. Only four women have ever served on the Supreme Court of the United States. President Trump, notably, chose to elevate two white men to the Supreme Court, who were later confirmed by the US Senate. Advocates for electing or appointing more women to political office maintain that it is inherently unfair in an elected democracy to have women represented in such low numbers compared to their presence in the population. Or, as the organization Political Parity, which seeks to increase women's political representation nationally, argues, "A more representative government leads to politics that represent more Americans" (Political Parity n.d.). Recent work by Political Parity and the Center for American Women and Politics, who interviewed 83 of the 108 women serving as senators, representatives, or delegates in the 114th Congress from both sides of the aisle, reinforces this point, as the women they spoke with overwhelmingly agreed that their presence and their voices mattered, even in an institution increasingly marked by partisan gridlock (Dittmar et al. 2017).

The third type of representation, symbolic, involves the use of symbols for eliciting a particular attitude or emotion. As Pitkin explains, "To say that something symbolizes something else is to say it calls to mind, and even beyond that evokes emotion or attitudes appropriate to the absent thing" (96). Political symbols often serve as powerful reminders of underlying shared values and possibilities. For example, Barack Obama's election as the first African American president of the United States is often interpreted to symbolize the democratic values of justice, equality of opportunity, and liberty to pursue one's dreams. In a similar way, electing Hillary Clinton to the presidency would have symbolized the country's greater openness to women's full participation in politics as well as the waning importance of the doctrine of separate spheres.

Symbolic representation is often employed to legitimize American politics as democratic and accessible to all. For example, a black female judge from Texas explained the importance of symbolic representation on the bench: "When I walk into that court and see all of the pictures of judges, I think there should be someone there who looks like me. And I think for all the people who are visiting the court, there should be judges who look like them" (quoted in Frederick 2014). When Professor Anita Hill accused future Supreme Court Justice Clarence Thomas in 1991 of sexually harassing her when they worked together at the Equal Employment Opportunity Commission, she was brought before the all-male, all-white Senate Judiciary Committee to share her story. The symbolism of having an all-male, all-white Senate Judiciary Committee interrogate an African American woman about sexual harassment was not lost, and many women were inspired to run for office to remedy the gender and racial imbalance in the US Congress in 1992 (Green 2013). Of course, sexual harassment claims did not stop Brett Kavanaugh from being confirmed by a Republican Senate in 2018, either, although several women who served on the Judiciary Committee during Kavanaugh's hearing won praise for their handling of Blasey Ford's claims at that hearing (Cillizza 2018).

Once elected, women are often reminded of their symbolic status as outsiders. Former Congresswoman Cynthia McKinney, an African American woman, was often asked to show her credentials when entering the US House of Representatives. She interpreted these routine stops from security guards as a comment on her position as an outsider, explaining that security guards "just don't think about people of color as members of Congress" (quoted in Hawkesworth 2003, 532). Stories like these suggest that symbolic representation can both enhance and call into question the legitimacy of government in the eyes of an increasingly diverse public.

Finally, substantive representation is defined by Pitkin as "acting in the interest of the represented, in a manner responsive to them" (209). For many scholars of politics, substantive representation is central to our notions of democratic accountability. Citizens and scholars alike are concerned not only with the appearance of representation in our political bodies but also with the actual policies and actions taken by those in formal power. In her widely acclaimed best seller on women's leadership, *Lean In*, Sheryl Sandberg (2013) argues that having more women at the top of corporate and political America will be good for all women, that women's experiences in a gendered world will shape their perspectives and lead them to make decisions that are more inclusive and sensitive to issues of diversity.

Many feminist scholars agree with Sandberg, arguing that increasing the descriptive representation of women in politics is a necessary but not sufficient condition for achieving the substantive representation of women's interests. Adding racial minority representation to the list as well, political theorist Jane Mansbridge (1999) has outlined several reasons why the presence of people of color and female group members will improve the representation of underrepresented groups' interests: such individuals are more inclined to represent the views of their group at the policymaking table; they bring new issues to the agenda that have thus far been neglected by the majority; they pursue more vigorous advocacy of the issues that affect their group; and they are often viewed as speaking with more moral authority on issues that disproportionately affect women and people of color.

Mansbridge also emphasizes potential symbolic benefits of representation: the presence of people of color and women in political institutions builds trust and legitimacy, especially where a history of discrimination and distrust exists between the majority and minority groups, and women and racial minorities serve as role models encouraging more people like themselves to consider a run for office. And although Mansbridge focuses almost entirely on women and people of color, the same benefits of symbolic representation can be extended to other marginalized groups, such as LGBTQ individuals and religious minorities.

Throughout the text, we discuss and analyze the different faces of representation across the American political landscape. Most chapters begin with basic descriptive information, including the percentage of women who have served in different areas of government and for how long they have enjoyed a seat at the table. We also emphasize the symbolic effects of women's presence in political arenas: Are they treated as full-fledged participants in politics or marginalized by their outsider status? Does women's presence in government inspire young girls and women to become more politically engaged and active? Finally, we focus on the substantive component of representation: Does policy look different, or is it more likely to incorporate or consider women's perspectives when women are incorporated into formal and informal positions of policymaking?

In the chapters ahead, we showcase a variety of political women, who are far from monolithic when it comes to which issues matter most to women or which public policies they believe will help women most. Women who identify as politically progressive often argue for a larger role for the state to play in providing social welfare programs for women and their families. Moreover, they often call on government to increase regulations on the private sector to ensure that women have equal opportunity in the work force or that such businesses provide benefits that make work/family balance easier for working parents. Liberal feminists insist that government allows for safe and legal access to abortion as well as marriage rights for all citizens, including LGBTQ individuals, as such rights are essential to women's full equality, they maintain. Socially conservative women, however, argue that government should restrict access to abortion and make access to marriage available only to heterosexual couples, as both policies, they believe, help reinforce traditional families and women's roles as mothers. Libertarian women, including many women active in the Tea Party, focus less on social issues and instead say government should dramatically reduce its scope and size on economic issues, as lower taxes and less business regulation, they insist, will unleash the free market, creating job growth and ensuring that individuals—both women and men—will be less reliant on government assistance. Like men, women engaged in politics bring with them no shortage of political ideas and policy prerogatives.

After reading this text, readers should have an excellent grasp of women's status as political actors in the United States, their paths to higher office, their behavior in office, the diversity of viewpoints and goals among political women, and the difference they make. We showcase diverse political women across the ideological spectrum and in all sorts of venues, not only because their stories are fascinating but also because we hope to inspire a new generation of women to become politically engaged. As we demonstrate throughout the book, women from all walks of life have stood up to make their voices heard. They did not start out as professional politicians but as women who thought they could make a difference and improve their communities by getting involved. The United States is a much richer place because of their efforts.

2

Women's Paths to Power

◆ ◆ ◆

WOMEN IN SOCIAL MOVEMENTS AND INTEREST GROUPS

Angered by president-elect Donald Trump's misogynistic behavior during his campaign and fearful about a potential rollback of women's rights during his administration, progressive women called for a Women's March. The day after Trump's inauguration, more than 4.5 million joined Women's Marches in over 600 cities across the United States and solidarity marches were held in more than 200 international locations (Berry and Chenoweth 2018; Frostenson 2017). Marchers rallied for a wide variety of causes including but not limited to equal pay, reproductive freedom, criminal justice reform, immigrant rights, opposition to sexual violence, LGBTQ rights, and a living wage for domestic workers, particularly women of color (Cauterucci 2017; Crockett 2017a).

One week later another group of women and men descended on Washington for the 44th annual March for Life to protest the *Roe v. Wade* decision. The conservative women who participated in the march were hopeful about the future, expecting the Trump administration and the Republican Congress to pass more restrictions on abortion and to appoint pro-life justices to the Supreme Court and lower federal courts (Desanctis 2017; Green 2017).

These drastically different marches demonstrate that there is no monolithic political view about what government actions are best to ensure that America's women and families thrive. While women today are actively engaged in social movements and in political interest groups, which enhances their descriptive representation, women's engagement in causes across the political spectrum raises fascinating questions as to substantive representation. Can women even agree on which issues would best serve their interests and what policy solutions will promote women's well-being?

This chapter takes a closer look at the significant social movements that changed the landscape of women's rights. It also examines the efforts of contemporary women's organizations on the left and right as they compete to frame political debates and offer policy solutions that reflect "what women truly want." The chapter begins with the first major movement for women's rights, the 70-year struggle for women's suffrage. We then examine the "second wave" of feminism that developed several decades after women gained the right to vote, as men and women adjusted to larger societal shifts in women's roles in the 1960s, including the increasing number of women in the workforce, the expansion of women's access to higher education, and rising divorce rates. Women organized to fight against the discriminatory behavior they faced at the workplace, in state and federal legislation, and in society. This chapter closely examines these struggles and how such battles culminated in the failed bid for an Equal Rights Amendment (ERA) to the US Constitution.

The unsuccessful battle over the ERA similarly revealed that women were not monolithic in their political views, as it sparked an intense backlash among more socially conservative women and men. These individuals believed that the second-wave feminist movement challenged women's traditional place in the home and undermined the American social fabric. Today debate about women's role in society continues, and women (and men) are of diverse opinions regarding numerous political issues relevant to women such as reproductive rights, childcare, and education. We consider how contemporary women activists on the left and right compete to frame political debates and offer policy solutions that address the challenges faced by women in today's workplace and at home.

EARLY WOMEN ACTIVISTS AND THE FIGHT FOR SUFFRAGE

Today we take for granted women's political rights and responsibilities. But for much of American history, politics in the United States was a "man's world" from which women were excluded on legal, moral, and social grounds. During the nineteenth and early twentieth centuries, women lost most of their legal rights upon marriage and were considered the property of their husbands. Married women had no right to own property, no right to an education, no right to their children in cases of divorce, no access to most professions, and no right to the wages they earned. Gender relations were guided by the principle of separate spheres in which men were the breadwinners for their families and represented their households in the public sphere. Women were expected to take care of the home, raise and educate the children, and conduct themselves on a higher moral plane (Kraditor 1981; Flexner and Fitzpatrick 1996).

Despite being largely excluded from the political world, including being denied the right to vote, some women still managed to participate in, and shape, public life. One early example of such political activism is in the abolitionist movement, in which many women worked alongside men to stop slavery. Elizabeth Cady Stanton and Lucretia Mott were two such women. They met each other at the 1840 World Anti-Slavery Convention in London. Skilled organizers in their own right, both were infuriated when they were denied seats at the convention and relegated to the balcony because they were women. Many female abolitionists began to realize that their lot in life was little better than that of slaves in that they shared few legal rights. As a result, Stanton and Mott organized the first women's rights convention in Seneca Falls, New York, in 1848, which marks the beginning of the American feminist movement. Issuing the Declaration of Rights and Sentiments modeled on the Declaration of Independence, these women called for a complete overhaul of the laws and traditions guiding relationships between the sexes (see appendix A for the full text of the Declaration of Rights and Sentiments). The women who gathered at Seneca Falls passed resolutions seeking to overhaul laws and achieve a more equitable social and legal standing for women, including the right to vote (Baker 1984; Hartmann 1989; Flexner and Fitzpatrick 1996).

The organizers at Seneca Falls, however, were far ahead of their time in terms of their conceptions about women's rights and had little real chance in the mid-nineteenth century of changing either the discriminatory laws against women or social views about women's place in public affairs. The organizers, however, began to see that women's ability to participate in elections was crucial to any changes in their status. As a result, the first widespread movement involving women was the fight for women's suffrage. Moreover, the 72-year fight (1848–1920) for suffrage reflects the evolution of different types of feminism. The women who organized the convention at Seneca Falls were feminists who sought a more radical restructuring of women's place in society, and many suffragists, such as Susan B. Anthony, would follow this rationale for attaining women's right to vote. Later, other women joined the battle for women's suffrage who were less interested in changing women's status, but instead used their moral authority as mothers to justify their participation in the movement. These women, such as temperance women who were opposed to the sale of alcohol, believed that the female vote would allow for the passage of legislation that would "clean up" corrupt government regimes along with society at-large. The battle for suffrage also illustrates the conflicts that emerged among women as they confronted issues of race, region, and class (Kraditor 1981; Flexner and Fitzpatrick 1996).

The early suffragists who forged their political consciousness in the abolitionist movement based their calls for the ballot on human rights, the equality of citizens, and the rights of all humans to achieve self-actualization. The Declaration of Rights and Sentiments adopted at the Seneca Falls convention included the first formal demand for women's suffrage based on the equality of humankind and the right to the pursuit of life, liberty, and happiness laid out by Thomas Jefferson in the Declaration of Independence. White and African American men and women including Horace Greeley, Henry Blackwell, and former slave and well-known orator Frederick Douglass as well as women leaders such as Elizabeth Cady Stanton, Susan B. Anthony, Lucy Stone, and Sojourner Truth, the former slave and author of the famous speech "Ain't I a Woman," worked to abolish slavery and gave speeches, organized petition drives, and lobbied legislatures on behalf of rights for African Americans and women.

To aid their cause, abolitionist leaders formed the American Equal Rights Association. After a successful campaign for the Thirteenth Amendment to abolish slavery, ratified in 1865, many believed that full citizenship rights for African Americans and women would soon be a reality. However, the introduction of the Fourteenth Amendment, which protects the privileges and immunities of citizens from infringement by the states and guarantees due process for citizens, created a major split in the movement for equal rights because for the first time the word *male* was used in the Constitution. It appeared in Section 2, which dealt explicitly with voting rights (Kraditor 1981; Flexner and Fitzpatrick 1996). Supporters of the amendment argued that because the Civil War was fought to abolish slavery and there was no public outcry in support of women's rights commensurate to the call for redressing the wrongs against former slaves, this was the "Negro's Hour." They believed that voting reform must be achieved incrementally. Tying women's suffrage to this already controversial proposal—which was geared at establishing full citizenship for the freed slaves and other African Americans—could doom the amendment. Those suffragists who opposed the amendment, including Susan B. Anthony and Elizabeth Cady Stanton, feared that including the word male in the Constitution would undermine women's claims to citizenship and the accompanying rights and privileges. Moreover, they believed that passage of the Fourteenth Amendment as written would require an act of Congress or even a constitutional amendment to grant women the right to vote in federal elections. Indeed, more than ten years later, in *Minor v. Happersett* (1875), the Supreme Court ruled that by refusing to register Virgina Minor, the president of the Missouri Woman Suffrage Association, to vote, the state of Missouri was not denying her the privileges and immunities of citizenship because voting was not a right of citizenship but a privilege granted by the states. Additional attempts to win the ballot by illegally registering women to vote and pursuing a citizenship claim through the courts were equally unsuccessful (Kraditor 1981; Flexner and Fitzpatrick 1996; Cushman 2001).

As a result of the conflict over the Fourteenth Amendment and the exclusion of sex from the Fifteenth Amendment, which bars denial of the right to vote based on "race, color, or previous condition of servitude," two competing organizations arose to fight for women's suffrage in 1869. The more radical group, the National Woman's Suffrage Association (NWSA), led by Anthony and Stanton, was dedicated to winning a federal amendment for women's suffrage. They restricted membership to women only and were active in a range of causes including working conditions for women, divorce reform, and elevating the position of women in the church. The more conservative organization, the American Woman Suffrage Association (AWSA), led by Lucy Stone and Henry Ward Beecher, both notable abolitionists, concentrated only on the right to vote and avoided other causes that could alienate important members of the political community. Rather than working for a federal amendment, they focused their energy on a state-by-state campaign for the ballot. After more than 20 years, with little to show for their efforts, the two organizations finally merged to form the National American Woman's Suffrage Association (NAWSA) in 1890, which would concentrate its efforts on obtaining the right to vote within individual states (Flexner and Fitzpatrick 1996; Kraditor 1981; McConnaughy 2013).

By 1890 the Progressive movement was in full swing, and many of the white middle-class women who adopted the fight for the vote subscribed to a vision of civic motherhood that required women as selfless, moral agents to emerge from the private sphere and engage in the public realm in order to properly fulfill their roles as mothers and wives. Rapid urbanization and industrialization created problems of public sanitation, education of new immigrants, and a need for more public services that aligned with women's traditional roles within the family. These dramatic changes in society required women to practice civic housekeeping, expanding their involvement from the home to the school, the local community, the state, and the national government (Baker 1984). On the basis of a desire to achieve a myriad of social reforms, Aileen Kraditor (1981) notes that the arguments made by suffragists in these years moved away from calls for the ballot on the basis of simple justice toward expediency, including why women deserved the vote and what women would do with the ballot. As Rheta Childe Door, journalist and member of the General Federation of Women's Clubs (GFWC), explained:

> Woman's place is in the home. . . . But Home is not contained within the four walls of an individual home. Home is the community. The city full of people is the Family. The public school is the real Nursery. And badly do the Home and the Family and the Nursery need their mother. (Door 1910, 327)

The Women's Christian Temperance Union (WCTU) was one of the first reform groups to adopt the fight for suffrage. Under the leadership of Frances

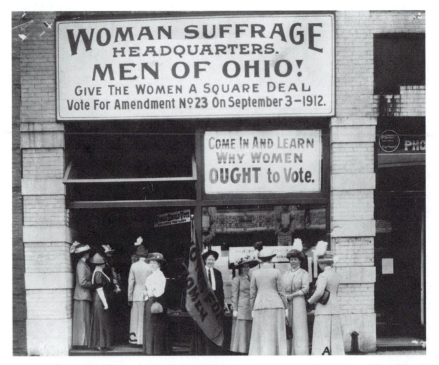

Woman Suffrage Headquarters in Cleveland, Ohio, in 1912. Pictured at far right is Miss Belle Sherwin, president of the National League of Women Voters. *Source*: Library of Congress.

Willard, in 1881, the group called for the vote as a Home Protection Ballot. Willard and other temperance leaders believed that women voters would pass local and state laws banning the manufacture and sale of liquor—an important goal that they argued would stop the impoverishment of families and the abuse of women and children who were harmed by husbands and fathers who succumbed to alcoholism. Thus, union literature disassociated itself from the natural rights arguments of suffragist organizations by pointing out that "the WCTU seeks the ballot for no selfish ends. Asking for it only in the interest of the home, which has been and is woman's divinely appointed province, there is no clamor for 'rights,' only a prayerful, persistent plea for the opportunities of Duty" (quoted in Bordin 1981, 119).

Through the WCTU, numerous conservative women who would eschew a rights-based movement that challenged traditional gender roles were drawn to the cause of suffrage. During many state initiative fights to grant women the vote, it was these temperance women who provided the majority of the activists in the campaigns. However, the prominence of the temperance movement in the suffrage cause also provoked the opposition of liquor manufacturers to suffrage and the industry utilized its considerable resources to finance campaigns against suffrage whenever states held a referendum on the question (Tyler 1949; Bordin 1981; Flexner and Fitzpatrick 1996).

Like the women of the WCTU, the white upper middle and middle-class club women of the GFWC also took up the cause of suffrage in the 1900s in order to achieve their reform goals. The GFWC grew out of the numerous local literary women's clubs established in urban areas in the late 1860s. Seeking to continue their education after marriage, clubwomen studied literature, art, and music. They presented papers and critiqued each other's works. By 1890, many of these clubs were involving themselves in social reform. The largest and most publicly active clubs included Sorosis, a club of career women in New York City, and the New England Federation of Women's Clubs, a group of elite reformers in Boston. Seeking to have a wider impact on public affairs, Jane Cunningham Croly, a journalist and leader of Sorosis, invited ninety-seven clubs to attend its twenty-first anniversary convention and to form a national organization. The GFWC grew to 500,000 members in 1910 and 1 million by 1914. These women viewed the ballot as a necessary tool to achieve their plethora of reform goals including the establishment of kindergartens and traveling libraries, improvement of the working conditions of women and children, public sanitation, and natural resource conservation (Wood 1912; Wells 1953; Blair 1980).

Although the incorporation of clubwomen and temperance crusaders expanded the ranks of those fighting for suffrage and united women across regions, the need to maintain the support of such a wide-ranging constituency also led to the adoption of tactics and policies antithetical to the cause of equal rights that suffrage represented. Reacting to the expansion of immigration in northern cities and racial relations in the South, many suffragists began to argue that women needed the vote in order to counteract the influence of the "undesirable" elements of society: the uneducated immigrants in the North who sold their votes to the political machines and black men in the South. Thus, speakers at suffrage conventions provided statistics to demonstrate that if granted the vote, the nativist educated white women would far outnumber the population of immigrant and black men who they believed contributed to the corruption of public affairs. To support the goal of limiting the vote to the more "deserving" elements of society, many suffragists advocated the adoption of educational requirements for the vote (Kraditor 1981; Flexner and Fitzpatrick 1996). Thus, Elizabeth Cady Stanton advocated an educational qualification for voters because:

1. It would limit the foreign vote
2. It would decrease the ignorant native vote by stimulating the rising generation to learning

3. It would dignify the right of suffrage in the eyes of our people to know that some preparation was necessary

As Stanton concluded,

"One of the most potent objections to woman suffrage is the added ignorant and depraved vote that would still further corrupt and embarrass the administration of our Government. . . . It is the interest of the educating working-men, as it is of the women, that this ignorant, worthless class of voters should be speedily diminished. With free schools and compulsory education, there is no excuse in this country for ignorance of the elements of learning." (quoted in Kraditor 1981, 133)

To win the suffrage referendum in the southern states, the movement needed the support of southern women. Therefore, the leaders of NAWSA adopted a state's rights position that allowed local suffrage groups to exclude black women from their organizations and did not repudiate the racist arguments used in favor of the suffrage cause (Kraditor 1981). At the same time, the National Association of Colored Women's Clubs argued for the ballot for all women and fought against lynching and Jim Crow laws. The group's leaders included Ida Wells Barnett, the journalist who at great risk to her own life chronicled in vivid detail the horror of lynchings across the South, and Mary Church Terrell, the group's first president. Terrell used her writings and speeches to draw attention to the problems of racism and sexism. She and Wells Barnett both helped found the NAACP (National Association for the Advancement of Colored People) (Robnett 2000; Dickerson 2018; Michals 2017).

Even with these changing tactics and coalitions, the suffrage movement endured years of defeats before the adoption of the Nineteenth Amendment to the US Constitution that granted women the right to vote federally. In 1890, Wyoming became the first state to enter the union with full suffrage for women, and Colorado adopted female suffrage in 1893. A few states adopted laws allowing women to vote in school board or municipal elections. However, after the 1896 state referendum in which Utah and Idaho became the third and fourth states to adopt women's suffrage, no other state voted to give women full suffrage until Washington in 1910 (Kraditor 1981; Flexner and Fitzpatrick 1996; McConnaughy 2013).

Campaign after campaign, suffragists were stymied by poor organization and a lack of resources as they faced opponents backed by business interests, the liquor industry, and political machines. These party machines feared that armed with the vote, women would seek to ban child labor, reform working conditions for women, pass prohibition, and support civil service reform. These antisuffrage groups had the support of important political figures, ranging from state legislators, members of Congress, and former president Grover Cleveland, who pointed to the destabilizing impact women's suffrage would have on the home, the family, and the nation. Additionally, antisuffragist women who came from wealthy families (and were often politically well connected) spoke out against suffrage as an unnecessary burden on women who did not want or need it because their men represented them and cared for their interests (Flexner and Fitzpatrick 1996).

Frustrated by the continued slow expansion of suffrage at the state level, in 1916 NAWSA leader Carrie Chapman Catt formulated a "winning plan." The plan called for abandoning the state-by-state campaigns that had yielded limited success in favor of a single-minded focus on a federal constitutional amendment. The Congressional Union for Woman Suffrage also championed the crusade for a federal suffrage amendment. Led by Alice Paul, these women had left the NAWSA because they believed the tactics of NAWSA leaders were too timid. Moreover, they rejected NAWSA's nonpartisan advocacy, and building on Paul's experience with the militants in the British suffrage movement, the Congressional Union women advocated a policy of holding the party in power responsible for the lack of suffrage. They also picketed the White House, as the then president, Woodrow Wilson—a Democrat—shared the same party affiliation as the majority party in Congress. Therefore, they actively worked to defeat Democratic congressional candidates and to hold the Wilson administration responsible for women's exclusion from the vote, particularly in those states where women had already been granted the right to vote and could be galvanized as a potential voting bloc to punish politicians who did not support suffrage.

Ultimately, Wilson changed his mind and supported the suffrage cause, and what became known as the Susan B. Anthony Amendment passed through Congress and was moved to the states for ratification. After 56 state referendum campaigns, 480 efforts to get state legislatures to allow state referenda, 47 campaigns for suffrage at state constitutional conventions, 277 attempts to include votes for women in state party platforms, and 19 campaigns to get a federal amendment through Congress and then ratified by three-quarters of state legislatures, this goal was finally achieved when Tennessee became the thirty-sixth state to adopt the women's suffrage amendment in 1920 (Kraditor 1981; Klein 1984; Flexner and Fitzpatrick 1996).

FEMINISM, THE SECOND WAVE (1960s–PRESENT)

After achieving the goal of suffrage, the women's movement lost its grassroots base. The country was recovering from World War I and desired a "return to normalcy" under President Warren G. Harding. Individual women leaders gravitated to new causes and became active in organizations promoting the interests of working-class women, peace, birth control, and equal rights. The leaders of NAWSA formed the League of Women Voters, a nonpartisan group dedicated to educating women about issues and their new responsibilities as voters so that women could cast intelligent ballots and participate effectively in politics. The more radical members of the Congressional Union established the National Woman's Party and promoted a new ERA, authored by Alice Paul, to eliminate sex discrimination in all areas of society. Other women began to move into the male-dominated major political parties. There were some efforts to coordinate the demands of women reformers, particularly through the Women's Joint Congressional Committee. Established in 1919, the group brought together women's groups including the League of Women Voters; the Business and Professional Women's Clubs; the American Association of University Women; the National Consumers League; the Women's Trade Union League; the National Association of Colored Women; and the National Council of Jewish Women to lobby the state and national governments for legislation dealing with education, child labor, peace, maternal health, and a range of other issues. However, after a few legislative victories, particularly the passage of the Sheppard-Towner Act providing federal funds for prenatal and maternal health-care education, the failure to deliver a unified women's vote nationally, and a dispute over the ERA quickly eviscerated the power of this union (Hartmann 1989; Andersen 1996).

The Rebirth of the Feminist Movement

The 1960s provided the confluence of factors that initiated the rebirth of the feminist movement. With regard to social conditions, the participation of women in the job market grew to 35 percent of the national workforce, birthrates declined, the introduction of the birth control pill allowed more women to control their fertility, and more women were enrolled in college. Additionally, an increased divorce rate and the decision of many women to marry later in life led to an increase in the number of unmarried women.

However, women's increased presence in the job market and in higher education did not translate into a transformation of attitudes concerning women's proper place among most Americans. After World War II, American society sent "Rosie the Riveter" and her female counterparts who worked in the war industries back home, and the country celebrated the ideal of female domesticity, taking care of home and children. Working women were concentrated in low-paying jobs and many college-educated women felt stifled by the routine of domesticity.

In 1963, Betty Friedan published *The Feminine Mystique*. Interviewing members of her class of 1942 at Smith College, Friedan found that these women were deeply dissatisfied with their lives as housewives and could not reconcile the intellectual and social stimulation of their college years with the isolation and routine of housework and child care. The book ignored the plight of minority and working-class women; however, it raised the consciousness of educated middle-class housewives who now realized that their feelings of powerlessness were shared, and they could use the political process to make changes (Hartmann 1989; Costain 1992). While *The Feminine Mystique* raised the consciousness of older educated middle-class women, younger college-aged women were coming to the conclusion that gender discrimination was pervasive in society rather than a consequence of personal failings. Moreover, these younger activists believed that this discrimination should be attacked through political action. Many college-aged women participated in the civil rights, student, and antiwar movements. Within these movements women learned how to gain attention to a cause and organize and mobilize a grassroots base.

While history books focus on leaders like Martin Luther King, Jr. and Malcolm X as the face of the civil rights movement, many women served as leaders in the cause (Robnett 2000). Precipitated by Rosa Parks refusing to give up her seat on the bus, the Montgomery Bus Boycott was a key moment in the effort to end racial segregation. To achieve success, the bus boycott had to be maintained. Jo Ann Robinson, an English teacher at Alabama State College, played a key role in building support in the black community to sustain the boycott for almost a year. Robinson led the Women's Political Council (WPC), an organization founded by local professional black women in 1946, to register black women to vote. Robinson and the WPC promoted the bus boycott by organizing WPC members and recruiting students and faculty at Alabama State College to prepare information sheets and distribute them throughout the black community. She also helped found the Montgomery Improvement Association. With Martin Luther King, Jr. as president, Robinson served on its executive board and edited its newsletter. She was a member of the team that negotiated with local and state officials and helped organize alternative transportation (Hartmann 1989).

Ella Baker was another key civil rights leader who often goes unmentioned. Baker was a founder of the Southern Christian Leadership Conference (SCLC) led by Martin Luther King, Jr. A community organizer, she served as NAACP field secretary and director of branches in the early 1940s and successfully developed NAACP chapters throughout the country. At great risk to her own life, Baker traveled the South enrolling blacks in the NAACP and helped to identify ways local leaders could combat segregation despite the fact that the NAACP was an outlawed organization in the South and its members were routinely tortured, killed, or run out of town (Omolade 2004). Although male ministers controlled the SCLC, in the 1950s Baker set up its office in Atlanta, was its first associate director, and temporarily served as executive director. Baker helped organize student protests and sit-ins and, through her position at SCLC, she provided the leadership and organizational support that led to the formation of the Student Non-Violent Coordinating Committee (SNCC)—a group committed to decentralized leadership and local control (Omolade 2004; Robnettt 2000). She was involved in SNCC's major projects and decisions throughout its lifetime despite being significantly older than its membership. SNCC leader and current member of Congress, John Lewis (D-GA), proclaimed, "In terms of ideas and philosophy and commitment, she was one of the youngest persons in the movement" (Hartmann 1989).

While participation in the social movements of the 1960s provided women with important political and organizing skills, women also found that their contributions were not equally valued, and they were inhibited from advancing to leadership roles in their respective movements. When the civil rights movement increasingly turned toward "black power," white activists were pushed out of the movement as new, more radical leaders like Stokely Carmichael had begun to emphasize that black men needed to regain their manhood. In the antiwar movement, women found themselves in supporting roles as only men could burn their draft cards. Women who participated in the student movement and organizations such as Students for a Democratic Society were shut out of leadership roles and their concerns for women's rights were largely dismissed. In 1967 the National Conference for a New Politics gathered 200 civil rights, antiwar, and radical organizations. When women tried to raise their concerns about sex discrimination, the conference rejected these demands as trivial compared to the needs of other oppressed groups. This led women activists to start their own women's groups in cities across the country (Freeman 1975; Hartmann 1989).

The Emergence of the Older and Younger
Branches of the Feminist Movement

Although feminism has been defined in many ways over the years, most would agree that feminism embraces a view of women's place in society that emphasizes equality, the social construction of gender, and group identity. Feminists believe that women and men are inherently of equal worth. While sex is a biological category, feminists view gender as a social construct. Historical social practices have elevated men, leading to the devaluation of women, their talents, and their role in society. In response, feminists devote themselves to eliminating sex discrimination by raising women's consciousness so that the personal becomes political and women embrace a group identity that sees their individual struggles through a politicized lens. Since the subjugation of women stems from an accumulation of private and public actions and traditions, government action is required to level the playing field and encourage social change (Cott 1987; Lorber 1994; Friedman 2002).

The development of group consciousness and the harnessing of women's political power required an active social movement. Organizationally, scholars note that the feminist movement developed along two tracks, each of which embraced different strands of feminism. These two branches of the movement have been referred to as the older and younger branches or the liberal and radical feminist movements. Liberal feminists utilized political action to effect social and political changes that would eliminate sex discrimination and allow women to achieve equal rights whereas radical feminists eschewed traditional methods of politics and attacked the ingrained sexism of society in order to raise feminist consciousness and achieve women's liberation (Freeman 1975; Hartmann 1989; Costain 1992; Ferree and Hess 1994). Both branches of the women's movement were mobilized at a time when the political system was open to the influence of new groups.

The younger branch focused its efforts on local activism and community building. Utilizing skills built in the protest politics of the civil rights, antiwar, and New Left movements, the activists in the younger branch devoted themselves to consciousness raising, which involved getting women to recognize that what they believed were personal problems actually stemmed from inherent sex discrimination in the institutions of society and through socialization processes. The consciousness-raising sessions and writings that came out of participation in the movement advanced the theoretical and ideological foundations of feminism. These women formed groups that emphasized equality and participatory democracy in both action and structure. Therefore, they did not have hierarchical structures with recognized leaders. Instead, they rotated leadership positions and made decisions based on consensus. One group, the Redstockings Collective, created a manifesto modeled on the Communist Manifesto that characterized women as an oppressed social class that must rise up in revolution against its oppressors (Freeman 1975; Shanley 1988) (see appendix B for the full text of the NOW Bill of Rights and the Redstockings Manifesto).

These younger branch feminists also sought to create new institutions devoted to women's needs. They established women's health clinics, feminist bookstores, childcare centers, and rape crisis centers. Their consciousness-raising groups allowed women to share their experiences, provide mutual support, and explore the societal and political foundations of discrimination. Many younger branch groups also gained notoriety for employing radical shock protest techniques. Group names like SCUM (the Society to Cut Up Men) and WITCH (Women's International Conspiracy from Hell) were designed to shock mainstream America. WITCH staged hexing events such as the hexing of the New York Stock Exchange and

Mrs. Pat Nixon during the First Lady's trip to Portland, Oregon, in 1968. Other younger branch feminists staged a protest at the 1968 Miss America Contest in which they threw underwear, cosmetics, and false eyelashes into a "freedom trashcan" and crowned a sheep Miss America. The groups also held protests at bridal fairs and staged hairy legs demonstrations. These techniques often embarrassed the older branch of the movement, which preferred to focus on traditional lobbying methods, and feared the impact of these protests on public support for the larger movement (Freeman 1975; Hartmann 1989; Costain 1992; Ryan 1992).

In contrast, the older branch grew out of women's involvement with President Kennedy's Commission on the Status of Women (CSW) and focused most of their efforts on dismantling discrimination through legal change. Victorious in the extremely close presidential election of 1960, President Kennedy recognized that the New Deal coalition of voters forged by President Roosevelt was declining and both Republicans and Democrats were looking for ways to mobilize new groups of voters to create a governing majority. Viewing women as a potentially emerging voting force, Kennedy agreed with a suggestion from Esther Peterson, assistant secretary of Labor and the director of the Women's Bureau of the Department of Labor, that he appoint a CSW to recommend proposals to combat sex discrimination in government and the private sector. The CSW would have the added benefit of deflecting attention away from the demand for an ERA to the Constitution put forth by women's groups such as the National Woman's Party, the National Association of Colored Women, and the Business and Professional Women's Clubs. The ERA could potentially split the Democratic Party since organized labor vehemently opposed its adoption, fearing that it would lead to the elimination of the protective labor legislation that Progressive Era reformers had fought for in order to improve the working conditions of women (Freeman 1975; Hartmann 1989; Costain 1992; Ryan 1992; Ferree and Hess 1994).

Chaired by Eleanor Roosevelt, the report issued by the CSW in 1963 documented social, economic, and legal discrimination against women across the country and led to the creation of a Citizen's Advisory Council on the Status of Women and an Interdepartmental Committee on the Status of Women. In response to the findings of the CSW and the pressure of women's groups, governors across the country created state-level Commissions on the Status of Women. These state commissions continued the work of documenting discrimination against women and met together in annual conferences to share their findings. Thus, the work of the federal and state commissions helped create the organizational capacity for a renewed feminist movement. With the support of the federal and state governments, commission members developed the data necessary to demonstrate pervasive discrimination against women. The national conferences brought women together from across the country to share their findings, network with fellow commission members, and develop contacts inside the federal government (Freeman 1975; Hartmann 1989; Costain 1992; Ryan 1992; Ferree and Hess 1994).

In addition to the creation of the State Commissions on the Status of Women, Congress passed two important pieces of legislation to advance women's rights. In response to the lobbying efforts of labor unions and women's groups organized by Esther Peterson, Congress passed the Equal Pay Act in 1963. Although the act would not address the fact that a sex-segregated workforce in which occupations predominantly composed of women pay less than occupations of similar skill levels that are predominantly composed of men, the act did mandate that employers could no longer pay women less than men who perform the same job and established a precedent of government action on behalf of economic equity for women (Hartmann 1989; Costain 1992).

The inclusion of sex in Title VII of the Civil Rights Act of 1964 constituted the second important legislative advancement for women. The act prohibits discrimination based on race, color, religion, sex, or national origin in public accommodations and employment. The law also created an Equal Employment Opportunity Commission (EEOC) to investigate job discrimination complaints. One of the crowning achievements of the civil rights movement, the inclusion of sex in Title VII was a contentious proposition (Freeman 1975; Hartmann 1989; Costain 1992; Ferree and Hess 1994; Gelb and Palley 1996). Although sincerely supported by some legislators, particularly Martha Griffiths (D-MI), who originally intended to introduce the addition of sex as her own amendment, other liberal members of Congress including Edith Green (D-OR), who sponsored the Equal Pay Act, opposed the addition of sex to the act for fear that it would doom the bill and its efforts to curtail racial discrimination. In fact, the incorporation of sex was added as an amendment in the House Judiciary Committee by an ardent opponent of the Civil Rights Act, Representative Howard Smith (D-VA), the chair of the House Rules Committee—who hoped to doom the entire bill. Numerous southern legislators voted in favor of the addition of sex and against the entire bill. During the House floor debate over the amendment, some liberal male members treated it as a joke. In response, Martha Griffiths (D-MI) scolded her colleagues, asserting that "if there had been any necessity to have pointed out that women were a second-class sex, the laughter would have proved it" (quoted in Hartmann 1989, 55; Costain 1992, 38). Representative Edith Green (D-OR), who opposed the amendment, nonetheless sought to reinforce the legitimacy of claims of sex discrimination by stating, "Any woman who wants to have a career, who wants to go into the professions, who wants to work, I feel, cannot possibly reach maturity without being very keenly and very painfully made aware of all the discrimination placed against her because of her sex" (quoted in Costain 1992, 39). Despite its inauspicious start, the Civil Rights Act of 1964 with the incorporation of sex into Title VII ultimately passed.

The controversy surrounding the inclusion of sex in Title VII impacted the calculations of the EEOC concerning how heavily to focus on enforcement of the sex provision. With limited resources and a belief that race was the major focus of their mission, EEOC commissioners did not devote much attention to the task of rooting out sex discrimination in employment. Two of the EEOC commissioners, Richard Graham and Sonia Pressman, as well as other women serving inside the government, encouraged Betty Friedan to form an interest group outside of government—an NAACP for women—to put pressure on the EEOC. When the EEOC refused to address the problem of sex-segregated want ads in which newspapers listed positions by sex, the delegates to the national conference of the State Commissions on the Status of Women drafted resolutions urging the EEOC to enforce the Title VII provisions concerning sex discrimination. However, the delegates were barred from introducing these resolutions, as they would be construed as a criticism of the Johnson administration.

Recognizing the need for a pressure group that was independent of the government, Betty Friedan and others formed the National Organization for Women (NOW) in 1966. Among the group's 126 charter members were former EEOC commissioners Richard Graham and Aileen Hernandez and seven former and current members of State Commissions on the Status of Women. Thus, the group began as an elite Washington-based network that later developed a grassroots base of chapters throughout the nation (Freeman 1975; Hartmann 1989; Costain 1992).

In contrast to the younger branch of the feminist movement, which emphasized consciousness raising to change societal norms, NOW and other older branch organizations worked to achieve equality through legal reform. They believed that changes in law and adoption of public policies such as expansion of education and childcare services and enforcement of antidiscrimination laws would allow women to achieve equality in society and the workplace. Therefore, the newly created NOW devoted itself to attacking sex discrimination by adopting a strategy that combined direct executive and legislative lobbying with mass protest and the litigation of test cases that had been perfected by the civil rights movement. Utilizing these multiple political tools, NOW convinced President Lyndon Johnson to expand the executive order that is the basis for federal affirmative action programs to include sex. They also forced newspapers to eliminate sex-segregated want ads after intensive lobbying and a protest campaign that included picketing the headquarters of the *New York Times* and a national day of demonstrations in five cities targeted at the EEOC. In addition to reversing its earlier ruling on sex-segregated job ads, NOW activities also contributed to the decision of the EEOC to withdraw its support for state protective laws that restricted women's access to employment (Freeman 1975; Hartmann 1989; Costain 1992; Ryan 1992; Carabillo, Meuli, and Csida 1993; Ferree and Hess 1994).

The litigation activities of NOW's Legal Defense and Education Fund (LDEF) also helped break down discriminatory barriers in all areas of society. For example, *Weeks v. Southern Bell* established the precedent that an employer must open all jobs to women who wish to apply by ruling that barring women from jobs that involve lifting more than 30 pounds constitutes a violation of Title VII of the Civil Rights Act of 1964. By 1974, NOW's LDEF had participated in more than fifty major legal cases concerning issues including family law, property rights, civil rights, and employment discrimination. Mass marches brought media attention to the movement and new members and supporters. For example, the 1970 "Women's Strike for Equality" held on the fiftieth anniversary of suffrage in favor of legalized abortion, government-sponsored childcare, and equal educational and employment opportunities attracted 500,000 women in New York City and 20,000 women in 90 cities across 42 states to demonstrations and rallies. These mass protests often brought together women from the older and younger branches of the movement (Freeman 1975; Hartmann 1989; Costain 1992; Ryan 1992; Carabillo, Meuli, and Csida 1993; Ferree and Hess 1994).

Although NOW enjoyed numerous successes, it also experienced internal and external conflicts concerning its goals, tactics, and methods of organization. Soon after its formation, Betty Friedan drafted a NOW Bill of Rights to present to the parties and candidates in the 1968 election and to create a plan for political action (see appendix B). The inclusion of demands for an ERA and support for abortion rights drove some activists out of the organization. In particular, support for the ERA drove away women associated with organized labor whose unions opposed the elimination of protective legislation for women, such as laws regulating women's working hours (e.g., preventing businesses from making women work night shifts) and the types of jobs they could perform. Other women objected to the inclusion of abortion rights. Some of these women formed the Women's Equity Action League, which devoted itself solely to issues regarding employment, education, and taxes. Other activists objected to the hierarchical decision-making structure of NOW that limited opportunities for local initiatives and sharing of power. Women like Ti-Grace Atkinson of the New York chapter of NOW left the group to form the Feminists, which adopted an organizational structure conducive to equal participation of all members (Freeman 1975; Hartmann 1989; Ryan 1992; Costain 1992).

Over time, NOW and other feminist groups have also received criticism as being organizations of middle-class white women that neglect the interests of working-class and minority women (Barakso 2004; Strolovitch 2007). For example, fighting for the right to work outside the home was not an overriding concern for black women who always had to work to support their families. The right to an abortion is not meaningful without securing access for those who cannot afford the procedure. Moreover, black women were also concerned with addressing the injustice of the forced sterilization of people of color and people with disabilities (Grady 2018; Ko 2016). Some black feminists began to identify themselves as womanists in an effort to include race and class issues in feminism. Womanists identify and criticize racism in the feminist community and sexism in the black community. Alice Walker, Bell Hooks, and Audre Lorde are some of the prominent writers and activists associated with the movement (hooks 1981; Walker 1983; Lorde 1984). Building on this work, Kimberlé Crenshaw, a law professor and activist, coined the term intersectionality to refer to the importance of understanding how the multiple overlapping identities of marginalized groups impacted their experience of discrimination based on race, class, gender, and sexuality (Crenshaw 1989).

Alienated by the mainstream feminist organizations like NOW, women of color formed organizations focused specifically on addressing the interests of black women including The National Black Feminist Organization and the Combahee River Collective. Active from 1973–77, the National Black Feminist Organization (NFBO) worked on a range of issues from welfare reform and the problems of unwed mothers to black women as consumers and media images and stereotypes of black women. They lobbied for the inclusion of domestic workers in the Fair Labor Standards Act. Since the majority of domestic workers were black women, their inclusion in the Fair Labor Standards Act would mean they were covered by federal labor laws giving them access to collective bargaining, minimum wage, and other benefits (Harris 2001, 2009).

The Combahee River Collective took its name from a Civil War battle that was planned and led by Harriet Tubman. The battle freed 750 slaves and was the only military battle organized by a woman. The collective had a more radical vision of change than NFBO. They supported socialist solutions to economic problems and wanted to give a voice to black lesbians. The group focused on consciousness raising and community organizing. For example, they led an organizing and protest campaign to draw attention to a series of twelve murders of black women in Boston that was being ignored by the press and police because the women were alleged prostitutes and not valued by society. Their work led to greater focus on the problem of violence against women. They also hosted annual retreats where members could share their writings and brainstorm for future activism. The group's Combahee River Collective Statement became an important foundational document for black feminists (Harris 2001, 2009).

In addition to these internal movement struggles, the women's movement began to face new barriers in the political system. The election of President Nixon in 1968 as an advocate for the conservative "Silent Majority" that was upset by the turmoil of the civil rights, New Left, antiwar, and women's rights movements closed the executive branch to women's influence. However, Congress was increasingly open to their demands. The civil rights movement—and the passage of the Civil Rights Act of 1964 and the Voting Rights Act of 1965—created a coalition of members of Congress that was responsive to initiatives framed as demands for equal rights. Between 1972 and 1974, Congress passed Title IX to the Educational Amendments Act barring gender discrimination in education, the Women's Educational Equity Act, the Equal Credit Opportunity Act, and the ERA (Hartmann 1989; Costain 1992).

Although members of Congress embraced these initiatives that were designed to achieve what Gelb and Palley call "role equity" for women, they would not address legislation that embraced "role change" (Gelb and Palley 1996). In fact, movement historian Anne Costain (1992) claims that the agenda of the women's movement was co-opted by Congress as the groups focused on the equal rights agenda and set aside the special needs demands such as maternity leave rights in employment, establishment of government-funded childcare centers, and tax deductions for home and childcare expenses for working parents that were all included in the 1968 NOW Bill of Rights (see appendix B). Such treatment by Congress convinced many women's groups that true equality under the law would require a new constitutional amendment that guaranteed women equal rights.

THE EQUAL RIGHTS AMENDMENT

Section 1. Equality of rights under the law shall not be denied or abridged by the United States or by any state on account of sex.

Section 2. The Congress shall have the power to enforce, by appropriate legislation, the provisions of this article.

Section 3. This amendment shall take effect two years after the date of ratification.

After women won the vote, Alice Paul, leader of the National Woman's Party, believed that women needed an amendment to ban all discrimination based on sex, so that they could achieve full equality. To achieve this end, she drafted an ERA. First introduced in Congress in 1923, the amendment was reintroduced in various forms every year through 1971. Both major parties adopted platforms proclaiming their support, Republicans in 1940 and Democrats in 1944, despite facing strong opposition from labor unions that feared its impact on protective legislation for women workers.

It would be another 30 years before Congress passed the ERA. Women's groups, including NOW and Business and Professional Women's Clubs, coordinated their actions with sympathetic members of Congress, who forced the ERA out of committee in order to achieve hearings on the issue and moved the amendment toward a vote by the full House and Senate. In 1972, the ERA was finally granted a floor vote and passed the House and Senate by wide margins: 354 to 23 in the House and 84 to 8 in the Senate. During the House and Senate debates, women's groups and their allies defeated unfriendly amendments, such as exceptions for state protective labor legislation for women workers (such as laws regulating the types of jobs they could perform) and the exclusion of women in combat that sought to weaken the ERA. Thirty states had ratified the amendment by early 1973 (Mansbridge 1986; Hartmann 1989).

However, the controversial 1973 Supreme Court decision *Roe v. Wade* activated a strong antifeminist movement that opposed the goals of feminists who supported abortion rights and the ERA. Led by conservative women like Phyllis Schlafly, founder of STOP ERA and Eagle Forum, and Beverly LaHaye, founder of Concerned Women for America, the women who participated in the anti-ERA effort and the larger New Right movement were often socially conservative Christians. Many of these women were from the middle and lower-middle classes, and a large proportion were homemakers (Conover and Gray 1983; Klatch 1987; Schreiber 2008). Often mobilized through activism in their churches, the opposition forces excelled at grassroots organization and lobbying at the state level. The women involved in the anti-ERA movement wrote notes by hand to their state legislators and engaged in daily lobbying of individual state legislators in key states. Just as the pro-ERA forces utilized mass marches and protest techniques to highlight the connection between the ERA and American ideals of equality and the women's suffrage movement, anti-ERA activists engaged in their own symbolic politics as they sought to play on the American public's attachment to the ideals of motherhood, home, and family. Thus, STOP ERA activists handed out apple pies to state legislators with poems that read, "My heart and my hand went into this dough. For the sake of my family please vote no" (Mansbridge 1986; Ryan 1992; Ferree and Hess 1994).

Feminist groups countered with national economic boycotts against states that had not ratified the ERA, hundreds of letters mailed to legislators, and protest marches on state capitols. However, women's groups did not have grassroots organizations in specific states that had not ratified the amendment, particularly the conservative strongholds in the South. Additionally, it was difficult for the pro-ERA forces to point to concrete policy changes impacting gender roles that would result from the passage of the ERA. For example, many ERA activists used 59 cents, the wage gap between men and women, as an argument in favor of the ERA.

However, since the ERA had passed Congress in 1972, several Supreme Court decisions and the actions of the EEOC had eliminated some of the most egregious examples of sex discrimination, such as the protective labor laws that prevented women from being hired for jobs in specific fields and regulated their hours. As an amendment to the federal constitution, the ERA's language was vague and would only apply to actions of the federal government. Therefore, it would provide limited authority to act on issues of sex discrimination by states or private employers. Although the impact of the ERA on sex discrimination in the workplace was a source of conflict, the one substantive impact that was not disputed by either the pro or anti-ERA forces was that the ERA would require women to be drafted into the military if the country was to institute another draft during wartime. Drafting women was widely unpopular. In fact, one of the most effective strategies of anti-ERA activists in battleground states involved bringing baby girls wearing signs saying "Please don't draft me" to rallies at state capitols (Mansbridge 1986).

An estimated 10,000 marchers descend on the Capitol building in Springfield, Ill to demonstrate for the passage of the Equal Rights Amendment, May 16, 1976. The IL state legislature ultimately voted against ratification. *Source*: Associated Press.

Although most Americans support the concept of equal rights, there is less agreement regarding appropriate gender roles in the realms of employment, family, and the military. Indeed, public opinion polls spanning from congressional passage in 1972 to its failure in 1982 indicated that a majority of the public supported the amendment (Mansbridge 1986). However, as shown in table 2.1, while Americans' attitudes regarding gender roles have changed dramatically in the last 40 years, many Americans both support the idea of equality for women in the workplace and yet continue to value the ideal of women as mothers and primary caregivers of children. This ambivalence about the role of women creates conflict over policies that potentially impact the structure of family life, from public funding of childcare to contraception and abortion. Opponents of the ERA capitalized on fears concerning the impact of the ERA and the larger feminist movement on the status of homemakers, the welfare of the nuclear family, the obligation of the husband to support his wife and children in marriage and in cases of divorce, and the moral fabric of society. Such fears contributed to the mobilization of a strong antifeminist backlash (Mansbridge 1986; Gelb and Palley 1996).

Activist Phyllis Schlafly wearing a "Stop ERA" badge, demonstrating with other women against the Equal Rights Amendment in front of the White House, Washington, DC, February 4, 1977. *Source*: Library of Congress / Warren K. Leffler.

Despite the activism of the opposition groups, the national lobbying efforts by pro-ERA women's groups, which sponsored a large mass march on Washington to renew efforts to pass the amendment, convinced Congress to pass an extension of the original seven-year deadline that had been set when the ERA initially passed Congress in 1972. However, only five more states had ratified by 1977 and anti-ERA forces successfully persuaded some states that ratified the amendment to vote to rescind their ratification. Although these votes were nonbinding, they had a detrimental impact on the movement. The amendment went down to defeat in June 1982, falling three states short of ratification. This represents a much stronger performance than other recent popular amendments that have failed to make it out of Congress, including amendments requiring a balanced budget and amendments banning flag burning and abortion (Mansbridge 1986). The ERA has been reintroduced in every congressional session since its defeat.

In subsequent years, many states added ERAs to their state constitutions. Most recently, in the 2014 elections, Oregon voters passed a ballot initiative to add the ERA to their state constitution (Phillips 2014). In response to renewed activism for women's rights sparked by the election of Donald Trump as president, the Nevada and Illinois legislatures voted to ratify the federal amendment in 2017 and 2018, respectively. The map in figure 2.1 indicates which states passed the federal ERA, which states adopted an ERA in their state constitutions, and which states have neither passed the federal ERA nor included the ERA in their state constitutions. Theoretically, only one more state needs to ratify the federal ERA for it to be added to the Constitution (Stewart 2018).

Table 2.1 Public Opinion and Gender Roles

It is much better for everyone involved if the man is the achiever outside the home and the woman takes care of the home and family.

	1972–1982(%)	1998(%)	2002(%)	2006(%)	2010(%)	2016(%)
Agree	65	34	38	35	36	27
Disagree	34	63	61	63	64	73

A working mother can establish just as warm and secure a relationship with her children as a mother who does not work.

	1972–1982(%)	1998(%)	2002(%)	2006(%)	2010(%)	2016(%)
Agree	48	67	63	67	75	75
Disagree	50	32	36	33	24	25

A preschool child is likely to suffer if his or her mother works.

	1972–1982(%)	1998(%)	2002(%)	2006(%)	2010(%)	2016(%)
Agree	66	41	45	40	35	27
Disagree	32	56	54	59	64	72

Source: General Social Surveys 1972–2016.

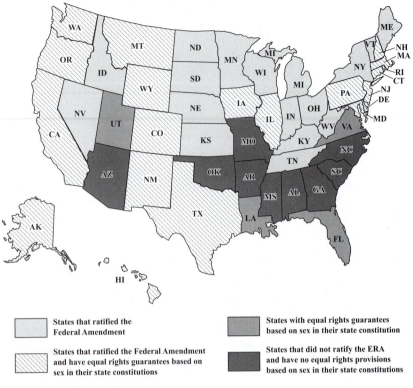

States that ratified the Federal Amendment

States that ratified the Federal Amendment and have equal rights guarantees based on sex in their state constitutions

States with equal rights guarantees based on sex in their state constitution

States that did not ratify the ERA and have no equal rights provisions based on sex in their state constitutions

Figure 2.1 ERA in the States

Source: Adapted from *Wall Street Journal* and Equalrightsamendment.org.

WOMEN AND INTEREST GROUPS

As a social movement, the first and second waves of the feminist movement sought to dramatically change American society by altering the accepted view of women's proper role in the public and private spheres. Social movements are both a cause and a consequence of dramatic social upheaval. By contrast, interest groups are more enduring factors of the American political landscape. Their narrower purpose seeks to effect policy change on a specific issue or set of issues (McAdam 1982; Costain 1992; Gelb and Palley 1996). Often, political interest groups emerge as a result of social movement protests, when the most committed protestors and activists formalize their involvement in actual groups. Thus, the feminist movement sought to change public perceptions as a social movement while also forming groups geared at enacting specific political and policy goals. Even before women won the right to vote, they had joined and formed groups to persuade local, state, and national officeholders to change the law on issues ranging from abolition to temperance. Women's groups including the National Congress of Mothers, the Women's Christian Temperance Union (WCTU), the National Consumers League, the National Association of Colored Women, and the General Federation of Women's Clubs (GFWC) contributed greatly to the development of government responsibility for social welfare programs in the Progressive Era (Skocpol 1992; Andersen 1996).

Advocating the philosophy of civic motherhood in which political activism was not a violation of the principle of separate spheres but a natural extension of women's duty to protect children and the home, these women lobbied the state and national governments for laws and programs addressing a wide range of issues, including maximum-hour laws for women and children, abolition of child labor, forestry and natural resource conservation, mothers' pensions (the precursor to modern-day welfare), public sanitation, civil service reform, and the creation of juvenile courts. These women's groups gained legitimacy by claiming to represent the interests and views of women, and they utilized their exclusion from traditional politics and the doctrine of separate spheres to claim authority as they sought reforms for moral and not political ends. Lacking the ability to vote politicians out of office, these groups were still able to sway officeholders because they had strong grassroots organizations in which local and state groups were connected to a national organization and could be mobilized to publicize issues and lobby government officials.

In her detailed study of the GFWC's involvement in the development of mothers' pensions, Theda Skocpol (1992) noted that for each issue engaged, club women consulted experts, undertook detailed investigations of current state practices, and studied the laws of other states. The clubs designed public education campaigns to gain support through moral exhortation and created model programs. Local and state legislatures were then lobbied to pass laws, establish regulatory commissions, and appoint women to these commissions. As a result of the activism of women's groups, women were appointed as factory inspectors, members of labor bureaus, truancy officers, police matrons, school board members, library commissioners, and members of social welfare agencies (Baker 1984; Skocpol 1992). Upon reviewing the efforts of the Harrisburg (PA) Women's Civic Club, a member reported:

> It is no longer necessary for us to continue at our own cost, the practical experiment we began in street cleaning . . . nor is it necessary longer to strive for a pure water supply, a healthier sewage system, or the construction of playgrounds. This work is now being done by the City Council, by the Department of Public Works, and by the Park Commission. (quoted in Door 1910, 37)

As a demonstration of the power of the activism of Progressive Era women's groups, surveying the development of state labor laws regarding women's working conditions, Skocpol found that state federations of women's clubs were active in lobbying for thirteen of the nineteen women's-hour laws that were passed from 1909 to 1917. Additionally, state federations actively lobbied for mothers' pensions to provide a source of financial support to widowed women with children in twenty-four states between 1912 and 1920. In those states where federations did not endorse pensions, the state legislature either failed to adopt pensions at all or adopted them much later than other states (Skocpol 1992). At the national level, the GFWC and other women's groups lobbied heavily for the Pure Food and Drug Act and the Sheppard-Towner Infancy and Maternity Protection Act.[*] They also worked for the establishment of the Children's Bureau and the reorganization of the Women's Division of the Bureau of Labor Statistics into a separate Women's Bureau to investigate the conditions of women workers and advocate for their welfare (Baker 1984; Skocpol 1992).

Like their Progressive Era counterparts, modern-day women's interest groups gain legitimacy by proclaiming to represent women's interests. However, groups have different and often opposing definitions of what constitutes women's interests and what women want. Many of the contemporary women's interest groups grew out of the feminist movement and the antifeminist countermovement. Additionally, there was an explosion in the number of national-oriented interest groups in the late 1960s and early 1970s. This interest group expansion stemmed from important changes that made the political system more open to interest group influence and from technological innovations that made it easier to contact and mobilize supporters (Berry 1997; Davidson et al. 2015). The increasing activism of the federal government during Lyndon Johnson's Great Society increased the number of government programs resulting in the creation of groups devoted to protecting and expanding their benefits and groups advocating for (or against) increased regulations on business and the environment, for example. In response to the Watergate scandal in the Nixon administration, Congress passed "sunshine laws" designed to open government activities to public scrutiny. As congressional hearings, committee meetings, and floor debates became open to the public, and information on the activities of the president and bureaucracy could be obtained through requests under the Freedom of Information Act, groups gained easier access to information impacting their interests.

Interest groups involved in elections also flourished as a result of the decline in the power of the political parties. Parties became weaker because

---

[*] The Sheppard-Towner Act was officially known as the Federal Act for the Promotion of the Welfare and Hygiene of Maternity and Infancy.

of the expansion of direct primary laws (state parties had less control over nominees to represent them in the general campaign), candidate-centered campaigns (in which parties became less important in terms of running campaign organizations), and campaign finance reform laws in the 1970s that decreased the power of the party to raise campaign money. Following passage of the Federal Election Campaign Act (FECA) in 1971 and its amendments in 1974, interest groups began establishing political action committees (PACs) to donate money to candidates, which in turn expanded their access to policymakers.* Finally, the advancement of technology, particularly the development of the internet and social media more generally, has reduced the costs associated with establishing a group and mobilizing activists (Hall and Wayman 1990; Berry 1997).

NOW remains the most widely known women's group. As mentioned earlier, the group grew out of the president's Commission on the Status of Women and was created in 1966 with the intention of establishing an "NAACP for women" to eliminate discrimination against women (Carabillo, Meuli, and Csida 1993). Today NOW claims to be the largest grassroots-based feminist organization in the United States with chapters in all fifty states (National Organization for Women 2017a). The group has a broad-based agenda advocating for policies to eliminate discrimination against women in the workplace, schools, the justice system, and all other sectors of society. Reproductive rights and other women's health issues, violence against women, the ERA, pay equity, family-friendly workplaces, and eliminating discrimination based on race and sexual orientation are also among the group's top priorities (National Organization for Women 2017b).

From the early years, NOW committed itself to being an action-oriented group dedicated to the mobilization of women at the grassroots level and to the pursuit of fundamental social change rather than to the more limited goal of legal equality with men. To that end, NOW combines traditional lobbying and education activities with more radical forms of political engagement such as mass marches and protests (Freeman 1975; Barakso 2004). In recent years, the group has held mass protests to support abortion rights, promote gay marriage, and rally against domestic violence (Barr and Williamson 2004; NOW 2017c). Former NOW president Patricia Ireland describes the benefits of marches and other mass actions:

---

*Political action committees, or PACs, were established by the federal government as part of the 1974 Federal Election Campaign Act in order to monitor and limit campaign spending by businesses and interest groups. Any corporation, union, or other interest group can form a PAC and register it with the Federal Election Commission, which monitors its spending on federal candidates. PACs are allowed to spend up to $5,000 on a federal campaign per election for each election cycle (meaning they can spend $10,000 if a candidate runs in a primary and in the general election).

We use them to organize and to inspire. A mass action builds our strength and our momentum—and shows that strength to politicians and to ourselves. Successful mass actions also have positive "hangover effects": the tremendous individual and group efforts needed to organize a big march expands our lists of contributors and supporters and provides an opportunity to develop skills and activism at the grass roots. These new community organizers can continue to expand that network and use it to turn out the vote or bring constituent pressure for an issue. (Ireland 1996, 249)

In addition to grassroots demonstrations and lobbying, NOW Foundation, the educational and legal arm of NOW, often uses the courts to pursue legal cases. With the courts playing such a key role in defining the parameters of women's rights, NOW Foundation has filed amicus (friend of the court) briefs seeking to expand or maintain women's rights in several recent high-profile cases including *Young v. United Parcel Services* regarding pregnancy discrimination, *King v. Burwell* concerning subsidies to help people pay for health plans under Obamacare, and multiple cases regarding gay marriage (National Organization for Women 2015a). The group works to mobilize younger generations of women through Campus Action Networks for women in college and NOW clubs for high school age teens. Finally, NOW, like many other organizations, has consistently been involved in presidential and congressional elections, conducting voter registration drives, endorsing candidates, and seeking to publicize its issues with the public and the major candidates. The group was an early and strong supporter of Senator Hillary Clinton (D-NY) in her race against Barack Obama for the 2008 presidential nomination. The group actively campaigned for Clinton in 2016 (National Organization for Women 2007, 2015b).

Groups like the Feminist Majority Foundation and the American Association of University Women are similar to NOW in their devotion to a broad range of issues and their focus on political activism utilizing a wide range of techniques from lobbying to litigation, issue research, and mass protest. There is also an increasing trend toward specialization in the feminist community in which groups concentrate their activism and research on one specific issue such as abortion, gay rights, domestic violence, or pacifism. The National Abortion Rights Action League (NARAL), Planned Parenthood, the National Coalition Against Domestic Violence, and CODE-PINK: Women for Peace are all groups that participate in grassroots activism for a particular cause. Still other organizations are brought together by a shared identity based on professional status or demographics such as age or race. Examples of these organizations include the Older Women's League, the Black Women's Health Imperative, The National Latina Institute for Reproductive Health, and Business and Professional Women.

Finally, there are numerous women's think tanks, which conduct public policy research on issues that impact women and families, and legal

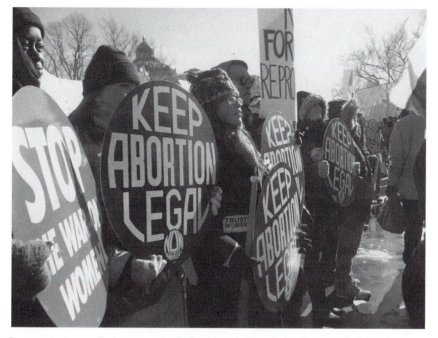

Demonstrators rally in support of abortion rights at the *Roe v. Wade* anniversary rally in January 2014. ***Source***: National Organization for Women / NOW.org.

advocacy groups, which focus their energy on activities such as providing legal representation for women in discrimination cases. For example, the Institute for Women's Policy Research publishes annual reports on the Status of Women in the States that rank each state based on women's status in political participation, employment and earnings, social and economic autonomy, reproductive rights, and women's health and well-being (Institute for Women's Policy Research n.d.). These reports are used to garner attention to these issues and spur legislation and policy change to address women's concerns. Similarly, the National Women's Law Center and the Center for Women's Policy Studies also focus on legal aid and public policy research rather than grassroots activism.

Conservative Women's Groups Fight Back

While there is great diversity in the activities and goals of organizations associated with the feminist movement, there is also a burgeoning conservative women's movement. In her book, *Women of the New Right*, Rebecca Klatch (1987) describes two archetypes of conservative women: the social conservative and the laissez-faire conservative. The political activism of the social conservative woman is strongly influenced by her religious beliefs and a desire to protect the traditional family, particularly regarding women's role in the home and in the care of children. Whereas the social conservative is motivated to activism by her moral code, the laissez-faire conservative is devoted to the ideals of individual rights, free market principles, and limited government. Thus, these women tend to eschew debates on social issues such as abortion and focus their efforts on economic concerns such as workplace issues. For example, laissez-faire conservative women oppose programs such as affirmative action as an unconstitutional preference and government intrusion that violates free market principles without improving the position of women and minorities (Klatch 1987; Schreiber 2002b, 2008). In contemporary politics, Concerned Women for America and Independent Women's Forum are two prominent conservative interest groups that typify the activism of right-leaning women's organizations.

Concerned Women for America is the largest group representing socially conservative women. Just as the awakening of a feminist consciousness in the early 1960s spurred the formation of NOW, Concerned Women for America grew out of the antifeminist countermovement. These women were mobilized in response to their opposition to the ERA, the *Roe v. Wade* decision on abortion, and the International Women's Year conferences and celebrations that elevated feminist principles concerning women's rights. Founded in 1979 in San Diego, California, by Beverly LaHaye, the group reaches out to Christian women as wives and mothers in an effort to protect the traditional family and reassert biblical principles as a foundation of public policy. LaHaye was at the center of the New Right movement in the 1970s and 1980s, traveling the country and giving speeches on family values and the moral decay of the nation, writing books, and conducting her own radio show. Her husband, the Reverend Tim LaHaye, was a founding member of Jerry Falwell's Moral Majority, one of the leading organizations in the mobilization of the New Right in the 1980s (Marshall 1995; Schreiber 2002a, b, 2008). According to the group's mission statement, "CWA protects and promotes Biblical values and Constitutional principles through prayer, education, and advocacy" (Concerned Women for America 2017a).

In her memoir *Who but a Woman?* Beverly LaHaye maintains that she founded CWA to "combat the goals of the feminist movement" after witnessing what she and other Christian women viewed as an attack on traditional families that occurred at the National Women's Convention in Houston, Texas, in 1977 to celebrate International Women's Year. LaHaye opposed the adoption of resolutions by the convention including "the ratification of the Equal Rights Amendment; the 'right' of homosexuals and lesbians to teach in public schools and to have custody of children; federally funded abortion on demand; approval of abortion for teenagers without parental knowledge or consent; federal government involvement in twenty-four-hour-a-day child care centers, and more" (LaHaye 1984, 27). The group built its membership through church networks, attracting the support of ministers, distributing literature to recruit evangelical Protestant women, and holding coffees with like-minded women.

Today CWA represents a national network of prayer/action chapters connected to a professional staff at the national headquarters, which opened in 1985 (Concerned Women for America 2017b). The prayer/action chapters mobilize grassroots women by meeting to learn and pray about issues and then take action on them, such as writing letters to Congress or newspaper editorial boards. In order to promote the return to biblical values, the group focuses on issues such as opposition to abortion, homosexuality, and pornography. It also opposes the United Nations as undermining American sovereignty, advocates for the expansion of religious liberty, meaning the ability to bring religion back into the public square, and seeks to restore Judeo-Christian values and parental authority in the public school system (Concerned Women for America 2017c).

Like its feminist counterparts such as NOW and AAUW, CWA conducts lobbying efforts and prepares voter guides to draw the attention of its members and legislators to its key issues. In recent years CWA and Susan B. Anthony List, a pro-life women's organization, have been particularly active in lobbying the federal and state governments to adopt more restrictions on abortion and to prohibit government funding to Planned Parenthood as an organization that provides abortions in addition to other women's preventive health services such as birth control and cancer screenings (Hodges 2017; Swers 2018).

In contrast to the social issue focus of Concerned Women for America, the Independent Women's Forum (IWF) concentrates on the economic and limited government issues that concern laissez-faire conservatives. Angered by the media coverage of the Clarence Thomas–Anita Hill hearings,[*] in which the feminist view was equated with the perspective of all women, a group of women who worked for the George H. W. Bush administration founded this organization in 1992. They decided to create an organization to counter the feminist establishment by providing a voice for conservative women who believe in individual freedom, self-government, and personal responsibility. IWF eschews moral debates and does not take a position on

---

[*] The hearings involved the confirmation of Clarence Thomas to be an associate justice on the US Supreme Court in 1991. The all-male Senate Judiciary Committee heard testimony from Anita Hill, who had accused Thomas of sexual harassment when she worked for him at the Equal Employment Opportunity Commission. Liberal women's organizations believed that Hill was mistreated but her allegations were not taken seriously by many of the senators during questioning. Thomas, who denied the charges, was eventually appointed to the bench.

abortion. Instead, it focuses on economic issues and on reducing government regulation (Schreiber 2002a, b, 2008).

The group believes that government programs designed to help women, in fact, disrespect women and limit their choices. For example, IWF opposes the Title IX program as it applies to athletics. Title IX is federal legislation that mandates that public schools that receive federal funds, both at the secondary and at the collegiate levels, must ensure that women's sports programs receive equal treatment and the same funding as men's programs. The IWF views Title IX as a quota system that demeans the legitimate athletic accomplishments of women and denies opportunities to men by requiring a strict measure of proportionality in participation in college athletics when women are relatively less interested in athletics than men (Schreiber 2002a, 2008).

Similarly, IWF and economic conservative activists argue that the gender pay gap is a myth and, instead, reflects women's choices (Schreiber 2008). Feminist advocates maintain that a combination of discriminatory practices and social expectations about women's roles contribute to a gender pay gap in which women as a group make less money than men. To close the gender wage gap, feminist groups believe the government should adopt policies that make it easier for employees to share salary information and engage in litigation to combat employment discrimination. They also advocate for changes in society that undervalue positions that are predominantly held by women compared to male-dominated fields. Thus, feminists ask why home health care and childcare workers make less than truck drivers and security guards. Feminist groups strongly advocate for policy changes that would make it easier for women to balance their work and family responsibilities such as paid family leave, paid sick days, and leave policies that encourage men as well as women to take leave (O'Leary and Kornbluh 2009; Boushey 2014).

By contrast, IWF and conservative women oppose the proposals as big government interferences into areas that reflect women's individual choices. They maintain that women are more likely than men to want to reduce their hours or to leave the workforce to take care of their children. Among college-educated workers, women are more likely than men to major in fields that emphasize caring and pay less. Thus more men major in various fields of engineering while more women major in early childhood education, social work, and psychology (Sommers 2014). Conservative women also assert that policies that mandate benefits like parental leave and seek to micromanage wages actually reduce women's choices, making it harder for them to negotiate flexible work schedules and pay, and reducing incentives for employers to hire more workers and more women (Lukas 2014). In sum, IWF leaders focus their efforts on providing research and gaining media attention to a conservative viewpoint on women's interests.

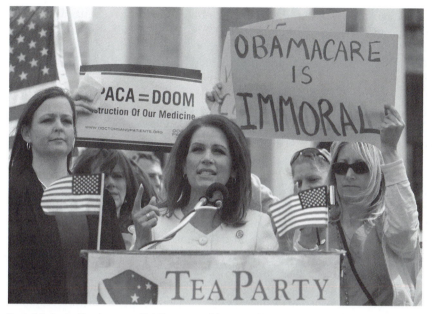

Rep. Michele Bachmann, R-Minn, speaking at a Tea Party Rally to oppose the constitutionality of Barack Obama's health care overhaul on March 28, 2012, the day the Supreme Court heard oral arguments about the Affordable Care Act. Bachmann is flanked by Tea Party women activists, including Tea Party Patriots cofounder Jenny Beth Martin (left). *Source:* Associated Press / Carolyn Kaster.

Reinvigoration of the Feminist Movement and Conservative Women's Activism

In 2016, feminist activists and Democratic-leaning women celebrated when Hillary Clinton became the first female presidential nominee of a major political party. These women were shocked and angered when she lost to Donald Trump, a candidate who had no political experience, made numerous racist and sexist remarks throughout the campaign, and bragged about making unwanted sexual advances against women in a video continuously replayed by the media. The day after President Trump's inauguration, thousands of women took to the streets in Washington, DC, cities across the United States, and around the world, to protest for women's rights. Soon after, the #MeToo and Time's Up movements arose to confront sexual assault and sex discrimination in the workplace (Grady 2018). By 2018, women driven to activism by issues ranging from women's rights to health care ran for local and national political office achieving the biggest electoral gains for women winning office since 1992 (Edmonson and Lee 2018). Does the renewed activism among women represent a reinvigoration of the feminist movement?

The place of women's rights in the political world has changed dramatically in recent years. During the 1960s and 1970s issues of women's rights were not strongly associated with either the Democratic or the Republican Party. Both parties had endorsed the Equal Rights Amendment in their platforms. Republican president Gerald Ford's wife, Betty, actively campaigned for the Equal Rights Amendment. Supporters and opponents of abortion could be found in both the Democratic and Republican ranks (Sanbonmatsu 2002; Wolbrecht 2000). The election of Ronald Reagan in 1980 marked a turning point in which the parties' positions on women's rights began to diverge. Reagan brought social conservatives into the fold of the Republican Party. The party dropped its support for the Equal Rights Amendment and in each successive presidential convention its platform concerning abortion became more strongly pro-life. Meanwhile, feminist organizations gained influence in the Democratic Party. In the 1970s, the Democrats adopted quotas that required proportional representation of women, minorities, and young people at conventions. As members of the party coalition, women's groups could pressure party leaders to address their concerns (Sanbonmatsu 2002; Wolbrecht 2000). Grossman and Hopkins (2016) have described the Democrats as a party of groups in which Democratic politicians espouse policies to address the interests of their constituent groups including women's groups, civil rights groups, environmental organizations, and labor unions. Similarly, social conservatives are firmly entrenched in the Republican Party. Today women's rights is a major fault line between the parties and abortion is among the most fiercely debated issues.

At the same time that women's rights became incorporated into the partisan divide, party competition for control of government became more intense. With a few exceptions, Democrats controlled Congress for most of the period from the New Deal in the 1930s through the early years of Bill Clinton's presidency (1990–1992). When Republicans won control of Congress in the 1994 Republican Revolution, Democrats had controlled the House of Representatives for more than 40 years. Since 1994 the parties have won and lost control of the presidency and both houses of Congress multiple times (Fiorina 2017). This heightened competition means that feminists and conservative women have gone through periods where the presidential administration and/or the congressional majority is responsive to their lobbying and periods when they are completely shut out of political decision-making. Thus, feminist groups celebrated when the Clinton administration and a Democratic Congress passed the Family and Medical Leave Act which, to date, is the only federal legislation mandating time off but not requiring pay for parental leave or other caregiving responsibilities. They hoped to see this program expanded and to require paid leave. However, the Republican takeover of Congress in 1994 stymied these efforts and the 2000 election and 2004 reelection of President George W. Bush meant that feminists had no allies among the ruling party in either the executive or the legislative branches of the national government. Feminist groups found themselves on the defensive trying to prevent the passage of policy changes that would restrict women's rights, particularly in the area of reproductive freedom.

The Democratic takeover of Congress in 2006, which included the selection of the first female Speaker of the House of Representatives, Nancy Pelosi (D-CA), and the election of a Democratic president, Barack Obama, in the 2008 election reenergized feminists as they again gained access to policymakers. The Lilly Ledbetter Fair Pay Act and various executive orders regarding equal pay moved the ball forward on pay equity. Obamacare, the president's health reform, expanded women's access to health care and provided important protections for women's health, including requiring coverage for prenatal care and contraception in basic health plans (Swers 2013; Deckman and McTague 2015).

While feminists celebrated these accomplishments, conservatives became increasingly incensed by the expansion of government into health care and efforts by the Bush and the Obama administrations to respond to the economic turmoil of the Great Recession in 2007. They seethed over the bailout of the giant financial institutions that helped cause the economic collapse and were alarmed by what they viewed as wasteful spending in Obama's economic stimulus bill. Conservative anger sparked the Tea Party movement. Many conservative women joined Tea Party groups and became active on social media to spread their views. Indeed, case studies suggest that there may have been more women than men in leadership positions at the local level (Lo 2012). Interviewing Tea Party women across the country, Melissa Deckman (2016a) found that these women felt an obligation as mothers to get involved in politics to protect their children against reckless government spending and rising debt.

Several women also emerged as national Tea Party leaders. Sarah Palin, the 2008 Republican vice presidential nominee, galvanized conservative women by appealing to "Mama Grizzlies who would rise up to protect their young against the oppressive hand of government" (Deckman 2016a). Jenny Beth Martin cofounded and became the president of the Tea Party Patriots, arguably the nation's largest Tea Party organization. She helped organize and lead the September 2012 Taxpayer's March on Washington to protest Obama administration policies on government spending, health reform, and abortion (Altman 2010). Michele Bachmann (R-MN) also catapulted to the forefront of the national movement espousing Tea Party principles during her time as a representative in Congress and briefly running for the Republican presidential nomination in 2012.

Many Tea Party women also strongly supported Donald Trump. Trump spoke to these women's fears that the country is moving in the wrong direction both culturally and economically. They responded to his proposals to crack down on illegal immigration and bring back jobs to the United States. Some Tea Party women took leadership roles in his campaign, including Katrina Pierson, the founder of a Texas Tea Party organization who became Trump's national spokesperson, and Amy Kremer, the former chair of the Tea Party Express's PAC, who co-founded the pro-Trump Super PAC known as The Great America PAC (Deckman 2016a, b).

By contrast, feminist women's groups actively supported Hillary Clinton's run for the presidency and eagerly anticipated a renewed focus on women's rights. Clinton promised paid family leave, affordable childcare, and greater protections for women's reproductive rights and the LGBTQ community (Paquette 2016; Sussman and Meckler 2016). Donald Trump's unexpected victory alarmed progressive women. With full Republican control of the presidency and Congress, President Trump's administration began implementing plans to restrict abortion and defund Planned Parenthood (Crockett 2017b; Haberkorn 2017). President Trump moved quickly to install more conservative jurists on the Supreme Court, making feminists worry that the future of *Roe v. Wade* and abortion rights are at risk. Whereas the Obama administration focused heavily on enforcement of

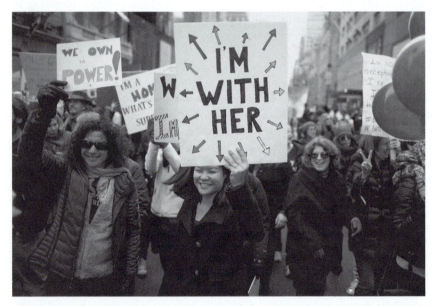

Outraged at the election of Donald Trump, millions of women took to the streets in Washington, DC, and around the world, on January 21, 2017, one day after his inauguration, to express their support for reproductive, civil, and human rights and other progressive causes that they believe may be threatened by the Trump administration. *Source*: Associated Press / Mary Altaffer.

civil rights laws, the Trump administration turned its attention to restricting immigration and scaled back provisions aimed at protecting racial and ethnic minorities and LGBTQ rights (Calamur 2017).

Anger at President Trump's racist and sexist rhetoric and his past behavior toward women galvanized many women to action. Sparked by a desire to protect gains made during the Obama years and to prevent a return to a more conservative vision of women's place in society, progressive women began organizing and engaging in politics. Perhaps the most high-profile action was the Women's March. Occurring the day after President Trump's inauguration the Women's March mobilized an estimated 4.5 million people across the world including the primary gathering in Washington, DC, and marches in 654 cities across the United States and 251 locations across the world (Berry and Chenoweth 2018). The march organizers committed to building a march based around intersectionality that would emphasize the unique problems faced by women of color, immigrant women, and LGBTQIA (Lesbian, Gay, Transgender, Queer, Intersexual, and Asexual) people. Their platform of unity principles included broad goals that "women's rights are human rights and that gender justice is economic justice is racial justice" and more concrete policy actions calling for paid family leave and a right to clean water (Berry and Chenoweth 2018; Frostenson 2017).

Even with these efforts the Women's March as an organization and movement has faced criticism from various quarters. Pro-life feminist women were angry about being excluded from the march (Deckman 2017). The leadership of the march has been criticized for ties to anti-Semitism (Stockman 2018). Despite the commitment to intersectionality, the marchers across the United States were disproportionately highly educated, white, middle-aged women (Shulevitz 2017; Fisher, Dow, and Ray 2017). With white women dominating the march attendees, minority women worried that not enough attention would be paid to the problems faced by women of color and other groups outside of the white middle-class women that have dominated the feminist movement (Bates 2017; Desmond-Harris 2017; Brewer and Dundes 2018). For example, many local leaders in the Black Lives Matter movement, a movement founded by three black women to protest shootings of unarmed black men and violence against the larger black community, refused to attend the Women's Marches in 2017 and 2018 or voiced concerns about the sincerity of white women's commitment to their cause (Quarshie 2018) (For more on the grassroots presence of Black Lives Matter, see chapter 6.).

Still, research shows that the most successful social movements are able to draw from broad and diverse sources of support, building coalitions across groups and appealing to the moderate and wealthy members of society who have connections with those in positions of power in government and society (Chennoweth and Stephan 2012; Gade 2018; McConnaughy 2017). Women from all walks of life have participated in marches and protest actions broadly labeled as part of the "Resistance" (to President Trump and his policies more broadly), including The March for Science, A Day Without an Immigrant, A Day Without a Woman, The People's Climate March, and the March for Racial Justice (Heaney 2018; Berry and Chenoweth 2018).

Women also increased their engagement in traditional political activities, crowding town halls and flooding congressional offices with petitions in campaigns to save health-care reform from Republican efforts to repeal and replace Obamacare. Surveying organizers and participants in local groups active across the swing state of Pennsylvania, Skocpol and Gose found that 70 percent of participants were educated middle-aged suburban women between age 30 and 60, many of whom had not previously been active in politics (Putnam and Skocpol 2018).

Other women became active in the #MeToo and Time's Up movements. #MeToo originated with Tarana Burke, who founded the movement to draw attention and support for young women of color who had

Tarana Burke, the founder of the #MeToo movement. *Source*: Lev Radin/Pacific Press/Newscom.

been sexually assaulted or abused. The emergence of accusations of sexual assault and harassment against Hollywood mogul Harvey Weinstein led to a viral #MeToo movement on Twitter, Facebook, and Instagram initiated by well-known actresses that raised the consciousness of women as they learned of others who had endured similar experiences. Powerful men in media, business, and politics who had previously avoided consequences for their actions were now driven out of their positions and some faced criminal charges. Despite the media's focus on high-profile white women's experiences of assault, women of color remain disproportionately likely to be victims of sexual assault, and Native American women experience the highest rates of sexual violence among all groups of women (Hemmer 2017; Burke 2017; Langone 2018).

Seeking more concrete changes in law and business practices, Hollywood women created Time's Up, an organization focused on combating sex discrimination and sexual harassment in the workplace. The group also created a Time's Up Legal Defense Fund administered by the National Women's Law Center to help working-class women who do not have the means or the celebrity status to attract media attention and fund lawsuits against their employers (Buckley 2018; Corkery 2018).

The increased political organizing among women helped spur more women to run for office and support political campaigns in 2018. The heightened activism of women led to a record number of women running and winning office at the local and national level. Indeed, the new Congress that was elected in 2018 was striking for its diversity with a record number of women of color elected, including the first two Native American women and the first two Muslim American women elected to Congress (Edmondson and Lee 2018). As we discuss in more detail in chapters 4 and 7, we can expect newly activated women will continue to seek change in law and society moving forward.

CONCLUSION

Our discussion of women's participation in social movements and interest groups highlights a long, rich tradition of political activism among women. This activist tradition is marked by a great deal of diversity in the causes advocated by women, the ideological viewpoints of female activists, and the organizational tactics employed. Thus, during the fight for women's suffrage, women were active as both opponents and proponents of votes for women. Among the suffragists, women supported the movement for different reasons and they varied in the extent to which they sought to challenge traditional gender roles. Some women advocated for women's rights based on principles of human rights and individual freedom whereas others viewed the ballot as a means to achieve other social reforms by allowing women to act as civic mothers, viewing politics as a natural extension of women's private sphere responsibilities. Still other women sought the vote for more nefarious reasons, seeking to counteract the influence of minorities and immigrants in an effort to preserve white supremacy.

During the second wave of feminism, activists sought to expand women's rights in society and government. Through lobbying and legal reform, older branch groups like NOW sought to eliminate discriminatory employment practices and expand women's access to reproductive health services from abortion to contraception. Meanwhile, younger branch groups worked to raise women's group consciousness and to achieve women's liberation through profound changes in societal gender relations. Black women organized to empower themselves and gain attention to issues of racism and sexism. As the nation becomes more diverse, many women are emphasizing the importance of intersectionality, paying attention to women's overlapping identities and addressing the interests of previously marginalized groups. Women from a diverse array of backgrounds are both challenging and reinvigorating the feminist movement as they react against the policies of the Trump administration and organize on behalf of causes including immigrant rights, climate change, criminal justice reform, health care, sexual assault, and reproductive freedom.

In contemporary politics, women's organizations represent a wide range of issues and ideological perspectives. Thus, feminist groups promote equal rights for women and the elimination of barriers to women's full participation in society whereas socially conservative women's organizations promote the values of the traditional family and the primacy of motherhood. Economic conservatives seek to reduce government barriers to women's exercise of their free choice and pursuit of their goals in the free market. As women's place in society continues to evolve, women's organizations on the left and right will continue to promote their vision of "what women want."

3

The Gender Gap in Elections and Public Opinion

◆ ◆ ◆

HILLARY CLINTON LAUNCHED HER 2016 presidential campaign promising to put a focus on the needs of women and their families. According to Clinton and her Democratic supporters, women want equal pay, an increase in the minimum wage, access to paid leave, and affordable high-quality childcare (Allen 2015). Her opponent Donald Trump focused his campaign on blue-collar voters who had been hurt by trade deals and who were uneasy about immigration. Trump was also heavily criticized for his long history of inappropriate comments toward and about women, which he insisted was merely "locker room talk." In an effort to appeal to suburban women voters, Hillary Clinton tried to capitalize on Trump's misogynistic statements by running advertisements showing young girls looking into a mirror while they listened to a litany of insulting comments Trump had made about women (Merica 2016). While Trump's campaign largely portrayed him as a strong, decisive leader who would "Make America Great Again," Trump also recognized the importance of outreach to women voters and tried to mobilize them with a plan developed by his daughter Ivanka to provide paid maternity leave and increase the affordability of childcare through expanded tax credits for working mothers (Rucker 2016).

The contest between the first female presidential candidate and a candidate who continually highlighted his masculinity meant women voters were central to the 2016 campaign. Similarly, in recent elections, candidates, parties, and their interest group allies have typically crafted messages that will mobilize particular groups of women. Democrats such as Barack Obama and Hillary Clinton have focused on equal pay, health care, reproductive rights, childcare affordability, and other policies targeted at women (Roarty 2012; Thompson 2012; Allen 2015). Meanwhile, Republicans like George W. Bush and Mitt Romney have focused on women as entrepreneurs who will benefit from Republican tax policies and as mothers who are looking to protect the security of their families (Martinez and Carey 2004; Reinhard

2012). Such approaches by these campaigns raise an important set of questions: What do women voters want? Do women and men actually have distinct views about politics and divergent patterns in their voting behavior? How do other factors such as race, class, education, and marital status influence the worldviews of men and women?

In this chapter we examine differences in the voting behavior and political attitudes of men and women. The chapter traces the emergence of the gender gap in voting and explores the causes of this much talked about phenomena of American politics. We explore the efforts of the political parties to attract the votes of different demographic subgroups of women and examine whether women's position as a potential swing-voting group translates into political power and women-friendly policy. Finally, the chapter examines whether women voters constitute a key group of supporters for women candidates and we take a closer look at the 2016 and 2008 presidential campaigns of Hillary Clinton and her support among various groups of male and female voters.

COURTING THE WOMEN'S VOTE: THE EARLY YEARS

As chapter 2 recounts, the struggle to achieve the right to vote for women spanned over seventy years of American history (1848–1920). (See table 3.1 for a list of countries and when they granted women the right to vote.) During the campaign female reformers promised that when given the right to vote, women would "clean up" government and elect politicians committed to reforms that would help women and children, often involving enhanced regulation of industry. Wanting to court this new group of potential voters and facing pressure from women's organizations such as the General Federation of Women's Clubs and the National Congress of Mothers (today known as the PTA), members of Congress passed several important bills to help women and their families. These laws included the Sheppard-Towner Act (1921), the first government-supported program for educating mothers about infant and prenatal care, the Packers and Stockyard Bill (1921), requiring meat inspections to protect consumers, and the Child Labor Act (1924), an effort to pass a constitutional amendment limiting child labor (Klein 1984; Skocpol 1992; Flexner and Fitzpatrick 1996).

While reform-minded politicians eagerly anticipated a women's vote, others marshaled their resources against suffrage out of fear that women's votes would yield a flood of progressive legislation. Thus, business interests, including railroad, oil, meatpacking, and general manufacturing groups, opposed women's suffrage because they feared that women would vote to outlaw child labor and demand improved conditions for workingwomen. The political machines opposed voting rights for women because they doubted their ability to control women's votes and feared their reform proposals for clean government. The liquor manufacturers were among the most ardently opposed to suffrage because of the leadership of women in the temperance movement (Flexner and Fitzpatrick 1996). Speaking at the 1912 convention of the National Retail Dealer's Association, Neil Bonner, the association president, declared: "We do not fear the churches, the men are voting the old tickets; . . . we need not fear the YMCA, for it does no aggressive work; but, gentlemen, we need to fear the Woman's Christian Temperance Union and the ballot in the hands of women; therefore, gentleman, fight woman suffrage" (quoted in Tyler 1949, 159).

Yet proponents and opponents of women's suffrage, who foresaw the potential of having women vote en masse, were wrong. In the years immediately following the adoption of the Nineteenth Amendment, women did not vote in large numbers and a women's bloc of votes loyal to a specific set of issues or a particular party did not emerge. A generation of women who were raised to believe that politics was a male domain did not cast a ballot. Instead, like other new groups of voters, women had to develop the habit of voting (Corder and Wolbrecht 2016). In the 1920 election, only one-third of eligible women voted, and among those women, party affiliation, class, religion, and ethnicity, rather than sex, influenced their voting decisions. The greatest differences in turnout among women occurred among groups where sex role differences were most entrenched. Immigrant, rural,

Table 3.1   Women's Suffrage in Select Democratic Countries

Year	Country
1893	New Zealand
1902	Australia*
1906	Finland
1913	Norway
1915	Denmark
1918	Germany, United Kingdom
1919	Netherlands, Sweden*
1920	United States
1944	France
1945	Italy
1952	Greece
1971	Switzerland

Note: In 1971, Switzerland became the last democratic country to adopt women's suffrage. In contrast to the United States, where the Nineteenth Amendment to the Constitution mandated full suffrage for women, in Switzerland, the constitutional amendment passed allowed local cantons (the equivalent of states in the United States) to adopt their own laws concerning suffrage in local elections and for one house of the Swiss Parliament. As a result, two Swiss cantons did not adopt full suffrage for women until 1989 and 1990 (Banaszak 1996).

Source: Inter-Parliamentary Union: 2005. "A World Chronology of the Recognition of Women's Rights to Vote and to Stand for Election." www.ipu.org/wmn-e/suffrage.htm.

*Indicates that the right to vote was subject to conditions or restrictions.

Southern, and poor women voted in much smaller numbers than their male counterparts, whereas the turnout rates of native-born, middle-class women were closer to that of men (Klein 1984; Andersen 1996).

During the Great Depression, New Deal Democrats courted women voters based on Roosevelt's social welfare policies. Thus, in 1936, First Lady Eleanor Roosevelt and Mary Dewson, the head of the Women's Division of the Democratic Party from 1932 to 1937, organized 60,000 women to canvass door-to-door for the Democrats (Klein 1984). Still, in presidential elections from 1920–1936 Corder and Wolbrecht (2016) find that women voters did not consistently favor any particular party's candidates more than men did. As new voters, in comparison to men, women's turnout levels varied more as a result of the competitiveness of the parties in their state and the restrictiveness of their state's electoral laws, such as registration requirements. Women's voting participation first exceeded 50 percent of eligible women in the hotly contested presidential race of 1948 in which Harry Truman survived a split of his party that led Strom Thurmond to run on a Dixiecrat ticket and Henry Wallace to run under the Progressive banner (Klein 1984). The race

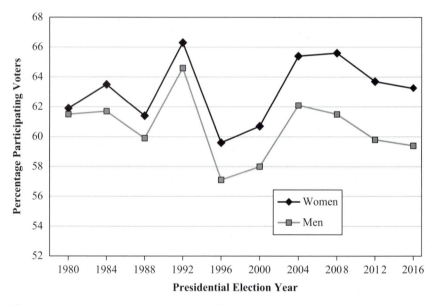

Figure 3.1 Male and Female Eligible Voter Turnout in Presidential Election Years 1980–2016

Note: Numbers are based on the U.S. Census which relies on self-reports in post-election surveys resulting in some inflation of the numbers of actual voters.

Source: "Gender Differences in Voter Turnout" Center for American Women and Politics 2017. http://www.cawp.rutgers.edu/sites/default/files/resources/genderd iff.pdf.

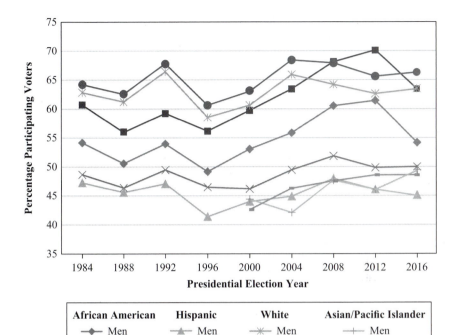

Figure 3.2   Voter Turnout by Race and Gender in Presidential Elections 1984–2016

Note: Numbers are based on the U.S. Census which relies on self-reports in post-election surveys resulting in some inflation of the numbers of actual voters.

Source: "Gender Differences in Voter Turnout" Center for American Women and Politics 2017. http://www.cawp.rutgers.edu/sites/default/files/resources/genderd iff.pdf.

was so close that the *Chicago Tribune* mistakenly declared Republican Thomas Dewey the winner in its early morning edition (Norton et al. 1986).

By 1968 women's voting rates had largely caught up to the participation rates of men. Signaling the complete political integration of women in the realm of voting, since the 1984 election, women's participation rates in presidential elections have exceeded the rates of men across racial categories with the largest differences among African Americans (see figures 3.1 and 3.2).*

---

*According to the Center for American Women and Politics (2014), in 2000, the first year for which data are available, Asian /Pacific Islander men voted at a higher rate than Asian/Pacific Islander women at 42.5 percent for women and 44.3 percent for men. Since 2000, voter turnout of Asian/Pacific Islander women has equaled or exceeded the turnout rates among their male counterparts. However, in 2016 turnout among Asian/Pacific Islander women lagged men 48.4 to 49.7 percent.

Between 1984 and 2004 white women were the most likely voters across all racial and gender groups. However, reflecting their enthusiasm for the election of the first African American president, Barack Obama, in 2008 and 2012 African American women exhibited the highest turnout (Center for American Women and Politics 2017). By 2016, with Barack Obama no longer on the ballot, the voter turnout rates for African American men and women reverted back to 2004 levels. Some analysts argued that this decline in black turnout hurt Hillary Clinton's chances in swing states like Pennsylvania and Michigan where turnout among black voters in cities like Philadelphia and Detroit was down (Fraga et al. 2017). While we cannot definitively say that one particular factor swings a race, campaigns work feverishly to mobilize voting blocks that favor their party, a point we will return to in our discussion of Clinton's race for the presidency.

THE EMERGENCE OF THE MODERN GENDER GAP

When most people think of the gender gap, they assume that it refers to the tendency of women to favor the Democratic Party. The media began paying attention to the gender gap in 1980 when Ronald Reagan's strong conservative politics, particularly his stances on the military and social welfare issues, gave him stronger support among men than women (Gilens 1988; Burrell 2005). However, this has not always been the case. Figure 3.3 identifies the gender gap in voting for the Democratic presidential candidates since 1992, measured as the difference between the percentage of men and women who support the Democratic candidate. Surveys of party identification since the 1950s demonstrate that women were aligned more closely with the Republican Party until 1964. This partially stems from the fact that in the 1950s and early 1960s, the majority of women were home-makers, whereas the majority of men were employed in blue-collar jobs. Homemakers and those in professional/managerial and clerical/sales jobs tend to vote Republican, whereas employees in blue-collar/service jobs who are often unionized are more likely to vote Democratic. Thus, the fact that, in 1956, 64.5 percent of women were homemakers and only 16.9 percent held blue-collar jobs, whereas less than 1 percent of men were homemakers and 64.8 percent were blue-collar workers, helps explain the gender gap in partisanship and voting during this period (Seltzer, Newman, and Leighton 1997; Norrander 2008).

Other scholars point out that the gender gap resulted more from men leaving the Democratic Party than women realigning toward it (Kaufmann and Petrocick 1999; Norrander 1999, 2008; Kanthak and Norrander 2004). Beginning in the 1960s, men, particularly white Southern men, increasingly became more Republican because of their opposition to the ascendancy of liberal views on civil rights and social welfare issues in the

Democratic Party. At the same time, white Southern women also became more Republican but at half the rate of white Southern men. Outside the South, white men also affiliated more with the Republican Party but at a rate slightly lower than Southern white women. However, white women's partisan preferences outside the South showed no change over time (Norrander 1999, 2008; Kanthak and Norrander 2004; Ondercin 2017). The change in the demographics of the party elite since 1980 also spurred more women to associate with the Democratic Party as feminist groups became more strongly associated with the party and more women were elected to office (Ondercin 2017). In the 1990s, there is some evidence that white women began to turn toward the Democratic Party because of the Democrats' more liberal positions on cultural issues (Kaufmann 2002).

Reflecting the slow but steady movement of white men, particularly white Southern men away from the Democratic Party, in 1960, men were 5 points more likely than women to vote for Democratic presidential candidate John F. Kennedy. However, by 1964, at the height of the civil rights movement, men were 4 points less likely than women to vote for Democratic president Lyndon Johnson and Democrats Hubert Humphrey

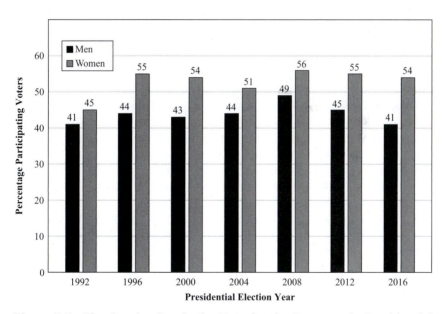

Figure 3.3   The Gender Gap in the Vote for the Democratic Presidential Candidate 1992–2016
Source: Exit Polls Compiled by Center for American Women and Politics 2017 "The Gender Gap" http://www.cawp.rutgers.edu/sites/default/files/resources/gg presvote.pdf.

and George McGovern in 1968 and 1972, respectively, drew slightly more women voters than men. In 1976, Jimmy Carter, a Southern moderate governor of Georgia running in the aftermath of the Watergate scandal, was able to win enough votes from men to eliminate the gap (Seltzer, Newman, and Leighton 1997; Norrander 1999, 2008). However, the gap reemerged and began to gain media attention when conservative Republican Ronald Reagan was elected in 1980. Since the Reagan years, the gender gap is a consistent feature of American politics, averaging around 7 points. The exit poll data since 1992 in figure 3.3 demonstrates that Hillary Clinton's 13-point gender gap in 2016 was on the higher end of recent Democratic presidential candidates. In fact, Clinton's gender gap was most similar to the other contemporary Democratic candidate who won the popular vote but lost the Electoral College, Al Gore in 2000. Exit polls show a 13-point gender gap for Clinton, in which she won the support of 41 percent of men and 54 percent of women. Similarly, Al Gore won the support of 43 percent of men and 54 percent of women (Center for American Women and Politics 2017).

The persistence of the contemporary gender gap in which Democratic presidential candidates increasingly rely on women voters may reflect larger trends in the polarization of the political parties. The ideological polarization of the parties in which Republicans became more consistently conservative and Democrats increasingly liberal began at the elite level among officeholders and activists. The election of Ronald Reagan in 1980 and his delineation of strong conservative policies in combination with a more strongly partisan Congress, particularly after the 1994 Republican Revolution, sent strong signals to voters about what the parties stand for and precipitated an ideological realignment in the partisan preferences of voters (Abramowitz and Saunders 1998; Norrander 1999). There is also evidence that over time, the gender gap expands when the country becomes more ideologically conservative, when the economy declines, and when there is an increase in the number of single women (a group that is more likely to need the social welfare services provided by the government) (Box-Steffensmeier, De Boef, and Lin 2004).

While the gender gap is an important feature of contemporary electoral politics, it is smaller than other significant voting gaps in American politics. The greatest differences in American voting behavior are based on race. White voters are more likely to vote for Republican candidates while racial and ethnic minority voters, including African Americans, Hispanics, and Asian Americans, lean toward Democrats. African Americans in particular vote overwhelmingly for Democrats. According to exit polls, in 2016, Hillary Clinton won 89 percent of African American voters, a proportion similar to the 88 percent of black voters won by John Kerry in 2004. Barack Obama, the first African American candidate and president, earned even more minority votes, winning 95 percent of African American votes in 2008 and 93 percent of these voters in 2012. Meanwhile, white voters' support for the Democratic Party has steadily declined. From 1992 through 2008, Democratic presidential candidates garnered between 41 and 43 percent of the white vote. By 2012 only 39 percent of white voters supported Barack Obama and Hillary Clinton garnered only 37 percent of the white vote in 2016 (Cilliza and Cohen 2012; CNN 2004, 2016a).

While the gap between African American and white voters remains both large and stable, the gap between white voters and other minority groups is expanding, particularly among Hispanics and Asian Americans. Thus, in 2004, 53 percent of Hispanic voters supported the Democratic presidential candidate, John Kerry, in his bid to unseat incumbent president George W. Bush. By 2012, 71 percent of Hispanic voters chose Democratic president Barack Obama. Similarly, Asian American support for the Democratic presidential candidate grew from 56 percent in 2004 to 73 percent in 2012. Hillary Clinton had less support from these minority voters than President Obama. Still, nearly two-thirds of Hispanic and Asian American voters supported Clinton, indicating that the Democratic Party is increasingly reliant on the support of minority voters as it continues to lose ground among white voters (Luhby 2016; Ramakrishnan 2016; Tyson and Maniam 2016).

Like the race gap, religious observance is a larger divide in American politics than the gender gap. Since 1992, those who attend weekly religious services are much more likely to vote for Republican presidential candidates than less observant voters. Thus, in 2016, 62 percent of secular voters who never attend religious services supported Hillary Clinton while only 41 percent of voters who attend services weekly supported Clinton, a 21-point gap. The religiosity gap stems from the increased association of social conservatives with the Republican Party and a countermovement of secular voters to the Democratic Party (Fiorina 2011; CNN 2016a). The smaller size of the gender gap in comparison to other voting gaps in American politics may come as a surprise, given the level of attention devoted to the gender gap by the media and political candidates. However, women constitute a larger potential pool of voters than the voters in other categories, women have higher turnout rates than men, and women are often perceived as swing voters by both the Republican and Democratic Parties (Burrell 2005; Norrander 2008).

THE GENDER GAPS: VOTING TRENDS ACROSS DIFFERENT GROUPS OF WOMEN

Since voting is influenced by a variety of demographic factors from race to education and marital status, it is important to examine trends in the voting behavior of different groups of women. While Hillary Clinton won more votes from women overall, she lost white women. Fifty-two percent of white women voted for Donald Trump while only 43 percent of these women supported Clinton (CNN 2016a). Media commentators decried the lack of female solidarity. "Clinton Couldn't Win Over White Women," "Why Hillary Clinton Couldn't Win Over Female Voters," and "White Women Sold Out the Sisterhood and the Whole World by Voting for Trump" were just some of the shocked headlines after the election (Anderson 2016; Malone 2016; Newton-Small 2016). Given Trump's salacious comments directed toward numerous women during the campaign, as well as the outcry after the leaked audiotape in October 2016, which heard him brag about his ability to sexually assault women because of his fame, many commentators assumed that women would abandon Trump in November. Comedienne Samantha Bee fumed "a majority of white women, faced with the choice between the first female president and a vial of weaponized testosterone, said, 'I'll take Option B. I just don't like her.' Hope you got your sticker, ladies. Way to lean out" (Bradley 2016). Yet in contemporary politics, white women consistently lean Republican, and the 2016 results were very similar to white women's voting behavior in the past several election cycles. While fewer white women vote Republican than white men, in the 2012 election 56 percent of white women voted for Republican Mitt Romney, while only 42 percent of white women (compared to 35 percent of white men) supported Barack Obama (CNN 2012; Dittmar 2016a). Indeed, since 1952, a majority of white women voted for the Republican candidate in all but two elections, 1964 and 1996 (Junn 2017).

Reflecting the fact that race is such a fundamental divide in American politics, African American and Hispanic women are much more likely to support Democratic candidates than white women. The growth of minority voters as a proportion of the voting population and their strong support for Democratic candidates drives the modern gender gap. Women of color constituted almost one-third of female voters in 2016. These women overwhelmingly voted for Hillary Clinton with 94 percent of black women, as compared to 82 percent of black men, and 69 percent of Latino women, as compared to 63 percent of Latino men, supporting Clinton. As the first African American president, Barack Obama received even more support from minority voters. In 2012, 96 percent of African American women and 87 percent of African American men voted for President Obama, and 76 percent of Latina women, compared to 65 percent of Latino men, favored Barack Obama (Center for American Women and Politics 2012; Junn and Garcia Bedolla 2013; CNN 2016a; Junn 2017).

The gender gap is also more pronounced at higher education and professional levels and between single men and women in comparison to married men and women. Some scholars argue that we should expect a larger gender gap among highly educated professionals because labor force participation exposes women to gender inequalities they would not see as homemakers and gives these women a means of economic independence that shapes their political behavior. Thus, the expectation is that professional women will be attracted to Democratic Party proposals related to equal pay and employment discrimination (Carroll 1988; Box-Steffensmeier, De Boef, and Lin 2004; Huddy, Cassese, and Lizotte 2008). Alternatively, other scholars maintain that the professional advancement of highly educated women leads to more shared experiences with men and will lead to a convergence of the political views of educated, professional men and women (Box-Steffensmeier, De Boef, and Lin 2004).

The education divide was a major factor in 2016. Clinton won college-educated white women by 7 points (51 to 44 percent), the only group of white women that favored Clinton. In 2012, a majority of these women had supported Mitt Romney. However, the dramatic shift of noncollege-educated voters to Donald Trump propelled him to victory, particularly in key swing states, including Ohio, Pennsylvania, and Wisconsin. White voters without a college degree favored Trump by 39 points, a margin larger than Ronald Reagan's 1984 landslide against Walter Mondale (Brownstein 2016). By contrast, in 2012 noncollege-educated whites voted for Romney 61–36, a healthy 25-point margin but 14 points less than Trump's support from these voters. Clinton did particularly poorly with white men without a college degree, losing them by 48 points (23–71 percent) but white women without a college degree also favored Trump by 27 points (34–61 percent) (Brownstein 2016; Dittmar 2016a; Tyson and Maniam 2016).

Finally, marital status is also an important influence on voting behavior. Single women are the strongest supporters of Democratic candidates, while married women are more likely to favor Republicans. Indeed, in 2016, 63 percent of single women supported Hillary Clinton. While Clinton won unmarried women by 31 points (63–32), she only won married women by 2 points (49–47), and 57 percent of married men supported Trump (CNN 2016a). This small victory with married women represents the first time a Democratic presidential candidate had won married women in the last 20 years (Dittmar 2016a). For example, 53 percent of married women favored Mitt Romney in 2012 (CNN 2012). While there are currently more married than single voters, larger social trends indicate that marriage rates are declining. For example, the percentage of voters that were married dropped from 66 percent in 2008 to 60 percent in 2012 (Deckman 2012). The preference of single women for the Democratic Party is attributed to the fact that these women are the most economically vulnerable and thus the most likely to need the social welfare programs supported by the Democratic Party. Meanwhile married women are more likely to be older, white, more religious, and financially secure—all groups that lean Republican (Box-Steffensmeier, De Boef, and Lin 2004; Huddy, Cassese, and Lizotte 2008; Norrander 2008).

In sum, it is too simple to say that women as a group favor Democrats while men vote Republican. Instead, the gender gap varies across all types of men and women. Women of color heavily favor Democrats, while white women lean to the Republicans. College-educated women are increasingly moving to the Democratic Party, but women who did not attend college swing Republican. Unmarried women strongly support Democrats, while married women generally favor Republicans. In the competition for votes, the parties try to create policy platforms that will appeal to particular subgroups of men and women as they work to create a coalition that will propel them to victory.

ISSUES THAT EXPLAIN THE GENDER GAP

To understand the nature of the gender gap and how likely it is that this gap will continue to manifest itself in electoral politics, it is important to examine the underlying causes of the gender gap in men's and women's political attitudes and concerns. Beginning in the 1970s, survey research has demonstrated that women evince greater support for social welfare spending and a more activist government role in assisting the poor, in guaranteeing jobs, and in guaranteeing a standard of living (see figure 3.4). In addition to differences in attitudes on social welfare issues, women are more likely to express feelings of insecurity and pessimism about the general economy and their own personal finances (Shapiro and Mahajan 1986; Seltzer, Newman, and Leighton 1997; Chaney, Alvarez, and Nagler 1998; Kaufman and Petrocik 1999; Norrander 1999, 2008; Box-Steffensmeier, De Boef, and Lin 2004). There are also some gender differences on environmental issues. Because women are more risk averse than men, a gender gap emerges on environmental regulations related to reducing risks such as health risks. However, there is no gender gap on issues where environmental protection is weighed against taxes or job growth (Norrander 2008).

Women's greater support for social welfare spending and government intervention in the economy may stem from the fact that, on average, women are more economically vulnerable than men. Women earn less than men, are more likely to receive welfare benefits, and are more likely to be employed in public sector and social welfare occupations that rely on government funding (Norrander 1999, 2008). Women of color, particularly African American and Latina women, are more likely than white women to be single mothers with children under age 17 at home and are more likely to be low-income. Thus, these women have a stronger need for social safety net programs (O'Leary and Kornbluh 2009; Junn and Garcia Bedolla 2013). Additionally, there is some evidence that men are more likely to be pocketbook voters, basing their vote on their personal economic situation, whereas women are more likely to be sociotropic voters who weigh societal conditions more heavily. Therefore, women's greater empathy for the

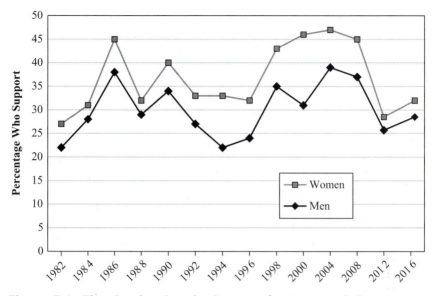

Figure 3.4 The Gender Gap in Support for Increased Government Services and Spending
Source: National Election Study https://electionstudies.org/resources/anes-guide/second-tables/?id=161.

poor may drive their support for increased social welfare spending (Huddy, Cassese, and Lizotte 2008). Since social welfare issues and government spending have constituted a major fault line between the Republican and Democratic Parties since the New Deal, the gender gap will likely continue to be a feature of American politics for the foreseeable future.

Sex differences in support for the use of force constitute another important component of the gender gap. Over time, women have been less supportive of military intervention than men and less supportive of increased defense spending (see figure 3.5). These issues played a particularly important role in determining the gender gap in the 1980s when women were less supportive of Ronald Reagan's defense buildup and more in favor of a freeze on nuclear weapons development than were men (Smith 1984; Shapiro and Mahajan 1986; Seltzer, Newman, and Leighton 1997; Norrander 1999, 2008). Looking specifically at the issue of war, figure 3.6 brings together public opinion polls from World War II through current debates about whether to send ground troops to defeat the Islamic terror group known as ISIS. Although the question wording differs slightly in each case, depending on the source and year, there are some clear patterns. While a majority of women have often supported the deployment of troops, in every case women are less inclined to support war than men are. Interestingly, in the most recent conflicts, the Iraq War and the campaign against ISIS, only a bare majority of women, 51 percent, supported going to war against Iraq in 2003, while men (67 percent) were strongly supportive of the war. Once the war became unpopular as a result of mounting casualties and costs to the economy, women were still more likely to oppose the war than men. Similarly, while a bare majority of men, 52 percent, would support sending troops to combat the terror group ISIS, only 41 percent of women favored sending ground troops to defeat ISIS as of May 2015.

Delving into opinions about terrorism, research on torture and the war on terrorism demonstrates that women are more likely than men to oppose the use of harsh interrogation techniques. Because women are more conscious of sexual violence than men, gender differences were largest regarding techniques that make the detainee feel the most personally vulnerable, such as sexually humiliating a detainee, forcing a detainee to go naked, or holding a detainee's head under water (Haider-Markel and Vieux 2008). With regard to use of force issues on the home front, women are more likely to oppose capital punishment and to support gun control measures (Seltzer, Newman, and Leighton 1997; Norrander 1999, 2008).

In contrast to conventional wisdom, feminist or women's issues are not an important component of the gender gap. Men and women express

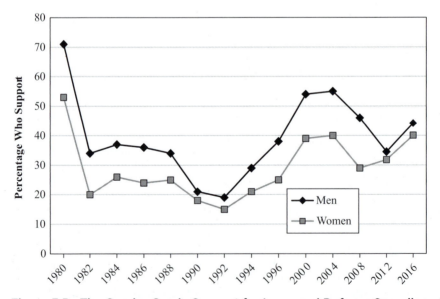

Figure 3.5   The Gender Gap in Support for Increased Defense Spending
Source: National Election Study https://electionstudies.org/resources/anes-guide/second-tables/?id=242.

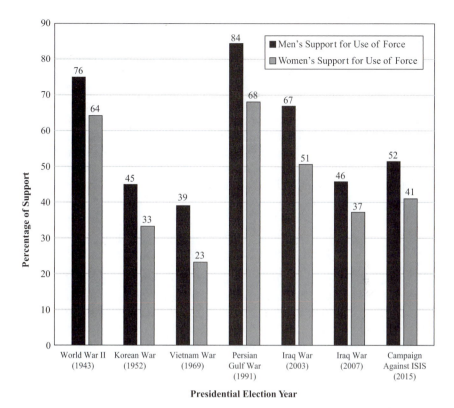

Figure 3.6   Support for Use of Military Force by Sex
Sources: World War II (Gallup, October 1943); Korean War (Roper Organization, October 1952); Vietnam War (Gallup, October 1969); Persian Gulf War (CBS/New York Times 1991); Iraq War 2003 (ABC News/Washington Post 2003); Iraq War 2007 (Gallup 2007); Campaign against ISIS (Pew Research Center 2015). In most cases, the surveys ask respondents about the use of force, but in the case of the Vietnam War question, Gallup asked respondents to describe themselves as hawkish or dovish when it comes to Vietnam. Respondents who described themselves as hawkish are listed above.

similar attitudes on gender roles, equality for women, and abortion. Although the media attributed the emergence of the gender gap in 1980 to Ronald Reagan's opposition to the ERA and his conservative position on abortion, research has shown that men and women were equally supportive of the ERA and equally likely to utilize it as a determinant of their vote (Mansbridge 1986). More recently, a study of support for the Obamacare mandate requiring that insurers provide contraceptive coverage found that greater female support for the birth control mandate stemmed from women's stronger commitment to the social safety net and government's role in providing social services and not to their attitudes about abortion (Deckman and McTague 2015).

However, there is some evidence that women do feel more intensely about their abortion position, particularly pro-life women. Moreover, women are more likely to hold positions at the extremes, either supporting abortion in all cases or prohibiting it in all circumstances (Seltzer, Newman, and Leighton 1997; Norrander 1999, 2008; Kaufmann 2002; Jelen and Wilcox 2005). Perhaps related, there is also evidence that women are more religious and they express slightly more conservative attitudes on some additional social issues, including school prayer, sexual mores (such as pornography), and civil liberties (Seltzer, Newman, and Leighton 1997; Norrander 1999, 2008).

COURTING THE WOMEN'S VOTE IN A COMPETITIVE POLITICAL CLIMATE

Throughout the 1990s and 2000s, political competition between Republicans and Democrats intensified at all levels of government, aided in part by the realignment of many white Southerners to the Republican Party. Since 1994, when the Republican Revolution election gave Republicans control of both houses of Congress for the first time in more than 40 years, party control of the House and Senate has rested on a handful of seats, and control of each chamber has shifted multiple times. At the presidential level, races have been so tight that twice in the new millennium the winner of the popular vote did not win the Electoral College and the presidency. In 2000, the contest between Al Gore and George W. Bush was decided by such a small number of votes that the recounting of votes in Florida and the dispute over how to count those votes kept the outcome from being decided long after Election Day. Like 2000, in 2016 the Democratic candidate Hillary Clinton won the popular vote but lost the Electoral College. President Trump secured victory in the Electoral College by winning three states, Michigan, Wisconsin, and Ohio, by less than 1 percent of the vote—0.2, 0.7, and 0.8 percent, respectively. Thus, Trump won these states by less than 80,000 votes in an election where Clinton won the popular vote by almost 2.9 million (Bump 2016).

In such a volatile and competitive electoral climate, both parties scramble for ways to motivate their base and attract the elusive swing voter to expand their voting coalition in order to achieve a governing majority. Consequently, each election cycle, the parties target specific groups of women voters. Women are particularly courted because they routinely vote at higher rates than men, are less likely than men to be strong partisans, and are more likely to decide on their vote later in the election cycle (Burrell 2005; Norrander 2008).

Republican vice presidential candidate, Alaska Gov. Sarah Palin appears at a campaign stop at the airport in Colorado Springs, Colo., Monday, November 3, 2008. *Source*: Associated Press / David Zalubowski.

The Republican Party focuses the most attention on white, married, suburban women with children. Married voters lean Republican more than single voters, and married voters are more likely to turn out to vote than single voters. Married women are also more religious than singles, making them more open to the traditional family values message of the Republican Party (Brownstein 2008; Elder 2008; Norrander 2008). Indeed, religiosity is now a better predictor of voting behavior than religious affiliation, meaning, for example, that an observant Catholic or Protestant is more likely to vote Republican than a Catholic or Protestant voter who rarely attends services (Brownstein 2013). Thus, married, suburban, white women were the "soccer moms" that Bill Clinton and Bob Dole competed over in 1996. They were the voters that George W. Bush tried to appeal to in 2000 with his message of "compassionate conservatism." In 2004, these married, white, suburban women became "security moms" who were concerned about the threat of terrorism and the security of their families (Kanthak and Norrander 2004; Martinez and Carey 2004; Norrander 2008). Similarly, in 2016 Trump's tough talk on immigration and terrorism appealed to Republican women's concerns about their children's safety (Deckman 2016).

Responding to the economic recession, Republicans focused even more attention on noncollege-educated white women in 2008 and 2012. The media described these voters as "waitress moms" or "Wal-Mart moms" who "shop at Wal-Mart at least once a week, earn less than $60,000 a year, [and] have less than a college education" (Zernike 2008; Trotta 2012). John McCain's selection of Alaska Governor Sarah Palin in 2008 as his running mate was an important part of his effort to reach working-class women voters and evangelical women. Palin frequently described herself and her female supporters as "hockey moms" or "mama grizzlies" seeking to protect their families from government overreach and trying to put the government's fiscal house in order (Healy 2008; Kaufman 2008). While noncollege-educated women are less likely to turn out than college-educated voters, married women without college degrees voted strongly Republican in 2012. Donald Trump was particularly successful with noncollege-educated voters. These voters powered his destruction of the traditional "blue wall" as he won Rust Belt states, including Michigan, Pennsylvania, and Wisconsin, that had voted for Democratic presidential candidates in five or more of the previous presidential contests (Brownstein 2016; Collingswood 2016).

As an antiestablishment candidate stirring up populist anger, Trump focused very little attention on courting women voters compared to previous Republican nominees. Instead, his "Make America Great Again" slogan was aimed at mobilizing male voters, particularly those rural and working-class voters displaced by the loss of manufacturing jobs. Emphasizing a protectionist message on trade and a crackdown on illegal immigration, Trump appealed to these voters' feelings of economic anxiety and racial resentment (Collingswood 2016; Cramer 2016; Guo 2016).

Throughout the campaign, Trump portrayed himself as the strong alpha male who would never back down from a fight. During the primary, he belittled his opponents by portraying them as too feminine and weak to exercise leadership. He ridiculed Jeb Bush as low energy and characterized Marco Rubio as "Little Marco" (Chavez and Stracqualursi 2016). He dismissed Carly Fiorina, declaring, "Look at that face, would anyone vote for that?," and he took aim at Ted Cruz by posting an unflattering picture of Cruz's wife Heidi next to a picture of his model wife Melania (Estepa 2015; Green 2016). Trump even touted the size of his manhood in a presidential primary debate when he pushed back on Marco Rubio's campaign rally taunt that Trump had "small hands" (Flores 2016).

Trump's appeal to male vigor was reflected in his primary numbers. Throughout the primaries, Trump earned a plurality of male and female voters in a majority of states. However, Trump consistently earned stronger support from men. Looking at the states where exit polls were conducted, Trump earned an average of 7 percent more votes from male than female primary voters, winning an average of 46 percent of men and 39 percent of women. By contrast, Ted Cruz and John Kasich ran relatively evenly with men and women, with women narrowly favoring both candidates by one point. Before he dropped out of the race, Marco Rubio did an average of 4 points better with women than men (author analysis of CNN 2016b; Dittmar 2016b). This strong support from men helped propel Trump to victory since more men than women vote in Republican primaries (Norrander 2003; Dittmar 2016b).

In the general election campaign, Trump continued his appeal to masculinity. He claimed Hillary was playing the woman card and repeatedly questioned her stamina (Ball 2016; Deckman 2016). Clinton responded by selling a woman card on her campaign website and declaring "if fighting for women's health care, paid family leave, and equal pay is playing the woman card, then deal me in" (Bellstrom 2016). Trump campaign rallies featured T-shirts emblazoned with macho and sexist messaging, including "Trump: Finally Someone with Balls" and "Trump That Bitch" (Ball 2016). After a video tape emerged where Trump described grabbing women by the genitals against their wishes, he and his campaign surrogates dismissed it as locker room talk (Reily 2016).

While Trump largely focused his efforts on mobilizing men, particularly noncollege-educated white men, he did try to appeal to subgroups of women that traditionally support Republicans. Like previous Republican candidates, Trump sent female surrogates to court women voters. Trump's campaign manager Kellyanne Conway made a career of advising male Republican candidates on how to speak to women voters (Rubin 2016). Sarah Palin was an early supporter of Donald Trump, endorsing him right before the Iowa caucuses, the first contest in the Republican nomination battle. Other high profile and conservative Tea Party women also campaigned for Trump, including Ann Coulter and Phyllis Schlafly, the head of Eagle Forum and champion of the STOP ERA movement (Deckman 2016). In September, his campaign kicked off a Women's Empowerment tour headlined by his daughter-in-law Lara Trump and featuring female supporters, including his national spokeswoman Katrina Pierson and a pair of African American women, Diamond and Silk, who had a popular YouTube channel supporting Trump (Glueck 2016). His strongest surrogate to women voters, particularly white, suburban women, was his daughter Ivanka Trump, an accomplished businesswoman and mother. Speaking at the Republican National Convention, Ivanka Trump called for paid family leave and tax credits for childcare, policy positions that have not been embraced by contemporary Republican presidential candidates. She helped Trump craft a policy plan to make childcare more affordable and provide

Reality TV personality Omarosa Manigault and other Women for Trump members endorse Republican presidential candidate Donald Trump during a campaign rally at the Charlotte Convention Center in Charlotte, N.C., on Friday, October 14, 2016. *Source*: David T. Foster III/TNS/Newscom.

women, but not men, with six weeks of paid maternity leave (Drabold 2016; Sullivan and Costa 2016).

While Republicans work to increase turnout among subgroups of married, white women, Democratic strategists target single women, college-educated women, minority women, and millennials. Single heads of households are more economically insecure and, therefore, expected to be more inclined to support Democratic social policy initiatives. Single women under 40 and older women with grown children are particular targets of the get-out-the-vote efforts of the Democrats (Brownstein 2008, 2013; Norrander 2008). The group Women's Voices, Women's Votes was created to register and mobilize single women, as these women are less likely to vote than their married counterparts (http://www.wvwvaf.org/). To appeal to single women, Democrats emphasize issues such as abortion rights, access to emergency contraception for young single women, affordable health care, equal pay, and, for senior women, improvements to Medicare and Social Security (Martinez and Carey 2004; Roarty 2012; Tumulty 2012).

Throughout the Obama years, Democrats increasingly focused on courting these groups of minority, college-educated, single, young millennial, and minority women. This coalition is often referred to as the "Rising American Electorate" because these demographic groups constitute a growing proportion of the American electorate. For example, between 2000 and 2012 racial minorities grew from 19 percent to 26 percent of the electorate (Frey, Teixeira, and Griffin 2016). According to exit polls, nonwhite voters constituted 29 percent of the electorate in 2016 (CNN 2016a). These voters are projected to make up 40 percent of voters by 2032 because of immigration trends and the fact that younger generations coming up are more racially mixed (Frey, Teixeira, and Griffin 2016).

In 2008 and 2012, Barack Obama heavily courted the minority, single, college-educated, and millennial women that are a part of the Rising American Electorate. To mobilize these voters, Obama highlighted women's issues, including health care, equal pay, and reproductive rights. In 2008, he touted his support for equal pay by campaigning with Lilly Ledbetter, the woman who unsuccessfully sued the Goodyear Tire Company for years of being paid less than her male colleagues and who was ultimately denied redress by the Supreme Court (Zerinke 2008). The Lilly Ledbetter Equal Pay Act was the first bill that Obama signed as president (Murray 2009). In the 2012 and the 2014 congressional midterm elections, Obama and congressional Democrats accused Republicans of waging a "war on women" in which they opposed efforts to achieve equal pay for women and wanted to deny women access to the contraceptive services that were guaranteed under the preventive health provisions of Obama's Affordable Care Act (Reinhard 2012; Roarty 2012; Thompson 2012).

President Barack Obama applauds Lilly Ledbetter, left, with Vice President Joe Biden, right, before signing the Lilly Ledbetter Bill for equal pay for equal work Thursday, January. 29, 2009. The pay discrimination Ledbetter experienced at Goodyear Tire and Rubber Co. became a rallying cry for women across the country. Ledbetter campaigned heavily for President Obama in 2008. *Source*: Associated Press / Pablo Martinez Monsivais.

Furthermore, in his campaign speeches, Obama frequently paid tribute to his mother, who was a single mother, and to his grandmother, who helped raise him. He celebrated his wife's strength and accomplishments and spoke of his hopes for his two daughters (Levey 2008). Prominent celebrities like Oprah Winfrey and female officeholders from Democratic leader Nancy Pelosi to Obama's former primary opponent and future Secretary of State Hillary Clinton worked to mobilize women voters during his first race for the presidency (Healy 2008; Vedantam 2008).

As the first female presidential nominee of a major party, in 2016 Hillary Clinton openly embraced her gender. Outreach to the Democratic-leaning groups of women who constitute the Rising American Electorate was central to her campaign strategy. Clinton drafted detailed policy proposals to reduce childcare costs, raise the minimum wage, tackle student loan debt, and safeguard reproductive rights (Ehrenfreund and Tankersley 2016; Paquette 2016a; Siddiqui and Gambino 2016). She touted a plan for 12 weeks of paid family leave and promised to appoint a cabinet that was half women (Sussman and Meckler 2016; Crockett 2016). The video introducing Clinton at the Democratic National Convention included a montage of the previous male presidents and ended with Clinton shattering a virtual glass ceiling (Fang 2016). When she accepted the nomination, Clinton came out in a white pantsuit to evoke the white dresses suffragettes wore when they marched for women's voting rights (Jamieson 2016).

In her campaign appearances and her television advertising, Clinton spoke of her long career fighting for women and children, including her work for the Children's Defense Fund and her focus on education and health care as First Lady (Baird 2016). She also touted her commitment to women's rights across the world, including her speech as First Lady at the UN World Conference on Women in Beijing where Clinton declared women's rights are human rights and her work to empower women in the developing world during her time as Secretary of State (Newton-Small 2015). Clinton appeared frequently with prominent women leaders, including Senator Elizabeth Warren (D-MA), former Secretary and State Madeleine Albright, and first lady Michelle Obama, as well as female celebrities from Katy Perry to Beyoncé (Gass 2016; Phillip 2016). Pushing back against Donald Trump's sexist rhetoric, Clinton denounced Trump's attacks on her and other women. She ran commercials showing young girls looking at themselves in the mirror and listening to Trump's insulting remarks about women's looks (Merica 2016; Siddiqui and Gambino 2016).

Ultimately, college-educated, minority, single, and millennial women strongly supported Hillary Clinton, helping her win the popular vote by nearly three million votes (Walsh 2016). However, Clinton's support from these women was offset by Trump's gains among noncollege-educated

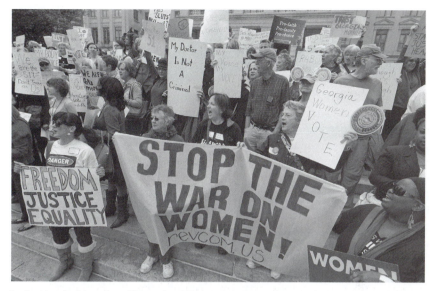

Protestors hold a sign, "Stop the War on Women," during the "Walk in My Shoes, Hear Our Voice" protest Monday, March 12, 2012, at the state Capitol in Atlanta. The rally protests legislation passed by the Georgia State Senate banning abortion coverage under state employees' health-care plans and exempting religious health-care providers from having to cover birth control. *Source*: AP / Atlanta Journal-Constitution, Jason Getz.

white men and women in the Rust Belt states, propelling Trump to victory in the Electoral College (Brownstein 2016).

Post-election, there were numerous analyses that showed that elements of the Rising American Electorate had not turned out as strongly for Clinton as they did for Barack Obama. As the establishment candidate in a change election year, Clinton had trouble building enthusiasm and mobilizing some of the voters in her coalition (Blake 2016; Brownstein 2016). In the key states of Wisconsin, Michigan, and Pennsylvania, African American turnout fell from 2012 levels (Fraga et al. 2017; Jackson 2016). Similarly, in 2016, millennials, voters between age 18 and 35, were now as large a share of eligible voters as the baby boomers (age 52–70) (Fry 2016). However, younger voters turn out at lower rates (Fry 2016). Thus, in 2016 voters between 18 and 44 made up 44 percent of the electorate, while voters over 45 constituted 56 percent of the electorate (CNN 2016a).

Mobilization of single, minority, and young voters is a continuing challenge for Democrats. While these voters pushed Barack Obama over the finish line in 2008 and 2012, they are less likely to vote than older, married, and white voters. Indeed, in midterm elections, when congressional candidates are up for reelection but the president is not on the ballot, voter turnout falls from an average of 60 percent to about 40 percent (Kernell et al. 2014). Compared to presidential years, the voters in midterm elections are generally older, whiter, and wealthier, a profile that favors Republican candidates (Brownstein 2013). Thus, between Obama's 2012 presidential election and the 2014 midterm elections, turnout among young voters (18–29) dropped 6 points from 19 percent to 13 percent of the electorate, and turnout among single women dropped from 23 percent to 21 percent of the electorate (CNN 2012, 2014). A two-point decline might seem small, but these differences represent millions of voters (PBS Newshour 2014). For Republicans, their challenge is that their most reliable voters constitute a shrinking proportion of the electorate, particularly in presidential years. With increasing racial diversity, Republicans must win a greater share of white voters to prevail. Yet the population of white voters continues to decline. When Ronald Reagan won the presidency in 1980, white voters made up 88 percent of the electorate (Brownstein 2013). By 2016, only 71 percent of the electorate was white (CNN 2016a).

In contrast to previous midterm elections, the 2018 midterms set a record for a non-presidential year with 50.3 percent of eligible voters turning out to vote. This is the largest turnout in a midterm election since 1914, which was before women got the right to vote. Midterm elections are generally a referendum on the sitting president. As a result, the president's party usually loses seats. The 2018 elections saw a Democratic wave that elevated Democrats to the majority in the House and brought a large new diverse freshman class. Voting groups that lean Democratic including women, college-educated voters, racial minorities, and young people, propelled the wave (United States Elections Project 2018; Bump 2018; Stewart 2018). While younger voters continued to turn out at lower rather than older Americans, compared with 2014, voters under thirty increased their turnout by more than 50 percent and heavily voted for Democratic candidates (Gontchorova 2018). Moreover, polls conducted shortly before the midterm elected showed that young women indicated they were more likely to turn out to vote than young men and were far more likely to support Democratic candidates (Zhou 2018).

Looking to the future, Democrats hold an advantage with the fastest-growing groups in the electorate (minorities, youth, single women), but they need to work harder to mobilize their voters. Meanwhile, Republicans need to grow their coalition to capture some of the expanding groups in the electorate, including racial minorities, college-educated women, and single women. As a result, we should expect both parties to continue targeting subgroups of women that might favor their candidates.

DOES THE GENDER GAP BRING WOMEN POLITICAL POWER?

In the early 1980s, feminists and women's organizations, particularly the National Organization for Women (NOW), coined the term *gender gap* and worked to draw the attention of the media and party leadership to the potential importance of women as a voting bloc. Sending a monthly "Gender Gap Update" to several thousand reporters, Ellie Smeal (president of NOW) and other women leaders sought to parlay the gender gap into stronger support for the ERA and, in 1984, to pressure Walter Mondale, the Democratic nominee for president, to select a woman as his running mate. Although the campaign for the ERA ultimately fell three states short of ratification, women's groups and concerns about the gender gap did play a key role in Walter Mondale's decision to tap Congresswoman Geraldine Ferraro to be his vice presidential candidate (Bonk 1988; Frankovic 1988). Similarly, Ronald Reagan's concerns about his lack of support among women voters in 1980 led him to promise to appoint the first woman to the Supreme Court, a promise that he fulfilled with the appointment of Sandra Day O'Connor (Burrell 2005). Does the gender gap empower women and pressure politicians to adopt policies that benefit specific groups of women? Or do politicians pay lip service to the needs of particular subgroups of women in an effort to win elections and then ignore the needs of women when governing?

At the presidential level, Burrell (2005) argues that incumbent presidents running for reelection will use the power of their office to create initiatives that will appeal to women voters. Thus, in an effort to mobilize women voters for the 1996 election, President Clinton increased the number of grants to combat violence against women, convened an Early Child Development and Learning Conference and a White House Conference on Child Care, held a roundtable on pay equity, and created a White House Office for Women's Initiatives and Outreach that held roundtables across the country on women's issues. He also proposed new legislation on pay equity and an expansion of family and medical leave (Burrell 2005). Underscoring the effort to reach female voters, the Family and Medical Leave Act was the first bill President Clinton signed into law.

Similarly, Barack Obama used his executive authority to pursue policies for women. Upon winning office in 2008, the first piece of legislation Obama signed into law was the Lilly Ledbetter Fair Pay Act (Murray 2009). He supported inclusion of a broad mandate for contraception in the Affordable Care Act. Obama used executive orders to provide some paid leave for federal workers and to further equal pay by requiring government contractors to disclose more details about what their employees earn and to let their employees share salary information to reduce pay secrecy (Eilperin 2014; Wheeler 2015).

While these initiatives are meant to help women and their families, Susan Carroll argues that the courting of ephemeral swing-voting groups like soccer moms actually disempowers women. Examining the 1996 reelection bid of Bill Clinton, Susan Carroll (1999) argued that the competition for the votes of "soccer moms" between Bill Clinton and Bob Dole in 1996 did not lay a foundation for significant policy changes to benefit women and left out broad segments of women voters. During the campaign, Clinton appealed to "soccer moms" by touting his support for policies, including v-chips in televisions, school uniforms, and an expansion of the Family and Medical Leave Act to allow parents to attend parent-teacher meetings. Bob Dole campaigned with soccer moms at his side and promoted the ways in which his tax cuts would help these women and their families. According to Carroll, the focus on the soccer mom and policy proposals related to children essentialized women as mothers and deflected attention away from the concerns of other subgroups of women (including women of color, older women, women on welfare, and professional women). This focus on soccer moms gave the campaigns the appearance of being responsive to the concerns of women while ignoring the majority of women. Therefore, despite the largest gender gap in presidential voting history—one that was not caused by the votes of soccer moms—activists representing various women's groups could point to no specific campaign promises that gave them a mandate to demand action on behalf of women on issues such as health care, abortion, welfare, employment, or childcare (Carroll 1999).

By contrast, in her research on gender differences in the policy activities of members of the House of Representatives and Senate, Swers (2002, 2013) found that concern about the gender gap among the leadership of the Democratic and Republican Parties raises the profile of women members of Congress, facilitates their efforts to gain positions of power in the party and committee structures, and enhances their ability to pursue policy initiatives related to women.

Due to their traditional advantage with women voters and the identification of many social welfare and feminist issues with the Democratic Party, Democrats are particularly eager to highlight issues and themes that will reinforce voters' perception of Democrats as the party advancing women's rights. To solidify this image, the party seeks out women members to speak on the House floor and in the media on women's issues, ranging from reproductive health to family and medical leave. Accepting these roles enables female Democrats to raise their public profile and enhance their standing with the party leadership. These Democratic women can then use their political capital to persuade party leadership to advance legislative proposals related to women's issues, sometimes even pushing leadership to take a stronger position in favor of women's rights (Swers 2002, 2013). In recent years, female Democratic senators acting individually and as a group pressured the Obama administration and Democratic leaders to include broad provision of contraceptive services among the preventive services covered by insurance companies under the Affordable Care Act, and they pressured the administration to narrowly limit the types of employers that could gain a religious exemption from providing contraceptive services (Swers 2013). In the midst of the #MeToo movement, Democratic women in Congress spearheaded the efforts that led to the resignation of fellow partisan senator Al Franken and they worked with their Republican colleagues to overhaul the way Congress handles accusations of sexual harassment and assault among members and staff (Traister 2018; Murphy 2018; Tully-McManus 2018).

In sum, the question of whether the gender gap brings women political power is a complicated one. Women's groups have long tried to harness the power of the gender gap to lobby politicians to champion proposals that advance women's rights. As women increase their presence in Congress, some female members have utilized the gender gap to push their parties to support policies that will help women and their families. Still, parties are electoral coalitions working to solidify their base and expand their outreach to swing voters. Subgroups of women that don't fall into these categories of coveted voters can find their needs ignored.

DO WOMEN VOTE FOR WOMEN?

It is often assumed that women provide a natural constituency of voters for women candidates. However, this is not necessarily the case, and current research provides conflicting evidence. The most important predictor of an individual's vote is party identification. Voters who identify as Democrats tend to vote for Democratic candidates. Similarly, voters who identify as Republicans are more likely to vote for Republican candidates. In 2016, there were many articles suggesting that Republican women would turn away from Trump, but in the end, women largely voted their party, and Clinton's support among women largely followed the trajectory of previous Democratic candidates. Indeed, Trump won 88 percent of self-identified Republican voters even though four of the last five Republican presidential nominees refused to endorse him and Trump took policy positions that conflict with the conservative ideology espoused by traditional Republican elites and officeholders, particularly his stance against trade deals and his advocacy of a large infrastructure spending program (CNN 2016a; Enten 2016).

At the congressional level, voters are increasingly voting a straight party ticket, aligning their votes for the House and Senate with their presidential votes. In 2016, for the first time there were no split tickets, meaning that every state that voted for the Democratic presidential candidate,

Hillary Clinton, also supported the Democratic Senate candidate and states that voted for the Republican, Donald Trump, also sent a Republican to the Senate (Enten 2016; Phillips 2016). Beyond party, incumbency plays a powerful role in vote choice as incumbents, particularly House incumbents, are routinely reelected at rates above 90 percent. Incumbent members of Congress, who are largely men, enjoy significant advantages over their male and female challengers, including superior fundraising, higher name recognition, and a large staff assisting them in helping constituents and building a policy record to run on (Herrnson 2012; Jacobson 2013).

Given the overwhelming importance of party identification and incumbency, is there any room for a voter's sex to impact his or her candidate choice? Some research suggests an affinity effect does exist in which voters are more likely to support a candidate of the same sex. For example, Sanbonmatsu (2002) finds that voters have a standing baseline gender preference to vote for a male or a female candidate and women are more likely than men to express a gender preference and to prefer a female candidate. Alternatively, women may vote for women because they trust them more on "group salient" issues that have a larger impact on women such as sexual harassment, childcare, or abortion, especially when an election emphasizes these group-salient issues (Paolino 1995; Dolan 2008b).

Others claim that women may be more likely to vote for women because of a shared gender consciousness that recognizes that women are underrepresented in government and that women's political futures are tied together (Rinehart 1992; Rosenthal 1995; Lewis 1999). However, race consciousness among blacks is more widespread than gender consciousness among women, as African Americans are more likely to express a sense of linked fate. The social organization of race is based on separation between whites and blacks, whereas the social organization of gender incorporates intimacy among men and women. Moreover, as a majority in the population, women are divided by race, class, education, and other identities, creating a large array of opinions among women (Huddy, Cassese, and Lizotte 2008; Burns and Kinder 2011; Tesler 2016). Yet much of the research on gender and candidate evaluations is based on experiments in which voters are asked about hypothetical candidates rather than real-world elections where the ratio of female to male candidates is smaller. Examining election results, scholars find that women may be more inclined to vote for women candidates when gender issues are primed and highly salient to the campaign, most notably during the 1992 Year of the Woman elections (Paulino 1995; Sapiro and Conover 1997; Dolan 2004, 2008a). This could very well be the case for the 2018 midterm elections, in which a record number of Democratic women candidates ran for office and the need for more women's voices at the policymaking table was an important theme.

Indeed, exit polls showed that 45 percent of Americans stated that it was very important to elect more women to public office; notably, 82 percent of Democrats said it was very important compared with just 17 percent of Republicans (CNN 2018).

Outside of 1992 and 2018, analyses of elections for the House, Senate, and governorships indicate that partisanship-driven voting leaves little room for a separate gender effect (Dolan 2004, 2014; Hayes 2011). Fulton (2014) did find a gender affinity affect among independent voters, but it was independent men who favor male candidates and independent women are not swayed by candidate gender. It is possible that women might vote for women candidates in low-information elections where less is known about the positions of the candidates (McDermott 1997). For example, many state and local elections are non-partisan. A recent study of State Supreme Court elections shows that in the non-partisan contests, women were more likely to support the female candidate (Badas and Stauffer 2019).

Finally, the ability to determine whether women vote for women is complicated by the fact that the gender gap in women's voting patterns favors Democrats, and more women candidates run as Democrats. For example, in the 2016 election, among the 167 women running for the House of Representatives, 120 candidates were Democrats while only 47 candidates were Republicans (Center for American Women and Politics 2016). Similarly, in the 2018 election that saw a record setting 102 women elected to the House, 181 of the 233 female candidates were women, while only 52 women were Republicans (Center for American Women and Politics 2019). Therefore, it is possible that women are not voting for women but are simply more likely to vote for Democrats (Norrander 1999, 2008). Indeed, analyses of voter opinions about the parties demonstrate that voters trust Democrats to handle issues that align with stereotypes about the issue expertise of female candidates, including health care, education, and family issues, while preferring Republicans to handle the male issues of national security and tax policy (Dolan 2004, 2014; Winter 2010). This alignment of partisan and issue stereotypes has led to characterization of the Democratic Party as the "mommy party" and the Republican Party as the "daddy party" (Winter 2010). Moreover, Palmer and Simon find that certain districts are more likely to elect women candidates to Congress and these districts are more urban, more diverse, and have higher median household incomes. In the current political climate, these are also more likely to be Democratic districts (Palmer and Simon 2012). Just as particular subgroups of women are more likely to vote for Democratic presidential candidates, research indicates that certain groups of women are more likely to support female candidates, including feminists, liberals, African Americans, and well-educated women (Rosenthal 1995; Smith and Fox 2001; Lynch and Dolan 2014).

HILLARY CLINTON AND THE WOMEN'S VOTE

Hillary Clinton's historic run for the presidency provides the first opportunity to test whether women are more likely to support female candidates at the presidential level. As noted earlier in the chapter, Clinton's
13-point gender gap was on the higher end but in line with previous Democratic candidates. She had strong support from the minority, single, and
college-educated women that have tilted toward the Democrats in recent
elections. Clinton did better than previous candidates with college-educated
white women and married women. Indeed, her 2-point advantage with
married women marks the first time a Democratic presidential candidate
had won married white women in the last 20 years (CNN 2016a; Dittmar
2016a). Clearly there was not a large gender affinity affect that helped
Clinton in the general election.

However, there was a male backlash. As compared to President
Obama, who won men by 1 point (49–48) in 2008 and lost men by 7
points (45–52) in 2012, Donald Trump beat Hillary Clinton among male
voters by 11 points (52–41). It seems that more men voted for third party
candidates in 2016, as 7 percent of men supported a third party candidate
as compared to only 3 percent in 2012 (CNN 2008a, 2012, 2016a). However, Al Gore and John Kerry also lost men by 11 points, as Bush beat Gore
among men 54–43 and Kerry by 55–44 (Center for American Women and
Politics 2017).

Clinton's biggest problems were with white men. While Clinton lost
white women to Trump by 9 points (52–43), she lost white men by a gaping
31 points (62–31). Yet in 2012, Obama also lost white men by 27 points
(35–62) and white women by 14 points (42–56). Noncollege-educated
white men most vehemently opposed Clinton. She lost them by 48 points
(23–71), but she also lost noncollege-educated white women by 27 points
(34–61). The education gap among white voters was a major shift in 2016
as there was not a large education gap in 2012 (CNN 2012, 2016a). It is
not clear how much of Clinton's problems with white men are based on
gender bias against a female candidate or responsiveness to the heightened
masculinity in Trump's campaign. However, group solidarity based on a
shared gender consciousness was clearly not a strong factor in the general
election (Tesler 2016).

Instead, the 2016 election was unique from previous elections in the
importance of what political science research calls "hostile sexism" as
a predictor of the vote. Hostile sexism refers to the extent that a voter
discounts the existence of gender discrimination and instead believes that
women are inappropriately using claims of gender discrimination to gain
benefits from government and advance their status. Hostile sexism also
reflects an antipathy toward women who are viewed as usurping men's

power. Donald Trump's focus on masculinity and gender-based taunts against Clinton, combined with Hillary Clinton's status as potentially the first female president which could destabilize traditional gender roles, activated hostile sexism as a predictor of vote choice in a way that it had not been relevant in the 2012 Obama-Romney presidential contest. Both white men and white women who exhibited high levels of hostile sexism were much more likely to support President Trump while these views had no influence on an individual's propensity to vote for Mitt Romney. While low-income white women supported Obama in 2012, the low-income female voters without a college degree who scored high on hostile sexism were much more likely to support Donald Trump (Cassese and Barnes 2018; Schaffner et al. 2018). By contrast, women of color who scored high on hostile sexism were actually less likely to vote for Donald Trump, indicating that hostile sexist attitudes had the greatest impact on the votes of white men and women (Frasure-Yokley 2018; Bracic et al. 2018). Other research suggests that voters who believe that "American society has become too soft and feminine," a concept known as gendered nationalism, were also significantly more likely to vote for Donald Trump in 2016 (Deckman and Cassesse 2018).

While being a woman created additional obstacles for Hillary Clinton in the general election, there is some evidence of women voting for women in the Democratic primary. Since the Reagan years, feminists and women's groups are an increasingly important part of the Democratic Party (Freeman 1986; Grossmann and Hopkins 2015). Furthermore, more women than men vote in the Democratic primary (Norrander 2016a). In both 2008 and 2016, Hillary Clinton's strongest support came from women voters. Table 3.2 reports the average proportion of the vote Hillary Clinton, Barack Obama, and Bernie Sanders won from various subgroups of men and women across the states. For example, across 37 states that conducted exit polls in the 2008 Democratic primary, Hillary Clinton won an average of 51 percent of women's votes and 42 percent of men's votes, a 9-point gender gap. In 2016, across 27 states that utilized exit polls, Clinton won an average of 60 percent of women's votes and 49 percent of men's votes, an 11-point gender gap (author analysis CNN 2008b, 2016b).

Comparing Democratic primaries from 1980 to 2000, Norrander finds that a gender gap emerged in one-quarter of these primaries. The largest gap was in 2000 when in half of the primaries, women voters favored Al Gore by a margin of 5 percent (Norrander 2003, 2016a). Clearly, Clinton had robust support from Democratic women in both her primary runs. The larger gender gap in the 2016 primary likely reflects the fact that in 2008 Clinton downplayed her gender while in 2016 Clinton decided to emphasize women's issues and the historic nature of her candidacy (Lawrence and Rose 2010; Traister 2016). This more overt discussion of gender

Table 3.2 The Gender Gap in the 2008 and 2016 Democratic Primaries

	2008 Average Gender Gap Across States						2016 Average Gender Gap Across States					
	Clinton			Obama			Clinton			Sanders		
	Women	Men	Diff.	Women	Men	Diff.	Women	Men	Diff.	Women	Men	Diff.
All	51	42	+9	45	52	−7	60	49	+11	38	49	−11
Race												
White	60	49	+11	35	44	−9	58	44	+14	41	55	−14
Black	18	13	+5	81	86	−5	80	80	0	19	19	0
Latino	69	59	+10	31	40	−9	72	63	+9	28	36	−8
Marital Status												
Married	50	41	+9	45	53	−8	68	61	+7	38	46	−8
Single	48	37	+11	48	57	−9	53	34	+19	45	65	−20

Notes: Numbers are average % support from each group across states that held exit polls in the 2008 and 2016 Democratic primaries. 37 states conducted exit polls in 2008 and 27 states held exit polls in 2016.
Source: CNN Primary Exit Polls 2008 and 2016.

and women's issues may have garnered the support of more Democratic women while also driving away some Democratic men. Indeed, Clinton struggled the most with unmarried men losing them to Obama by 20 points (37–57) in 2008 and to Sanders by a wider 31-point margin (34–65) (CNN 2016b; CNN 2008b) (see table 3.2).

Among groups of women, Clinton's support varied across the two primary campaigns depending on how voters responded to her opponent. Thus, in 2008 when Clinton ran against Barack Obama, black voters enthusiastically supported the first African American president. Running against Bernie Sanders, after serving as President Obama's Secretary and State, Clinton garnered large majorities among black voters (CNN 2016c; Norrander 2016b). Across both 2008 and 2016 more Latino voters chose Hillary Clinton over her Democratic primary opponent and she performed particularly well with Latina women (CNN 2008b, 2016b) (see table 3.2).

As the establishment candidate touting her experience and extensive policy knowledge, in both 2008 and 2016 Clinton earned the most support from older voters while she had more trouble connecting with younger voters who were looking for a change. Indeed, in 2008 Clinton lost 18–29-year-olds to Obama by an average of 26 points (35–61). In 2016, the gap widened as younger voters favored the septuagenarian Sanders by an average of 43 points (71–28) and Sanders won younger women by an average of 37 points (CNN 2008b, 2016b; Reston and Ramirez 2016). While Clinton earned more support from women than men in all age categories, media commentators frequently noted the contrast between older women who strongly supported Clinton and their younger counterparts who embraced the message of change promised by Obama in 2008 and Sanders in 2016 (Kantor 2008a, 2008b; Steiger 2016).

Older women most closely identified with Clinton's struggles as a woman competing in the male-dominated political world. These women witnessed the feminist movement and are more likely to have faced employment discrimination and the challenges of balancing work and childcare responsibilities (Kantor 2008a, 2008b; Huddy and Carey 2009; Steiger 2016). Growing up in a society changed by the feminist movement and just starting out in their careers, younger women did not feel as much of a sense of urgency to elect a female president. In 2016, facing a tough job market after the Great Recession and high rates of student loan debt, many young women were more drawn to Sanders's broadly progressive economic message of raising the minimum wage, reducing student debt, and health care for all (Bruenig 2016). Interestingly, one study found that younger women who had already experienced workplace discrimination and/or having childcare responsibilities limit their employment prospects were more likely to support Clinton than other young female voters (Poloni Staudinger, Strachan, and Schaffner 2016).

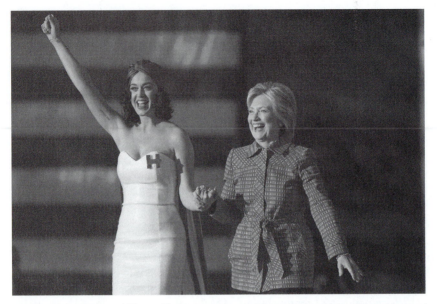

Presidential nominee Hillary Clinton appears with pop star Katy Perry to court younger women voters; while younger Democratic women tended to side with Bernie Sanders in the primary election, Clinton's strong support among older women ensured that she won the women's vote during the Democratic primaries. Clinton also extended the gender gap in the presidential race, although her margin with women voters was not enough to win the presidential election. *Source*: REUTERS / Alamy Stock Photo.

Moving beyond 2016, it remains to be seen how much of Clinton's experience with male and female voters related to her gender and how much related to her status as a Clinton and her long career in the public eye. Will a future female presidential candidate who runs on a message of change attract more young voters? How will stereotypes that associate the presidency with male leadership affect the issue and style emphases of the next female presidential nominee and their ability to appeal to different subgroups of primary and general election voters? The 2020 election may give us some more insight as multiple women are competing to become the Democratic nominee who will challenge President Trump.

CONCLUSION

Since the 70-year-long struggle for the right to vote, candidates, political parties, and the media have tried to identify and attract the women's vote. Scholarly evidence indicates that the modern gender gap, in which women are prone to favor Democratic candidates, stems from men leaving the

Democratic Party—not from women flocking to it. Social welfare issues and an increased support for government spending on these programs constitute a major source of the gender gap. Women's lower levels of support for defense spending and military action have also played a role in explaining the gender gap over time.

Although smaller than other voting gaps, particularly race, the gender gap expanded in the 1990s and became a major focus of presidential candidates during this period of close party competition as campaigns tried to mobilize their base and lure swing-voting groups of women from white, middle-class "soccer moms" to blue-collar "Wal-Mart women" and single mothers. It is an open question whether the aggressive courting of subgroups of women leads to policy changes to benefit women in society. Still, given that more women vote than men and that women are more likely than men to be undecided voters, it is likely that the gender gap will continue to play a role in future elections and political parties will work to target different groups of women voters.

4

Gender and the Decision to Run for Office

◆ ◆ ◆

ASHLEY BENNETT, an African American health-care worker from New Jersey, surprised even herself deciding to run for a seat on her local county commission in 2017. She had never run for political office, was not recruited by any political party, and, despite identifying as a Democrat, lived in a Republican stronghold district. As she herself offered, "I never saw this coming, ever. If you would have asked me back in November, would you run for office? I would have looked at you strangely" (Schmidt 2017).

So what made her decide to run? With an estimated three million women marching in Washington the day before Donald Trump's presidential inauguration, one of her elected officials posted a Facebook meme of a woman at a kitchen stove, stirring a pot, and asked, "Will the protest be over in time for them to cook dinner?" As Bennett tells it, she was furious and decided to confront the man, John Carman, at a town meeting the following day. His response, claiming that his post was a joke and that "'strong confident" women were not offended by it, did little to mollify her. Instead, Carman's disrespect toward fellow community members and their concerns deeply disturbed her. After venting to her family, who encouraged her to do something about it, she decided to challenge the county official for his seat and soundly defeated him in the November 2017 elections (Schmidt 2017).

Bennett's story is particularly instructive because it illustrates a number of truisms about women's experiences as political candidates in the United States. First, receiving encouragement from family, friends, colleagues, and others is one of the most important factors in women's decisions to run. As Susan Carroll and Kira Sanbonmatsu (2013) argue, such calculations reflect that women's candidacies are deeply embedded in their personal relationships—with family, friends, members of their community, and political parties—to a greater extent than are men's. In what they term women's "relationally embedded candidacies," women contemplating a run for office seek out and require support from a web of connections more so than men. Consistent with this theory, Bennett credits the support and encouragement of her family as key to her decision to run (Schmidt 2017).

A second distinction between the sexes is that female candidates are more likely to attribute their decisions to run to a desire to help their communities and to address policy issues of particular importance to their districts (Carroll and Sanbonmatsu 2013; Schneider et al. 2016), an approach that reflects the importance women place on sustaining relationships with others. Women of color are even more likely than white women to cite policy concerns as a motivating factor and often build political capital by serving their communities in other ways before considering a run for office (Carroll and Sanbonmatsu 2013; Garcia and Marquez 2001; Hardy-Fanta et al. 2016; Takash 1993). True to form, Bennett characterized her decision to run as an act to serve her community and expressed great disappointment that the incumbent showed such disregard for those he was elected to represent.

Bennett was not alone in feeling dismissed by those in power. Similar concerns rang true for many first-time female candidates in 2017 and 2018 who expressed deep concern and frustration with the direction of the country, shrinking access to health care, deepening income inequality, the prevalence of sexual harassment and assault illuminated by the #MeToo movement, President Trump's misogyny, and Hillary Clinton's defeat (Alter 2018; Dolan and Shah 2019). Yet despite the historic wave of women running in 2018, they still constituted less than 25 percent of all congressional candidates (Dittmar 2018a).

Nearly 100 years after women won the right to vote, why is it that women are so much more reluctant to try their hand at politics? Does it matter if women, who constitute more than 50 percent of the population, typically make up such a small fraction of the candidate pool? What explains the persistent gender gap in political candidacies? What does it suggest about the nature of our democracy when women are so much more reluctant than men to put themselves forward as candidates?

This chapter takes up these questions, focusing on three explanations that increasingly dominate the scholarly discussions: women don't run because they underestimate their own qualifications; they are less likely than men to be recruited by parties and other political players; and their greater family responsibilities discourage them from undertaking the demanding and erratic hours necessary for political candidacy and subsequent officeholding. But noting the historic influx of female candidates, we also attempt to explain what changed the calculus for so many women between 2016 and 2018: with a newly elected president who had zero political experience, were they less apprehensive about their own qualifications? More heavily recruited by the parties and other political players? All of a sudden less encumbered by family responsibilities?

Noting the record numbers of diverse new women who launched candidacies in 2018, we also argue for greater intersectional analysis of women's decisions to run for office. Women of color constituted more than one-third of female candidates running for the US House, with African American women making up nearly half of these candidates (Dittmar 2018b). To appreciate the historic significance of black women's record numbers, consider the following: between 1980 and 2012, a grand total of 130 different African American women sought out a seat in the US Congress (Silva and Skulley 2018). In contrast, more than 80 individual African American women threw their hat into the ring in 2018 alone. Similarly, record numbers of Latina, Asian, and Native American women decided to run in 2018 (Lai et al. 2018).* The number of LGBTQ women running was also higher than usual. The Victory Fund, an organization that aims to increase the number of LGBTQ individuals serving at all levels of government, reported record numbers of LGBTQ candidates winning their primary elections for the US Congress in 2018, with women-identified candidates constituting the majority of those who ran (Imse 2018).

Yet because most of the existing scholarship fails to differentiate motivations by considering women's various identities, our assumptions about female candidates' experiences and their decisions to run may be off the mark. For example, as we discuss later, many women in politics today suffer what might be termed as a confidence gap: even when they are qualified by all objective measures, women are far more likely than men to question their own qualifications and decide against running (Fox and Lawless 2004). Yet Ashley Bennett expressed no such reservations, at least not publicly, perhaps corroborating research that finds African American women more politically engaged and ambitious than their sisters of other races (Darcy and Hadley 1988; Hardy-Fanta et al. 2016; Holman and Schneider 2018). With a candidate pool that increasingly looks like the US population, there are good reasons to question whether the existing scholarship sufficiently describes and explains different women's decisions to run for office. We do so here.

Finally, we also pay special attention to questions of symbolic representation. When Bennett was elected in 2017, she encouraged others to follow in her footsteps, tweeting, "representation matters, and if you don't see

---

*Because not all candidates publicly indicate their racial identity, very few sources share precise numbers. Nonetheless, in an analysis of female candidate website biographies and associated media in 2018, Dolan and Shah (2019) estimate the following numbers of women of color launched candidacies: 89 African American women, 59 Latina women, 31 Asian women, and 4 Native American women. Silva and Skulley (2018) report that from 1980 to 2012, the TOTAL numbers of women from these different racial backgrounds was 130 African American, 89 Latinas, 18 Asian American. They do not report any numbers for Native American women.

Freeholder Ashley Bennett Speaks at Women's March in New York at Central Park West. *Source*: Pacific Press/Sipa USA/Newscom.

yourself reflected in your elected officials, maybe you should run to be an elected official" (Bennett 2018). And when women run and serve in elected office, research suggests that their presence signals that politics is no longer a man's domain and inspires and engages other women to become more politically engaged and active (Atkeson 2003; Campbell and Wolbrecht 2006; Silva and Skulley 2018; Stokes-Brown and Dolan 2010). Was Hillary Clinton's candidacy an impetus that inspired many more women to run? Were once-complacent women finally inspired to throw their own hats into the ring? Can we expect to continue to see a trend of more and more women running for office in subsequent years, or might 2018 prove to be a blip?

A CONFIDENCE GAP: WOMEN UNDERESTIMATE THEIR POLITICAL ABILITIES

Filling the pipe at one end does not, it turns out, guarantee a robust result at the other end.

—Melody Rose (2012)

Throughout the 1970s and 1980s, female candidates began making steady, incremental progress into elected office, winning their elections as frequently as their male counterparts and leading scholars to conclude that "when women run, women win" (Darcy, Welch, and Clark 1994). Women certainly lagged behind men, but their numbers in lower level positions were especially encouraging and suggested that once they developed the requisite skills and experience in lower level offices, they would progress through the political pipeline and reach the highest ranks of the political hierarchy. Far fewer women were running compared to men, a point many scholars attributed to the different occupational and professional career paths of men and women. But increasing numbers of women were also breaking into and building experience in springboard occupations, such as law and business, again fueling speculation that we would see accompanying increases in the numbers of women running for (and winning) office. The presumption was that these women would begin their candidacies with lower level offices, such as school boards and city councils, and gradually work their way into higher and higher offices. Thus, it would be just a matter of time before women reached parity in elected offices.

But as the quotation given earlier suggests, the pipeline theory has not panned out the way scholars expected. By relying on the experiences and pathways of white men as the norm, scholars perhaps shortsightedly expected women to follow those well-trodden paths to office once they developed the same professional experiences as men. Male politicians continue to come disproportionately from law and business backgrounds, and women have made steady inroads into these two types of occupations. Yet female candidates come from a wider array of occupational backgrounds than their male counterparts. In their study of female and male state legislators, Susan Carroll and Kira Sanbonmatsu (2013) find that women are significantly more likely than men to hail from professional backgrounds in teaching, health care, and nonprofit work. So even though women are populating the ranks of business and law like never before, women in those fields are not necessarily mounting political candidacies.

In addition, before women can begin to traverse the pipeline to set their careers in motion, they must first decide they are ready to run for office. And many women appear to have much greater apprehensions about their own qualifications for office than do men. As political consultant Cathy Allen puts it, "Men decide to run in two hours after someone in the law firm says, 'You've got to run.' . . . The average woman takes two years to decide. She'll wait until she has the perfect campaign manager, the right 17 endorsements, until she's gotten down to a perfect size 10 and the kids are out of school" (Collins 1998).

In their pathbreaking analyses of thousands of women and men in business, law, and education positions, Richard Fox and Jennifer Lawless find a similar story: even when highly qualified by all objective standards, women are still more likely than men to cite their own qualifications as a reason not to run, convincing themselves they are not worthy candidates (Fox and

Lawless 2004, 2011). Journalists Katty Kay and Claire Shipman (2014), in their interviews with many highly influential women in politics and other fields, noticed a similar pattern. Simply put, they deduced that many professional women suffer from an "acute lack of confidence." In study after study, they find that women generally underestimate their own abilities and are more risk averse when it comes to putting themselves forward for promotions or for risky ventures like running for political office. As the quotation earlier suggests, women typically wait until they are 100 percent qualified before undertaking a new venture, while men hold themselves to a much lower threshold. Building on Facebook COO Sheryl Sandberg's exhortation to women to lean in to their careers, Kay and Shipman (2014) posit that "underqualified and unprepared men don't think twice about leaning in. Overqualified and overprepared, too many women still hold back. Women feel confident only when they are perfect." And if female candidates wait until they are perfect and men do not, we will continue to see far fewer women running for office: far fewer women than men will populate the pipeline.

But why do women hold themselves to such impossible standards? Kay and Shipman (2014) suggest that it is, in part, because women and men experience and process failure and success in different ways. They argue that women are more likely to internalize failure and externalize success, whereas men are inclined to do the opposite. So when things go poorly, women tend to blame themselves and conclude that their own personal shortcomings are responsible. Yet, when women are successful, they tend to downplay their own efforts and assume that their positive outcomes are due to luck or to factors and forces outside of their control. For men, the reverse is often true: they often shrug off failure as the result of circumstances outside of their control and take full credit for their own successes. As such, they are more likely to engage in risky behavior like running for office because failure is less costly to their psyches—if they fail, it's not because they were not good enough, but because other mitigating circumstances caused the failure. If they win, they gain the confidence that comes with successfully managing a risky venture.

It's a troubling combination, according to Kay and Shipman (2014), because it means that women are less likely to undertake risks and thus have fewer opportunities to deal constructively with failure. In contrast with men, women will avoid taking risks like running for office for fear that losing will signal that they are out of their league and have no business running in the first place. If they win, they derive few confidence-boosting benefits because they downplay their own agency in creating the victory.

And for women, these apprehensions are likely compounded by fears that voters will not take them seriously or will scrutinize them more closely because of their status as outsiders (Piscopo 2018). This tendency may be particularly true for women of color and LGBTQ women. When asked if any factors made her reluctant to run, a Democratic woman running in a Republican-leaning district in 2018 offered, "I thought that the odds were stacked against me as a gay woman" (Dolan and Shah 2019). To her surprise, her sexual orientation never became an issue on the campaign trail. But one can understand her worry as a recent study found that nearly half of LGBTQ candidates faced harassment by voters or an opponent during their campaigns, and other research shows that many voters discriminate against LGBTQ candidates (Doan and Haider-Markel 2010; Magni and Reynolds 2018; Kluttz 2014). Pearl Kim, a Korean American woman running for Congress in 2018, also expressed frustration with some voters' implicit assumptions about her qualifications for office saying, "sometimes there's a stereotype that maybe Asian Americans are perceived as foreigners, there might be a perception to some that I'm somewhat less American than someone else." And Debra Haaland, one of two Native American women to make history by getting elected to Congress in 2018, similarly offered, "from the very start I think people doubt your abilities" (*"This Is Our Time": Women of Color Break Barriers in 2018 Midterms* n.d.).

So were women in 2017 and 2018 suddenly less concerned about their own qualifications? Might a surge of newfound confidence explain the record-shattering number of women (476) who sought their party's nomination for a seat in the US House of Representatives in 2018, obliterating the previous record of 298 set in 2012 (Center for American Women and Politics 2018a)? In interviews with many of these congressional hopefuls, Dolan and Shah (2019) uncovered evidence that many women squarely confronted such apprehensions about their qualifications, convincing themselves that the stakes were too high to worry about whether they had the perfect resume or how voters might perceive them. One first-time candidate spoke directly to the point. Two years prior, she had contemplated running for a lower level office, ultimately convincing herself that the time was not right and that she was insufficiently prepared. But those self-doubts evaporated after the 2016 presidential election. Appalled by the election of Donald Trump, she explained, "I can't wait around for someone to save me. Men like Donald Trump are going to keep getting elected." She recognized her earlier misgivings as a barrier limiting not only herself but also her larger community, suggesting the power of the relationally embedded candidacy. She offered that worrying about her resume essentially held her back "from doing something that could benefit other people and make other people's lives better." Chrissy Houlahan, a first-time candidate and an Air Force veteran who ran successfully in Pennsylvania's 6th congressional district, similarly offered, "I always thought [running] was for other people, and I was not qualified." But she also characterized the 2016 elections as a wake-up call, begging the question, "Why not me?" (Alter 2018).

Many other women reported similar calculations, saying things like, "If not now, when?" And "If not me, who?" (Dolan and Shah 2019). For many women, the perceived costs of continuing to sit quietly on the sidelines were enough to put worries about qualifications or voter discrimination in perspective.

As mentioned previously, record numbers of women of color also ran for Congress in 2018, giving us the opportunity to explore how racial identity might shape women's decisions to run (Dittmar 2018b). Emerging research suggests that women of color are more often self-starters than white women, often having to contend with political parties who discourage rather than encourage their candidacies (Carroll and Sanbonmatsu 2013; Frederick 2013, 2014). In addition to Ashley Bennett's story, an African American woman running for Congress in 2018 expressed impressive confidence in explaining her motivations for running, despite being harassed by members of her party and community, in the following way: "You have to be persistent and you have to be willing to stand up and take a risk" (Dolan and Shah 2019).

Yet we need to remember that not all women of color are the same. Alexandria Ocasio-Cortez, one of five new Latinas elected to Congress in 2018, clearly did not wait to amass a typical political resume before ousting a sitting incumbent from her own party, suggesting a certain level of confidence. She was working as a waitress and bartender and had never run for office, let alone Congress, when she defeated 10-term incumbent Joseph Crowley to represent New York's 14th district. Yet she, too, expressed hesitation as a potential candidate. After her brother nominated her to Brand New Congress, an organization committed to electing regular, working people to Congress, Ocasio-Cortez attended one of the organization's summits. While there, she recalls thinking, "Where did I get off? I mean, I'm going to tell people that I, as a waitress, should be their next congresswoman?" (Remnick 2018).

As mentioned earlier in this chapter, many women report that encouragement from friends, family, advocacy groups, and party officials is key to their decision to run. Indeed, scholars find that women need more encouragement to overcome the confidence barrier yet are less likely than men to be recruited by the parties or by other political actors (Carroll and Sanbonmatsu 2013; Fox and Lawless 2004). For relationally embedded candidacies, these connections weigh heavily on women's decisions to run.

Many women's organizations recognize this gap and host training seminars and schools to provide skills and know-how for women considering a run for office. In 2018, female hopefuls shattered previous records by enrolling in such trainings offered by organizations like EMILY's List, She Should Run, Vote Run Lead, and Emerge. For example, in February of 2018, EMILY's List reported that 34,000 women had contacted them to express their interest in running, obliterating the previous record of 920 set in 2016 (Emily's List 2018) and representing an increase of nearly 3600 percent in two short years.

Yet, we know that these schools cannot possibly reach all potential female candidates or draw reluctant women out of the woodwork. In the United States, parties play an essential role in developing and recruiting candidates for elected office. We turn next to examine the parties' checkered past in terms of incorporating and supporting women over time.

POLITICAL PARTIES' EFFORTS TO INCORPORATE WOMEN

Today, much research confirms that the confidence gap can be overcome when women are actively recruited to run for office. Potential female candidates begin with less confidence in their abilities to wage a successful campaign, but this confidence gap can be overcome when women are actively recruited and supported by power brokers, especially party leaders. Rashida Tlaib, one of two Muslim American women elected to Congress in 2018, reports that it took seven different people encouraging her to run before she first took the plunge to run for state legislature (MAKERS n.d.). Yet the parties are more likely to recruit men than women, a long-standing pattern in the United States. Why is this so? And did the parties behave differently in 2018, explaining the surge of female candidates?

As Kira Sanbonmatsu (2010, 36) argues, "Too often, political parties have been an obstacle that women must overcome." Political parties have historically stood in the way of women's candidacies, using a number of mechanisms to keep women on the outside. First, parties kept women marginalized to the party apparatus by assigning them volunteer rather than candidate-grooming roles. Second, after realizing that women were not likely to form a voting bloc following passage of the Nineteenth Amendment, parties disbanded their women's divisions and placed little emphasis on developing female leaders. Third, once women became active in the party, they were often offered up as sacrificial lambs, or candidates who had little chance of success. Fourth, party leaders, drawing on their own social networks, selected individuals like themselves (mostly white men) to stand for office. Because women and people of color are treated as outsiders, they are less likely to be perceived as candidate material than white men. And for women of color, the parties often went an extra step in actively discouraging their candidacies (Carroll and Sanbonmatsu 2013; Dolan, Shah and Stripp 2019; Williams 2018).

We later provide a brief history of women's involvement in the political parties below, also emphasizing the ways in which the Republican and Democratic parties have diverged over time. As we discuss in more detail in chapter 7, Democratic women have enjoyed much greater gains than

Republican women in securing elective office over the last few decades. More Democratic women run for office and more of them win their elections, with the result that Democratic women continue to make gains in state legislatures and the US Congress while Republican women's numbers are declining (Crowder-Meyer and Lauderdale 2014; Shames 2015). Case in point: after the 2018 elections, 35 new Democratic women were elected to the US House, the single largest increase in female representation in congressional history. On the Republican side, only one new woman was elected and 11 lost or did not seek reelection, leading to a net *loss* of 10 seats (Center for American Women and Politics 2018b). Put another way, Republican women went from constituting 26 percent of the female faces in Congress to 17 percent in just two short years, between 2017 and 2019. Yet, despite being greatly outnumbered by Democratic women, record numbers of Republican women ran for US Senate seats in 2018 and came close to matching their historic numbers for House seats (Dittmar 2018b). Did both parties do more to recruit women in 2018 than in previous years?

Although scholars will certainly investigate this question in more detail, preliminary data indicate no such change in party recruitment patterns. In fact, there are a number of high-profile female candidates who launched candidacies and won their party's nomination without their party's backing. Perhaps the most well-known case is Democrat Amy McGrath. A first-time candidate challenging Republican incumbent Andy Barr in Kentucky's 6th district, McGrath served 20 years in the Marine Corps becoming the first woman to fly in an F-18 fighter jet in combat. The video announcing her candidacy went viral, helping her raise nearly a million dollars and secure valuable media coverage. But despite the Democratic Party's stated goal of recruiting more women and veterans to run for Congress in 2018, they reportedly encouraged former Lexington Mayor Jim Gray to enter the race, which he did months after McGrath announced her candidacy (Nilsen 2018). McGrath defeated Gray in the primary before eventually losing to Barr in the general election.

Many other women running in 2018 tell similar stories, about approaching their party to seek support only to be told that the timing was not right or that the party had someone else in mind for the position (Dolan, Shah, and Stripp 2019). Although first elected some 20 years ago, Senator Tammy Baldwin's experience as the first female congresswoman from the state of Wisconsin and the first openly lesbian woman in the US Congress is strikingly similar to the treatment many women received by their parties in more recent elections. As Baldwin explained,

> I was projected to lose every competitive race I entered. People told me that I wouldn't be able to win, that I should get out of the race to ensure a clean primary, or that I should step aside to ensure that a candidate who "could win in

the general election" would win our primary. Well, I proved them all wrong, having won every race I was supposed to lose. ("No Limits for Women: The Official Word" 2002, 12)

Republican Marsha Blackburn, who became the first woman from Tennessee elected to the US Senate, faced similar pressures by party colleagues not long after she announced her decision to vacate the US House seat she had held for 15 years to run for the Senate in 2018. Learning that fellow partisans had approached incumbent Republican Senator Bob Corker in an attempt to convince him to postpone retirement to ensure the seat remained in Republican hands, Blackburn's campaign manager fired back, "Anyone who thinks Marsha Blackburn can't win a general election is just a plain sexist pig" (Mattise 2018).

So even in an historic year like 2018, the major political parties appear reluctant to share the levers of power with women. In fact, interviews with numerous women running in this electoral cycle indicate that individuals and organizations outside of the party provided more encouragement and recruitment than their respective parties (Dolan, Shah, and Stripp 2019). About twice as many of these women report being recruited by family, friends, colleagues, and progressive groups like Indivisible, Brand New Congress, and 314 Action than were recruited by the parties.

Why would the parties behave in such a way? As mentioned earlier, some argue that in their recruiting efforts, party chairs have discriminated against women because they are more likely to recruit candidates like themselves—other men (Niven 1998; Sanbonmatsu 2006; Carroll and Sanbonmatsu 2013). David Niven (1998) suggests that unconscious discrimination by party elites is to blame. As he argues, party leaders have a tendency to select candidates who look and behave like themselves. Because women traditionally enter politics through community service or activism in local organizations, their qualities and credentials are often discounted by male party elites, who more often rise through the ranks of the party leadership or enter politics through business connections.

Or perhaps male party elites are opposed to or even hostile to the idea of sharing power with women. The major political parties have historically been bastions of male power that often dismissed women's political ambitions and kept them out of leadership positions. Women struggled to gain entrance into the major political parties in the same way that they had to fight for the right to vote. Throughout the 1800s and early 1900s, party politics was also a major part of male social life. According to Paula Baker (1984), parties united white men across the social classes by providing entertainment, a definition of manhood, and the basis for male ritual.

In fact, it was through third parties that women first gained meaningful influence. Associated with reform movements such as temperance, cleaning up government, and social welfare reform, third parties including the Prohibition Party, the Populists, and the Progressives gave women leadership positions on party committees, allowed them to serve as delegates to party conventions, and even supported their candidacies for office on their tickets. Women gained support from these parties both because of their devotion to the party's reform causes and because of the parties' hope that the mobilization of women as a new voting bloc could help them build the majority coalition that would lead them to become a major force in American politics (Andersen 1996; Freeman 2002).

In contrast, it wasn't until the 1970s that the national Democratic and Republican parties began creating programs to support women candidates. For example, in 1974, the Democratic Party sponsored a Campaign Conference to help train Democratic women to run for office. In 1976, the National Federation of Republican Women began publishing a booklet, *Consider Yourself for Public Office: Guidelines for Women Candidates*. Since the 1992 "Year of the Woman" elections highlighted the underrepresentation of women in office and the potential benefit of women as outsider candidates, both parties have created various programs to recruit and train more women to run for elective office. The Republican Party's Excellence in Public Service Series is a political leadership development program led by groups of Republican women in several states. The typical program includes eight monthly sessions and a three-day leadership seminar in Washington, DC. The first program, the Richard Lugar Series, was founded in 1989 and subsequently spread to a number of other states. Over the years, the Democratic and Republican parties and their associated campaign committees have spearheaded various initiatives to try to recruit and support more female candidates (Burrell 2018). Elected women in both parties have also done their part to support other female candidates leading recruitment and fundraising efforts through the party committees including the Democratic and Republican House and Senatorial Campaign Committees and forming their own leadership Political Action Committees (PACs) and organizations dedicated to recruiting and electing women such as Senator Kirsten Gillibrand's (D-NY) Off the Sidelines and Representative Elise Stefanik's (R-NY) Elevate-PAC (E-PAC) (Burrell 2018; Pathé 2019).

Yet even with such initiatives in place, female candidates remain at a disadvantage for a couple of reasons. First, Kira Sanbonmatsu (2006) finds that party leaders say they recruit fewer women because they do not think all districts are equally winnable by female candidates. But blaming voters for party recruitment decisions may be a clever way to disguise discriminatory intent among party leaders themselves, a refusal to allow more than a handful of women to join their ranks. For example, one African American woman who ran for Congress in 2018 told of being physically as well as verbally threatened by fellow Democratic party members, being denied access to local party events, learning from supporters that they were afraid to contribute to her campaign because of the potential blowback from powerful men in the community, and otherwise being harassed and ostracized by (mostly) white men in charge of the party (Dolan, Shah, and Stripp 2019). Some might interpret such treatment not only as sexist and racist but also as evidence of these men's fears in creating a more diverse party where they would certainly lose some of their power.

Second, Republican women fight an uphill battle trying to convince their party that women's voices are distinct and valuable addition to the ranks of elected officials. In her analysis of the two major parties, Jo Freeman argues that by 1992, it was clear that the Democratic Party embraced feminism and expanded roles for women while the Republican Party valued family values and more traditional gender roles (Freeman 1993). As she explains, distinct cultures define the political parties: Democrats are much more inclined to make gender equality a core component of the party platform and consider women an important constituency, while the Republican Party is more likely to downplay gender equality and eschew identity politics in their efforts to field candidates and secure votes among their base.

Reflecting these distinct party cultures, the coalitions of interest groups that have grown up to support party candidates also differ in the extent to which they prioritize the election of women. One of the most important factors in a race is the ability to raise money. To successfully campaign for a House seat, candidates must raise at least $1 million and Senate races typically require multiple millions (Jacobson 2013). A network of outside groups has arisen to help candidates raise money. The most successful of these organizations is EMILY's List. Established in 1984 to elect more pro-choice Democratic women to office, EMILY's List stands for Early Money is Like Yeast (it makes the dough rise) and is one of the most influential groups in Democratic politics. Their influence comes from their ability to recruit and endorse strong female candidates and support them with a large fundraising network. Women's PACs supporting Republicans, such as Maggie's List, are newer to the scene and have greater difficulty raising money than EMILY's List because they are not as widely known and because Republican donors are not as responsive to calls to elect more women, rejecting the idea of identity politics (Burrell 2014, 2018). In fact, examining congressional elections in 2010 and 2012, Thomsen and Swers (2017) find that Democratic women enjoy some important fundraising advantages over their Republican counterparts. Among Democrats, female donors prioritize the election of female candidates and contribute disproportionately to their campaigns. Yet on the Republican side, neither male nor female individual donors prioritize the election of female candidates and give about equally to men and women (Thomsen and Swers 2017). Moreover, women's Democratic PACs such as EMILY's List are more integrated into their party's culture than Republican PACs, meaning that Democratic donors are more likely to recognize and take cues from EMILY's List when deciding which candidates to give money to, while Republican donors generally have never heard of the Republican-aligned PACs that are trying to elect more women (Crowder-Meyer and Cooperman 2018).

Women's electoral fortunes reflect such differences between the parties. In 2018, record numbers of women threw their hats into the ring and won their party nominations (see Figure 4.1). Yet the increase among Republican women occurred only in contesting Senate seats, and not surprisingly, their gains were far more modest than Democratic women's. In fact, Democratic women constituted approximately three-quarters of the female candidates as well as nominees. And in a year in which the Democrats flipped the House with a gain of 41 new seats, Democratic women won the majority (59 percent) of these new seats (Dittmar 2018b; Edmondson and Lee 2018). Out of the record numbers of new women elected in 2018, the vast majority were Democrats (38 of the 42), suggesting that 2018 was more of a blue than pink wave. As an important component of the Democratic Party base, women typically do well when their party does well.

For Republican women, the picture is more complex. Perhaps reflecting the Republican Party's less diverse base and its move away from prioritizing gender issues when compared to the Democratic Party (see also chapter 3), Republican women constitute a much smaller share of their party's candidates in any given year and their fortunes do not appear to be as closely linked to those of their party as they are for their Democratic sisters. The 2010 elections are illustrative. Republicans took control of both the House and Senate in 2010, gaining a total of sixty-three new House and six new Senate seats. Yet, Republican women won a paltry share of these seats, less than 20 percent of the newly acquired seats. As figure 4.1 shows, the Republican Party fields far fewer female candidates in any given election year than does the Democratic Party. Without some changes, the partisan gap will likely continue to grow. After developing a creative measure to estimate the potential supply of female candidates in each party's base, two scholars find that women constitute more than half of the potential candidate pool for Democrats and only about one-quarter of the pool among Republicans (Crowder-Meyer and Lauderdale 2014). The nonprofit organization Political Parity is particularly attuned to this partisan gap and is working to identify remedies and strategies for encouraging more Republican women to run. More recently, after having lost nearly half of its female members in the House, Representative Elise Stefanik (R-NY), one of the youngest members of Congress, launched a new PAC in 2019 geared at recruiting more Republican women to run for office. At the launching of her new organization, called E-PAC, she warned that the gender gap for the GOP had hit a crisis level (Schultz 2019). She told the *New York Times*,

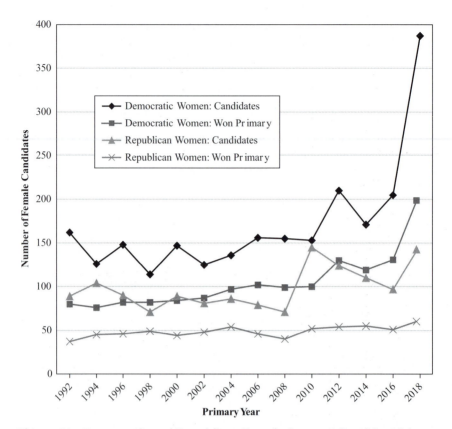

Figure 4.1 Democratic and Republican Female Congressional Candidates Over Time

Source: 1992–2014 Data generously provided by Political Parity, from Political Parity. 2015. Primary Hurdles Report. Available at https://www.politicalparity.org/research/primary-hurdles/. 2016 and 2018 data available from Center for American Women and Politics. 2016 data from *Women Candidates 2016*. Available at http://cawp.rutgers.edu/sites/default/files/library/cansum16.pdf. 2018 data from *2018 Summary of Women Candidates*. Available at http://cawp.rutgers.edu/potential-candidate-summary-2018.

"We have to take the time to do a deep dive and get to the why. This is not a time to stick our heads in the sand" (Pager 2018).

One encouraging piece of evidence suggests that the parties do not need to entirely revamp their recruitment efforts or develop and fund new training schools to support women's candidacies. In fact, one study focusing on Republican Party recruitment efforts found that simply having local party officials vocalize their support for female candidates at party caucus meetings was sufficient to significantly increase the numbers of women running for spots as party delegates. So while good old fashioned one-on-one recruitment will continue to be effective in persuading reluctant women to run for office, smaller gestures that signal that the Republican Party is open to women are seemingly effective, and much less costly, for increasing the numbers of Republican women in the pipeline (Karpowitz, Monson, and Preece 2017).

FAMILY CONSTRAINTS

Finally, scholars argue that situational constraints effectively diminish women's likelihood of putting themselves forward as candidates. As Ruth Mandel (1981, 86) explains,

> The political world does not work on the steady, weekly routine of an office, factory, or retail business schedule. Mothering requires predictable scheduling, whereas politicking requires availability for erratic scheduling.

Holding public office is notoriously time consuming, often demanding long and irregular hours and trips away from the home district to conduct legislative business in the state or national capital. Because American women continue to bear a disproportionate share of childrearing and housekeeping responsibilities, many women simply postpone their political careers until their children are grown and have left the household (Burrell 2014). Although men certainly face family constraints in their pursuit of public office, they do not appear to weigh as heavily on their decisions to run as women's. For men considering a run for public office, having small children at home is not all that atypical. For women, however, it remains fairly atypical (Carroll and Sanbonmatsu 2013). In fact, it wasn't until 2018 that Senator Tammy Duckworth became the first female Senator to give birth while holding office (Kirby 2018). Shortly thereafter, she sought out and achieved a rule change to allow infants on the Senate floor and became the first woman to bring her infant onto the Senate floor (Kliff 2018).

The challenges of balancing career and family may help explain why women run far more often for seats on school boards and city councils than for state legislative or congressional seats. Local offices are closer to home and are often part-time positions with more flexible hours. Many city councils meet once a week or less, and school boards typically meet even less frequently. As such, women considering a run for public office may decide to begin locally so as to more easily balance their work and family responsibilities.

Even among young women, those who are single without children, it appears that expectations about future family responsibilities weigh heavily on their career ambitions. In an experimental design that asks male and female undergraduates to indicate their likelihood of running for political offices, Rachel Silberman (2014) finds that female undergraduates are twice as likely as male undergraduates to say they would run for state legislature if the legislature were close by (less than 15 minutes away). In addition, she finds that districts that are further away from state capitals are significantly less likely to have female candidates running for office than are those that are less distant. Silberman concludes that professional women tend to avoid inflexible careers, such as politics, and concludes that young women are already figuring out ways to balance work and family in ways that men are not.

But in addition to the time constraints, women appear to care deeply about the emotional impact their candidacies have on their families. These concerns reflect Carroll and Sanbonmatsu's (2013) theory of relationally embedded candidacies. As they explain,

> women's decision making about office holding is more likely to be influenced by the beliefs and reactions, both real and perceived, of other people and to involve considerations of how candidacy and officeholding *would affect the lives of others with whom the potential candidate has close relationships.* The candidacy decision-making process takes place in the context of a network of relationships and is deeply influenced by relational considerations. (emphasis added)

In interviews with congressional candidates in 2018, many women voiced such concerns. After being warned that her life would become an open book should she decide to run, one mother of four explained,

> "I was a little bit apprehensive about what it would mean for my family, the scrutiny. I wondered what the time commitment would do. I have kids. I've got four kids and so I didn't know what my day-to-day life would really look like. Like how many hours of the day this would take for me and for my family . . . And how much will they dig into my family's life?" (Dolan and Shah 2019)

Another woman worried that her position on gun control, at odds with her conservative district where many owned guns, could lead to herself and her children being targets of gun violence.

But like Ashely Bennett, many women also spoke about the positive, often key impact their families had on their decisions to run. Referring to her middle school aged daughter, one woman shared, "I felt like one day she would ask me what were you doing when all this stuff was happening in our country." By throwing her hat into the ring, she continued, "I can tell her I've been fighting for a long time." After thinking about a potential run, another woman offered, "my grandson was the reason I finally said yes . . . And the way he said it, and the look in his eyes, I knew I had to do it." Many others credit their spouses for their unflagging support and encouragement.

Finally, 2018 ushered in a legal change that may facilitate more political candidacies among women and men with small children. While running for Congress in 2018, Liuba Grechen Shirley asked the Federal Election Commission (FEC) to rule on whether or not she could use campaign funds to pay childcare costs for her two toddlers. In a unanimous decision, the FEC ruled in her favor, opening the door for other parents to follow suit (North 2018). While the legal ruling addresses some of the financial constraints associated with caregiving responsibilities that fall disproportionately on women's shoulders, it does not necessarily resolve the relational concerns that more often shape their decisions to run.

SYMBOLIC REPRESENTATION: DOES IT MATTER IF WOMEN RUN FOR OFFICE?

Scholars have also begun to question whether the gender gap in pursuing elected office may be a function of women's poor descriptive representation among candidates and officeholders. That is, since political women remain the exception rather than the rule, perhaps seeing so few women like themselves running for or serving in office signals to women and girls that politics is men's business and that they are unwelcome. Some political theorists argue that previously excluded groups like women and people of color will find politics and governance more legitimate when they see more people that look like themselves standing for and serving in office, so termed the "role model effect." According to Jane Mansbridge (1999), improved descriptive representation serves a number of symbolic purposes: it helps to lower distrust among previously excluded groups and increase the legitimacy of the state, it demonstrates that once marginalized groups are fit to rule, and it gives these groups faith that someone is looking out for them. As Barbara Burrell (1988, 51) offers,

> Women in public office stand as symbols for other women, both enhancing their identification with the system and their ability to have influence within it. This subjective sense of being involved and heard for women, in general, alone makes the election of women to public office important because, for so many years, they were excluded from power.

Until 2008, very few women had been highly visible in US politics at any one given time. But in 2008, Hillary Clinton made her historic bid for the Democratic nomination for the US presidency, Sarah Palin ran as the first female vice presidential candidate on the Republican ticket, Congresswoman Nancy Pelosi served as Speaker of the House of Representatives, and Condoleezza Rice served as Secretary of State. All of these women appeared regularly on television and in the print media and were highly visible to even the most casual observer of US politics. Did their presence increase political interest and engagement among women and girls? Eight years later, did Hillary Clinton's presidential run and unexpected loss to Donald Trump serve as an impetus for the (mostly) blue wave in 2018?

The research findings are mixed. National surveys consistently show that men are more politically engaged than women: they report greater interest and pay closer attention to politics. Since 1960, 12 percent more men than women, on average, indicate that they pay attention to public affairs most of the time.* With so many high-profile women in the public eye in 2008, were female citizens particularly attuned to politics and energized by women's historic gains? Not exactly. Only 20 percent of women in 2008 indicated that they followed public affairs most of the time, down from 21 percent in 2004. In contrast, men were slightly more interested in 2008 compared to 2004 (33 and 31 percent) (American National Election Studies n.d.).

But the picture was slightly different in 2016. Previous scholarship reveals that women demonstrate much greater interest and engagement in politics when they live in states in which elections pit a competitive woman against a man (Atkeson 2003). Among other things, women in these states discuss politics more often and are more likely to try to influence someone else's vote compared to women in states where no competitive women are running for office. These effects are even stronger when a woman in their own party is running, suggesting that women are most engaged and interested in politics when a viable woman from their own party is on the ballot (Reingold and Harrell 2010).

And since Clinton was favored to win the presidency and appeared on the ballot in all 50 states, perhaps her 2016 candidacy had stronger engagement effects than did her 2008 campaign. Indeed, preliminary analysis suggests that Clinton's presence at the top of the ticket may have piqued more women's political interest than ever before. For example, the percentage of women indicating they planned to vote was higher in 2016 than 2012 and exceeded the percentage of men planning to vote, suggesting women were particularly attuned to this election in a way that men were not (Matthews 2016). And 6 percent more women indicated that they regularly followed politics in 2016 compared to 2012, again suggesting that they were more engaged than usual. Larger percentages of men also paid greater political attention in 2016 than 2012, but their gains were smaller than women's. Finally, consistent with historical patterns, more women than men turned out to vote in 2016, both in sheer numbers and the proportion of eligible

---

*1960–2008 data accessed by authors through The ANES Guide to Public Opinion and Electoral Behavior at https://electionstudies.org/resources/anes-guide/top-tables/?id=84. Data for 2012 and 2016 accessed through Survey Documentation and Analysis (SDA) Archive at University of California Berkeley at https://sda.berkeley.edu/index.html.

voters (Center for American Women and Politics 2017). So, on balance, Clinton's historical presidential run did appear to increase interest and engagement levels among women.

Scholars have also looked beyond political engagement to determine whether or not highly visible female candidates shape girls' and women's likelihood of becoming more politically active and perhaps running for office in the future. On this score, the results are mostly encouraging. Anecdotally, many women credit other pioneering women with influencing their decision to become active in politics. Nikki Haley, the first female governor of South Carolina and former Ambassador to the United Nations, credits Hillary Clinton with inspiring her own entrance to politics. As she explains, Clinton gave a speech at a local conference she attended and encouraged women to run. As Haley retold it, Clinton emphasized, "There will be all of these reasons that people tell you can't do it. She said that there's only one reason for you to do it, and it's because you know it's the right thing. I walked out of there thinking, I've got to do this" (Cox 2012).

So did Clinton's candidacy prompt women to run in 2018? Even though she lost, was her presence at the top of the ticket enough to create a role model effect that inspired thousands of women to run? Or was the election of Donald Trump the impetus behind the wave? According to Jennifer Lawless and Richard Fox (2017), the election of Trump did more to energize and mobilize Democratic women than did Clinton's campaign. Drawing from a national sample of potential candidates in the months following Trump's inauguration, they find that Democratic women were disgusted and appalled by Trump's victory and spurred to greater political activism post-election. Democratic men were likewise disturbed by the election of Trump and more politically active following the election than before the election but did not experience the same surge in political activity as their female partisans. For example, nearly half of the surveyed Democratic women indicated paying greater attention to the news after Trump's victory while about one-third of Democratic men did so. On the other hand, compared to their male colleagues, Republican women actually became *less* attentive to national news after the election. Again among Democratic women, about half (47 percent) took to social media to communicate about politics, while 38 percent of Democratic men did so.

But did such interest translate into a desire to run for political office? Lawless and Fox (2017) find mixed evidence. For one, men of both parties remained significantly more likely than women in their party to say that they were considering a political candidacy. The gap was largest among Republicans, with 41 percent of Republican men and 20 percent of Republican women expressing an interest in running. As we might expect, Democratic women were more inclined to run than Republican women (24 percent vs. 20 percent), but less likely than Democratic men (35 percent to do so.

But what is perhaps most striking is *when* potential candidates started thinking about running. Nearly one-third (28 percent) of the Democratic women began thinking about running in the months immediately following Trump's election, nearly triple the numbers of Democratic men, Republican men and Republican women who made their decisions in the same time frame.

Additional interview evidence from female candidates in 2018 confirms the potency of the Trump effect. When asked whether Clinton's campaign and subsequent loss had any impact on their decisions to run, less than 10 percent of these women agreed. In contrast, close to 40 percent indicated that Trump's campaign and election played into their decision (Dolan and Shah 2019). Typical are the following responses: "Around January, I started to feel like, okay, you can sit around and just be so frustrated and angry and upset or you can decide to do something." For this woman, the election of Trump lay squarely at the foundation of her decision to run. Another woman, whose parents immigrated to the United States, worried deeply about Trump's hostility and rhetoric toward immigrants and how his presidency could lead to the undoing of the American dream for so many people. Responding to that threat, she indicated, was key to her decision to run: "It was feeling that Trump was going to threaten and undo a lot of the good that I had worked so hard for [in my own career] and really what brought my parents here."

The 2016 elections also appeared to spur additional activism among young women. Melissa Deckman (2018) finds young women (15–24 years old) significantly more politically engaged and active than their male peers following the election: they are more likely to attend rallies, volunteer for groups and causes they care about, donate money to a campaign or political cause, and use social media to engage others and sign petitions. But again, determining whether these women were inspired by Clinton, outraged by Trump, or some of both is difficult to tease out. In earlier years, David Campbell and Christina Wolbrecht (2006) find a clear relationship between the presence of high-profile political women and girls' intentions to be politically active in the future. After Geraldine Ferraro made history as the first major party vice presidential candidate in 1984 and again after the historic 1992 "Year of the Woman," girls were significantly more likely to indicate that they intended to become politically active in the future. Not only did their political interest levels spike upward compared to previous years, but they also became significantly more interested than boys in these same years. The same effect occurs when girls see high-profile women running for political office in their home states, suggesting the efficacy of a role model effect. When no viable women are running, girls and boys give similar answers when asked about their future political involvement. But when one or more viable women runs for office, girls envision themselves as being much more politically active in the future when compared to boys.

But in our polarized political landscape today, new scholarship finds that seeing viable women in powerful positions is more likely to have a role model effect on fellow partisans than on young women from the opposite party. So while Speaker Pelosi and Hillary Clinton may inspire young Democratic and liberal women and increase their likelihood of being politically active in the future, it guarantees no comparable effects on young Republican and conservative women (Mariani, Marshall, and Mathews-Schultz 2015).

Finally, what can we deduce about the motivations of the record numbers of women of color running in 2018? Were they inspired by the first female presidential candidate? When Sarah Palin and Barack Obama were on their respective tickets in 2008, black women exhibited considerable gains in their feelings of political efficacy, or beliefs that government was responsive to them and that they could understand politics. These gains were much larger for black women than for black men and women of other races, leading the authors to conclude that "as double minorities, Black women may respond more enthusiastically to bids by numerically under-represented groups. They may see more meaning in the advancement of the politicians from socially disadvantaged groups" (Stout and Tate 2013). Additional research finds that African American female candidates have positive role model effects on both African American and white women in the population (Stokes-Brown and Dolan 2010). But perhaps most promising for future years, Silva and Skulley (2018) uncover evidence that greater numbers of women mounting congressional candidacies begets even more female candidates the next time around. Even more important, they find racial congruence matters: when more black, Latina and Asian women launch candidacies, win or lose, we see greater numbers of women in each racial group running in subsequent elections.

So, to return to one of the questions posed at the beginning of this chapter, is it more likely that the recent "Year of the Woman" is the beginning of a new era in women's political engagement in the United States, or a blip unlikely to be repeated anytime soon? The continued increased engagement is encouraging, but so are the words and actions of many women who ran and lost in 2018. Democratic hopeful Lisa McCormick mounted a primary challenge to fellow Democrat and incumbent Senator Bob Menendez in New Jersey in 2018. She lost, but secured 38 percent of Democratic primary voters on a shoestring budget of less than $5,000 (Dolan and Shah 2019). Subsequent to her loss, she launched a female candidate network with the goal of bringing progressive women together to share their experiences, work together, and expand political opportunities moving forward. Many other women voiced similar commitments and initiatives, pledging to run again in the future and/or recruit and train other women to run. And as long as women continue to be motivated by community and policy concerns, 2018 is not likely to be a blip. Indeed, issues like income inequality, access to health care, immigration, and women's rights weighed heavily on many women's decisions to run in 2018. If little progress is made in addressing the issues near and dear to their hearts, we can expect to see women continue launching candidacies.

CONCLUSION

As this chapter makes clear, there is no single explanation why women continue to lag significantly behind men as candidates. Rather, it is likely a mix of factors that inhibit women from becoming candidates: worries about their qualifications or voters' perceptions of their qualifications, party leaders who consciously or unconsciously discriminate against women in their recruitment efforts, and the pull of women's greater family and household responsibilities.

Yet the 2018 elections provide a unique opportunity to revisit the three leading explanations and consider the impact of women's various identities on their decisions to run. First, these elections demonstrate that although many women struggle with self-doubt, they appear to be able to rise above those doubts when the stakes are high enough. Returning to the theory of women's relationally embedded candidacies, these findings make sense. If women run out of a sense of responsibility to their larger community, perhaps such a push is the powerful antidote they need to get past their own apprehensions. With the support of their communities, which was perhaps more tangible for progressive women in 2018 as the Trump presidency upended any sense of normalcy in American politics, perhaps these women's calculations shifted. Second, while party recruitment still matters, the creation of many new organizations to inspire and promote women's candidacies may prompt the major parties to take a broader look at who makes a good candidate, although Democratic and progressive organizations have made the recruitment of women candidates a much higher priority to date. Third, while family responsibilities will likely continue to sideline some women, their deep relationships and commitments to family members can also serve as powerful motivators.

In sum, we contend that greater representation of women as candidates in American politics is crucial for democracy. The record numbers of women seeking political office in 2018, which included the most diverse and inclusive set of female candidates in terms of race, ethnicity, sexual orientation and age ever, is a step in the right direction. Women have long expressed less interest in politics than men, but promising new evidence suggests that women's interest levels and their likelihood of considering politics as a career will grow as the number of viable women running for office continues to increase. That is, we tend to agree that "political engagement among the American electorate is gendered, in part because political representation is gendered" (Reingold and Harrell 2010). As young girls and women see more and more women like Ashley Bennett, or Alexandria Ocasio-Cortez, or Debra Haaland, or Pearl Kim, or Elise Stefanik and many others like themselves running for office, they will begin to receive the message that politics is open to them, that women are fit to rule, and that their contributions to the polity are valued.

5

Women on the Campaign Trail

◆ ◆ ◆

IN THE 2018 ELECTIONS, record numbers of women ran for elective office and made history with their bids. Across the country, diverse women were running in positions where few had gone before: if successful, Stacey Abrams would have been the first African American woman elected governor of any state in the nation, Christine Halquist's gubernatorial candidacy in Vermont made her the first transgender woman to win her party's nomination for such a seat, Native Americans Peggy Flanagan and Donna Bergstrom squared off against one another for the position of Lieutenant Governor in Minnesota, and Alexandria Ocasio-Cortez challenged and defeated a sitting incumbent of her own party before becoming the youngest woman ever elected to Congress (Ball 2018; Heim 2018; Ring 2018; Shannon 2018). Along with other records that went down in flames in 2018, the number of female veterans who threw their hat into the ring was unprecedented. By one count, at least 34 female veterans sought their party's nomination for Congress and 14 went on to the general election. They came from all branches of the military and ran as both Democrats and Republicans (Jordan 2018; Shane 2018).

Gina Ortiz Jones was one of those record-breaking women. A veteran of the Air Force who also worked in the Obama and Trump administrations on national security issues, Ortiz Jones waged one of the most competitive battles of the year, losing to incumbent Will Hurd by less than 100 votes in the 23rd congressional district of Texas (*The New York Times* n.d. 23). In her campaign communications, she emphasized her status as an Air Force Veteran with 14 years of national security experience and characterized herself as a tough, independent woman ready to fight for her constituents. In one campaign ad, she narrated, "When you're a first generation American from Texas, an Iraq War veteran, and national security expert, the toughest fights are what you run towards, not away from" (*Gina Ortiz Jones for Congress—I Run Towards* n.d.). Other ads introduce us to her mother, who we learn is also tough. Not only did she raise Gina as a single mother, but left her native Philippines to come to the United States to provide a better life for Gina and her sister. Her mother also waged and won her own battle against colon cancer.

As we argue in this chapter, female candidates must navigate gender to convince voters that they belong in the masculine world of politics. To make sure that voters do not dismiss them as too feminine for the job, women often play up their masculine qualities (Dittmar 2015b). Nearly all of Ortiz Jones's campaign communications highlight her status as a military veteran, and her campaign slogan of "One of Us, Fighting for Us" serves to remind voters that she is tough enough for the job. In another ad, she assures voters of her independence and resolve, saying, "I don't need a party or anyone to tell me to do what's right for Texas. I'll just do it" (*"No One Had to Ask"—Gina Ortiz Jones for Congress* n.d.).

But Ortiz Jones, like many other female candidates, also took steps to showcase her feminine side, explaining that she moved home to take care of her ailing mother because it was the right thing to do. She also promised to champion policy issues like health care, an issue for which women are presumed more competent than men, telling voters that she would fight to make quality health care available for all. And although she does not highlight her sexual orientation in any of her ads, she did showcase her

Gina Ortiz Jones, the 2018 Democratic candidate for the 23rd congressional district seat in West Texas. *Source*: Associated Press / Eric Gay.

empathy, explaining how serving in the military under the "Don't Ask, Don't Tell" policy that forbade LGBTQ individuals from disclosing their sexual orientation helped her understand the fears of Dreamers in the United States under Donald Trump, offering "I'm not a DACA recipient, but I can only imagine what . . . those folks must feel like to know that they've earned something, they've worked hard for it, and through no fault of their own, that opportunity could be ripped away from them" (Ortiz Jones, quoted in Young 2018).

This chapter examines women who have made the decision to run for office, investigating the ways in which female candidates across the spectrum navigate challenges on the campaign trail. We focus especially on women's attempts to manage the often gendered expectations of voters and media by drawing on Kathleen Hall Jamieson's (1995) concept of the double bind. Conventional wisdom has long held that female politicians are judged by different, and more unforgiving, standards than their male colleagues, and emerging research suggests race and gender interact to shape those standards (Brooks 2013; Ward 2016b; Cargile 2016). The growing academic scholarship also suggests that Republican women face a slightly different set of gender-based constraints on the campaign trail than do Democratic women (Sanbonmatsu and Dolan 2009; Lawrence and Rose 2012). Indeed, before she became Donald Trump's campaign manager in

Georgia Gubernatorial Candidate Stacey Abrams Speaks to her Supporters During her Election Night Watch Party at the Hyatt Regency in Atlanta, Wednesday, November 7, 2018. *Source*: Alyssa Pointer/TNS/Newscom.

2016 Republican pollster Kellyanne Conway advised Republican women to avoid running "overtly as a woman" (Stolberg 2014). Because Democratic and Republican women must appeal to different bases of voters, Democratic women typically get more mileage out of gender-based appeals than do Republican women (see also chapter 4).

With record numbers of women running for and winning office in 2018, can we conclude that the playing field is beginning to level? Or, alternatively, might it simply reflect that female candidates are more astute and adept campaigners than ever before, preemptively fashioning strategies for counteracting voter misgivings about their abilities to succeed in a man's world?

The research in this area is still growing, and scholars will undoubtedly study the historic 2018 elections with these questions in mind. But the preliminary evidence suggests that the double bind is alive and well—particularly at the executive level. In the 2016 presidential elections, for instance, many voters disliked both Trump and Clinton, but the media hyped Clinton's likability problem more than Trump's, despite the fact that more voters found Trump unlikable than Clinton. Moments after Senator Elizabeth Warren announced her presidential candidacy for 2020, the chatter about her likability began, comparing her to Hillary Clinton for being "cold and aloof" (Korecki 2018) instead of highlighting her passion and progressive ideals and the ways in which she compared positively to firebrand Bernie Sanders. And when former gubernatorial candidate Stacey Abrams was chosen to deliver the Democratic Party's response to President Trump's 2019 State of the Union Address, at least one news outlet featured a photo of Abrams appearing angry and aggressive. As one commentator noted, "There are countless photos of Stacey Abrams and her glorious smile" and went on to surmise that the news organization must have had to search to find a photo that framed her as not only unlikable, but as an angry black woman, a long-standing trope leveled against African American women (McElrath 2019; Collins 2008).

Yet, despite these obstacles, the historic election of so many women to Congress and state legislatures in 2018 might reflect that there has never been a better time to run as a woman. For instance, Deckman (2018) found that across a variety of issues, likely midterm voters in 2018 perceived women as either equally qualified as men or better able to handle the demands of political office—even on traditionally "masculine" issues such as law enforcement or foreign affairs. Across a wide array of issues, whether it was health care, gun control, environmental issues, or economic issues, large numbers of respondents said men and women handle such issues equally well. On issues that overtly pertain to gender, such as sexual harassment or reproductive rights, likely voters gave female politicians a more substantial advantage. Likely Democratic voters were more likely to rank women as better equipped to deal with a host of issues than Republicans, but the overall data provide encouraging evidence that voters may now be more receptive to women as political leaders and believe in their abilities. Whether this is a fluke in 2018 or more a growing trend in future elections remains to be seen.

In this chapter, we delve into the literature on gendered voter stereotypes and media coverage and pay special attention to the 2016 presidential race, analyzing both Hillary Clinton's general and primary election campaigns as well as the primary campaign of Republican presidential hopeful Carly Fiorina to illustrate the unique challenges women still face in seeking elected offices.

CHALLENGES ON THE CAMPAIGN TRAIL AND STRATEGIES FOR SUCCESS

Even though women are more reluctant than men to contest office, women's success rates at the polls are encouraging. Scholars argue that voter discrimination worked against women in the 1960s and 1970s, but most public polls today demonstrate that very few voters flat out refuse to vote for female candidates. The result is that most scholars today conclude that "when women run, women win." Whether in primary or general election contests, female candidates now compare very favorably to their male counterparts (Darcy, Welch, and Clark 1994; Burrell 2014).

If women tend to win about as often as men, why are so few women sitting in elected office? First, as detailed in chapter 4, women are significantly less likely than men to run. Until female candidates reach parity with men in the candidate pool, their progress into elected office will continue to be slow and incremental. Second, incumbency is a major factor. The majority of incumbents are still men, and it is very difficult to unseat incumbents in the United States (Jacobson 2013). Combined with the fact that the vast majority of incumbents seek reelection year after year, quality electoral opportunities arise relatively rarely for women and other underrepresented groups. Third, a limited number of congressional districts have sent a disproportionate share of women to Congress, and an even smaller number have elected women of color (Palmer and Simon 2012). If women are electable in some, but not all, districts, we may reach a plateau where women continue to replace other women in office, but fail to increase their numbers overall as they cannot make inroads into less friendly districts. At the state legislative level, this may already be occurring. Over a time span of nearly 20 years, women's representation in state legislatures has remained fairly stagnant, inching up a mere 6 percentage points between 1999 and 2019. Even after the historic 2018 elections, female representatives still hold less than 25 percent of the seats in the US Congress. (Center for American Women and Politics 2019a, 2019b). Thus, even if women begin running and winning in similar numbers, the power of incumbency, combined with a limited number of "women friendly districts," virtually ensures that it will take many years to significantly alter the existing gender imbalance in elected positions.

In addition, relatively similar success rates at the polls do not necessarily mean that women and men face the same challenges and constraints on the campaign trail (Dittmar 2015a). Rather, the historical evidence indicates that voters perceive female and male candidates through different lenses and that the press treats their candidacies inequitably. In addition, scholars are beginning to better understand the way in which race and gender intersect on the campaign trail, suggesting that voters and the media use different frames for evaluating and reporting upon female candidates depending on their racial background. Finally, in an era of great party polarization, we are uncovering evidence that Republican and Democratic women are confronted with slightly different challenges on the campaign trail.

Voter Stereotypes about Female Candidates

All political candidates must figure out a way to appeal to a general public that pays relatively little attention to politics and election campaigns. Most citizens devote very little time to learning about candidates, relying instead on cues like party identification and incumbency when casting their ballots. Especially true in local, low-stimulus elections such as city council or school board elections, voters tend to take shortcuts when deciding for whom to vote. That is, most people simply do not have the time or interest to research all of the candidates running, compare and contrast their policy positions and experiences, and select the candidate who most closely approximates their own ideals. It is far easier to rely on a few shortcuts, such as party identification and/or incumbency. If the incumbent has performed relatively well in office, or has avoided scandal or controversy during his or her tenure, voters more often than not decide to return him or her to office (Jacobson 2013). Voters also rely on partisan identification to simplify their voting decisions. Thus, if all else is equal, voters tend to pick the candidate who shares their own partisan identification.

Gender likewise serves as a voting cue, but in a more complicated way than party identification and incumbency. For voters, the generic male and female candidates simply stand for different things (McDermott 1998; Sanbonmatsu 2002). In assessing candidates, especially those for lower level offices where information is scarce, voters tend to use identity stereotypes and apply them to the particular candidates running for office, regardless of whether or not the individual candidates fit the stereotypes. As Kim Fridkin Kahn (1996) explains the process,

> When developing impressions of others, people routinely give priority to judgments based on stereotypes rather than judgments based on new information. People prefer to limit their cognitive efforts by drawing stereotypical impressions rather than processing new information that may alter their initial assumptions. (4)

As such, voters presume that female candidates possess certain feminine personality traits whereas men possess certain masculine traits. Female candidates are seen as more compassionate, moral, honest, and ethical than men. Voters perceive men as tougher, better able to handle crises, more qualified, and more decisive than women (Alexander and Andersen 1993). If both sets of personality characteristics were equally valued, female candidates would be on relatively equal footing with male candidates. But voters historically have valued masculine traits over feminine traits (Rosenwasser and Dean 1989; Huddy and Terkildsen 1993). As such, we can expect that voter stereotypes will hurt women more often than they will help them. In the widely acclaimed "Year of the Woman" in 1992, voters were said to be in the mood for change and eager to throw out incumbents who were guilty of overdrawing their official checking accounts in the House of Representatives. Believing that women were more honest, moral, and ethical, the political climate was favorable for women in that year and 24 new women were elected to the United States House. Ten years later, in the aftermath of September 11, 2001, and with war against Iraq on the horizon, voters were presumably looking for tough, masculine candidates. Only seven new women were elected to the House of Representatives.

Second, voters presume that women are more competent in dealing with issues such as health care, social security, and education whereas men are better at dealing with the economy and taxes, the military, and crime (Rosenwasser and Dean 1989; Alexander and Andersen 1993; Sanbonmatsu 2002). More recent surveys of voters show that women may no longer face a gendered penalty on issues that are often associated with male leaders, such as law enforcement or foreign affairs, and may be perceived as better equipped to deal with the additional issues of sexual harassment and reproductive rights (Deckman 2018). Accordingly, women's electoral fortunes can be expected to rise and fall depending on the issues deemed most salient immediately preceding an election. If voters are particularly concerned about the economy, terrorism, or military crises, they tend to assume that male candidates are more capable for the job. On the other hand, women can be expected to do better in election years in which education, health care, or other social issues are on the forefront of citizens' minds. With health care at the top of most voters' lists of important issues in 2018, and in an era in which concerns about sexual harassment and women's rights appear to be prominent, 42 new women were elected to Congress (CNN 2018; Edmondson and Lee 2018).

Third, voters tend to overestimate liberalism among female as well as candidates of color (Fulton and Gershon 2018; Koch 2000; McDermott 1997). For certain women, such as Republican women running in moderate to liberal districts or women of color running in liberal or very liberal districts, such perceptions may work to their advantage. For women of any racial background running in more conservative districts, however, the public's overestimation of female candidates' liberalism may work against them at the polls, and maybe especially problematic for conservative women of color. In her 2018 bid for Arizona's 2nd congressional district, Latina Lea Marquez Peterson squared off against three male opponents in the Republican primary. Perhaps to squelch any voter misperceptions about her ideological leanings, the first line of her website biography reads, "Lea Marquez Peterson is a lifelong conservative Republican."

Voter assumptions about female candidates' ideology, combined with increasing party polarization, may also help to explain why fewer Republican women than Democratic women have been running for Congress over the last decade. Although the percentage of Republican and Democratic female congressional candidates was relatively equal until 1988, Democratic women now lead the way. Substantially more Democratic women seek their party's nomination in the primary, and substantially more Democratic women win their party's nomination to go on to the general election (Palmer and Simon 2001; Lawless and Pearson 2008; Dittmar 2018). If the public assumes that Republican women are more liberal than they are, contesting a Republican Party primary may prove quite difficult for these women because primary voters are typically more ideologically extreme than are those who vote in the general election. Even if female Republican candidates are sufficiently conservative, primary elections are often low-information races, the type of races in which voters are most likely to rely on voter stereotypes. For Republican women of color, these voter stereotypes are likely to be doubly damaging, especially when reinforced by journalists. In her analysis of the media coverage surrounding former Representative Mia Love, the first Republican African American woman to serve in Congress, Orlanda Ward (2016a) finds news stories subtly calling into question Love's conservative bona fides, suggesting she was a puppet of the party rather than a woman of her own convictions.

Beyond ideology, candidates of color face additional voter stereotypes: they are presumed to bring different traits to the fore when compared to white candidates. Among other things, candidates of color are expected to be more empathetic, more competent on issues such as civil rights, race relations, and poverty than white candidates (McDermott 1998; Schneider and Bos 2011; Sigelman et al. 1995). As such, we might expect women of color to face two sets of potentially competing stereotypes: those that are typically attributed to women, and those that apply to men of color. In fact, scholars have long speculated that women of color may face a double dis-advantage, with voters likely to punish them for their status as women and racial minorities (Beal 2008). Yet because most of the existing scholarship focuses primarily on white women or black men, we are only beginning to understand the impact of these intersecting identities. However, numerous scholars have pointed out that women of color constitute a larger share of elected officeholders within their racial group than do white women. For example, African American and Asian women made up more than 40 percent of their racial group's membership in the 116th Congress, Latinas constituted 30 percent of all Latinx members, while white women consti-tuted just 24 percent of the white membership (data collected by authors). Thus, better descriptive representation among women of color, at least compared to white women, seems inconsistent with the supposition that they are facing more discrimination than their male colleagues.

In fact, Christina Bejarano (2013) argues that Latinas are actually *less* electorally disadvantaged than Latino men. Her evidence suggests that two dynamics are at work. First, white women are more likely than white men to hold positive attitudes about minority women's candidacies, making them more inclined to vote for Latina women compared to white male vot-ers. Second, she argues that racial minority voters are much more likely to vote for someone who looks like them, reflecting the value of descriptive representation. As such, Bejarano argues that "minority females encounter a positive interaction of their gender and race/ethnicity that results in fewer electoral disadvantages" (2). They benefit from "their multiple community identifications" (Smooth 2006) in a way that white women do not.

However, other scholars find evidence to the contrary, suggesting that women of color's success might reflect that they are incredibly adept at responding to and counteracting voter discrimination. For example, one study found that Latinas received significantly fewer votes than Latino men *and* white women in low-information local elections in Miami-Dade County, Florida. They reason that because voters knew very little about any of the candidates, they relied on both gender and racial stereotypes in select-ing candidates, with Latina women encumbered by more negative stereo-types than white women or Latino men (Matson and Fine 2006). Another study found that Latinas are considered less competent than white women on stereotypically feminine as well as masculine issues. When compared to Latino men, Latinas are given the edge for their mastery of feminine issues, but fall short on masculine issues. As such, they do not appear to benefit from a double advantage, at least in terms of voters' beliefs about their competencies (Cargile 2016). But if Latinas are disproportionately running in districts with large Hispanic populations, such voter stereotypes may have less of an impact on their electoral fortunes. In fact, in this same study, Latinx respondents were far more likely to find the sexes relatively comparable on their mastery of feminine and masculine issues than were non-Latinx respondents, suggesting a more level playing field.

For African American women, preliminary evidence suggests the possibility of a double advantage. One study reported that voters give black female candidates the edge on dealing with civil rights issues compared to other candidates (Gordon and Miller 2005). Another, focusing more specifically on their character traits, finds African American women are deemed more compassionate than all other groups, more hardworking than white females, and more trustworthy than whites more generally. They are also presumed to be more liberal than white women, black men and white men (Carew 2016), perhaps, again, circumscribing the types of districts in which they are most likely to be successful.

When necessary, what can female candidates do to counteract voter stereotypes about their capabilities and ideological leanings, particularly in low-information elections? Like Gina Ortiz Jones, many female candidates take proactive steps to present themselves as both masculine and feminine and to communicate their ideological dispositions so that voters need not resort to stereotypes. And according to new research, these strategies appear to be working. In her analysis of the impact of gendered stereotypes on voters' decisions regarding for whom to vote, Kathleen Dolan (2014) finds that voters are savvier than we previously thought. She surveyed voters across the country before and after the 2010 elections, gauging their thoughts about generic male and female candidates. She finds, like many before her, that when asked about hypothetical candidates, voters typically give stereotyped responses: women are more compassionate and bring policy expertise in domestic policy issues like health care, while men are more decisive and competent in dealing with defense issues. But when they are presented with an opportunity to vote for an actual male or female candidate, these stereotypes matter very little. As Dolan and Lynch (2014) explain, in actual elections, voters "don't treat . . . candidates as abstractions but instead draw on traditional political criteria in making vote-choice decisions." Partisan affiliation is chief among these criteria in predicting a citizen's vote: Democrats vote for Democrats and Republicans vote for Republicans, almost regardless of their attitudes about the strengths and weaknesses of generic female candidates.

Yet, the relationship is a bit more complex for Republican women: some stereotypes help and others hurt their election chances. Republican voters who think that female candidates are more compassionate and honest than male candidates are more likely to vote for a female Republican than those who hold no such attitudes. When it comes to their policy expertise, a different pattern emerges: Republican voters are *less* likely to vote for female Republican candidates on the ballot when they assume that women are better suited than men in dealing with stereotypically feminine policy issues like health care and education. Additional research corroborates Dolan's (2014) findings: Republican voters consider Republican women less conservative than Republican men, have greater misgivings about their presumed policy strengths, and are less likely to vote for them in primary elections (King and Matland 2003; Sanbonmatsu and Dolan 2009).

However, additional research suggests that voter stereotypes may be waning as voters are being exposed to more and more female candidates. As Deborah Brooks (2013) characterizes the early research, most studies found that female candidates were held to a double standard: they were expected to act like ladies as well as leaders, control their emotions, especially crying and displays of anger, and had to work twice as hard to get half as far as male candidates. If they did not successfully traverse this tightrope of gendered expectations, voters would punish them, but would not hold male candidates to the same expectations. In a nutshell, Brooks argues that in the absence of many high-profile women running for office, voters perceived female candidates as women first, politicians second. But in today's world, she suggests that voters evaluate women as leaders first and ladies second, especially when considering candidates with a great deal of experience. In what she terms the leaders-not-ladies theory, she uncovers preliminary evidence that voters no longer apply double standards when evaluating female candidates, at least when evaluating fictional candidates under experimental conditions. In the 2018 midterms elections, at least for Democratic women, their gender may have even been somewhat of an advantage, given that Democratic voters were almost three times more likely to say that electing more women to public office would make the country better (72 percent) than Republican voters (26 percent) (Public Religion Research Institute 2018).

Yet as we discuss later in the chapter, our analysis of Hillary Clinton's campaign reveals that Brooks's research likely underestimates the role played by the media and political opponents in caricaturing female politicians, including those with a great deal of experience (see also Bauer 2015). If these women already have been tagged as unsuitable for office, voters will have more difficulty in honestly evaluating their generic leadership qualities and may choose instead to base their assessments on whether or not the woman in question possesses gender appropriate, or ladylike, traits. Recent research by Erin Cassese and Mirya Holman (2017) supports these suppositions. They find that voters are more likely to punish female politicians who do not display sufficient feminine traits than they are to punish similar male politicians. In particular, they find that Democratic female candidates, like Hillary Clinton, are the most vulnerable to attacks on their perceived feminine character traits. As such, being tagged as "Crooked Hillary" by rival Donald Trump likely went a long way toward convincing undecided voters that Clinton was insufficiently ladylike for the job.

As much as candidates can control their own messaging and the ways in which they communicate their strengths to voters, in this day and age of 24-hour news cycles and social media, they must also take careful aim to generate positive and deflect negative media coverage. When it comes to media, how do female candidates fare? Does the press hold them to different standards than their male colleagues?

Media Coverage of Female Candidates

Depending on the level of office sought, most candidates must secure media coverage. Local races for mayor, city council, or school board often receive coverage in local newspapers and radio programs. As one moves up the hierarchy of elected offices, candidates generally rely more heavily on media coverage to communicate with voters. Some state legislative candidates and virtually all congressional and gubernatorial candidates attempt to secure some sort of television coverage. What types of media coverage do male and female candidates report? Do they receive similar amounts of coverage by media outlets? Are more stories devoted to men's or women's candidacies? Does the press take seriously women's policy positions? Do they focus disproportionately on their status as outsiders?

Communications scholars Diana Carlin and Kelly Winfrey (2009) argue that much media coverage of female politicians is problematic because journalists interpret and report on women's campaigns using a narrow set of gendered frames. Journalists use frames in order to "guide the selection, presentation, and evaluation of information . . . by slotting the novel into familiar categories" (Norris 1997, 2). For example, a frame frequently employed by journalists covering elections is the "horse race," in which stories are pegged around which candidate leads or lags in the polls. Journalists could, instead, choose to focus on different components of the campaign, such as the candidates' backgrounds or policy positions, but they rely on the competitive nature of the campaign as a convenient and conventional frame for structuring their stories. For women, whose candidacies are typically more novel than men's, journalists resort to familiar and gendered frames such as the mother, the pet or child, the seductress, or the iron maiden in covering their campaigns (Carlin and Winfrey 2009).

None of these frames are particularly flattering or helpful for women seeking the trust of the voting public. The mother frame implies a candidate who is nurturing and compassionate, but who will have trouble balancing her public leadership and maternal responsibilities. For example, reporters often relied on this frame in covering Sarah Palin's 2008 vice presidential candidacy. Typical was this front-page story in the *New York Times*, which ran during the Republican National Convention entitled "A New Twist on the Debate on Mothers," in which two female reporters interviewed dozens of women as to their opinions about Sarah Palin's candidacy: "With five children, including an infant with Down syndrome and . . . a pregnant 17-year-old, Ms. Palin has set off a fierce argument among women about whether there are enough hours in the day for her to take on the vice presidency, and whether she is right to try" (Kantor and Swarns 2008).

Other women report similar treatment, suggesting that the media could not see past their maternal roles and responsibilities in evaluating their candidacies. When Joan Growe was running for a US Senate seat from the state of Minnesota, she lamented that reporters would steer conversations toward questions about her children when she was in the midst of discussing arms control policy (Watkins and Rothchild 1996). Additional research confirms that the press pays less attention to female candidates' policy positions than they do for men, even when female candidates devote greater attention to policy issues in their own political communications (Kahn 1996). An unfortunate implication of such slanted coverage is that voters may come away with the impression that female candidates are light on policy details, incapable of balancing their maternal responsibilities with the rigors of public office.

But on rare occasions, female candidates have successfully employed the mother frame in their campaigns. Running in 1992, when voters were fed up with incumbents and seeking change, Democrat Patty Murray played up her status as an outsider, referring to herself as "Just a Mom in Tennis Shoes" and going on to win her race, becoming the first female senator from the state of Washington (Schroedel and Snyder 1993). In 2018, far more women seemed eager to show themselves in maternal roles. Kelda Roys and Krish Vignarajah, running for the Democratic gubernatorial nomination in their respective states of Wisconsin and Maryland, were shown breastfeeding in their campaign advertisements. Despite making a splash and receiving considerable media attention, both women lost their elections, perhaps suggesting that voters are not quite ready for such overt gender appeals. Yet other women more successfully drew on their roles as mothers in emphasizing the impact their children had on their policy priorities as well as decisions to run (Chira 2018, see also chapter 4). Lucy McBath, who defeated the Republican incumbent in Georgia's 7th congressional district, emotionally shares how the tragedy of losing her teenage son, Jordan Davis, prompted her to advocate for tighter gun control and run for office. An African American, Jordan was shot and killed at a gas station by a white man who didn't like the music playing in his car ("About Lucy" n.d.). In a campaign video, she offers, "I lost my son Jordan. But I'm still his mother, and I still continue to mother him through making sure that I preserve the lives of other children like him" (Lucy McBath for Congress n.d.). Whether women will continue to draw positively on their status as mothers remains to be seen.

A second frame, the sex object or seductress, draws attention to the physical appearance, attributes, and feminine characteristics or mannerisms of the subject. During the 2008 presidential election season, the media paid a great deal of attention to Sarah Palin's appearance. Early profile stories almost always mentioned her background as a beauty pageant contestant and *New York Times* columnist Maureen Dowd referred to her as Caribou Barbie in at least one column (Carlin and Winfrey 2009). Other members of the media frequently used sexist terms to describe her physical appearance. For example, Rush Limbaugh referred to her as a "babe" (Limbaugh 2008) while talk show radio host Chris Baker referred to her as "a smoking-hot chick from Alaska" (Media Matters 2008). According to Jane Danowitz, former director of the Women's Campaign Fund, such coverage "knock[s] women down a peg or two on the credibility ladder. . . . News stories focusing on appearance detract from and dilute a candidate's message" (Jahnke 1992). If a woman is too attractive, the implication is that she cannot be taken seriously as a political candidate.

The third frame, the iron maiden or iron lady, suggests that a woman is so masculine that she has lost touch with her feminine side. Former British prime minister Margaret Thatcher is often used as the classic prototype for this frame. As the first female prime minister of the United Kingdom, Thatcher was given credit for her toughness and command, especially surrounding her decision to wage war against Argentina in the Falkland Islands, but was less often portrayed as having a compassionate or sympathetic side. When Congresswoman Michele Bachmann was campaigning for the Republican presidential nomination in 2012, she embraced the iron lady moniker. Leading up to the Iowa caucuses, she referred to herself as "America's Iron Lady" and encouraged Iowa voters to send a strong woman to the White House ("Michele Bachmann Plays Gender Card as Iowa GOP Vote Nears" 2012). Despite having made history as the first woman to win the Ames Straw Poll a few months earlier, Bachmann ultimately bowed out of the race after finishing a distant sixth in the Iowa caucuses (Cillizza 2011; *The Washington Post* 2012).

Some of Hillary Clinton's media coverage in the 2016 and 2008 campaigns similarly played into the iron lady frame by focusing on her toughness and suggesting that her masculine traits overwhelmed her feminine ones. For example, the top positive character narratives in media stories about Clinton concerned her qualifications and preparedness to lead the country, but questions about her likability, trustworthiness, and whether or not she represented the "status quo" also appeared frequently in media narratives (Pew Research Center's Project for Excellence in Journalism 2007; Shorenstein Center on Media, Politcs and Public Policy 2016b). Conservative talk show host Rush Limbaugh likened Hillary's power within the Democratic Party to a "testicle lockbox," saying that "her testicle lockbox can handle everybody in the Democratic hierarchy." He later claimed that "Clinton reminds men of the worse characteristics of women they've encountered over their life: totally controlling, not soft and cuddly. Not sympathetic. Not understanding" (Smith 2008).

Finally, the pet or child frame suggests that the subject lacks agency as well as the ability to make things happen. A child must rely on the good graces of others to help her navigate her way in unfamiliar territory; she has neither the experience nor the knowledge to lead on her own. For example, when Elizabeth Dole ran for the Republican presidential nomination in 2000, reporters frequently drew connections to Robert Dole, her spouse, a former senator and presidential candidate himself. An analysis of editorial cartoons found Dole disproportionately portrayed in domestic settings with her husband and relatively mute on political issues. In contrast, her male colleagues were almost always portrayed in public settings and engaging the political issues of the day, the contrast implying "that Dole is unfamiliar with or has no opinions on issues of vital importance to the office of president, and is, therefore, unqualified for the post" (Gilmartin 2001).

Hillary Clinton was likewise discussed in relation to her husband, former president Bill Clinton, but reporters rarely employed the pet or child frame in these stories, perhaps because the iron lady frame more appropriately characterized her candidacy. The McCain campaign was guilty of employing the child frame from time to time in its portrayal of Sarah Palin (Carlin and Winfrey 2009). When reporters started pressing Palin on her lack of foreign policy experience, the campaign tried to deflect attention away from her inexperience by emphasizing that McCain was at the top of the ticket, not her, or they emphasized that she was part of a team, a quick study who would learn much as vice president. When CNN anchor Campbell Brown asked campaign spokesman Tucker Bounds why he thought Sarah Palin was ready to be commander-in-chief, he responded, "Governor Palin has the good fortune of being on the ticket with John McCain, who . . . is the most experienced and has shown proven judgment on the international stage" ("Brown: Tucker Bounds Interview Becomes Lightning Rod" 2008). Whether it was poor planning on the part of the campaign or an honest reflection of their concerns about Palin's abilities, such treatment did not convince the public that Palin was cut out for the job.

Black women are framed in even more narrow terms—as mammies, jezebels, or sapphires (West 2008). The mammy frame is similar to the mother frame in emphasizing black women's nurturing and caretaking roles; mammies are self-sacrificing women, but are also portrayed as content, taking on multiple responsibilities, happily living under discrimination, and crushing workloads. The jezebel is comparable to the sex object frame, with the added characteristics of promiscuity and immorality, suggesting that sexual violence against black women is not problematic or even unwelcome. The sapphire image is comparable to the iron lady frame, an overbearing masculine woman who emasculates men with her aggressive and dominating behavior.

The angry, black woman frame is a variation of the sapphire frame. Some commentators used this frame to depict Michelle Obama during the 2008 presidential campaign, taking issue with the comment she uttered during a campaign event that "for the first time in my adult life, I am proud of my country because it feels like hope is finally making a comeback" (Merida 2008; Gillespie 2016). More recently, Gloria Bromell Timubu ran as the Democratic candidate in South Carolina's 7th congressional district in 2012. In a competitive race with no incumbent, the local paper contrasted her "belligerent" behavior with the "calmer temperament" of her white Republican male opponent, playing into the angry, black female frame (Ward 2016b). After defeating three men in the Democratic primary, Bromell Timubu ultimately lost the race. Unfortunately, Bromell Timubu's experience is not unusual for women of color. In fact, emerging research shows that women of color receive less media coverage than both white women and men of color, and that the coverage they receive is decidedly more negative (Ward 2016a, 2016b; Gershon 2013; 2012). Gershon (2012, 117), in her analysis of media coverage of incumbent members of Congress seeing reelection, finds much the same, leading her to conclude that the "combination of being both a woman *and* a minority leads to coverage that tends to be more negative in tone than the coverage other members receive."

Early scholarship focusing entirely on white women found a similar pattern: female candidates for high-ranking offices received less but more negative media coverage than similarly situated men, making it more difficult for them to communicate their message to voters (Kahn 1996; Aday et al. 2000). More recent research analyzing female candidates for the US House finds a more gender-neutral balance in terms of both quantity and tone of news reporting, but also does not account for race, leaving open the possibility that racial differences persist, and that only some women receive relatively equitable coverage (Lavery 2013; Hayes and Lawless 2015).

Yet white presidential candidate Hillary Clinton enjoyed no such balance. She received more news coverage than primary opponent Bernie Sanders, but it was significantly more negative. Looking solely at news covering her policy positions as reported in eight national media outlets, one study found 84 percent of Clinton's issue coverage negative in tone, four times the amount of negative coverage Bernie Sanders received (Shorenstein Center on Media, Politcs and Public Policy 2016a). Facing off against Donald Trump in the general election, Clinton received less media coverage, but the coverage she received was slightly more positive than was Trump's.

Perhaps this is not particularly surprising considering that Trump railed against the mainstream media, often labeling their coverage as phony or dishonest, and revoked press credentials for numerous journalists covering his campaign (Farhi 2016). What is perhaps more surprising is that there was not a greater discrepancy between the two candidates in the tone of their coverage. Even on the issue of their overall fitness for office, the vast majority of Trump's as well as Clinton's media coverage was negative in tone (87 percent for both) (Shorenstein Center on Media, Politcs and Public Policy 2016b), despite the fact that the public judged Clinton much more favorably on this dimension.

Does the double bind continue to shape women's candidacies? Gina Ortiz Jones's story at the beginning of this chapter suggests that female candidates proactively attempt to counter damaging stereotypes by simultaneously portraying themselves as both masculine and feminine. Or, might the historic number of women elected to legislative office suggest that the double bind is less relevant—or perhaps more relevant for Republican women, who have the added challenge of convincing their party faithful that they are conservative enough for the job? Analysis of Carly Fiorina's and Hillary Clinton's 2016 presidential bids suggests the double bind still matters for women contesting political office, particularly for the nation's highest office (Heldman, Conroy, and Ackerman 2018). Before we explore these candidacies in more detail, we provide a brief history of women running for the presidency.

FEMALE PRESIDENTIAL CANDIDATES

In July 2016, Hillary Clinton made history by becoming the first woman to receive a major party's nomination for the office of the US presidency. After a hard-fought battle with Democratic rival Bernie Sanders, Clinton's victory in the California primary gave her the necessary number of party delegates to claim the mantle of party nominee, an honor she accepted one month later at the national convention in Philadelphia, Pennsylvania.

Yet the road to secure the Democratic nomination was not easy. Many pundits assumed that Clinton would easily secure her party's nomination, given her huge initial fundraising advantage and the fact that she had earned the endorsement of most of the Democratic Party's elected officials nationally, including respected party elders such as Representative John Lewis (Politico 2016). Senator Bernie Sanders mounted a stronger than anticipated challenge and, despite trailing Clinton by more than three million votes at the end of the primary season, refused to concede the nomination until just a few weeks before the Democratic National Convention, fueling much speculation that he was intending to mount a challenge at the convention (Frizell 2016). His refusal to exit gracefully, combined with many of his delegates chanting "Bernie or Bust" during convention proceedings and vowing not to support Clinton in the general election, was a striking contrast to Clinton's concession to Barack Obama eight years earlier. Despite waging a much closer race in terms of both votes and superdelegates, Clinton conceded to Obama four days after he clinched the nomination (Parlapiano and Yourish 2016). In their analysis of Clinton's 2008 campaign, Regina Lawrence and Melody Rose (2011) find that Clinton faced great pressure to drop out of the race, even before the last of the primaries were held and while remaining mathematically competitive. Sanders did not appear to face such comparable pressures, despite the much steeper hill his campaign would need to climb to secure the nomination. And as we detail later in the chapter, some of Sanders's followers could hardly contain their disdain for Clinton and took to social media to harass and belittle her followers.

Nine years before, when Clinton announced her first presidential candidacy in 2007, she immediately became the most viable female candidate ever to run for the US presidency and was, again, the presumptive nominee. Not only did Democratic voters prefer her by a margin of nearly 2–1 over Barack Obama, her closest competitor for the nomination, but she also matched up very well in the general election against Republican hopefuls such as John McCain, Mitt Romney, and Rudy Guiliani (Polling Report 2008b; Gallup 2007). During the campaign, she amassed more votes (nearly 18 million) and delegates (1,896) than any other female presidential candidate in history. In a less crowded primary field in 2016, she received fewer votes, but broke her previous record by securing 2,807 delegates (RealClearPolitics 2016). Her 2008 victory in the New Hampshire primary, edging out Barack Obama by two points, made her the first woman to win a major party's presidential primary for the purpose of delegate selection (Center for American Women and Politics 2016).

In contrast with Clinton, the vast majority of women who have run for the US presidency dropped out long before their party's nominating conventions and very few of them earned any delegates along the way. Before Clinton, Republican senator Margaret Chase Smith held the record for most votes in the presidential primaries. Competing in five states in 1964, Smith received over 200,000 votes before eventually dropping out of the race. Shirley Chisholm, a sitting congresswoman from New York, became the first Democratic and African American woman to run for the office when she competed for the 1972 Democratic presidential nomination. She ran in state primaries in 12 states and secured 151 delegates at the Democratic National Convention before dropping out of the race. In the same year, Congresswoman Patsy Mink became the first Asian American woman to run for the office, but appeared on few state ballots and did not receive any delegates (Center for American Women and Politics 2016).

Before Clinton's historic runs, most gender politics scholars expected a Republican woman to be the first truly viable female candidate for president (Clift and Brazaitis 2000), someone such as Elizabeth Dole, a relatively moderate woman who had amassed substantial executive experience inside and outside of government. Indeed, before Clinton, Dole was the most viable woman to seek her party's nomination for the presidency. She served in both President Ronald Reagan's and President George H. W. Bush's cabinets, worked as a White House aide for two additional presidents, and had led the American Red Cross as president for eight years before announcing her own candidacy (Watson and Gordon 2003). Future president George W. Bush was the clear favorite among Republican voters in 1999, but public opinion polls regularly showed Dole in second place. Until she dropped out of the race in October of 1999, Dole was running ahead of all the other Republican candidates, including Senator John McCain, businessman Steve Forbes, and former vice president Dan Quayle, her closest competitors. Dole performed similarly well in the presidential trial heats. When likely voters were asked for whom they would vote if the presidential election pitted Elizabeth Dole against Vice President Al Gore, Dole routinely received more support than did Gore (Polling Report 2000). Dole withdrew from the race in October of 1999, citing her difficulties in raising money.

Two additional Republican women have waged campaigns for their party's presidential nomination. In 2016, Carly Fiorina was the sole woman running on the Republican side, facing a crowded primary field against 16 men. Fiorina made her name and fortune as the first woman to be named the CEO of a Fortune 50 company, Hewlett Packard, in 1999, where she served in that capacity until 2005. She later became a major fundraiser for the Republican Party and in 2010 won the GOP's nomination for Senate in her home state of California, only to lose to incumbent Democratic senator Barbara Boxer. In 2015, she decided to run for president, claiming that her status as a businesswoman and political outsider was just what the country needed. Her campaign for the nomination, however, yielded little success in a very crowded GOP field, and she dropped out of the race after finishing seventh in the New Hampshire primary (Center for American Women and Politics 2016).

In 2012, Michele Bachmann, a congresswoman from Minnesota and founder of the congressional Tea Party Caucus, was the sole female candidate seeking the presidency. Bachmann made history by winning the Ames Straw Poll, an early poll used to gauge the strength of the competing Republican presidential candidates, but ultimately withdrew from the presidential race after a disappointing finish in the binding, and more important, Iowa caucuses (Center for American Women and Politics 2016).

Clinton's 2016 and 2008 candidacies demonstrated that women can be serious contenders for the presidency, and likely opened the door a little bit wider for future female presidential candidates like Bachmann, Fiorina, and the numerous Democratic women who have announced their presidential candidacies as this edition goes to press: Senators Elizabeth Warren, Kirsten Gillibrand, Kamala Harris, Amy Klobuchar, Representative Tulsi Gabbard, and author Marianne Williamson (CAWP 2019c).

Navigating Gender on the Campaign Trail: the 2016 Elections

"Look at that face! Would anyone vote for that? Can you imagine that, the face of our next president?"

(Donald Trump, referring to Republican primary opponent Carly Fiorina, September 2015)

"Such a nasty woman."

(Donald Trump, referring to Hillary Clinton during third presidential debate, October 2016)

Gender was on full display in the 2016 presidential elections. Donald Trump's hyper-masculine behavior served to persuade voters that he, and only he, was man enough for the job. As both of the quotes above illustrate, Donald Trump employed barbed, gendered critiques to discredit his female opponents, focusing on Carly Fiorina in the primary and Hillary Clinton in the general election. He also leveled gendered attacks against his male competitors, suggesting Jeb Bush was weak and effeminate, and calling Marco Rubio a lightweight, and "Little Marco" (Tani 2016; Kreig 2016). In this section, we look back at the 2016 elections to illustrate the challenges of navigating gender in seeking the highest office in the land. Neither Hillary Clinton nor Carly Fiorina lost her election bid simply because of her status as a woman, but in a country that has elected only male presidents, masculinity is so thoroughly infused in the presidency that men are privileged as the default category (Borrelli 2002; Duerst-Lahti and Oakley 2018; Dittmar 2015b). In both the primary and general election campaigns, Clinton and Fiorina faced gendered critiques from their campaign opponents and the media, critiques that reinforced gender stereotypes and reminded voters of the candidates' status as interlopers, attempting to tread where no woman has gone before.

As Kelly Dittmar (2015b) explains,

For most of American history, [navigating gender] has meant that presidential candidates—male *and* female—have worked to prove they are man enough for the job. Whether by emphasizing their roles as paternal protectors, displaying toughness and strength, or proving their "manliness" in campaign activities and photo-ops, candidates have long engaged in the business of gender performance to meet the masculine credentials of executive office.

But in addition to demonstrating their manliness, women, much more so than men, must also prove their femininity. As discussed earlier, the theory of the double bind posits that our notions of leadership conflict with our preconceptions of what it means to be womanly, often to the detriment of women seeking entrance into the masculine world of politics. We examine the ways in which both Fiorina and Clinton performed gender on the campaign trail and also focus on the ways in which election opponents, voters, and the media subjected their candidacies to gendered critiques.

Carly Fiorina Navigating Gender in 2016 Elections

We start with Carly Fiorina's unsuccessful bid to win the GOP presidential nomination. As the only woman on the Republican side, Fiorina's YouTube campaign announcement took an early jibe at Hillary Clinton, perhaps to dispel any voter assumptions that women in politics are interchangeable. Fiorina's video announcement begins with her clicking off a television that was airing Clinton's own presidential announcement video, turning to the cameras, and declaring that our founders "never intended for us to have a professional political class," instead wanting "citizens and leaders to step forward." She implored voters who were tired of political corruption, and who believed it is "time to declare the end of identity politics," to join her campaign.

Despite impressive debate performances, former businesswoman Carly Fiorina's campaign for the GOP nomination in 2015–2016 stalled. *Source*: Associated Press / John Locher.

The rejection of identity politics is a theme long embraced by conservative activists, including many Republicans. Roughly speaking, identity politics can be described as a political approach employed by progressive activists who advocate for the civil rights of marginalized groups in society, based on race, ethnicity, sexual orientation, class, or gender. While liberals view such activism as vital to addressing structural or socioeconomic barriers that they believe contribute to the continued discrimination of such groups in society, conservatives argue that such an approach is divisive and misguided. When it comes to women's rights, in particular, right-wing women such as Carly Fiorina take issue with liberal feminists' claims that federal regulation and more government programs are necessary for women to make greater gains in the workplace or help lift women out of poverty (Deckman 2016a). They also fiercely disagree with liberal feminists' position that the legalization of abortion is essential to women's fundamental rights. This rejection of identity politics in many ways made the double bind even more daunting for Fiorina.

Carly Fiorina garnered much attention in her presidential campaign for being willing to attack Planned Parenthood, a nonprofit health organization for women that is also the leading provider of legal abortions nationally. For several years, Republicans in Congress have tried to deny federal funding to the group, which also provides basic health care services to poor women nationwide; polls show that most Americans support the organization and believe the federal government should fund it (Page and Firozi 2015). Federal law already prohibits federal funding of abortion services for low-income women, but conservatives opposed to abortion believe that the organization is able to spend more on abortions because it receives federal funds to cover its other expenses. In the summer of 2015, at the start of the contentious GOP presidential race, a series of secretly filmed videos of Planned Parenthood employees suggested that the organization was selling fetal organs and tissues for profit. A later investigation of the allegations determined them to be false. However, Fiorina passionately took Planned Parenthood to task in an early debate over the films, and while critics denounced her claims of footage she had viewed in the film as inaccurate, she managed, in the words of the *Atlantic*'s David A. Graham (2015), to "make Planned Parenthood a national story."

Notably, during the campaign Fiorina showed a willingness to embrace the term feminist, and although a strong opponent of abortion rights, she shares with more liberal feminists the view that women often must navigate sexism in their professional lives. In one well-received video she filmed for Buzzfeed news in July 2015, titled "What If Men Were Treated Like Women in the Office?," she asked puzzled men in an office setting questions often lobbed at women workers that are never addressed to male professionals, such as "How do you walk in those shoes?" and "How do you manage the work life balance?" (Buzzfeed News 2015). In addition, Fiorina penned an essay, "Redefining Feminism," for a popular website, urging businesses and society to embrace women as leaders, noting "we still can make our country a better place by fully tapping the potential of every woman" (Fiorina 2015).

Fiorina acknowledged facing her share of sexist treatment on the campaign trail as well. In one debate, when asked by the moderator about her biggest weakness, she said "after the last debate, I was told I didn't smile enough," adding "but I also think these are very serious times" (Paquette 2015). She told the *Boston Herald*'s Herald Drive Show that her critics often called her "bimbo" and another "b word" (Villani 2015). Many people in the media denounced her business-like, no-nonsense approach as being too unfeminine and harsh. For example, one online newsmagazine criticized Fiorina when her campaign put out a video of the candidate holding a puppy with the headline "Not Even a Room Full of Puppies Can Make Carly Fiorina Likable" (Boggioni 2015). Even the women co-hosts of the daytime show *The View* claimed that Fiorina's face looked "demented" during her performances in presidential primary debates (Richardson 2015). Fiorina called *The View* hosts to task, arguing that they would never pick on Hillary Clinton's appearance, saying conservative women politicians are often held to a different standard even than liberal women politicians.

As mentioned earlier in this chapter, the best-known dig Fiorina had to endure during the campaign came from Donald Trump in a September 2015 article with *Rolling Stone*. In the interview, Trump maligned Fiorina, who at the time was experiencing a brief surge in the polls thanks to her strong debate performances. Of Fiorina he said, "Look at that face! Would anyone vote for that? Can you imagine that, the face of our next president?" (Estepa 2015). When Trump tried to defend his statement in the debate that followed, claiming that his comments were about her "persona" and not her looks, Carly Fiorina's response—"I think women all over this country heard very clearly what Mr. Trump said"—drew praise from the debate audience and Americans nationally (Gambino 2015). In a speech to the National Federation of Republican Women, Fiorina told the audience, "Ladies, look at this face. This is the face of a 61-year-old woman. I am proud of every year and every wrinkle. . . . And look at all of your faces—the faces of leadership" (Glueck 2015).

In their in-depth analysis of Fiorina's campaign, Heldman, Conroy, and Ackerman (2018) provide numerous additional examples of Fiorina navigating gender on the campaign trail: responding to speculation that she was running only to be selected as the vice presidential candidate, answering questions about her pink nail polish, facing questions about whether women's hormonal natures might make them poor presidential material, and being called by her first name in the first debate while her male colleagues were more deferentially referred to by their professional titles.

Fiorina dropped out of the race after a disappointing performance in the New Hampshire primary. Her name did briefly reappear in the context of the primary contests—toward the end of the presidential primary, Texas senator Ted Cruz told supporters that he would select Fiorina as his running mate if he were selected as his party's nominee, and she briefly campaigned with the senator before he conceded the race to Donald Trump in May 2016.

Hillary Clinton Navigating Gender in 2016

Despite developing valuable experience during her 2008 run for the Democratic nomination, nothing could have prepared Clinton for the nasty and gender-infused battle of 2016, when she became the first woman to ever be selected as a major party presidential nominee. Her unpredictable

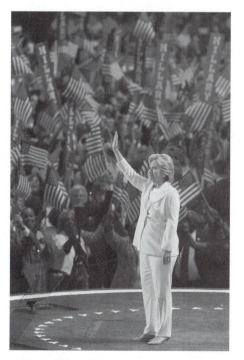

Former Secretary of State Hillary Clinton accepts the Democratic Party's presidential nomination in July 2016, becoming the first woman in American political history to become a major party presidential nominee. *Source*: Xinhua / Alamy Stock Photo.

opponent, Donald Trump, adopted a hyper-masculine campaign style in the general election. He routinely displayed his own masculinity in crude and exaggerated ways while at the same time faulting Clinton for being insufficiently masculine. His campaign likewise called into question Clinton's femininity, referring to her as a "nasty woman" and an unfaithful wife (Ball 2016). Similarly, Clinton also contended with sexist treatment and misogynist rhetoric during her primary battle against Bernie Sanders and, much like during her 2008 campaign, received more negative than positive media coverage (Pew Research Center's Project for Excellence in Journalism 2007; Shorenstein Center on Media, Politcs and Public Policy 2016). We discuss both campaigns here.

As mentioned earlier in this chapter, Senator Sanders refused to concede to Clinton after the California primary gave her the necessary number of delegates to sew up the nomination. Perhaps his behavior was not particularly surprising, considering his pattern of dismissing and belittling her throughout the campaign. In April of 2018, Sanders told a group of supporters that Clinton was unqualified to be president, echoing a similar comment made by Trump. Months before, Sanders's campaign manager suggested Clinton would make a great vice president, not president, and even went so far as to suggest they would interview her for the position (Heldman, Conroy, and Ackerman 2018). And some of Sanders's most ardent young (mostly) male supporters—dubbed "Bernie Bros" by the *Atlantic*—were called to task for their sometimes hateful, misogynist rhetoric on social media aimed toward Hillary Clinton and her supporters (Meyer 2015). One common meme involved lambasting Clinton's female supporters for showing gender solidarity for their candidate, such as one Bernie Bro supporter who tweeted the following comment under a photo of then-New Hampshire governor Jeanne Shaheen with Hillary Clinton at a campaign rally: "their vaginas are making terrible choices" (Rothkopf 2016). Several female reporters, such as Joan Walsh, the national-affairs correspondent with the left-leaning the *Nation* magazine, also reported receiving misogynistic hate tweets from Sanders's supporters after they expressed criticism of Sanders (Walsh 2016).

Bernie Sanders and his campaign team quickly moved to distance themselves from such tactics. For instance, Sanders told *Ebony* magazine that some of his followers went "over the edge" in their support, apologizing for their behavior (Lemieux 2016). Sanders's deputy communications director, Mike Casca, implored their followers on Twitter to "please follow the senator's lead and be respectful when people disagree with you" (Casca 2016). Yet despite such appeals, a study by the *Washington Post* found that among gendered slurs directed at Clinton on Twitter, nearly 15 percent of such tweets were issued by Sanders's supporters (Tromble and Hovy 2016). Male supporters were responsible for about twice as many of these tweets as were female supporters, reminding us that many young women preferred Sanders to Clinton. In fact, Sanders received substantially more support from 18 to 29 years old women in the primaries than did Clinton. Older women, in contrast, were much more supportive of Clinton (see also chapter 3).

Turning to their rhetorical styles, some commentators pointed to unequal treatment faced by the candidates in the Democratic primaries that was rooted in gender stereotypes. Much was made, for example, of Bernie Sanders's frank, no-holds-bar style on the campaign trail, particularly his penchant for shouting from the podium at his rallies (Healy and Berenstein 2015). While some argued that Sanders should tone down the yelling during his rallies and his debate performances, most of his supporters largely viewed Sanders's strong delivery style as a hallmark of his passionate views (Roberts 2015). As political scientist Kelly Dittmar (Dittmar 2016) reminds us, voters often expect men to be more "assertive and loud in proving masculinity, while women's femininity is expressed by being polite, reserved, and soft-spoken." Hillary Clinton, herself, brought up this point at an early debate with Bernie Sanders, when the two clashed about gun control. Coming from a predominantly rural state, Sanders's record on guns was one of the few areas in which his position was more conservative than Clinton, who has always been an outspoken critic of the NRA and the progun lobby. As she responded in one debate about her passion on gun control, "I've been told to stop shouting about ending gun violence. Well, I haven't been shouting. But sometimes, when a woman speaks out, some people *think* it's shouting. But I won't be silenced, and I hope you won't be either" (emphasis in original, Marcotte 2015).

After sewing up the Democratic nomination, Clinton faced a broader electorate who remained skeptical about women's capacity to govern. Despite women's continuing inroads into political office in the United States, one out of five voters polled in 2016 did not believe the United States was ready for a female president (Dutton et al. 2016). Why not? Approximately 20 percent of the American population expressed reservations about a female president's ability to handle a military crisis, keep the country safe from terrorism, deal with the economy, and make difficult decisions. Such a finding reflects years of scholarship that historically finds that voters believe men are better than women in handling masculine policy issues (Rosenwasser and Seale 1988; Sanbonmatsu 2002; Dolan 2014).

Especially when seeking the office of the presidency, these stereotypes work to men's advantage and women's disadvantage. Simply put, voters especially value masculine traits and policy expertise over feminine ones in their presidential candidates (Rosenwasser and Seale 1988). Men must demonstrate sufficient masculinity to be taken seriously for the presidency, but their status as men gives them a leg up. Voters have little reason to question how their male gender affects their capacity to govern: some male presidents have performed better than others, but because only men have held the office, one particularly poor performer is not read as an indictment on all men, but reflects rather on the individual himself (see also chapter 8). By virtue of their historical monopoly on the position, male candidates benefit from being presumed competent and capable from the start, even when compelling evidence suggests otherwise.

Second, because female candidates for the nation's highest offices are novel, voters scrutinize them more closely for how well they satisfy traditional feminine norms like compassion, honesty, and likability (Brooks 2013). As discussed before, Deborah Brooks terms such behavior as treating female candidates as "ladies, not leaders." The essence of treating women as "ladies" is that they are expected to exhibit both feminine characteristics and stereotypically masculine leadership qualities and face a formidable challenge in trying to figure out how to strike the right balance. And lacking any successful female predecessors in their quest for the Oval Office, both Clinton and Fiorina had to figure out how to navigate this tricky terrain on their own.

The essence of the double bind is that men are free to exhibit their full masculine selves without worrying too much about convincing voters that they also have a feminine side. As a man, Trump's masculinity was never really in doubt: he showed a willingness to humiliate his opponents, denigrate those who dared disagree with him, and brag about his ability to get away with sexual assault, as evidenced in the leaked audiotape of an interview he had done earlier in his career with *Access Hollywood*. Moreover, for his claims that he, and only he, could fix America's problems, and that he knew more about destroying ISIS than the Generals in charge of the military, Donald Trump has been referred to as an alpha male, "a cartoon of masculinity," and a "parody of machismo" (Ball 2016). And voters appeared to give him a pass on feminine qualities, pooh-poohing his lack of empathy and compassion as well as well-documented dishonesty. At the end of the day, it appeared that many voters chalked up his boorish behavior and his open hostility toward women and other groups as irritating, but hardly disqualifying (Blake 2016).

Indeed, it may very well be the case that many of Trump's supporters were drawn to this hyper-masculine behavior. Melissa Deckman's analysis of PRRI data shows that two-thirds of Trump supporters believed that "society as a whole has become too soft and feminine," compared with just 17 percent of Clinton supporters (Deckman 2016b). Little wonder, then, that Trump and his vice presidential nominee Mike Pence routinely declared on the campaign trail that "broad shouldered" leadership was the only way to keep Americans safe from danger. The Trump campaign routinely cast Hillary Clinton as weak and ineffectual, and one television ad, "Dangerous," went so far as to show clips of Clinton coughing and stumbling when she went through a brief bout with pneumonia during her campaign, juxtaposed against the sound of Trump saying, "Hillary Clinton doesn't have the strength or stamina to lead in our world." As the research of Erin Cassese and Mirya Holman (2017) finds, such attacks on stamina and toughness can be especially effective against female candidates who are Democrats, a party that is often viewed by voters as being weaker on national security.

Thus, Hillary Clinton faced a formidable challenge in presenting herself as sufficiently masculine. In trying to differentiate herself from Trump and give undecided voters a reason to vote for her, Clinton was caught between a rock and a hard place. If she came across as too masculine in an attempt to rival Trump, voters could dismiss her as unladylike, as a woman who has lost touch with her softer, more feminine side. Indeed, in the aftermath of Clinton's 2008 loss to Barack Obama, gender politics scholars dissecting her defeat concluded she should have run a *less* masculine and more feminine campaign (Lawrence and Rose 2014). Because voters were already convinced that Clinton was tough enough for the job, they counseled that Clinton could have gained more mileage by playing up her lifelong advocacy on behalf of women and children and reminding voters of her softer side. Her 2016 campaign appeared to take such advice to heart. When she announced her candidacy, Clinton promised to be a champion for every-day Americans. In positioning herself as someone committed to fighting income inequality in the United States, Clinton also paid special attention to policy issues that disproportionately affect women, such as pay equity, affordable day care, and paid family and medical leave (Chozick 2015). She also seemed far more comfortable acknowledging and even embracing the important symbolic importance of her quest to become her party's first female presidential nominee. Early in the 2016 contest she told the *Des Moines Register* that she expected "to be judged on my merits," and continued, "and the historic nature of my candidacy is one of the merits that I hope people take into account" (Des Moines Register 2015). She routinely talked about her grandchildren on the campaign trail as well, and poked fun of critics who decried both her gender and age by telling an audience in a campaign stop in South Carolina in 2015, "Now I may not be the youngest candidate in the race. But I have one big advantage: I've been coloring my hair for years. Nooooooo . . . you're not going to see me turning white in the White House" (Karni 2015).

Despite adopting a more distinctly feminine tone in 2016, Clinton again struggled to convince voters of her feminine strengths. Most voters readily acknowledged her impressive presidential qualifications, but evidence suggests that their final vote choices were based on factors other than her leadership capacity, no doubt shaped by her political rivals' sustained efforts over many years to paint her as cold and calculating, as quintessentially unfeminine (Gates 1996; Petri 2016). As one voter said of her, "She doesn't wear a dress ever. . . . She'll probably show up in a pantsuit for the inaugural. She's not a typical woman—she's not soft. She's so power-hungry, which is not becoming of a woman" (Ball 2016).

What made 2016 such a unique presidential race is that Clinton and Trump were the two most unpopular presidential candidates nominated by their parties in years. Voters had misgivings about both Clinton and Trump's trustworthiness and likability, and even though Trump was rated as more unlikable and dishonest, these character flaws seemed much more damaging to Clinton's candidacy than Trump's (Newport 2016). The media clearly played a role in priming voters to hold such a double standard. In an analysis of 88 *Washington Post* articles that mention favorability polling numbers for the two candidates, likability is mentioned much more frequently for Clinton than for Trump. In fact, we found only two mentions of a likability problem for Trump and 21 mentions for Clinton. Journalists also framed the issue differently: they often referred to Trump's high unfavorables in polling numbers but Clinton's likability problem.[*]

Analyzing speeches at the two nominating conventions provides additional evidence that the candidates recognized these gendered standards. Trump trailed in the popularity contest, yet very few speakers at the Republican convention attempted to soften his image or vouch for his positive character traits. Instead, most people who spoke on behalf of Trump emphasized his business accomplishments and leadership skills. On the flip side, speakers at the Democratic convention spent much of their speech time attempting to humanize Clinton by telling personal stories and attesting to her good heart and character. For voters, Clinton's likability "problem" was a larger hurdle to overcome than was Trump's. For men, being masculine is sufficient. For women, being masculine without being sufficiently feminine is highly problematic. According to Adrienne Kimmell, the executive director of the Barbara Lee Family Foundation, "For women candidates, likability is linked to electability, and that's not the case for men" (quoted in Page 2016). As this edition goes to press, Donald Trump is no more likable than he was when elected. However, in the wake of the 2018 midterm elections, the Republican National Committee took the unusual step of passing a resolution to throw their "undivided support" behind the president, widely interpreted as a mechanism to deter any primary challengers (Michel 2019), and illustrating that for men, likability is separate from electability.

---

[*] Analysis conducted by authors, with assistance from Rose Allen.

Donald Trump's campaign also behaved in ways that suggest he was attempting to negate any perceived advantage Hillary Clinton might have in feminine character traits, labeling her "Crooked Hillary" to cast doubt on her honesty as well as moral and ethical compass. Because women are expected to be more ethical and honest, by tagging Clinton as "crooked," Trump could continuously prime voters to scrutinize and penalize her for falling short of "ladylike" behavior while simultaneously engaging in more egregiously dishonest behavior himself. Because the public begins with lower expectations about men's honesty (Pew Research Center 2015), Trump could essentially fabricate stories to keep the issue of trustworthiness in the public eye, expecting that voters would use gendered notions of proper behavior and hold Clinton to a higher standard. As journalist Susan Page of *USA Today* suggests, "Male candidates face lower expectations they will be honest, and voters are quicker to forgive them when they aren't." Adrienne Kimmell adds, "When women are pushed off of or fall off their honesty-and-ethical pedestal, it is very, very hard for them to climb back up, and that isn't the case for men" (Page 2016). Indeed, new research finds that female Democratic candidates are punished more severely than any other candidates for perceived shortcomings in feminine traits, suggesting the Nasty Woman and Crooked Hillary monikers negated many of Clinton's own attempts to convince voters of her softer side (Cassese and Holman 2017).

For Clinton, climbing back up on the pedestal proved nearly impossible. Months after she was cleared by the FBI of any criminal wrongdoing for setting up her own email server while Secretary and State, FBI director James Comey made the highly controversial decision to re-open the investigation a mere two weeks before the November election. The decision was particularly suspicious for a number of reasons, but particularly because Comey broke with standard protocol by commenting on an ongoing investigation and potentially violated federal law by behaving in a way that could reasonably be interpreted as attempting to influence the outcome of the presidential election (Hodges 2016). The reopened investigation turned up absolutely nothing new, but led many Clinton campaign staff and supporters to conclude that Comey's actions sealed the deal for Trump. Not only was the timing particularly problematic as undecided voters were running out of time to make up their minds, but the narrative played perfectly into Trump's strategy of painting Clinton as fundamentally corrupt (McElwee, McDermott, and Jordan 2017).

And Trump's strategy appeared to work. Despite much evidence to the contrary, voters persisted in evaluating Clinton and Trump as about equally trustworthy (36 percent viewed Clinton as honest and trustworthy and 33 percent viewed Trump similarly). Examining nearly 400 candidate statements on the campaign trail, however, PolitiFact rated Clinton as far and away the more truthful candidate: 52 percent of her statements were rated true or mostly true while only 15 percent of Trump's received the same rating. At the other end of the spectrum, a full 70 percent of Trump's statements were rated as false, well over twice the number reported for Clinton (28 percent). In the most egregious category, statements dubbed so dishonest as to be "pants on fire," Trump was the far worse offender. Nearly one out of five of his statements received such a designation (18 percent) while a mere three out of one hundred (3 percent) of Clinton's did (Sharockman 2016).

And according to both *Washington Post* journalist Paul Waldman and scholar Thomas Patterson, the mainstream media contributed to voters' distorted assessment of the candidates' trustworthiness by employing remarkably different and unfair standards in their coverage of Clinton and Trump. Waldman (2016) suggests that the media essentially locked in on different frames for the respective candidates: Trump the crazy/bigoted one and Clinton the corrupt one. Once these frames were in place, every one of Clinton's steps was investigated and reinvestigated for evidence of corrupt wrongdoing. As he argues, "even when the new information serves to exonerate Clinton rather than implicate her in wrongdoing, the coverage still emphasizes that the whole thing just 'raises questions' about her integrity." In contrast, he continues, "when it comes to Trump . . . we've seen a very different pattern. Here's what happens: A story about some corrupt dealing emerges, usually from the dogged efforts of one or a few journalists; it gets discussed for a couple of days; and then it disappears." Political scientist Thomas Patterson goes a step further, taking the media to task for failing to distinguish between the two candidates' weaknesses and thereby implying that both were equally flawed. As he puts it, "when journalists can't, or won't, distinguish between allegations directed at the Trump Foundation and those directed at the Clinton Foundation, there's something seriously amiss" (Shorenstein Center on Media, Politcs and Public Policy 2016).

So how did voters respond? When we look at other public opinion measures for the two candidates, the results are initially encouraging but ultimately suggest the power of the double bind. Zeroing in on two key leadership traits, qualifications and temperament for office, reveals substantial advantages for Clinton. A majority of voters agreed that Clinton was qualified (52 percent) and had the right temperament to be president (55 percent), while much smaller minorities agreed that Trump satisfied such criteria (38 percent and 35 percent) (CNN 2016). On this score, there appears to be no double standard: Clinton undeniably possessed greater government experience than Trump and was far less combative and reckless on the campaign trail.

But when we examine how voters' assessment of both candidates affected their actual votes, we find evidence of a double standard. Trump secured 94 percent of the votes of those who thought he had the right temperament to be president and 94 percent of the votes of those who thought he was qualified to serve as president. For Trump, convincing voters that he had the right temperament and qualifications for office virtually assured their votes for him. For Clinton, these same two indicators were less reliable predictors of vote choice. She secured 83 percent of the votes from those who agreed that she had the temperament to be president and 86 percent of the votes from voters who agreed she was qualified to serve as president (CNN 2016). Clinton convinced plenty of people that she possessed the necessary leadership qualities to be president, but these sentiments were not enough to sew up their votes in the way in which they were for Trump. The differences are not extraordinary, but certainly large enough to shape the final electoral outcome. These findings suggest that at least some voters downplayed Clinton's experience and qualifications, or did not draw on their perceptions of the candidates' qualifications and temperament in gender-neutral ways.

The double standard is even more obvious when we examine voters who thought Trump and Clinton compared favorably on leadership traits, roughly 20 percent of the voting population. Despite such similar evaluations, these voters overwhelmingly chose Trump over Clinton. Among those who deemed both Clinton and Trump suitable in temperament, a whopping 77 percent ultimately voted for Trump and 20 percent for Clinton. A similar pattern exists when we consider voters' perceptions of the candidates' qualifications. Among those who thought both were qualified, 71 percent voted for Trump and 22 percent for Clinton (CNN 2016).

Looking at the voters who held more negative attitudes about each candidate, the same pattern persists. Among those who thought neither candidate had the right temperament to be president, 67 percent ultimately voted for Trump, more than four times the number (12 percent) who selected Clinton. For those who found neither candidate particularly qualified, 66 percent voted for Trump and 15 percent for Clinton (CNN 2016). If voters were gender neutral in their assessment of these candidates' suitability for the presidency, these numbers should be much more comparable. The fact that Trump received nearly four times more votes across all of these categories suggests that voters were using other criteria to determine their final vote choices. And since they compared favorably on feminine qualities such as trustworthiness and honesty, the evidence seems to suggest that Clinton was penalized for her perceived feminine failings while Trump was never expected to exhibit them in the first place.

Of course, the decision to cast the ballot for president involves multiple influences, not merely perceptions of the candidates' temperament, trustworthiness, and leadership qualities. For instance, voters in the same exit poll were asked whether empathy, experience, good judgment, or the ability to bring change was the single candidate quality that mattered most to them when they voted in 2016. Among the roughly 57 percent who cited the first three qualities listed above as mattering most to their vote choice, Clinton was the candidate far more likely to have been selected by such voters. Yet the single criteria that mattered most to a clear plurality of voters—roughly 4 in 10 voters—is also revealing in terms of the election's ultimate outcome: 82 percent of voters who prioritized the ability to bring change selected Trump compared with just 14 percent of these voters who chose Clinton.

While it is impossible to know the extent to which gender alone influenced the election, our preliminary analysis and evidence suggests that long-standing gendered assumptions about women in politics, exacerbated by media narratives and the attitudes and comments of Republican candidate Donald Trump, posed a significant set of barriers to Clinton's quest to break the glass ceiling. Given the closeness of the final results, it is very likely the double standard faced by Hillary Clinton on her historic quest for the presidency mattered. How future women candidates for president navigate these tricky terrains remains an open question.

CONCLUSION

As the discussions of both Hillary Clinton and Carly Fiorina reveal, female candidates today must continue to navigate gender on the campaign trail, particularly when seeking the presidency. As such, women running at the highest levels cannot count on plentiful information about their candidacies driving out gendered stereotypes about their capabilities and character traits. Nor can female candidates expect media coverage that is entirely equitable. Reporters continue to rely on simplistic frames that suggest political women are novelties and outsiders in the manly world of politics. Not only does such coverage give voters reason to call into question women's fitness for office, but it may also discourage other women from running in the future.

As this edition goes to press, scholarly analysis of Hillary Clinton's historic presidential campaign is still getting underway. But as we argue in this chapter, voters' perceptions of Clinton in 2016 very much mirrored those from the 2008 campaign: Clinton failed to strike the elusive balance between masculine and feminine—her impressive credentials were recognized by voters, but many harbored concerns about her lack of stereotypically feminine characteristics such as honesty and likability. Only time will tell whether the next female presidential candidate, Republican or Democrat, will face similar challenges, but the evidence from 2016 suggests that many voters and journalists continue to struggle in reconciling their notions of power and femininity.

6

Women in Local Politics and Government

❖ ❖ ❖

THE FEDERAL GOVERNMENT DOES NOT forbid discrimination based on sexual orientation or gender identity, as it does for sex, religion, and race. However, as Americans grow more accepting of LGBTQ Americans, with younger Americans increasingly comfortable being more "gender fluid" and challenging gender norms (Davis and Fisch-Friedman 2018), calls for such civil protections have grown louder. Currently, the United States has what is essentially a patchwork of civil rights protections for this group nationally: some states have passed civil rights protections that make it illegal to discriminate against any members of the LGBTQ community in terms of public accommodations and in the workplace, while others have not.

In February 2016, the city of Charlotte, North Carolina, joined many other American cities in passing a law to add gay and transgender people to the list of classes protected against discrimination within its borders. These types of city initiatives have been more common in states, such as North Carolina, whose legislatures are dominated by Republicans, a political party that tends to look less kindly on enhancing civil rights for queer Americans. As *Vox* noted "the city of Charlotte was trying to fill this gap in civil rights laws. . . . The city council hoped to make it clear that LGBTQ people should be able to go to a restaurant or hail a taxi without the fear of legally allowed discrimination" (Lopez 2017). The newly elected mayor of Charlotte, Jennifer Roberts—who had led previous efforts to pass such an ordinance the year before as a council member—told *Charlotte Magazine* that guaranteeing civil rights for all of Charlotte's citizens was vital: "You don't have partial equality. You have full equality" (quoted in Lacour 2016). She also noted that more than 200 cities nationally had passed similar legislation, hardly making the city ordinance a radical proposition that many critics of the bill claimed it was.

However, many socially conservative North Carolinians viewed the passage of Charlotte's anti-discrimination ordinance with disdain, and they had allies in the state legislature, which promptly passed legislation (HB 2), which pre-empted the Charlotte measure and banned other North Carolina cities from passing legislation that protected LGBTQ individuals from discrimination (Gordon, Price, and Peralta 2016). The legislation went further by specifically prohibiting transgender people from using school and public restrooms and locker rooms in North Carolina that align with their gender identity, legislating that individuals must use the bathroom that corresponds with their biological sex at birth. Opponents of Charlotte's measure claimed that the bathroom bill was needed in order to protect women and girls from predatory men who would use the measure as an opportunity to pose as women and harass or attack women in the public restrooms. However, studies find that there is no link between bathroom safety and trans-inclusive policy (Moreau 2018). The state's Republican governor at the time, Pat McCrory, fully supported the measure, signing the bill within 24 hours.

National condemnation of HB 2 was swift, as corporations located in North Carolina, such as PayPal and Deutsche Bank, pulled projected expansions from the state; artists such as Pearl Jam and Bruce Springsteen canceled concerts in the state; and both the NBA and NCAA pledged not to hold major championship games in Charlotte (Lopez 2017a). Ultimately, McCrory lost his reelection in November 2016 to Democrat Roy Cooper, who opposed HB 2, and who later supported a compromise deal with the Republican-controlled legislature to overturn parts of HB 2, essentially forbidding state and local agencies from regulating who uses what bathroom or locker room; however, the compromise still forbids cities such as Charlotte from passing broader anti-LGBTQ discrimination ordinances, at least until 2020 (Lopez 2017c).

As the case with Charlotte details, the politics of anti-discrimination laws at the local level of government can be contentious. Many LGBTQ activists look to cities as natural allies in their struggle to attain greater rights, given that urban areas often have more liberal populations (Graham 2017) than rural areas in many states. But even in places that have high-profile LGBTQ elected officials, such attempts are far from certain. For instance, Annise Parker, who served two successful three-year terms as the first openly lesbian mayor of Houston from 2010 to 2016, was unable to win passage of the Houston Equal Rights Ordinance or HERO ordinance, which would have banned discrimination against LBGTQ people in housing, employment, and public spaces (Kuruvilla 2014). To date (2019), Houston has yet to pass a civil rights ordinance that protects LGBTQ Americans living in its borders. Yet, other major cities in Texas, including San Antonio, Austin, Dallas, and Fort Worth, have much better records of passing civil rights protections, including with respect to public accommodations, according to the Human Rights Campaign (HRC 2016).

Debates about greater inclusion for LGBTQ Americans at the local level of government reveal several things that have political implications for women in politics. First, local governments can have a profound impact on the daily lives of Americans, including where it is safe to use the restroom and whether some citizens can be subject to discriminatory treatment more broadly, including lesbians and transgender women. At the same time, however, given the ideological diversity of the United States, not all cities, towns, or local governments provide protections for vulnerable populations at equal rates. Second, the decision-making capability of local elected officials can be limited by state governments, which ultimately provide the governing authority to cities and localities, a concept known as Dillon's Rule. As Americans have become more politically polarized, states have increasingly begun to preempt the abilities of cities and localities to pass public policies, particularly when liberal city governments clash with state legislatures dominated by more conservative majorities (National League of Cities 2018). Preemption battles apply not just to debates about the rights of LGBTQ citizens, but to other policy areas that disproportionally impact women and families, including whether cities can independently raise the minimum wage or pass policies requiring businesses to provide paid family and sick leave. For instance, as of 2018, 19 states currently preempt cities from passing laws that mandate paid leave (ibid.). At the same time, some cities, such as San Francisco and San Diego, have passed employer mandates that go beyond state protections in providing paid leave, making for more gender-inclusive workplaces (McFarland 2018). The politics and policies that occur locally, then, can have big impacts on the lives on women and minority populations, so examining the gender dynamics in local government is important.

Analyzing women in local politics is also crucial because women are more likely to serve at the local level of government than at the state or national level. One reason is obvious—there are many more opportunities to participate. The US Census Bureau (2018) reports that there are more than 90,000 government units in the United States, ranging from school boards, townships, counties, municipalities, and "special districts," which are independent government units designed for a specific special purpose, such as handling public transportation. Table 6.1 lists the numbers and types of local governments according to the US Census Bureau (data are reported for 2012, the last time such data were collected). Combined, these local governments allow for the election of almost 500,000 public officials nationwide. Women are also more likely to be elected at the local level than at other levels of government because such offices are often part-time, non-partisan, less costly to campaign for, and less high profile. Thus, running for local office involves fewer resources and less media scrutiny (Van Assendelft 2014). Serving in local elected offices means that women do not have to relocate or spend as much time away from their families. As Silbermann's (2014) research on state legislative districts shows, distance from the state capital correlates with women's representation in state politics: the farther away the legislative district, the smaller the odds that the representative will be a woman and that candidates for that office will be women. However, Silbermann found no such correlation between the proportion of women serving in local government and distance from the state capital, leading her to speculate that geographical distance from where the work of government gets done can influence a woman's decision to run for office. Hence, women are likely to find local-level politics more appealing than state-level politics.

Not only are women more likely to be elected at the local level of government, but enhanced opportunities to affect public policy also exist for women in local bureaucracies and in grassroots, nongovernmental organizations (Palley 2001). In many ways, the daily lives of women (and men) are deeply touched by local governments. Though local-level politics is less glamorous than national or state politics, local politicians grapple with issues that impact women and children disproportionately, such as education, social services, and domestic violence. In addition, local government is where public access to elected officials is greatest. Given that decentralization is a hallmark of American government and politics, examining the impact and activism of women in local politics is essential.

This chapter takes a look at women in local politics and taps into the larger themes of representation that we consider in the book. First, we examine women in local elected office, both as elected executives and as part of local legislatures such as city councils and school boards. With an eye toward the question of descriptive representation, we consider how many women

Table 6.1 Type of Local Governments

Type of Government	Number
Federal Government	1
State Governments	50
Local Governments	
General Purpose:	
County	3,033
Municipal	19,519
Township	16,360
Special Purpose:	
School Districts	12,880
Special Districts	38,266

Source: US Census Bureau. 2018. "Government Units in 2012." *US Census of Governments.*

are elected to these positions and what factors may inhibit or help women achieve parity in such positions. We also consider whether these local offices actually serve as political stepping-stones. Many advocates who desire seeing more women elected to state legislatures, Congress, or statewide executive office often look down the political pipeline at women serving in local politics as potential prospects for higher office, given that time spent in local government gives potential candidates vital political experience.

Second, turning to the issue of substantive representation, once women are elected to serve in local government, we consider whether their presence actually improves the status of women in their communities. Do women pursue different policies than men at the local level of government, or do they govern in a different manner? Moreover, how does race, class, or sexual orientation impact the opportunities for women to serve and participate in local government? Research finds, for instance, that women of color are far more likely to be elected at this level of government—and often at higher rates than white women in proportion to their share of the population—than in state or federal office (Hardy-Fanta et al. 2016).

Lastly, we also examine the role of women in grassroots activism, recognizing that participation in these areas often results in demands for government to address a variety of concerns like environmental issues and economic development. We also touch on the role of women, particularly younger women, in more current political movements such as Black Lives Matter and the Never Again movement, which aims at curbing gun violence. We profile several cases of local activism in which women made a unique contribution, showcasing how women of all ages and walks of life have been involved in both progressive and conservative politics within their communities.

DESCRIPTIVE REPRESENTATION: WOMEN SERVING IN LOCAL GOVERNMENT

We begin the chapter by providing the most recent data available to consider how well women are represented in various local offices, including mayors or executives, council members, and more local elected positions such as school board, sheriffs, and clerkships. We use a variety of sources to piece together an accurate picture of where women are serving in local governments, whether as elected executives or on councils or other local legislatures. Where available, we consider the racial, partisan, regional, and ideological breakdown of the types of women who serve in local offices. Next, we consider factors that might help to explain women's descriptive representation at these levels of office, arguing that the combination of electoral structure, political context, and desirability of office factor into the number of women serving locally. Lastly, we tackle whether such positions at the local level serve as political stepping-stones for higher office.

Generally speaking, women are better represented at local positions that have less autonomy, such as elected clerks, and fewer or narrower responsibilities, such as school boards. Such elections are generally less expensive, less competitive, and often conform to women's perceived stereotypical strengths. Women are less likely to be represented in local executive positions such as mayoralties or county executives, or in positions that may be viewed as more stereotypically masculine, such as elected sheriffs. To illustrate this phenomenon, just look at the data in table 6.2, which summarizes women's descriptive representation in various local offices with the most recent data available. While women are overrepresented at the clerk position, the school board is the local legislature in which women come second closest to parity with men, with women serving on 44 percent of such seats, followed by city and town councils, in which women hold approximately 30 percent of such positions. Compared with congressional or state legislative seats, women's representation as local legislative councilors is slightly better, but again does not come close to their numbers in the general population. Fewer than 1 in 10 elected sheriffs are women.

Table 6.2 Percentage of Women as Local Government Officials: Estimates and Sources of Data

Position	Percentage	Year of Data Collection	Source
Executives			
Mayors (Cities with more than 30,000)	22	2018	Center for American Women and Politics
Mayors of Municipalities (All sizes)	20	2016	American Municipal Officials Survey
Elected County Executives	8	2014	National Association of Counties
City/Town Council	30	2016	American Municipal Officials Survey
County Councils	13	1992	US Census of Governments
School Boards	44	2015	National School Boards Association
Elected Clerks	50–90	2012–2014	National Association of Counties (Bernick and Heidbreder 2018)
Sheriffs	Less than 10	2015	Farris and Holman (2015)

The Numbers: Women as Mayors and Local Executives

Most municipalities have mayors, although they vary with respect to their selection style and their formal powers. Mayors who are elected directly by the public and have independent executive powers, such as budget authority or the veto, are known as strong mayors. Weak mayors, by contrast, are largely ceremonial. Selected by the city council, weak mayors share an equal vote with the council and govern in what are known as council-manager systems. Often, the day-to-day job of running cities in such systems falls to a hired city manager. According to the National League of Cities, most cities (55 percent) use the council-manager system. More than one-third of municipalities, especially those in the Northeast and Mid-Atlantic states, use the mayor-council systems (National League of Cities n.d.); however, the nation's largest cities are more likely to have separately elected mayors. Smaller municipalities, townships or counties sometimes have governments without a formal executive, such as commissions or town meetings, although roughly 400 counties have a separately elected county executive (Smith and Greenblatt 2017).

In November 2018, Angela Alsobrooke, age 45, was elected County Executive of Prince Georges County, home to more than 1.25 million people just outside of the nation's capital and the second largest county in Maryland. The first African American woman elected to this leadership position in Maryland's history, in 2010, she was the youngest person ever elected State's Attorney in Maryland as well. *Source*: Associated Press / Manuel Balce Ceneta.

The first woman elected mayor in the United States was Susanna Madora Salter, who in 1887 was elected mayor of Argonia, Kansas, as part of the Prohibition Party (Kansas Historical Society n.d.). Salter, however, was the exception, and not the rule, for most of America's history. The Center for American Women and Politics at Rutgers University has long tracked the progress of women as mayors in cities with a population of 30,000 or more residents. In 1971, just 1 percent of such cities had female mayors. While women are currently better represented as mayors of larger cities than in higher ranking executive positions such as governors, scholars who study women mayors note that their progress as the city's top official has largely been stymied in the last two decades. For example, in the late 1990s, women crossed the 20 percent threshold as mayors in cities with more than 30,000 residents and have largely hovered around that mark for nearly two decades. In 2018 women made up 21.8 percent of mayors of large cities (CAWP 2018). In the state of California, however, women fare slightly better—in 2017, 28 percent of cities had a woman mayor (California Women Lead 2017). Women also make up a minority among mayors of the nation's most populous cities. Table 6.3 lists the 23 women serving as mayors among the 100 largest cities in America as of 2018 (Center for American Women and Politics 2018). Of those, almost half are women of color.

One path-breaking study that has tracked the number of women and men of color serving in local office is the Gender and Multicultural

In 1887, Susanna Madora Salter was the first woman elected as mayor in the United States, in the prairie town of Argonia, Kansas, running on a Prohibitionist platform to ban alcohol. She served one term before moving to Oklahoma. *Source*: Kansas Historical Society.

Table 6.3   Women Mayors of 100 Largest US Cities, 2019

Mayor	City	Rank	Population
Thelda Williams	Phoenix, AZ	8	1,626,078
London Breed	San Francisco, CA	15	884,363
Betsy Price	Fort Worth, TX	16	874,168
Vi Alexander Lyles	Charlotte, NC	20	859,035
Muriel Bowser	Washington, DC	24	693,972
Jenny Durkan	Seattle, WA	28	724,745
Carolyn Goodman	Las Vegas, NV	32	641,676
Jean Stothert	Omaha, NE	42	466,893
Keisha Lance Bottoms	Atlanta, GA	43	486,290
Nancy McFarlane	Raleigh, NC	45	464,758
Elizabeth "Libby" Schaaf	Oakland, CA	49	425,195
Karen K. Goh	Bakersfield, CA	53	380,874
LaToya Cantrell	New Orleans, LA	54	393,292
Angie M. Carpenter	Islip, NY	57	333,700
Lyda Krewson	St. Louis, MO	60	996,726
Debra March	Henderson, NV	71	302,539
Nancy Vaughan	Greensboro, NC	73	290,222
Mary Casillas Salas	Chula Vista, CA	82	270,471
Lori Barnett Dodson	Garland, TX	89	238,002
Sharon Weston Broome	Baton Rouge, LA	90	225,374
Hillary Schieve	Reno, NV	93	248,853
Lily Mei	Fremont, CA	98	234,962

Note: Women of color are itacilized.
Source: Center for American Women and Politics, Fact Sheet 2019; Population sizes and ranks are drawn from US Census Bureau estimates.

Leadership (GMCL) National Database and Survey, undertaken by political scientists Carol Hardy-Fanta, Pei-te Len, Dianne Pinderhughes, and Christine Marie Sierra (2016). Their work finds substantial growth in the numbers of African American women, Latina women, and Asian American women serving as mayors over the past three decades. However, women of color, like their white counterparts, are still far less likely than similar men to be elected mayors. Women of color are best represented as mayors in smaller cities with populations of fewer than 5,000 residents than their male counterparts of the same race (ibid. 99). When it comes to LGBTQ Americans, the Victory Institute, a political organization dedicated to training and promoting LGBTQ Americans for service in government, tracks the number of openly LGBTQ Americans serving in political office. Their data show that as of 2019, 40 LGBTQ Americans serve as mayors across the country, including 7 lesbian women (The Victory Fund 2019).

To gain a better understanding of the type of women who serve as mayors, Susan Carroll and Kira Sanbonmatsu (2010) surveyed America's women mayors in 2008 in cities with 30,000 or more residents as well as a random sample of male mayors for comparison purposes.[*] Their study finds that most mayors—both women (64.3 percent) and men (68.7 percent)—come into office through direct election and that the vast majority of these offices are nonpartisan. An additional one-third of women mayors preside in council-manager systems, which means that they were selected by their fellow council members to be mayor after they were elected to serve on the council. Predominantly non-Hispanic and white in terms of ethnicity, women mayors were both less likely to be married than their male counterparts and less likely to have children under the age of 18 (ibid.). Before being elected to office, most women mayors were very active in women's organizations such as the League of Women Voters and other civic groups such as religious organizations, local service organizations, and business/professional groups. Compared with their male counterparts, women are much more likely to be involved in organizations that focus on children's issues (ibid.). Politically, women mayors also engaged in more partisan and electoral activities than men prior to their time before serving as mayor, including holding previous elective or appointed positions. In short, women mayors "have had as much or more experience than their male counterparts before becoming mayors" (11), echoing other findings about women and political office, which shows that women who become candidates are often *better* qualified than men before they decide to run for office (Pearson and McGhee 2013). A more recent longitudinal analysis of elected mayors in California also finds that female mayors were significantly more likely than male mayors to have prior political experience (Crowder-Meyer, Gadarian, and Tronstine 2015).

The American Municipal Officials Survey (AMOS), a nonpartisan survey conducted jointly by scholars at Brigham Young University and the Washington University of St. Louis[†] found that in metropolitan cities with more than 10,000 residents, 20 percent of mayors are women. While the dataset is not large enough to break down the sample by race, the data do allow

---

[*] Carroll and Sanbonmatsu report that their overall response rate was 48.2 percent for a total sample size of 189. Women mayors were more likely to respond, and the authors express confidence with the generalizability of the results for the women mayors given that more than half of them (52.4 percent) responded to their survey request. They argue that the results for the male respondents should be viewed with more caution given that fewer than half—43.9 percent—of the men responded.

[†] The results of the American Municipal Officials Survey should be viewed with some caution, as the survey is not a truly random sample of officeholders. For more information on how the study was conducted, see the survey's website: http://www.municipalsurvey.org. The authors are grateful to the Directors of the survey, Adam Dynes, Hans Hassell, and Michelle Torres, for sharing their data with us.

for partisan, ideological, and regional analysis by gender. The AMOS study shows that there are no statistically significant regional differences when it comes to the likelihood that a woman or a man will serve as a mayor. Partisanship does not emerge as a significant difference between men and women—although women are more likely to identify as Democrats (43 percent) compared with their male counterparts (33 percent), while male mayors are slightly more likely to identify as Republicans or as Independents. However, female mayors are significantly more likely to self-identify as liberal (37 percent) compared with male mayors (21 percent), and men are more likely to identify as middle of the road (26 percent) than women (17 percent). Yet, 46 percent of women mayors describe themselves as conservative, serving as a reminder that women in elected office are far from politically monolithic.*

The Numbers: Women on City and County Councils

We next consider how many women serve on local legislatures such as city and county councils. Counties and cities are still viewed as arms of the states, which confer all formal powers to local governments through state constitutions or by acts of the state legislature (Ross and Levine 2001). Local legislatures at the county level are typically known as county councils, boards of supervisors, or boards of commissioners. In municipalities and cities, they are typically known as city councils. Traditionally, counties performed state-mandated duties such as record keeping, assessing property, maintaining and building local roads, administering local elections, law enforcement, and judicial functions—tasks that still make up the bulk of what county governments do. But many counties in the twenty-first century have increasingly taken on more responsibilities when it comes to tackling poverty, health care, economic development, and education (Smith and Greenblatt 2018).

In 1992, the Census of Governments reported that almost 13 percent of elected county council members were women, which marked a significant gain in women's descriptive representation since the 1970s, when their numbers were in the single digits (Manning 1988). Yet women's progress at the county level of government remains slow. For instance, a more recent study that examined a random sample of 394 of the nation's more than 3,000 counties found that half did not have any women serving on them (Kellogg et al. 2017); moreover, women held fewer than 30 percent of the seats on county councils or commissions in at least two-thirds of the sample (ibid.).

Women appear to be making greater gains on city councils. Data from the International City/County Management Association (ICMA) show

---

*Numbers calculated by the authors.

that women in 1991 held 18.7 percent of city council seats, a number that increased to 22.1 percent by 2001. In 2018, ICMA reports that women hold approximately two out of seven city council seats nationally, for an average of about 28 percent (Oztekin-Gunaydin 2018). However, the representation of women varies dramatically on city councils and women appear to be underrepresented in the nation's largest cities, including New York, Chicago, and Los Angeles. As of 2018, women fared best in Chicago, representing 14 of the city's 50 wards (28 percent). In New York, women held 11 of its 51 elected positions (22 percent), while just two women were seated on Los Angeles's 15-member council (11 percent). Women do fare better on other city councils in the Golden State: one 2017 study found that 31 percent of California City Council members are women, up from 28 percent three years earlier. However, while 15 percent of city councils (72 out of 482) in California have a female majority, 12 percent (56 out of 482) have no women serving on them (California Women Lead 2017). One city council, in California, Blue Lake in Humboldt County, has a city council made up of all women.

The 2016 American Municipal Officers Survey also surveys the men and women who serve on local legislative councils of cities of more than 10,000. In 2016, roughly 30 percent of women in city and county councils were women—which, again, corresponds closely with other studies that track the number of legislators in local offices by gender. Compared with men, local women legislators are slightly more represented in the West and slightly less represented in the Midwest. They are also more liberal and Democratic than their male counterparts. For instance, 42 percent of women city or county councilors describe themselves as liberal compared with just 28 percent of men; close to half (48 percent) of women identify as Democrats at this level of government compared with just 31 percent of men. Similar to female mayors nationally, then, women on locally elected councils appear to be more liberal and Democratic than their male counterparts.

With respect to racial diversity, the GMCL project found that women of color are significantly more likely to serve in municipal office than in county office compared with their male counterparts. Isolating their analysis to just people of color, the members of the project found that women of color make up 30 percent of municipal elected officials of color but only 18 percent of county elected officials compared with men of color who serve in such elected offices (Lien 2014). Breaking down those categories by specific racial or ethnic groupings in 2006, they also found that approximately one-third of black city council members, a quarter of Latino councilors, and about one-fifth of Asian American council members were women (Hardy-Fanta et al. 2016). Yet it is worth noting that over several decades beginning in 1990 to 2014, Hardy-Fanta and her colleagues (2016) find that the percentage of women of color serving in elected office at the local level has grown at a faster pace than that of both men of color and white women. Moreover, women of color are more likely to serve in municipalities that are majority nonwhite than women who are white; however, among those African American women who serve in county elected positions, the majority of their residents are white. Latinas elected at the county level—although there are relatively few across the country—tend to reside in more racially diverse counties compared with African American women (Lien 2014). Finally, the Victory Institute reports 66 women who identify as lesbian, queer, or bisexual serve on locally elected city councils, county commissions, or other local legislatures (The Victory Institute 2019). Moreover, four transgender women report serving on city councils in 2019 in Fairbanks (AK), Palm Springs (CA), Minneapolis (MN), and Doravile (GA) (ibid.).

The Numbers: Women Serving as School Board Members, Clerks, Sheriffs, and Other Local Officers

Next we consider women serving in more specialized positions at the local level such as school board, sheriff, and county clerks. In the late 1860s, several women were elected to school boards in Massachusetts (where they are known as school committees), marking the first elected political position held by women in the nation (Darcy, Welch, and Clark 1994). Moreover, many states granted women the limited right to vote in school board elections long before women gained universal suffrage in 1920. Historically, education has been viewed as a special prerogative of women, given many women's status as mothers. Even today, women devote more of their civic activism to education than to other political issues (Schlozman et al. 1995).

Because school boards make many important political decisions, school board elections have sometimes become a hotly contested venue in the "culture wars" of American politics. As pitched battles over sex education, censorship, and school prayer demonstrate, the school district is one arena in which moral values often intersect with education (Deckman 2004). School boards help to establish the direction of local education policy by selecting and monitoring school administrators and they also establish district priorities through budgeting. School boards represent the local political office to which women are most likely to be elected. The most recent data show that 44 percent of board members are women (National School Boards Association 2015). The ranks of women at the school board level have increased greatly from the early 1970s, when the National School Boards Association estimated that 12 percent of board members were women (Blanchard 1977). Data from the GCML database shows that women of color are somewhat more likely to serve on school boards than men of color—about 40 percent (39.6 percent) of all women of color who are elected serve on school boards, compared with about 29 percent of men of color (Hardy-Fanta et al. 2016). Women of color, as well as men of color, are also more likely to serve in school districts that are majority nonwhite, with African American women being elected primarily to districts that are majority black while Latinas are elected to districts that are majority Hispanic (Lien 2014). The Victory Institute reports that at least 10 lesbians currently serve on school boards, in addition to one transgender woman (The Victory Institute 2019).*

While women have almost reached parity with men on school boards, women are actually overrepresented in many states that have elected county clerkships. While their official duties vary from state to state, county clerks often are responsible for maintaining electoral paperwork, certifying elections, record keeping with respect to businesses and/or licensing, and overseeing budget and payroll services (Byers 2008). In 24 states, the position of county clerk is an elected office, while in California and New Year, only some counties have clerk elections; in other states, the position is appointed or there are no clerks (ibid.). Bernick and Heidbreder's (2018) analysis of data from the National Association of Counties from 2012 to 2014 shows that in 960 counties in 12 states that hold clerkship elections, no state had less than a majority of women serving in this position, and in some states, as many as 9 in 10 clerks were women. Another study found that, in California, women held 81 percent of clerkships from 1995 through 2011 (Crowder-Meyer, Gadariaian, and Trounstine 2015). One earlier study of local offices in nine Southern States also found a majority of women were elected to clerkships and that women often won majorities of other "process-oriented" elected positions such as assessor, probate judge, or treasurer (Lublin and Brewer 2003).

Women are far more underrepresented in another important elected position at the local level of government—the county sheriff, who is the leading law enforcement officer elected by voters in 47 states at the county level (all states except Hawaii, Alaska, and Connecticut). According to the National Sheriff's Association (2018), there are currently 3,081 elected sheriffs, most of whom serve four-year terms. As Farris and Holman (2015) note, the position of elected sheriff is particularly important compared with other local law enforcement officials since the legal authority of the elected sheriff's office often derives from the state constitution, making the elected sheriff a more autonomous position with substantial independence. Yet, Farris and Holman find that fewer than 10 percent of the nation's elected sheriffs are women (ibid.).

---

*The Victory Institute tracks openly known LGBTQ officeholders at all levels of government and encourages LGBTQ officeholders to add their names to their website database. There are likely more LGBTQ Americans who serve on school boards and other local offices that are just not reported to the Institute.

Paula Dance became the first African American woman elected Sheriff in North Carolina's history in Pitt County in 2018, also becoming one of the few black women to serve in this elected position. *Source*: Photo courtesy of Paula Dance.

Lastly, some states have appointed boards or commissions at the local level that handle duties such as historic preservation, parks and recreation, planning and zoning, or running the library, although such forms of local government are woefully understudied. However, the case of Iowa is particularly interesting, given that it is the only state whose state legislature has mandated that local governments should seek gender balance on such voluntary boards—although there are no penalties for local governments if they do not comply (Wang, Harrop, and Kieffer 2018). To be part of a local board or commission, individuals can apply to and must be approved by current board members, the mayor or the city council (Hannagan, Larimer and Hibbing 2016). Shortly before the law went into effect, nearly two-thirds of library boards had women serving on them and women made up about half of historic preservation boards, yet they were underrepresented on boards concerning zoning (ibid.). In the nearly 10 years since the gender-balance law passed in 2009, 63 percent of city boards and commissions have equal numbers of men and women, which represents a 13 percent increase since 2014 according to data collected by the Carrie Chapman Catt Center for Women in Politics (Cannon 2018). Overall, women are better represented on voluntary boards in cities (42 percent) compared with counties (34 percent). Service on such voluntary boards may represent an opportunity for women to become more knowledgeable about local politics and potentially help such participants consider running for elected office. Indeed, Iowa state representative Mary Mascher, who helped cosponsor the initial legislation, told the *Des Moines Register* that her inspiration to run for the state legislature came from first serving on her local parks and recreation board (Cannon 2018). Unfortunately, outside the case in Iowa, there are no systematic studies of the gender dynamics on such boards in other communities nationally.

What Determines Women's Representation in Such Offices?

Next, we consider the three major factors that help to explain why women are better represented on some local government positions than on others. First, the desirability of office may be an explanation for women's representation in politics. For instance, some women may be attracted to offices that are less competitive, require fewer resources, are closer to home, and reinforce traditional gender stereotypes. Second, the political context of local elections may help explain women's representation or lack thereof. For instance, the more liberal the community or the preexisting presence of women in other local offices may impact women's descriptive representation at the local level of government. Finally, the electoral structure or rules may factor into women's representation, particularly on city councils. In fact, political scientists have looked long and hard into whether the design of city councils into at-large versus single-member districts either helps or hinders women's representation. Another electoral rule is whether or not local elections are partisan. We turn first to electoral rules and their impact on women's descriptive representation in local offices.

Rules of the Game: Council Size, Apportionment and Partisanship

By rules of the game, we first consider if women's representation on local legislatures is linked to how seats on councils are apportioned or to the overall size of the elected body in terms of the number of seats available. Generally speaking, having a larger council improves the chances that at least one woman will serve on a city council (Alozie and Manganaro 1993; Trounstine and Valdini 2008; Smith, Reingold, and Owen 2012): the more seats, the more opportunities there are for women to serve.

Whether the electoral structure of city councils impacts the number of women serving on councils, however, is less clear. Political scientists have found that racial minorities benefit from single-member districts because waging a campaign in a single district is less expensive, and hence less competitive, than running at-large, typically in multimember seats, in which candidates compete citywide for the position as opposed to within a smaller district (see, for example, Browning, Marshall, and Tabb 1994). Racial minorities also maintain that it is easier to be elected in single-member districts because neighborhoods tend to be segregated racially; hence, the odds of electing a racial minority from a majority-minority district are higher than facing several opponents at-large as most black voters prefer black candidates (for an excellent summary of this literature, see Trounstine and Valdini 2008).

By contrast, many feminists argue that at-large elections, or those in which multiple candidates are selected to represent the entire locality rather than a narrow segment of the population, provide more opportunities for women to serve on city councils than single-member districts. Unlike racial minorities, women, as a group are not geographically isolated in city neighborhoods. The thinking is that women overall do better in such citywide races because voters are not faced with a zero-sum choice like in single-district races that elect just one member, in which voting for a woman would mean not choosing a man. When voters can make several choices for at-large positions, as opposed to one choice in a single-member district, they may be more likely to want to balance and diversify the ticket in terms of gender (Thomas 1998). In fact, Trounstine and Valdini (2008) find that white women, but not African American women, appear to benefit slightly from competing in at-large as opposed to single-member elections.

Yet other research, much of it conducted more than 20 years ago, concludes that women do not reap any particular advantages from running in at-large elections (Bullock and MacManus 1991; Alozie and Manganaro 1993; MacManus and Bullock 1993; Darcy, Welch, and Clark 1994; Smith, Reingold, and Owens 2012). One study of women running in California local elections over a decade found that women actually performed better in single-member districts than in at-large ones (Crowder-Meyer, Gardarian, and Trounstine 2015, 319). A more recent study of local elections in Louisiana also found that electoral structure had no bearing on women's success rates in local legislative elections; however, women were significantly more likely to *run* as candidates in at-large elections than in single-member districts (Crowder-Meyer and Smith 2015).

As suggested above, not all women may be impacted the same by whether a district is single member or at-large. In their analysis of the electoral outcomes of more than 7,000 cities, Jessica Trounstine and Melody E. Valdini (2008) find that having a majority of council members elected by district seats as opposed to at-large seats greatly improves the odds of electing African American women and men by more than 10 percent. African American *men*, however, benefit the most from this electoral arrangement, suggesting the intersection of race and gender complicates electoral dynamics for African American women. Data from the 2006–2007 GMCL Survey shows that there are relatively few major differences in terms of the descriptive representation of women minority elected officials with respect to the structure of the council, although in contrast with the findings reported above, both black women and Latinas report being slightly *more* likely to be elected to multiple-member district seats than their male counterparts (Hardy-Fanta et al. 2016) while African American men and Latinos fare slightly better in single-member districts. Of course, most early research of descriptive representation at the city level examined race or gender but rarely combined the two, so teasing out how and whether women of color are advantaged or disadvantaged by electoral structure apart from white women, for instance, is an area that needs further research.

Finally, most studies find that women's representation as council members or mayors is not related to whether the election is partisan or nonpartisan (Carroll and Sabonmatsu 2008; Trounstine and Valdini 2008). However, some research suggests that women are more likely to emerge as candidates when local elections are competitive in terms of partisanship, unlike in elections in which one party strongly dominates, given that there is more incentive for political parties to recruit candidates (Crowder-Meyer and Smith 2015). For mayors, however, women are more likely to be elected in nonpartisan races than in partisan ones, at least in large cities (Smith, Reingold, and Owens 2012), which may support previous research that suggests that parties aren't always adept at recruiting women to run for higher office (see chapter 4 for more on candidate recruitment by parties).

While more analyses on the impact of partisan recruitment have been done at the congressional or state legislative level, women's *perception* of the parties as being particularly effective at recruiting them to run for office at the local level has been mixed. Roughly a third of women of color who are elected to municipal office, for instance, agree that they received less support from parties in their bids for local office than other candidates; however, men of color who serve in local politics report receiving even less support overall from parties than do women (Hardy-Fanta et al. 2016). A more recent survey of municipal officeholders in 2014 found that women officeholders are more likely than male officeholders to believe that there are gender disparities when it comes to recruitment for seeking higher office (Butler and Preece 2016). Such disparity in recruitment by the parties may be worse for the GOP: field studies suggest that Republican women, especially, may be less responsive to party overtures to consider a candidacy than men (Preece, Stoddard, and Fisher 2016).

For the most part, however, the role of parties in terms of recruiting women to run for local office remains understudied, as is the role of other organizations that foster or encourage individuals to run for this level of government more generally. One exception is Oliver and Conroy's (2018) work, which found among a national, random sample of city council members that women are significantly *more* likely to report being recruited or encouraged to run for city council than men, which defies previous research that shows that women are often at a disadvantage when it comes to recruitment for other levels of office (Carroll and Sanbonmatsu 2013, Crowder-Meyer 2013). However, Oliver and Conroy (2018) find that city councilors who self-identify as more masculine, regardless of being male or female, are significantly more likely to be recruited to run for city councils than respondents who identify with more feminine traits. This finding holds true even for women's organizations, which appear to be recruiting women who demonstrate more masculine traits than women who express more feminine traits. On the one hand, their research shows potentially that "women who do not identify with traditional gender roles are not necessarily punished, at least at the recruitment stage of candidate emergence" (1095), so women no longer may be at a disadvantage in terms of recruitment to run for city councils if they are willing or able to present themselves as masculine enough to do the job. On the other hand, making inroads into elected office may continue to be difficult for women and men who do not uphold such masculine norms. As a result, as long as "perceptions of the ideal candidate is masculine, women will be at a disadvantage" (116). At the very least, Oliver and Conroy's work shows that candidate recruitment is more nuanced than previous studies acknowledge, and demonstrates that political scientists have much more to learn about how gendered personality traits—and not gender alone—may contribute to understanding why women may or may not be represented in elected office at the local level.

How the Political and Social Context of Cities Matters

Apart from the structure of local elections, are women more likely to be elected in liberal enclaves or in areas in which women overall have more professional status in their communities? In essence, are some localities more "women friendly" than others (Simon and Palmer 2006)? Do women do better when they are seeking political office in localities that have vibrant women's organizations? Smith, Reingold, and Owen (2012) examine 230 cities with more than 100,000 residents from the 2000s, looking at how the representation of women as elected mayors and council members is shaped by the urban political context. They find that more liberal cities (in terms of past presidential vote choice) elect more women to their city councils. Similar to large cities, the percentage Democratic vote is also linked to women's substantive representation on county boards—the higher the percentage of vote for Barack Obama in 2012, the higher the percentage of women serving on a county governing body (Kellogg et al. 2017). Moreover, women are also less likely to be elected to county governing boards in counties that have high levels of religious adherence (Kellogg et al. 2017). So, the political and social context of local elections matters to women's representation in local office.

Women's socioeconomic status also more generally enhances women's descriptive representation on city councils in large cities. Smith, Reingold, and Owen (2012) find that women are more likely to be elected onto city councils in large cities in which women overall are more likely to own businesses, have more college degrees, and have higher incomes.

In the state of Louisiana, however, women's socioeconomic and professional status in districts does not appear to matter to the emergence of women candidates for local government (Crowder-Meyer and Smith 2015). However, the presence of women candidates is linked to whether women have had success in higher political offices: as more women are elected to the state legislature over time, more women decide to run for local office in Louisiana (ibid.). Similarly, women are more likely to be elected as mayors in cities that have women present on their city councils (Smith, Reingold, and Owens 2012).

Another factor to consider in terms of the political context of local elections is the presence of women's organizations in localities. For instance, it is reasonable to expect that if a city has an active array of women's political organizations, women maybe feel more emboldened to run for political office and have resources to back them up. For example, Melissa Marschall's (2002) qualitative study of members of the National Women's Political Caucus (NWPC) found that most members were quite active in helping women run for local office. Yet empirical research more broadly fails to find such a relationship. While having more women's groups active in large cities has no apparent effect on the representation of women on city councils, Smith, Reingold, and Owens (2012) interestingly find that when it comes to mayors, having more women's groups active in cities actually *depresses* the likelihood of a city having a female mayor; their reasoning is that women are far from monolithic, and having more women's organizations may result in fragmentation, which could do more harm to women's chances of seeking a mayoralty than help them. More systematic work as to the impact of women's political groups and the presence of women in local government needs to be undertaken, particularly given the recent uptick in women running for office in 2018.

Desirability of Office

Finally, women's descriptive representation in local offices may be linked to the desirability of the office. Some have argued historically that elected offices that have higher salaries, longer terms, or greater responsibility may be less attractive to women candidates than men essentially because these desirable positions are more competitive. While an intuitive theory, the empirical support for it is mixed, as little research suggests that women are more likely to serve on city councils with less pay or shorter terms (Bullock an MacManus 1991; MacManus and Bullock 1995; Troustine and Valdini 2008; Smith, Reingold, and Owen 2012). However, the mere fact that women are most likely to be found at the local level in political offices that are less prestigious, such as school boards, volunteer boards, or in clerk-ships, may lend support to the notion that women are overrepresented in political offices that are considered less desirable. The study of women's descriptive representation in Louisiana is again instructive, which finds that women are significantly more likely to be candidates and winners of elected local seats in cities, towns, and villages than in counties or parishes, as they are known in Louisiana (Crowder-Meyer and Smith 2015). Coun-ties often serve as stepping-stones for higher office, compared with town or city governments (Crowder-Meyer 2013), and are likely perceived as more competitive and more desirable.

Moreover, locally elected offices that are viewed as overtly gendered in nature, such as school boards or clerkships, could be considered less pres-tigious. Given that most such positions are also nonpartisan, gender ste-reotypes among voters may actually advantage women in such races given that such elections are typically low-information—without party cues; and knowing little else, voters may be primed to consider stereotypes as short cuts to their voting decisions (Bernick and Heidbreder 2018). Moreover, as Crowder-Mayer, Gadarian, and Trounstine (2015) argue, gender stereo-types may also factor into the selection process at the local level of office, whether that means that women are more likely to be encouraged to run for such offices or choose themselves to run, as such local offices may be viewed as more secretarial in nature or may deal with policies considered to be women's strength, such as education. In the case of clerkships, spe-cifically, where men are systematically underrepresented, gender dynamics may discourage men from seeking such offices, which itself is problematic. As Bernick and Heidbreder (2018) argue, "If society continues to look only for ways to increase the number of women in the male-dominated electoral world without encouraging men to see 'female' elected positions as accept-able and desirable options, women's work and their roles in political life will continue to be devalued" (ibid., 9).

Local Office as Stepping-stones: Filling the Pipeline?

Many argue that women will not go on to pursue higher political office until they have more experience at local offices such as school boards or city and county councils. While relatively few studies of progressive politi-cal ambition among local officeholders exist, the ones that do suggest that those who believe the local pipeline will generate much higher numbers of women candidates for higher office may be disappointed. For instance, Laura Van Assendelft's (2014) study of women mayors and city council members in rural Virginia shows that the vast majority of women—about 80 percent—holding these offices show little interest in pursuing higher office. Instead, these women worry that serving in higher office will negate the very features of serving locally that they enjoy, namely the ability to interact regularly with the people who live in their local communities and the nonpartisan nature of the work. One woman commented that she enjoyed solving problems in her small town, working as a collaborative team. Susan Abram Beck's (2001) study of town council members also finds little progressive political ambition among individuals serving at this level of government—either women or men.

At the school board level, Deckman's (2007) research shows that school board candidates, both male and female, are not likely to express much political ambition outside of this local elected office—and that they are more likely to consider their work as community service. The vast majority of candidates who run for school boards lists community goals as the primary reason they ran for office. By contrast, just 10 percent of women candidates and 16 percent of men candidates said they ran for school board because they wanted political experience in case they might want to run for higher office one day. A more recent study by Sweet-Cushman (2018) of school board officials in Pennsylvania finds similarly dismal numbers with respect to progressive political ambition, with just 3.5 percent of men compared with 2.9 percent of women indicating that they would definitely consider running for higher office. Although 83.6 percent of male school boards members would not rule out seeking higher office one day, compared with just 73 percent of women, gender is not a significant factor in terms of predicting progressive political ambition once additional controls in a multivariate analysis are considered. Moreover, neither male nor female school board members report being encouraged to seek higher office from traditional political sources, such as parties, or in the cases of women, from women's organizations.

At the same time, many mayors decide to seek election after serving terms on their local city councils. More recent work suggests that pursuing a gendered policy agenda contributes to enhanced ambition to seek a mayoral position among women council members. In their study of Texas city council members in cities of more than 30,000, Budd, Myers, and Longoria (2015) find that city council women who listed as among their top three priorities "gendered" issues such as housing, the environment, and health and education, as compared with more traditional issues such as taxes, development, and infrastructure, were far more likely than female city council members who did not prioritize those concerns to express mayoral ambition. Windett (2014) found that female gubernatorial candidates typically started their careers in local political office as well.

Of course, as others have noted about women's representation in Congress, the pipeline argument alone is not enough to promote women's presentation at upper levels of government, especially given incumbency rates—more women can't be elected to higher office when current officeholders, predominantly men, choose to stay in their seats. That being said, parties and other organizations looking to back or promote quality candidates for statewide or national office may be overlooking an untapped potential source for encouraging progressive political ambition among women. However, more analysis of progressive political ambition at this level is needed.

SUBSTANTIVE REPRESENTATION: DOES HAVING WOMEN IN LOCAL GOVERNMENT MATTER?

As we document in our chapter on women in legislatures (see chapter 7), women officeholders at the state and congressional level do sometimes govern uniquely compared to men. Here, we consider whether women in local government govern differently than men, which is a key consideration when it comes to substantive representation. Having more women serving in local politics could be important if women bring with them different experiences, leadership styles, and policy concerns than men. Indeed, political theorists and women's interest groups have often argued that only when women achieve greater numbers of elected seats in government will they, as a group, have their concerns and preferences reflected in policy outcomes. First, we examine the substantive impact of women serving in municipalities and then turn our attention toward school board office.

Historically, women's presence as urban reformers during the Progressive Era shows that women have always played a part in pressuring local government to address issues of special concern to women and families, whether that meant improving city schools, pursuing labor reform, or spearheading efforts to address hunger and homelessness (see chapter 2 for more details). Women such as Jane Addams launched the settlement house movement. Women volunteers in the early twentieth century largely ran settlement houses, which sought to address the underlying causes of poverty in inner cities (Blair 1980). Eventually, these settlement houses led to the establishment of the field of professional social work.

Given women's historical role in addressing numerous social issues in urban environments, and given studies of women lawmakers at other levels of government that show that women often prioritize concerns of special interest to women and families, it would stand to reason that women officeholders in municipalities and counties would perhaps champion different political causes than their male counterparts. Studies that examine women and men serving in local governments, however, find relatively few gender differences among such officeholders when it comes to identifying the most important issues facing their cities. Simply put, both men and women serving as mayors and on local councils spend most of their time dealing with economic development and service delivery (Mezey 1978; Crow 1997; Flammang 1987; Beck 2001; Boles 2001; Tolleson-Rinehart 2001; Weikart et al. 2006; Holman 2014). Urban scholars have long recognized that governing cities is particularly challenging given the outsized role that private actors often play in city politics. Cities tend to prioritize developmental policies, which include attracting businesses and new jobs to their cities. Of course, some scholars have argued that prioritization of business concerns at the local level of government is in itself a gendered concept, given that men, especially white men, often dominate as head of business (DeSena 2008). However, both job growth and basic service provision—that is, making sure that schools are open, snow is removed or trash is collected—are both viewed as vital to maintaining higher-income residents who may otherwise flee to the suburbs and whose exit would create a downward spiral of lower tax revenues (Peterson 1981). Or, as Susan Abrams Beck (2001) put it in her comparative study of councilwomen and councilmen in suburban towns, all local officeholders are "hostage to the tax rate, persistently seeking ways to keep it down" (55). The many everyday responsibilities that are charged to localities, whether city or county government, such as making sure the garbage is picked up, potholes are filled, taxes are collected, and public parks are open and safe, are largely done in a gender-neutral fashion.

Although much of the substance of local government can be described as gender-neutral, and women and men who serve in them tend to prioritize the same issues when it comes to the day-to-day implementation of such policies, scholars do find some gender differences even at this level of government. While the actual ability of local government officials to address concerns about what are traditionally viewed as "women's issues," such as domestic violence, child care, sexual assault, or childbirth in public hospitals, is often circumscribed by budget realities and development priorities, councilwomen and female mayors are more likely than their male counterparts to identify such issues as germane to the work of local government and to spend more time working on such issues than men (Flammang 1985; Boles 2001; Holman 2014). One early study by Schumaker and Burns (1988) also identified numerous "gender cleavages" among the policy decisions in the city of Lawrence, Kansas.* They found that male councilors and policy elites were more supportive of economic growth policies whereas

---

* Moreover, Schumaker and Burns found that gender cleavages were more frequent than other types of cleavages based on factors such as socioeconomic status, race, and partisan identification. Cleavages predicated on neighborhoods and ideology, however, were more frequent than those based on gender.

female officials and elites were more supportive of neighborhood preservation policies and increasing financial contributions to social services. However, similar to other studies, Schumaker and Burns discovered that the city prioritized economic policies at the expense of social welfare programs.

Studies of local women officeholders also suggest that women may have a different *style* of governing than men. For instance, women mayors are more likely to say that they value collaboration. In comparing how female and male mayors view the role of their staff, for instance, studies show that women are more likely to identify their staff as an important part of a government team, while male mayors are more likely to view their staff as sounding boards (Tolleson-Rinehart 2001). Studies also find that women in local government are more likely than their male counterparts to seek input from community actors, bring neglected groups into the decision-making process, spend more time on their jobs than men, and believe that their constituents place greater trust in them than they would in men (Merritt 1980; Antolini 1984; Manning 1988; Beck 2001; Ulbig 2007). In Beck's (2001) work on municipal councils, both women and men council members agreed that women are more responsive to constituents, but many councilmen found this attribute to be negative, claiming that such responsiveness means women are more likely to make council decisions based on sentiment or—in the words of one councilman—"sympathy thoughts" (56). Yet, most councilwomen Beck interviewed believe that such an approach makes them better representatives than councilmen. As one councilwoman stated, the women's desire to seek more input from the community is about a willingness to "listen, not look for a quick solution. Men were looking for the management solution" (58). Laura Van Assendelft (2014) finds that the women mayors she studied in rural Virginia towns thought women bring a unique perspective. Said one mayor in the study, "Women are better communicators. They bring balance, they look at the whole issue and make better decisions in a more timely process" (quoted in Van Assendelft 2014, 206).

Mirya Holman's book *Women in Politics in the American City* (2014) offers the most comprehensive work to date on how men and women govern as mayors and as city councilors. Holman gathered data on how the gender of mayors and city councilors influences city politics by selecting 100 matched cities (all with more than 30,000 residents), meaning that 50 had women mayors and 50 had male mayors. Like others, she finds that women's ability to effect change on women's issues, such as affordable housing, children's welfare, social welfare, and domestic violence, is circumscribed by budget realities and that in all cities, general government, development, and quality of life issues predominate at city council meetings over traditional women's concerns. Yet, she also finds that male officeholders felt a greater sense of duty to represent development groups than women and cultivated closer ties with such groups. Women, on the other hand, felt a greater obligation to represent racial groups, women, and the poor, and spent more time interacting with such constituencies. Moreover, women who expressed the strongest responsibility to represent women's issues, whom Holman describes as *preferable descriptive representatives*, are significantly more likely than men or other women to prioritize women's issues and to initiate discussion of women's issues in city council meetings.

In cities with female mayors, while development and general government discussions still predominate in city council meetings, Holman writes that "discussions of women's issues occurred at more than twice the rate, 26 percent of all discussions, than they did in cities with male mayors, where discussion of women's urban issues were 12 percent of discussions" (47). While she finds that discussion of women's issues increases in city council meetings as the percentage of women on the council grows, under female mayors especially, this relationship is even more significant. In other words, when cities have female mayors *and* women make up multiple members of such councils, women's issues get addressed more often than in other cities.

Women in Politics in the American City also confirms findings from previous studies that women's leadership in cities can have a transformative impact on the behavior and attitudes of constituents. For instance, the public tends to comment publicly more in city meetings with female mayors than in cities run by men, which suggests that women mayors have a more inclusive style when they govern. It may also suggest that female leaders encourage broader participation by changing the substance of policy discussions. As one female leader in Holman's study put it, "We [women] tend to discuss topics more readily, find compromises, and share feelings, not just ideas of agenda. This helps get citizens out: they think we will listen to them" (76).

Women's more inclusive approach to governing in cities also spills over into the budgeting process. In their study of 120 US mayors, composed of 65 female and 55 male mayors, Weikart et al. (2006) find that female mayors were more likely than their male counterparts to change budgeting procedures to address policy goals and were more likely to view the budgetary process as a way to encourage more community participation in government. Mirya Holman (2014) finds that cities with female mayors are more likely to fund some programming related to the issues of urban women, such as funding for domestic violence or education programs, (approximately 81 percent of cities) compared with cities with male mayors (61 percent) and those cities with female mayors spend more per resident on such programs. Funding for such urban women's issue programs also increases under female mayors when they have more women on the city council. Finally, cities that have women mayors are also more likely to hire women to work in city government, which enhances the opportunity for women's representation in local bureaucracies (Salzstein 1986; Holman 2014).

There is also some indication that women mayors are taking a leadership role in addressing sex discrimination and harassment as part of the larger #MeToo movement—an issue that has particular relevance for women. For instance, female mayors at the US Conference of Mayors winter meeting in January 2018 acknowledged that they had a special responsibility to address this issue. Libby Schaaf, Mayor of Oakland, California, said, "We have a responsibility to share our stories. Because we are in a place of power, we get believed when so many women before us have not had that privilege" (quoted in Farmer 2018). Schaaf and other women mayors shared how the #MeToo movement had compelled them to change some approaches to government and to look deeper into cultural practices in their administrations that harmed women. Tacoma, Washington, mayor Victoria Woodard noted that as a city council member, she helped create the Office of Equity and Human Rights, and was using that office to ensure that city leadership better reflected the community; as part of her commitment to diversity, Woodard hired Tacoma's first female city manager in 2017 (ibid.). In Seattle, in the wake of the #MeToo movement, Mayor Jenny Durkan ordered a review of how the city handles sexual harassment complaints (Brownstone 2018).

Yet, for all the progress that women mayors and councilors have made serving in local government, some women still report that they face obstacles based on their gender. Women mayors are far more likely to agree that they face particular obstacles because of their gender than do men (Weikart et al. 2006). These women often cite personal experiences of struggling to gain credibility and respect among many community and business leaders and lament not being taken seriously, particularly when it comes to business-related decisions. Other studies of female leaders in localities find that women are often judged by different criteria than are their male counterparts, reflecting the double bind discussed in chapter 5. The women Sue Tolleson-Rinehart interviewed in her comparative study of women and men mayors (2001) acknowledge that women often have to work harder to prove their qualifications and to overcome voter stereotypes about their toughness as leaders. One black woman mayor she interviewed also noted the "double whammy" of being black and a woman. As she relates, "People's perceptions of me—on the one hand, expectations are more, because women have a reputation for being exhaustive workers, and constantly reaching out and giving of themselves. And on the other hand, there's some misunderstanding about your intellectual capacity and ability to be tough" (160). Despite the recognition that women leaders can face different standards, Tolleson-Rinehart's study still finds relatively few gender differences in how men and women manage the day-to-day work of running cities. Both the women and men she studies "used their cities' needs as the criterion for assessing political problems" (164), identifying the same issues as the ones that demanded the most city attention.

Shifting our attention from women's substantive representation in municipalities, we now examine whether women and men govern differently at the school board level. For example, are women school board members more likely to advocate for policies that help girls? Although Jesse Donahue's research of school board or committee members in Massachusetts finds that 79 percent of women board members agree that "public education needs to do more to foster equality for girls," compared with just 50 percent of male board members, very few women (8 percent) have ever worked on gender equity measures designed to help girls in their school districts, which is comparable to the findings for men (Donahue 1999). Donahue believes this discrepancy is due to a lack of women's interest groups to lobby on behalf of these issues at the school board level, the lack of formal powers that many school boards have to address such changes, and the substantial minority of board members who strongly disagree that girls need extra help in public schools. As Donahue notes, "At best, women [school board members] demonstrate an informed interest in the topic [of gender equality] but frequently fail to pursue measures that would help girls in their system. At worst a substantial minority of women committee members are openly hostile to the very idea that they should be representing girls in their school systems" (Donahue 1999, 77). Instead, men and women board members spend more time discussing more "mainstream" agenda items such as budgeting, curriculum, staff, facilities, and class size (Donahue 1997).

Apart from policy advocacy, a second way that gender could impact school board service is related to *how* members approach their positions. In other words, do male and female board members behave differently once in office? In the mid-1990s, Donahue (1997) found that women school board members actually talk *less* on average than men during board meetings, a finding based on the condition that men are more likely than women to chair school boards, and board chairs have a larger speaking role as facilitators of the meetings. More recently, Karpowitz and Mendelberg also found similar gender disparities in school board deliberations in their book *The Silent Sex* (2014), which included analysis of the minutes of 87 school boards in 20 states. Men were more likely to speak out on school boards, even when women members outnumbered them. By contrast, women were less likely to speak in proportion to their numbers; women only spoke as often as men when they had achieved at least 60 percent of the board. For Karpowitz and Mendelberg, such findings show that gender role expectations—that men speak more about politics and that their voices carry more political authority—remain deeply internalized, including in local governments that deal exclusively with education politics. They speculate that women may need to be overrepresented on elected bodies such as school boards in order to reach true equality in political deliberations or that the rules that govern debate and deliberation might need to be changed to facilitate more engagement by women.

Does it matter substantively that women remain slightly underrepresented in school board politics? On the one hand, the most recent research suggests that advancing gender equity matters in principle to most women board members, but that few take actions to make gender equity a reality. On the other hand, gender might still impact school board governance in ways that have not been quantified or documented. For instance, some speculate that because school boards are still predominantly male in most districts, it is harder for women to be appointed as school superintendents (Czubaj 2002). Thus, this important administrative position remains male-dominated nationally, with only about 1 in 4 women currently serving as school superintendents (Kominiak 2016). More updated research is needed at the school board level to determine if women school board members govern differently than their male counterparts.

WOMEN AS POLITICAL ACTORS OUTSIDE OF GOVERNMENT

Women's involvement in local policy and politics is not limited to their roles as elected officials. In fact, women's activism is perhaps strongest in grassroots politics, in which women often become involved in community issues through more informal networks of friends, kinship, and the neighborhood. Indeed, as chapter 2 notes, women historically have led local social reform movements despite being formally disenfranchised from the political system. Often, such involvement stems from women's concerns as mothers and a need to improve their children's lives, whether that means seeking government assistance with poverty or job training or cleaning up polluted environments. Women's activism at the local level is sometimes geared toward the business community as well, with women leading the movement to unionize for greater rights and protections or to litigate against sexual discrimination and harassment in the workplace, which has taken on new urgency in the wake of the #MeToo movement.

Moreover, women of all ages, classes, and race and ethnicities have been at the forefront of other local political causes that have made national headlines, from the Black Lives Matter movement, which shines a light on police brutality against African Americans and other minority groups, to activism for greater expansion of LGBTQ rights. Younger women, in particular, have been at the forefront of fighting for greater political rights for women, curbing gun violence and promoting environmental causes. Not all women, however, are engaged in progressive causes. As the Tea Party movement that first emerged in 2010 shows, women have also been among the most powerful advocates for fighting for a reduction in the size and scope of government for several years (see chapter 2). The larger point here is that women are far from politically monolithic, and their efforts have been critical at impacting political change in their communities. Here we profile a few examples of such grassroots activism spearheaded by women.

Poor or working-class women engage in much local political activism in communities. Yet, too often, scholars who study the women's movement overlook poor women's efforts to gain a better life for themselves and their families, whether their efforts involve addressing environmental concerns, a lack of day care or good-paying jobs, or domestic violence, focusing instead on the efforts of middle-class or educated white women to affect public policy (Bookman and Morgen 1988; Boris 2002). But fighting for domestic rights such as welfare, as noted sociologists Frances Fox Piven and Richard Cloward have argued, means fighting for public rights (Piven and Cloward 1997). The efforts of poor, often minority, women in these struggles have important dimensions that broaden our understanding of politics as "an attempt to change the social and economic institutions that embody the basic power relations in our society" (Bookman and Morgen 1988, 4).

Political scientist Cathy Cohen (2003) also reminds us that much of the political organizing done by women of color, since it is not typical of white male political activity, is often overlooked. For instance, Latina women are deeply invested in their communities and build political capital through community activism as well as grassroots campaigns for policy change (Takash 1993; Garcia et al. 2008). But because national surveys of political activity rarely measure these types of activities, we remain largely unaware of the ways in which many women contribute their time and talents to improving the lives of people in their communities. For example, Carol Hardy-Fanta (1993, 1997) studies Latina political activism in Boston. She finds that Latina women—like many women—have a blurred perception between the private and public dimensions, in which their roles as mothers play heavily. For these Latina women, politics consists of helping others and providing support, serving as "connectors" linking the Latino community to city hall informally.

That legacy of grassroots activism by women of color continues in more recent years as women have been at the forefront of speaking out against gun violence and police brutality in their cities and neighborhoods, including most prominently as the founders of the #Black Lives Matter movement. The movement began in 2013 in the wake of the acquittal of George Zimmerman, who fatally shot Trayvon Martin, an unarmed teenager who lived in Zimmerman's neighborhood. The movement further took off after Michael Brown, another unarmed black man, was killed by police officers in Ferguson, Missouri, in 2014, which led to rioting in Ferguson and nearby St. Louis. Three self-described female radical black organizers—Alicia Garza, Patrisse Cullors, and Opal Tometi—formed #Black Lives Matter to "organize and build local power to intervene in violence inflicted on Black communities by the state and vigilantes" through community groups and through an active online presence (Black Lives Matter n.d.). Garza, Cullors, and Tometi note that their group is unique from other civil rights organizations in that previous black liberation movements have typically been led by straight men, "leaving women, queer and transgender people and others either out of the movement or in the background to move the work forward with little or no recognition" (ibid.). Making those at the margins "closer to the center" of the organization, #Black Lives Matter has formed more than 40 chapters nationally in cities throughout the country.

In recent years, local women, particularly women of color, have also been at the vanguard of the environmental racism movement, which seeks to combat the placement of locally undesirable land uses (LULUs) in poor and economically depressed neighborhoods (Prindeville and Bretting 1998; Rainey and Johnson 2009). In seeking environmental justice, defined as the "fair treatment for people of all races, cultures, and incomes, regarding the development of environmental laws, regulations and policies" (ibid., 147), people of color have often been denied access to traditional environmental organizations, despite feeling the impact of environmental hazards, such as lead poisoning and air pollution, disproportionately in their communities. Indigenous women have also been vocal in addressing environmental causes, through vehicles such as Seeding Sovereignty, a grassroots organization that seeks to empower and educate young people about the connection between violence against women and environmental justice. Among their causes are the opposition to both the building of the Keystone Pipeline and the expansion of fracking on or near native lands (Seeding Sovereignty 2019).

Increasingly, young women have taken leadership roles in protecting the environment in their own communities, drawing national attention to their activism. Take the case of Delaney Reynolds, a college student at the University of Miami, who founded the Sink-or-Swim Project, which brings attention to the impact of global warming and rising sea levels in South Florida, her home. Her activism includes filing a lawsuit against her state government, claiming that the state of Florida is violating her generation's constitutional rights to life, liberty, property, and the pursuit of happiness by "creating and perpetuating an energy system that is based on fossil fuels" (Our Children's Trust 2018). Her outspoken advocacy has led to both a Ted Talk and an address at the General Assembly of the United Nations in New York City (Delaney Reynolds n.d.)

Young women have also garnered national headlines as leaders in the movement against gun violence. In the aftermath of the tragic school shooting that left 17 students dead at Marjory Stoneman Douglas High School in February 2018, a group of teenage boys and girls, including Emma Gonzalez and Jaclyn Corin, organized the March for Our Lives, an anti-gun violence rally in Washington, DC, to change the nation's gun laws and to help other students around the country to advocate for a reduction in gun violence, including a voter registration drive. Their initial advocacy in their home state of Florida resulted in the state's Republican-controlled legislature passing the first statewide restrictions on some gun sales for the first time in decades, including raising the age for Florida citizens to buy guns to 21 and extending the waiting period for buying guns (Mazzei 2018). Their continued efforts, now known as Never Again MSD, calls for funding gun violence research, more regulations on the gun industry, and universal background checks and bans on the sale of semi-automatic weapons, among other initiatives. The 2018 International Children's Peace Prize awarded its annual prize in South Africa to these student organizers (Vassolo 2018).

However, it is important to recognize that not all women activists root their community involvement in progressive causes. Julia Wrigley (1998) writes a fascinating case study of white working-class women engaged in

Emma Gonzalez has become the visible face of the #NeverAgain movement, started by student survivors of the tragic shooting at Marjory Stoneman Douglas High School in Parkland Florida, including many young women. Here, Gonzalez gave a powerful speech at the March for Our Lives rally in Washington, DC, in which she stood at the podium for more than six minutes crying silently to represent the amount of time it took for the gunman to kill 17 victims at the school. *Source*: Associated Press/ Abaca Press.

the struggle against school busing in Boston, forced on Boston residents in the 1970s after federal Judge Arthur Garrity's decision to desegregate the public schools by busing black students into predominantly white schools and white students into predominantly black schools in two of Boston's poorest communities. Garrity ruled that forced busing was the only way to ensure equal protection for African American students, but his decision caused shock waves in the local communities, particularly in white neighborhoods. The antibusing forces organized ROAR—Restore Our Alienated Rights—that was led by white women who arranged school protests and boycotts, distributed flyers, made public statements, and put pressure on state and national politicians to stop busing. That women emerged as leaders of the movement was somewhat surprising in a city dominated by male involvement in politics. Yet, Wrigley argues that it was the "intense separation of women's and men's activities and daily lives in Boston that allowed women to take early command of the anti-busing movement" (253). In other words, education was viewed as a mother's domain, and activists, such as this one, linked their involvement directly to their maternal roles: "I always say it's like a lioness in her den. You know, these are my children. The father, I'm sure, feels that way, but the mother had a little more time. The fathers were out working" (261). ROAR engaged in mass demonstrations called Mother's Marches. These demonstrations—which were often raucous events and staged in illegal areas—allowed women to act outside the "appropriate" norms for femininity, and local police were hesitant to do much about them. Ultimately, Garrity's ruling held for more than two decades, and with ROAR unable to stop court-ordered busing, many white working-class parents fled to the suburbs or sent their students to parochial schools.

As chapter 2 details, conservative women were also active in the Tea Party movement, a political movement that emerged in the wake of the election of Barack Obama in 2008. Like the ROAR protestors three decades before, many women used motherhood as a rationale to become active in the Tea Party cause, arguing that policies promoted by Obama, such as ObamaCare, usurped parental rights and threatened to leave their children and grandchildren with more federal debt than their generation. The decentralized nature of the Tea Party, combined with the advent of social media, allowed many women to emerge as local leaders within the Tea Party (Deckman 2016). While the Tea Party's profile has waned since Obama's presidency, many conservative women activists at the local level have joined Women for Trump grassroots organizations. For instance, such conservative women activists have held rallies in support of Trump's efforts to build a physical wall along the Mexican border (Akers 2019).

CONCLUSION

At the local level of government, women are making an impact as elected officials and activists in nongovernmental and grassroots organizations. Yet, women at this level do not always act in ways that differ greatly from those of their male counterparts, whether as mayors or as elected officials. Part of the reason that relatively few gender differences are found in local politics could be related to the demands and limits found in local governance. For instance, budgetary concerns are an overriding burden on all types of local government, whether located in rural, suburban, or city areas. Such financial worries often proscribe the ability of women to pursue public policies that they might otherwise follow, such as those that might give greater assistance to women and families in need. Also, handling the day-to-day functions of local governments, such as determining zoning requirements, handing out licenses, or picking up the garbage, has few, if any, gender components.

Despite these limitations, however, there are still a few ways that gender does become a factor in local politics. For example, one theme that emerges when examining the behavior of women and men elected officials and grassroots activists is the priority that women place on communication. Studies find that the public confidence in local government institutions grows as more women serve in them. As Jane Mansbridge's (1999) classic work on descriptive representation argues, having more individuals represent constituencies that heretofore have been underrepresented is important because it helps make the work of government, and the policies it prescribes, more legitimate. It also fosters more trust because elected representatives who look more like their constituents may be better situated to engage in meaningful dialogue with them. As Mansbridge writes, "Representatives and voters who share membership in a subordinate group can also forge bonds of trust based specifically on the shared experience of subordination" (641). The growing public presence of LGBTQ Americans also reminds us that a more inclusive government and public space should include a wide range of American women—and men.

At the same time, however, women who do choose to become active in local politics are not monolithic. At the national and state levels, the majority of women tend to be Democrats and to have more liberal views than men. This chapter has demonstrated that the same cannot necessarily be said about women in local politics. Moreover, although women's involvement at the grassroots level is often felt in progressive or liberal causes—a trend that might be increasing with younger generations of women (Deckman 2018)—the case involving mothers against busing in Boston as well as women's active participation in the Tea Party movement or the Women for Trump organization shows that many conservative women choose to become active in local politics, too. Yet again, democracy at all levels of government is made stronger when more women's voices, from a range of perspectives, are heard. Given the great strides that women made nationally as candidates in 2018 more research is needed to consider the presence and impact of women in local governments.

7

Women in Congress and the State Legislatures

THE 2018 ELECTIONS BROUGHT THE LARGEST MOST ethnically and racially diverse new class of women to the House of Representatives. These thirty-six women each came with their own vision of what they want to do in Congress. Some want to give voice to previously unrepresented groups including Deb Haaland (D-NM), one of two Native American women elected in 2018, who said "Congress has never heard a voice like mine. After years of seeing my community at the whim of national politics while organizing in Indian Country, it was time for me to take the lead" (Herman and Sloman 2019). Similarly, Lauren Underwood (D-IL), an African American former nurse and health care official during the Obama administration proclaimed, "It's very clear that, for a long time, decisions being made in our country were a result of one point of view. Now, we have different voices, and we're representing people whose stories and concerns have not been heard in Congress, so that's going to be a tremendous change" (Arietta-Kenna 2019). While some of the new Democratic women embraced their multiple identities as important influences on their legislative priorities, Carol Miller (WV), the lone female Republican elected in 2018, asserted that being a woman gives her a different perspective but does not define her: "I'm a wife, a mother, a grandmother, a business owner, and a bison farmer. I don't think my gender defines who I am, but it does add value and perspective to the decisions I make" (Herman and Sloman 2019).

The new group of congressional women includes fiery progressive activists eager to take on the establishment like the now youngest woman ever elected to Congress, Alexandria Ocasio-Cortez (NY), who unseated a Democratic incumbent in the primary and has a huge social media following which she deploys to promote progressive priorities such as a Green New Deal to address climate change and Medicare for

All (Coy and Dmitrieva 2019). It also includes a group of female military veterans and former CIA operatives who ran for office to bring a more civil, problem-solving style of politics to Congress. Thus, Chrissy Houlahan (PA) explained, "I think that veterans—and women in particular—have a heritage of team-building, collaboration and pragmatism that I think is really needed right now when we're a very, very divided nation. I'm hopeful that we'll bring a fresh set of legs into what is kind of a dysfunctional environment" (Arietta-Kenna 2019). With the new first-term women coming from different constituencies, with different ideological orientations, and different life experiences, what should we expect regarding their legislative activities and their ability to accomplish their goals?

In this chapter, we look at the history of women's integration into the US Congress and the 50 state legislatures. We also examine the similarities and differences in male and female legislators' policy activities and their leadership styles. We discuss the factors in the political environment that influence the ability and willingness of female legislators to work for policy changes on behalf of different groups of women.

Newly elected members from left, Alexandria Ocasio-Cortez, D-NY, Debbie Mucarsel-Powell, D-Fla., Abby Finkenauer, D-Iowa, Sharice Davids, D-Kan., Haley Stevens, D-Mich., and other members of the incoming freshman class, pose for a photo on the East Front of the Capitol on November 14, 2018. *Source*: Tom Williams/CQ Roll Call/Newscom.

WOMEN AND REPRESENTATION

Today women are drastically underrepresented in Congress and the state legislatures. Even after a record-setting 2018 election that was widely heralded as another "Year of the Woman," women still hold less than one-quarter of the seats in Congress and fewer than 30 percent of the seats across the state legislatures (Center for American Women and Politics 2019a, b). Does it matter that there are so few women in public office? Would policy or the nature of politics look any different if there were equal numbers of men and women serving in Congress and the state legislatures? The question of how to adequately represent the various interests in society has long preoccupied politicians and philosophers. Indeed, the question of representation was a major point of contention in the fight to ratify the Constitution. Campaigning against ratification, the anti-Federalists believed that the design of Congress would elevate the interests of the wealthy at the expense of the middle classes, particularly the virtuous yeoman farmers (Storing 1981). Supporters of the Constitution argued that the different classes of men had overlapping interests and the design of the electoral process would ensure the responsiveness of the representative regardless of the background of the elected official (Storing 1981, 35). Thus, frequent elections in which all eligible citizens could vote would guarantee that a legislator would advocate for the needs of his/her district.

This debate over the contours of representation continues today with a focus on politically relevant social identities including gender, race, ethnicity, class, and sexual orientation. In her classic work, *The Concept of Representation* (1967), Hanna Pitkin draws a distinction between descriptive and substantive representation. She characterizes descriptive representatives as individuals who mirror certain social characteristics of their constituents such as race, class, or sex and thus are able to "stand for" those constituents. Meanwhile, substantive representatives "act for" the interests of the represented. Pitkin discounts the need for electing descriptive representatives to achieve substantive representation of constituent interests and asserts that the representative's descriptive characteristics will only be relevant if they affect the representative's actual actions and decisions.

More recently, feminist scholars have argued that increasing the descriptive representation of women and racial minorities in legislatures is a necessary but not sufficient condition for achieving the substantive representation of group interests (Phillips 1991, 1995, 1998; Mansbridge 1999; Dovi 2002). Political theorist Jane Mansbridge (1999) maintains that the election of previously excluded group members will improve the representation of group interests by strengthening the relationship between legislators and their constituents and improving policy outcomes. With regard to the constituent-legislator relationship, Mansbridge argues that electing descriptive representatives will build trust between underrepresented groups and the government, allowing policies to gain legitimacy in the eyes of these underrepresented group members. This improved communication between legislators and their constituents, and enhanced trust, is especially important in cases where there exists a history of discrimination between those who hold power and those who do not. Furthermore, electing descriptive representatives provides role models, encouraging more underrepresented groups like women and people of color to see themselves as potential candidates and legislators, providing symbolic representation. As more group representatives are elected, the majority group will also see these new groups as fit to rule, furthering their integration into the government and society.

Within the legislature, Mansbridge (1999) argues that expanding descriptive representation can improve the quality of deliberation among legislators and the nature of policy outcomes. Women and people of color will draw on their shared experiences as group members to bring new issues to the agenda that have not been adequately addressed by the majority. They will also provide a unique perspective on established debates by explaining how those issues will differentially impact various groups of women and/or minorities. When policy is being made, group members will be more likely to achieve the inclusion of group interests in policy outcomes because of the moral authority they wield as group members and because of the vigorous advocacy they will bring to issues on the basis of shared life experiences.

While expanding descriptive representation can improve the quality of representation, there are also risks. Most significantly, advocates run the risk of essentializing a group, thereby creating the impression that group members always agree on policy positions and share the same interests (Mansbridge 1999; Dovi 2002). As we will see, representation is more complicated and women like men are influenced by their multiple identities including race, ethnicity, class, party affiliation, and more. With more women of differing backgrounds entering legislative office, they will bring a broader range of experiences to legislating and ensure that a greater diversity of viewpoints influences public policy.

WOMEN'S REPRESENTATION IN LEGISLATIVE BODIES ACROSS THE WORLD

Compared to other countries, the United States ranks quite low in women's representation. Table 7.1 highlights the percentage of women serving in the lower houses of the national legislatures of countries around the world. A closer look at the electoral processes employed by these different countries reveals that the rules of the game matter. The democratic countries with the highest levels of representation for women such as Sweden, Finland, and Norway have electoral systems that encourage broader representation for groups. These countries utilize proportional representation in which political parties are awarded legislative seats based on the percentage of the vote they garner in the election and where voters have the option

Table 7.1 Women's Representation in the Lower or Single House of the National Legislature in Selected Countries around the World

Country	Percentage of Women (%)
Rwanda	61.3
Bolivia	53.1
Mexico	48.2
Sweden	46.1
Finland	42.0
Norway	41.4
France	39.6
Spain	39.1
Argentina	38.9
New Zealand	38.3
Iceland	38.1
Belgium	38.0
Denmark	37.4
Netherlands	36.0
Italy	35.7
Portugal	34.8
Austria	34.4
Switzerland	32.5
United Kingdom	32.2
Germany	30.7
Australia	28.7
Israel	27.5
Canada	26.9
Italy	31.0
Austria	30.6
United Kingdom	30.0
Australia	28.7
Israel	27.5
Canada	26.9
United States of America	23.4
Ireland	22.2
Greece	18.7
Japan	10.1

Source: Inter-Parliamentary Union. 2018. "Women in National Parliaments: World Classification." www.iup.org/wmn-e/classif.htm. Data are percentages reported by countries as of December 1, 2018.

of selecting more than one candidate in multimember districts (Inglehart and Norris 2003; Paxton and Hughes 2007; Krook 2009). By contrast, the United States usually relies on single-member districts where voters choose a single candidate rather than multiple candidates. The US system is candidate-centered rather than party-centered, meaning that instead of running as part of a party list in which the candidate's fate is tied to the performance of the party as a whole, American candidates must build their own campaigns, relying on their own networks to raise funds and canvass for votes. As a result, the US system favors incumbents who have already established these networks of donors and supporters. These incumbents, who are mostly men, are reelected at rates above 90 percent, making it difficult for new groups to break into politics (Herrnson 2012; Jacobson 2013).

In addition to employing proportional representation, to enhance electoral opportunities for women, some established and new democracies have adopted statutory mechanisms such as gender quotas designating a minimum number of seats for women, or mandates that require parties to reserve a certain number of seats on their party list for women. The success of these laws depends on where women are ranked within the party lists and the severity of the sanctions for noncompliance (Inglehart and Norris 2003; Paxton and Hughes 2007; Krook 2009). A couple of examples illustrate the point. In 1991, Argentina adopted a gender quota law that required all parties contesting seats in the Chamber of Deputies to submit lists including a minimum of 30 percent women. Additionally, the law required that women be placed throughout the list, not clustered near the bottom. Party lists that did not comply with the law were rejected, and the party was not allowed to compete in the district's election. Following the implementation of the law, the representation of women in the Chamber of Deputies rose from 4.6 percent in 1991 to 21.3 percent in 1993. Conversely, in 2000, France adopted a parity law that required parties to include 50 percent women in their lists or risk the loss of a percentage of their state funding. Although the law improved representation at the municipal level, in the 2002 election to the French National Assembly, women's representation rose by only 1.4 percent. This poor result was due to the fact that parties concentrated women in seats that could not be won or accepted the insubstantial financial penalty for noncompliance (Inglehart and Norris 2003; Paxton and Hughes 2007; Krook 2009; Norris and Krook 2014). As a result, women's representation in the French National Assembly continued to grow at a slow pace until Emanuel Macron, who had been an economic minister in the Socialist party government led by Francoise Hollande, decided to start a new party and run for president. Macron's new party committed to fielding a gender-balanced candidate list in which women were not relegated to districts the party could not win. In the end, Macron won the presidency and the number of women in the National Assembly jumped from 155 to

223 moving France from 64th to 17th in the world rankings for women's parliamentary representation (Kelly 2017).

Many Latin American countries utilize gender quotas adopted as part of their constitutions or legislative statutes. Women now constitute the majority of legislators in the Chamber of Deputies, the lower house in Bolivia's parliament (see Table 7.1). In 2014, the country implemented a law requiring equal numbers of men and women on parties' candidate lists for the upper and lower houses of the Legislative Assembly. As a result, the proportion of women in the lower house rose from 22 percent in 2009 to 53 percent in 2014 (Etoniru 2014). Rwanda—the country with the largest number of women in the lower house (61.3 percent)—also has quotas requiring equal participation by women. These quotas, as well as bans on discrimination based on gender, race, ethnicity, and religion, were adopted after the Rwandan genocide. Rwanda is not a democracy. However, in many post-conflict countries, the disruption of gender roles and relations allows for the emergence of new women's movements and the demand for greater rights for women. These demands are reinforced by international organizations like the United Nations and World Bank that require compliance with international treaties regarding women's rights as a condition for receiving aid (Tripp 2013, 2015).

More common than statutory quotas are voluntary gender quotas. Many European, Scandinavian, and Latin American parties, particularly those on the left, have adopted voluntary gender quotas that are not prescribed by law but are adopted within party rules. Yet, scholars find that these quotas are a facilitating condition and the representation of women is more likely to advance in countries where electoral mechanisms coexist with political cultures in which the public holds more egalitarian views on gender roles and women's leadership. Additionally, the parties of the left that adopt gender quotas are already the parties that are most likely to accept women candidates (Inglehart and Norris 2003; Paxton and Hughes 2007; Krook 2009; Norris and Krook 2014).

WOMEN'S REPRESENTATION IN CONGRESS AND THE STATE LEGISLATURES ACROSS TIME

The representation of women in Congress and the state legislatures has grown very slowly over time. In 2019, women constitute only 23.7 percent of the members of Congress and 28.6 percent (2,112) of state legislators (Center for American Women and Politics 2019a, 2019b). The number of women in office varies widely by state as women constitute 35 percent of the California congressional delegation including the Speaker of the House of Representatives, Nancy Pelosi (D-CA), while Vermont has never sent a woman to Congress (Center for American Women and Politics 2019a).

In 2018, Nevada became the first state to reach parity with 50.8 percent women in their state legislature, while less than 15 percent of the state legislators in West Virginia, Mississippi, and Louisiana are women (Center for American Women and Politics 2019b) (see Figure 7.1).

The first women elected to state legislatures in the United States came from the western states that were the first to grant women suffrage. Women state legislators from Wyoming, Utah, Colorado, and Idaho were often elected with women's votes, as women voters often made up 40 to 50 percent of voter turnout in those states. In 1894, three women were elected to the Colorado House of Representatives: Clara Cressingham, Carrie C. Holly, and Francis Klock. In 1896, Martha Hughes Cannon, a doctor and woman's suffrage activist, became the first woman to be elected to a state senate when she beat several candidates including her husband, Angus, in an at-large election for the Utah State Senate (Center for American Women and Politics 2004; Dolan 2004).

The greatest expansion in the number of women serving in state legislatures occurred between 1920 and 1925, right after the passage of the Nineteenth Amendment, which granted women the right to vote. Women who ran for office in these early years faced numerous obstacles from voters, parties, and even the state itself as they had to fight to overturn provisions in state constitutions that only men could serve in the legislature (Dolan 2004). Once in office, these women entered a male bastion that was not accustomed to the presence of women. When Ida Sammis became one of two women to serve in the New York State Assembly in 1918, it was said

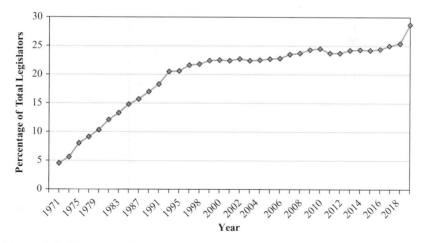

Figure 7.1 Progress of Women in State Legislatures Since 1970
Source: Women in State Legislatures 2019. Center for American Women and Politics 2019.

that her "first unofficial act was to take her brass spittoon—each member of the assembly was allocated one—and polish it to a brilliant shine. She filled it with flowers and placed it on her desk" (Andersen 1996). By 1930, there were 149 women serving in state legislatures across the country. Women's representation across the states ebbed and flowed as social attitudes about women's participation in the public sphere changed, with more support for electing women during periods of social and economic prosperity and less during times of national crisis. Thus, the number of women serving in state legislatures decreased during the years of the Great Depression, increased during World War II, declined in the postwar 1950s as Americans sought a return to traditional values, and increased again after the Korean War (Werner 1968; Dolan 2004).

The percentage of women serving in state legislatures grew rapidly through the 1970s and 1980s, increasing from less than 6 percent in 1973 to more than 13 percent in 1983 as more women gained the educational and occupational qualifications associated with a run for office (see Figure 7.1). By 1993 women made up 21 percent of the membership of state legislatures. However, in the decade from 1994 to 2004, women's representation stagnated, hovering around 22 percent. The number of women serving in state legislatures actually dropped between 2009 and 2011, declining from 24.3 percent to 23.7 percent after the Republican wave election of 2010. Since 2010 the representation of women in state legislatures barely increased, ranging from a low of 23.7 percent in 2011 and 2012 to 25.4 percent in 2018. With record numbers of women running for office in 2018, women now constitute 28.6 percent of state legislators (Norrander and Wilcox 2014; Center for American Women and Politics 2019c).

How do we explain women's slow advancement in state legislatures? Scholars point to a number of explanations: legislative structures, levels of professionalization and political culture within the state legislatures, and changing partisan dynamics. As already mentioned, one set of barriers is structural. The incumbency advantage and the high cost of campaigns make it difficult for new groups to make progress (Herrnson 2012; Jacobson 2013). Additionally, the elimination of multimember districts by many states and the adoption of term limits present further obstacles. Most state legislators are elected in single-member districts where voters select a single candidate to represent them. In multimember districts, more than one candidate is elected to represent citizens of a district. In those cases, voters are more likely to seek gender balance and vote for women when they can elect more than one candidate, and women may be more inclined to run if they are part of a team of candidates. Indeed, while the number of states using multimember districts declined from 13 in the 1990s to 10 in 2013, some of the states with the greatest number of women in office use multimember districts, including Arizona, Maryland, New Hampshire, Vermont, and

Washington (Norrander and Wilcox 2014; Sanbonmatsu 2018). Figure 7.2 identifies the states with the highest and lowest levels of women's representation in their state legislatures.

To reduce the power of incumbency and return power to citizen legislators, many political reformers of the 1990s advocated term limits. Today, 15 states place term limits on their legislators (NCLS 2015). It was thought that forcing out incumbents might also provide a path to office for new groups including women and racial minorities. However, particularly in the lower houses of legislatures, the number of women who are running for office has not kept pace with the number of women who are being kicked out when they reach their term limit. Whether it is because qualified women are less inclined to run for office than men or because the parties are not recruiting enough women to run, term limits have not been a path for expanding women's representation (Carroll and Jenkins 2001; Norrander and Wilcox 2014; Sanbonmatsu 2018). (See chapter 4 for further discussion of the reasons why there are fewer female than male candidates.)

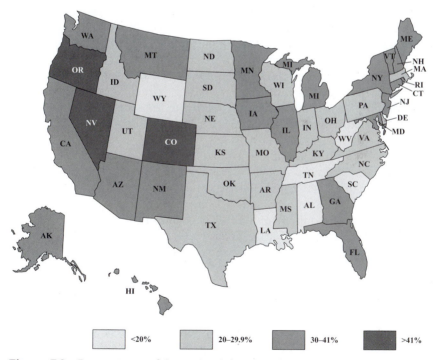

Figure 7.2 Percentage of State Legislators Who Are Women
Source: "Women in State Legislatures 2019." Center for American Women and Politics 2019.

The number of women in the state legislature is also impacted by the level of professionalization of the legislature and the political culture of the state. More professionalized legislatures have paid staff, provide a higher salary, and meet year round. There is more competition for seats in more professionalized legislatures (Norrander and Wilcox 2014). The states with the highest levels of female representation generally do not have highly professionalized legislatures. For example, New Hampshire has a part-time legislature whose members are paid $100 per year compared to California, whose full-time legislators earn more than $95,000 per year. Overall, women hold the largest proportion of seats in legislatures with moderate levels of professionalism (Sanbonmatsu 2018).

States also vary in political culture. Research demonstrates that fewer white women are elected in southern states with traditional political cultures, where women's voting participation lagged behind men's into the early 1970s (Norrander and Wilcox 2014). However, when differentiating by race and gender, Becki Scola (2013) finds that while white women fare best in moralistic political cultures, women of color fare much better in traditionalistic cultures and in states with more sizable racial minority populations. Both white women and women of color have had difficulty breaking into politics in Mid-Atlantic states like New Jersey and Pennsylvania, which have a history of strong political parties that controlled candidate recruitment. Meanwhile western states like Colorado have been friendlier to women politicians because they gave women the right to vote early, have political cultures that encourage participation, and they historically have weak party structures allowing for other avenues of political recruitment (Sanbonmatsu 2006, 2014; Norrander and Wilcox 2014; Scola 2006).

Beyond political culture, the changing partisan dynamics in the country have also impacted women's representation. Throughout the 1990s and early 2000s, the Republican Party made gains at all levels of elective office. By 2002, the formerly solidly Democratic South had moved toward the Republicans, and the Republican Party controlled more state legislative seats than the Democrats for the first time since the 1950s (Jacobson 2013; Davidson et al. 2015). For most of the twentieth century, Republicans did a better job of electing women to public office than did Democrats (Werner 1968; Cox 1996). Indeed, in a study of candidate recruitment to state legislatures, Sanbonmatsu (2002) finds that when Democrats have been the majority party in a legislature, they have recruited fewer women candidates. However, the contemporary parties are highly polarized, with Democrats trending more uniformly liberal and Republicans more conservative. In the 1980s and 1990s, the Republican Party included a growing and active socially conservative base with more traditional views about gender roles. The Tea Party movement that fueled the Republican electoral wave in 2010 called for a more conservative brand of politics that limits the role of government and scales back social welfare programs.

In the contemporary Republican Party, Republican women have not shared in their party's gains. Even as Republicans expanded their control of state legislatures from 41 percent of state legislative seats in 1993 to 53 percent of state legislative seats in 2011, the number of Republican women winning seats as a proportion of all Republicans remained stagnant or declined (Elder 2012; Carroll and Sanbonmatsu 2013; Norrander and Wilcox 2014). Indeed, Republican women and all women have their lowest levels of representation in the southern states that are currently the strongholds of the Republican Party. More Republican women are found in states with less professionalized legislatures. By contrast, as the Democratic Party has become more liberal and feminists have gained a more prominent foothold in the party, Democrats have placed a higher priority on recruiting women candidates and the gap between the parties has grown (Sanbonmatsu 2006, 2018; Elder 2008, 2012; Carroll and Sanbonmatsu 2013). As a result, in 2019, 67.8 percent (1,431) of female state legislators are Democrats while only 31.3 percent (660) are Republicans (Center for American Women and Politics 2019b). As we will see below, this partisan disparity in the number of women legislators persists at the congressional level.

THE ADVANCEMENT OF WOMEN IN CONGRESS

In 1916, Jeannette Rankin (R-MT) became the first woman to be elected to Congress, and she ultimately went on to serve two terms (1917–1919 and 1941–1943). A political activist who worked for social justice, Rankin had traveled the country working for women's suffrage and peace and against child labor and poverty in America's cities. In her campaign for Congress, Rankin expressed her desire to act as an advocate for women and children. She once noted that the country spent $300,000 per year to study hog fodder but only $30,000 per year to study the needs of children. She asserted, "If the hogs of the nation are ten times more important than the children, it is high time that we [women] made our influence felt." Asked why a woman should be elected to Congress, she answered, "There are hundreds of men to take care of the nation's tariff and foreign policy and irrigation projects. But there isn't a single woman to look after the nation's greatest asset: its children." As a member of Congress, she worked for the national women's suffrage amendment, against child labor, and for programs to improve mothers' and children's health. However, she is best known as the only member of Congress who voted against both World War I and World War II (Kaptur 1996).

Rankin's path to office was unique since most of the small number of women who served in Congress as late as the 1960s came to office as widows. After the death of a politician, political parties often turned to the spouse who had name recognition and the sympathy of the voters but who did not have larger political ambitions. The widow would serve one or two terms until the party decided who the next representative would be or until a candidate emerged, thus avoiding internal party strife. In fact, the first woman to be seated in the US Senate, Rebecca Latimer Felton (D-GA), served only one day. At the age of 87, she was appointed by the governor of Georgia to replace Senator Tom Watson after he died in office. She convinced the newly elected senator, Walter George, to delay taking the oath of office so that she could be seated and make a speech on the Senate floor. Felton was followed in the Senate by Hattie Carraway (D-AR) who replaced her deceased husband in 1931 and won the election in her own right in 1932, serving until 1945 (Kaptur 1996). From 1916 to 1940, 54 percent of women who served in the House succeeded their husbands and from 1941 to 1964, 37 percent of women serving were widows. After 1964, the number of widows in office fell to 15 percent (Gertzog 1995; Dolan 2004). Today this method of gaining election is quite rare.

Several female members who began their service as widows went on to have more accomplished careers in Congress than did their husbands. Perhaps the most famous is Senator Margaret Chase Smith (R-ME) who was first elected to the House of Representatives after the death of her husband in 1940. She then became the first woman elected in her own right to the US Senate in 1948 and served there for an additional 24 years until she was defeated in the 1972 election. She is most well known for her Declaration of Conscience speech in which she was the first Republican to come out against the communist witch-hunt conducted by Senator Joe McCarthy (R-WI) in the 1950s. Numerous careers and lives were ruined by his unsubstantiated accusations and televised hearings in which he searched for communists in government and society. In 1964, Smith became the first woman to seek her party's presidential nomination, receiving 205,690 votes nationally and winning 27 delegates at the Republican National Convention. She spent only $25 on her campaign in the first primary state, New Hampshire, but her campaign practice of handing out recipes and muffins on the campaign trail and posing for photos while cooking gained so much publicity that Republican candidate Nelson Rockefeller felt compelled to respond by distributing his fudge recipe (Kaptur 1996). Current Maine Senator Susan Collins (R) credits Smith with inspiring her to run for public office. On a high school trip to Washington, DC, Smith brought Collins into her office and spoke to her for several hours about her Senate career. Today, Collins holds Smith's seat in the Senate (Mikulski et al. 2001).

By the 1970s, most women serving in Congress were professional politicians elected in their own right. However, their occupational backgrounds and paths to politics continued to differ from those of men. For example, women were more likely than men to have begun their political careers as community activists spurred to activism for or against a particular local project or as members of the PTA, the local school board, or other community groups. For example, Senator Barbara Mikulski (D-MD), the longest serving female senator (elected in 1986 and retired in 2017), is a former social worker. Mikulski entered the political arena when she got involved in the fight to stop a highway project in her East Baltimore neighborhood. Similarly, when Patty Murray (D-WA) went to the state capitol to lobby against the elimination of a preschool program, a legislator dismissed her by saying, "You can't make a difference. You're just a mom in tennis shoes." In response, Murray organized a statewide parents' effort to revive the program. She was later elected to the school board and the Washington state Senate. When Murray ran for her first term in the US Senate, her campaign slogan was "just a mom in tennis shoes" (Mikulski et al. 2001).

Today, the educational and occupational backgrounds of male and female members of Congress continue to converge with more and more women entering Congress through the traditional pathways of law, business, or prior political office such as state legislator or city council member. However, elected women's occupational paths are still more diverse than their male colleagues, and women remain older and are more likely to wait until their children are grown up before running for office (Burrell 1994, 2014; Carroll and Sanbonmatsu 2013; Chinoy and Ma 2019). Indeed, House Speaker Nancy Pelosi (D-CA) had been heavily involved in Democratic politics as a party fundraiser and activist, chairing the California Democrat Party in the 1980s. However, she waited until her five children were grown up before she first ran for the House of Representatives in a special election in 1987, at the age of 47 (Sandalow 2008). Today, there are more women with young children serving in Congress than ever before, and they are pushing Congress to become more family friendly. In 2018, when Senator Tammy Duckworth became the first sitting senator to give birth, she pushed a rules change through the Senate, allowing senators to bring infants to the floor, so that she could more easily perform her duties as a mother and a senator (Haberkorn 2018). Since power in Congress is derived from seniority, the large class of young women elected in 2018 could lay the groundwork for more women to rise to committee chairmanships and party leadership posts.

Compared to the 1970s, women in the contemporary Congress are also more racially and ethnically diverse, with political views that span the ideological spectrum. Moreover, they serve in a much more partisan and electorally competitive Congress. The number of women in Congress grew steadily but slowly throughout the 1970s and 1980s (see Figure 7.3). Similar numbers of Republican and Democratic women were elected to the House of Representatives throughout the 1980s. As late as 1991, there were only two women in the Senate: Republican Nancy Landon Kassebaum (R-KS) and Democrat Barbara Mikulski (D-MD) (Center for American Women and Politics 2019a). The paucity of women in Congress became an issue in the 1992 election when Anita Hill accused her former employer, Supreme Court nominee Clarence Thomas, of sexual harassment. The spectacle of Anita Hill being questioned by an all-male Judiciary committee prompted women across the country to run for Congress including current Senators Dianne Feinstein (D-CA), Patty Murray (D-WA), and Barbara Boxer (D-CA) (Burrell 1994; Dolan 2001; Swers 2002). Referring to the fact that there were only two women in the Senate, Feinstein's campaign proclaimed that 2 percent was good enough for milk but not for women's representation in Congress (Feinstein 2006).

After the election, the number of women in Congress jumped from 32 to 54, still the largest increase in a single election cycle, and the 1992 election was dubbed "The Year of the Woman" (see Figure 7.3). Beyond the atypical focus on gender, there were structural features that facilitated the election of more women to Congress. Most importantly, the power of incumbency was weakened by the fact that 1992 was a redistricting year, and rather than facing election under new district lines, some incumbents decided to retire. Additionally, a series of congressional scandals reduced

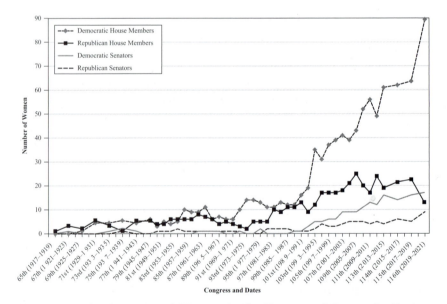

Figure 7.3   The Progress of Women in the House and Senate by Party
Source: "History of Women in the U.S. Congress." Center for the American Woman and Politics 2019.

public trust in Congress, spurring more incumbent retirements. As a result, the election featured an unusually large number of open seats and more women ran in these competitive elections. With the public in the mood for a change, women capitalized on the fact that they were not part of the establishment (Burrell 1994; Dolan 2001; Swers 2002).

The elections of the early 1990s also brought increased racial diversity to Congress through the creation of majority/minority districts. As a result of amendments to the Voting Rights Act that sought to prevent dilution of racial minorities' votes and ensure that people of color could elect a representative of their choice, the number of African Americans in Congress increased from 27 to 39 after the 1992 elections and the number of Hispanics in Congress rose from 10 to 17 (Manning and Shogan 2012; Bedolla, Tate, and Wong 2014). The first African Americans in Congress were elected during Reconstruction. However, when Reconstruction ended and Jim Crow laws were adopted to disenfranchise black voters, African Americans were excluded from Congress until Oscar DeLaPriest (R-IL) was elected to represent a Chicago area district in 1928 (Tate 2003; Manning and Shogan 2012).

The first African American woman did not come to Congress until the election of Shirley Chisholm (D-NY) in 1968. In that year, Chisholm was one of only ten women and nine African Americans in Congress. A former teacher and child care center director, she won her first election in her Brooklyn district with the campaign slogan "Unbought and Unbossed." This motto guided her career as she sought to serve the interests of groups that often go unheard, including the poor, children, women, and minorities. She was not afraid to challenge the political establishment. Upon election to Congress, she protested against her assignment to the Agriculture Committee by objecting to her committee assignment on the floor of the House of Representatives. Rather than punishing her, the leadership decided to move her from that committee to the Veterans' Affairs Committee as a result of her actions. Satisfied with the result of her protest, she remarked, "There are a lot more veterans in my [Brooklyn, NY] district than there are trees" (Kaptur 1996).

Throughout her congressional career, Chisholm challenged the establishment and championed both civil rights and women's rights. She called the seniority system that guides the advancement of members of Congress to positions of power on committees, the "senility system" that left control of Congress to "a handful of old men." Yet, while she criticized existing power structures, she managed to avoid alienating her colleagues and was able to advance first to her desired assignment to the Education and Labor Committee and later to the powerful Rules Committee. By 1972, Chisholm decided to take her message of change nationally and she became the first woman and the first African American to run for the

Shirley Chisholm gives the victory sign after winning the congressional election in Brooklyn's 12th District. She defeated civil rights leader James Farmer to become the first African American woman elected to Congress, November 5, 1968. *Source*: © Bettmann / CORBIS.

Democratic nomination for president. Although many of the male members of the Congressional Black Caucus actively opposed her candidacy, Chisholm was on the primary ballot in 12 states. Garnering less than 3 percent of the primary vote, she won 151 delegate votes at the Democratic National Convention (Kaptur 1996; Benenson 2005). When Kamala Harris (D-CA) announced her presidential run, she tied herself to Chisholm's legacy and adopted a red and yellow color scheme for her campaign logo that reflected the design of Chisholm's campaign buttons. Ayanna Pressley (D-MA), the first African American woman to win a House seat in Massachusetts, made a point of selecting Chisholm's former House office and taking her picture underneath Chisholm's portrait (Swenson 2019; Epstein 2019).

Hispanics first gained representation in Congress in 1822 when Florida was still a territory. The first Hispanic member to represent a state, Romualdo Pacheco (R-CA), entered Congress in 1877 (Office of the

Historian and Office of the Clerk, United States House of Representatives 2013). It was more than 100 years later that the first Hispanic female, Ileana Ros-Lehtinen (R-FL), was elected to Congress. Serving from 1989 to 2019, Ros-Lehtinen rose to chair the Foreign Relations Committee in the 112th Congress (2011–2012) where she fought against expanding relations with the communist regime in Cuba (Center for American Women and Politics 2019c, 2018).

A large and more diverse cohort of women was elected in 2018. The new freshman class included the first two Native American women ever elected to Congress, Deb Haaland (D-NM) and Sharice Davids (D-KS) and the first two Muslim women elected, Ilhan Omar (D-MN) and Rashida Tlaib (D-MI). Texas, which has one of the largest Hispanic populations in the United States, elected its first Latina women to Congress, Democrats Sylvia Garcia and Veronica Escobar. Alexandria Ocasio-Cortez (D-NY) became the youngest woman elected to Congress. Her surprise defeat of a Democratic incumbent in the primary, and her prolific social media presence catapulted her to political stardom. She uses her platform to promote progressive Democratic ideals from

Ileana Ros-Lehtinen (R-FL) chairing a session of the House Foreign Affairs Subcommittee on Middle East and North Africa. Serving from 1989–2019, Ros-Lehtinen is the first Hispanic woman to serve in Congress. *Source*: Tom Williams / CQ Roll Call via Associated Press.

climate change to the plight of working-class Americans. Most of the women of color in Congress represent majority/minority districts and these districts lean heavily to the Democratic Party. In the current 116th Congress, there is only one woman of color among House Republicans: Jamie Herrera-Beutler (R-WA). Two of the four nonvoting delegates, Jennifer Gonzalez from Puerto Rico and Amata Radewagen from American Samoa, are also Republicans (Center for American Women and Politics 2019c).

Compared with their white female counterparts, minority women hold more seats in proportion to the number of minority men in the House of Representatives. Yet, very few minority women have been elected to the Senate. Elected in the 1992 "Year of the Woman" elections, Carol Moseley Braun (D-IL) was the first African American woman to serve in the Senate. After Moseley Braun lost her reelection bid in 1998, there were no women of color in the Senate until Japanese American Mazie Hirono (D-HI) was elected in 2012. It was not until the 2016 election that there were multiple women of color serving in the Senate at the same time. These women include Kamala Harris (D-CA), who identifies as black and Indian American, and Catherine Cortez Masto (D-NV), who became the first Hispanic woman in the Senate. Tammy Duckworth (D-IL) identifies as Asian American and is a veteran of the Iraq War (Marcos 2016). One of the first women to fly combat missions for the army, Duckworth lost both of her legs when her helicopter was hit in battle (https://www.duckworth.senate.gov/content/about-tammy).

In addition to being more diverse, women in the contemporary Congress are much more likely to be Democrats than Republicans. In the 116th Congress, 106 women are Democrats compared to only 21 Republican women (Center for American Women and Politics 2019a). How do we explain this partisan disparity in which the gender gap in representation is larger than the gender gap in voting behavior?

The current partisan gap in women's representation did not emerge until after the 1992 elections (see Figure 7.3). Following that election, the number of Democratic women in Congress rose from 22 in the 102nd Congress to 40 in the 103rd Congress, while only four more Republican women were elected to the 103rd Congress, taking their combined numbers in the House and Senate from 10 to 14 (Center for American Women and Politics 2017a). Since 1992, the gap between the number of Republican and Democratic women has only grown wider. The 1990s and 2000s have seen several volatile electoral cycles in which control of the House and Senate majority has shifted between Republicans and Democrats. In the years when Democrats have done well including 2006, 2008, and 2018, the representation of Democratic women also advanced.

However, Republican women have not experienced concomitantly strong gains during Republican wave elections. Thus, in the 1994 Republican Revolution when Republicans took over the House majority for the first time in 40 years, the party gained 52 House seats but Republican women only expanded their presence from 12 to 17 seats. Similarly, in the wave election of 2010, Republicans won 63 House seats, but the representation of Republican women only increased by seven seats, from 17 to 24 House seats (Davidson et al. 2015; Center for American Women and Politics 2019a). The 2018 elections were particularly difficult for Republican women as their representation in the House dropped from 23 to 13, leading Representative Elise Stefanik (R-NY) to sound the alarm that women's representation in the Republican Party is at crisis levels, and the party needs to do something to expand women's representation. To address the problem, Stefanik announced that going forward, her Political Action Committee, E-PAC, will focus exclusively on recruiting and electing Republican women (Hagen 2019).

How can we explain these trends? Some scholars find that certain types of districts are more likely to elect women. These districts are generally more diverse, more urban, and have a higher median income. In contemporary politics, these types of districts are more likely to vote for Democrats (Palmer and Simon 2008; Pearson and McGhee 2013). Meanwhile, rural districts and the southern states, which are the stronghold of the Republican Party, are also less likely to elect women (Elder 2008; Pearson and McGhee 2013). Dynamics within the parties also contribute to the disparity. The contemporary Democratic Party is a more liberal party and its voters are more likely to prioritize diversity and embrace positive stereotypes about female candidates (Burrell 2014; Elder 2014). Meanwhile, the Republican Party focuses more on candidate ideology than identity (Cooperman 2013; Elder 2014).

Additionally, women's groups and civil rights organizations are more central to the Democratic coalition. These groups prioritize the election of more diverse candidates and are heavily engaged in efforts to recruit more women and minorities. EMILY's List is the most successful of these groups. They recruit women to run in primaries, raise money for candidates, and provide them with polling and other services that are important to campaigns. While Republicans have groups dedicated to electing more Republican women, their efforts lag behind the more established and successful Democratic groups (Crespin and Dietz 2010; Burrell 2014; Political Parity 2015). Indeed, a study of party campaign donors found that most Democratic donors recognized EMILY's List and considered it an important influence on their decision of which candidates to support. By contrast, most Republican donors had never heard of political action committees devoted to electing Republican women candidates including the most prominent Susan B. Anthony's List, which supports pro-life women and pro-life men running against pro-choice women (Crowder-Meyer and Cooperman 2018; Cooperman and Crowder-Meyer 2018).

Looking more closely at candidate fundraising in the primary and general election as a potential cause of the partisan disparity in representation, Kitchens and Swers (2016) found that Democratic women actually raise more money than Democratic men. Among Republicans, Republican women generally raise as much money as Republican men. However, when the analysis is limited to quality candidates, meaning candidates with previous electoral experience, the Republican women raise less money than the Republican men. This suggests that the most viable female challenger and open seat candidates may have more trouble accessing Republican fundraising networks than the quality candidates who are Republican men.

Based on current trends, women will continue to grow their ranks in Congress and state legislatures. However, the partisan gap among legislators is likely to continue and grow. Moreover, as more women of color are elected, these women are disproportionately likely to be Democrats. As we will see below, the increasing concentration of female legislators in the Democratic Party has important consequences for the ability of female legislators to influence policy with women having more access to the levers of power in legislatures controlled by Democrats and less influence in Republican-controlled legislative bodies.

WOMEN IN CONGRESS AND STATE LEGISLATURES: A DISTINCTIVE IMPACT ON POLICY?

The election of more women to Congress and the state legislatures raises the question of whether women legislate differently than men. Returning to the expectations of representation theory, do women espouse different policy priorities that focus more attention on the needs of women, children, and families? Do women exhibit a different leadership style or bring a unique perspective to existing policy debates that emphasizes how policy proposals will impact different groups of women? Examining the legislative activities of male and female members of Congress and the state legislatures, scholars find that the election of women does have a distinctive impact on policymaking.

One of the key arguments for descriptive representation is that descriptive representatives as members of the group will be more likely to understand group concerns based on shared life experiences and will prioritize policies that are important to group members. Examining legislators' perceptions of their representational roles, scholars find that female legislators in Congress and the state legislatures view women as a distinctive part of their constituency and feel a special responsibility to advocate for their interests (Reingold 1992, 2000; Thomas 1997; Carroll 2002; Dittmar et al. 2018). Surveys of legislators' policy priorities show that women are also more likely to consider women's issues an important part of their agenda than are their male colleagues (Dodson and Carroll 1991; Thomas 1994; Poggione 2004; Dittmar et al. 2018).

Gender differences in legislative behavior are most prominent at the agenda-setting stage where members decide which causes to champion and work to craft bills and build coalitions to advance their policy proposals. Studies of bill sponsorship and cosponsorship demonstrate that women offer more bills on issues related to women, children, and families. This includes feminist or women's rights bills that promote role equity or role change for women, such as bills concerning family leave, equal pay, sexual harassment, and reproductive rights. Female legislators also offer more initiatives on the social welfare issues that underlie the gender gap among voters, such as health care and education. Generally, sex differences in legislative behavior are greater the more directly an issue can be connected to consequences for women as a group. Therefore, gender is a stronger predictor of which members will champion feminist initiatives such as reproductive rights than social welfare policies such as education reforms (Thomas 1994; Gelb and Palley 1996; Bratton and Haynie 1999; Reingold 2000; Wolbrecht 2000; Swers 2002, 2013, 2016a; Dodson 2006; Osborn 2012).

The advancement of more women into legislative office has also impacted the deliberative process among legislators. Women bring a distinctive perspective to policy debates based on their life experiences as mothers, daughters, and women of various backgrounds. In their committee activity and on the floor, women utilize their positions to advocate for women's concerns and influence how issues are framed and solutions are crafted. Congressional studies of policies ranging from welfare and health reform to violence against women and abortion indicate that women use their positions on key committees and within their party leadership to ensure that women's interests are included in legislation and to prevent the legislation from faltering at key points in the process. For example, during the development of the welfare reform in the early 1990s, women in the Republican and Democratic parties who served on the House Ways and Means Committee and held positions in party leadership were pivotal in getting Congress to include child support enforcement and more funding for child care to support working mothers in the final bill (Swers 2002; Hawkesworth 2003; Dodson 2006; Johnson, Duerst-Lahti, and Norton 2007). When President Obama's health reform proposal was going through Congress, women in the House and Senate worked to ensure that women's health needs were included in the bill. For example, female senators pushed the administration to include prenatal care and broad coverage of contraception as part of a package of preventive services that insurance companies are required to offer (Swers 2013).

Analyses of floor speeches indicate that women act as vigorous advocates for women's interests. Women draw on their moral authority as women by referring to their roles as parents, mothers, and grandmothers. They are more likely than men to discuss the impact of policies on women and children (Shogan 2001; Cramer Walsh 2002; Levy, Tien, and Aved 2002; Swers 2002, 2013; Osborn and Mendez 2010; Pearson and Dancey 2011a). They highlight issues of women's rights in broader policy debates. Analyzing the Senate floor debates surrounding the nominations of John Roberts and Samuel Alito to the Supreme Court, Swers (2013) finds that among Democrats, Democratic women focused more attention than Democratic men on the nominees' positions on women's rights. The Democratic women were more likely than men to highlight women's rights issues outside of abortion, such as equal pay, family leave policy, and the representation of women on the federal courts (see also Swers and Kim 2013).

There is some evidence that women have influenced the way that men view and discuss women's issues. For example, in a study of congressional debate on abortion since the 1970s, Levy, Tien, and Aved (2002) found that over time, women have moved the debate from one that emphasizes the morality of abortion to one that increasingly includes a focus on the health of the pregnant woman. As a result, both pro-choice and pro-life proponents frame their arguments with an eye to the impact on women and women's physical and mental health.

In sum, female legislators clearly prioritize women's interests in their work. They perceive themselves as representatives of women and women's interests. They have introduced more initiatives concerning women, children, and families to the legislative agenda, and they act as vigorous advocates for these interests in the committees and on the floor. These findings reflect general trends in legislative behavior. There are numerous factors that affect whether an individual female legislator perceives herself as an advocate for women's interests and whether she has the ability to pursue these preferences in the legislative process. We turn now to the important political and institutional constraints that shape legislators' choices about what policies to champion.

Party, Ideology, and Constituent Interests

Party affiliation, ideology, and constituent opinion are among the most important predictors of how representatives behave. In recent years, the Democratic and Republican Parties have become more ideologically homogeneous and further polarized from each other. As the formerly solid South moved away from the Democratic Party and liberal Northeastern Republicans left the GOP, commentators began referring to red states and blue states to represent the ideological divides in the country (Jacobson 2013). In response to this polarization, voting among members of Congress increasingly falls along party lines (Poole and Rosenthal 1997; Davidson et al. 2015).

In this partisan atmosphere, it is hard to see how gender might have an independent effect on legislative behavior. While early studies of voting in Congress suggested that female representatives are more liberal than their male colleagues, the voting records of male and female Democrats and Republicans in the House of Representatives converged by the early 2000s (Frederick 2009). Much of the gender difference in voting behavior stemmed from the more liberal voting records of moderate Republican women. However, there are few moderates left in Congress and the new women being elected from the South and West are just as conservative as their male counterparts (Frederick 2009; Thomsen 2015; Swers 2016b, 2017). Women in the Senate remain more liberal than their male colleagues (Frederick 2010). However, this may change with the election of more conservative Republican women including Deb Fischer (NE), Joni Ernst (IA), and Marsha Blackburn (TN) who all have ties to the Tea Party movement. Focusing on women's issues, scholars find that women often vote more liberally on policies regarding women's rights such as pay equity and abortion (Burrell 1994; Dolan 1997; Norton 1999; Swers 1998, 2002; Frederick 2009). However, this trend may be declining among Republican women as more socially conservative women who are strongly pro-life are being elected to the House and Senate (Swers 2017, 2018).

Even in a partisan atmosphere, female members of Congress and state legislatures remain more committed to proposing and cosponsoring legislation related to women, children, and families. Numerous studies show that women are more likely to sponsor and cosponsor bills on women's issues even after accounting for the legislator's party affiliation, ideology, constituency effects, and committee position (Thomas 1994; Bratton and Haynie 1999; Wolbrecht 2000, 2002; Swers 2002, 2013; Dodson 2006; Osborn 2012; but see Reingold 2000).

Voters in a congressional or state legislative district have a general ideological view on issues. However, a legislator has wide discretion in choosing which specific policies to champion as long as they fall within the spectrum of policy views that his or her constituents can support. One would not expect a representative of a conservative district to support liberalized abortion laws. However, the member may advocate for increased funding for women's health research or programs to combat violence against women.

Analyzing bill proposals across ten state legislatures, Osborn (2012) finds that Democratic and Republican men and women advocate for distinct women's issues and offer different solutions to address specific problems. Democratic women offer the most bills regarding women's issues and their proposals span a wide range of women's interests. They are particularly aggressive advocates of policies regarding employment discrimination and women's health concerns ranging from cancer screening to services for pregnant women and breastfeeding mothers. Republican men offer the most bills to restrict abortion. Other proposals offered by Republican men focus on legal issues regarding marriage and divorce and efforts to increase punishment for sex offenders and expand child support enforcement. The bills of Democratic men span the range of issues and align more with the proposals of Democratic women, except in the areas of child support enforcement and sex offenders where they, like Republican men, focus more on punishment of offenders and less on victim's rights. Finally, Republican women offered the fewest proposals on women's issues. Their initiatives align more with the proposals of Republican men than Democratic women except in the area of women's health where their bills correspond more to the proposals offered by Democratic women including bills regarding breast cancer, services for pregnant women, and IVF insurance coverage. Republican women also offered more child care proposals than Republican men (Osborn 2012; Osborn and Kreitzer 2014). Thus, within the large category of women's issues, men and women from different parties have different ideas about what women need.

Beyond the policy preferences of individual legislators, the parties as a whole have developed reputations for expertise on particular issues. Women's issues have become a contested fault line between the parties. In a polarized era, women's rights issues are increasingly associated with the Democratic Party (Wolbrecht 2000; Winter 2010). Indeed, Osborn (2012) finds that more women's issue bills pass in state legislatures controlled by Democrats than in legislatures where Republicans are the majority party. Capitalizing on the party's presumed ownership of these issues and voter stereotypes concerning women's perceived expertise, Democratic women are generally the most active advocates of women's issue bills. When Democratic women advocate for expansion of equal pay or reproductive rights, they are pursuing legislation that both reflects their own policy priorities and helps the Democratic Party improve its standing with voters, particularly the activist base that donates to campaigns and mobilizes voters (Swers 2002, 2013; Dodson 2006). For example, Swers (2013) recounts how female Democratic senators were pivotal in drafting and building support for the Lilly Ledbetter Fair Pay Act. First brought to the floor in the run up to the 2008 presidential election, the media campaign female senators engaged in to build public support for the bill also served a dual purpose of portraying Republicans as opposing equal pay for women and acting against women's interests. Democratic women in Congress continue to combine their interest in seeking policies that expand women's rights with their roles as partisan warriors. In the 2012 and 2014 election cycles,

Democratic women promoted additional pay equity proposals as well as contraception coverage and other benefits for women's health in the Affordable Care Act. As they promoted these policies, they also accused Republicans of engaging in a war on women in which Republican policy prescriptions would harm women's rights and their families (Swers 2013; Deckman and McTague 2014).

While advocating policies related to women's rights is generally a natural fit for Democratic women, the political calculus for Republican women is more complicated. Women's issues are not central to the platform of the Republican Party and many of these policies conflict with the views of social conservatives, an important constituency within the Republican Party. If Republican women advocate for women's rights legislation, they could alienate Republican Party colleagues and risk losing their support on other issues important to the legislator's constituency (Swers 2002, 2013). At the same time, in this era of tight electoral competition, women represent a key swing-voting group that both Republican and Democrats want to court in their efforts to become the majority party in Congress and across the state legislatures. Therefore, the leadership of both parties utilizes female legislators as spokespersons for the party's position on women's issues. Republican women are often asked to speak at press conferences and on the House and Senate floor to defend the party against charges that it is unfriendly to women's interests or to explain how Republican policies will help women (Swers 2002, 2013; Dodson 2006; Dittmar et al. 2018). Serving as Republican Conference Chair for the 112th–115th Congresses (2013–2019), Cathy McMorris Rodgers (R-WA) considered reaching out to women voters and pushing back on the Democratic narrative of a war on women an important part of her job (Mimms 2015). Republican women hold press conferences to explain how small business tax cuts benefit women since women-owned businesses are one of the fastest growing groups of small business owners. Pro-life Republican women are asked to speak on the floor when abortion is being debated to demonstrate that not all women are pro-choice and that Republicans are not anti-women (Swers 2002, 2013, 2018; Dodson 2006).

As the ranks of moderate Republican women continue to dwindle and more conservative women are elected, it remains an open question whether Republican women will choose to engage on women's issues from a conservative perspective or whether they will prefer to focus on policies more central to Republican constituencies such as lowering taxes and rolling back regulations on business. Will they limit themselves to defending the party against Democratic attacks that characterize Republicans as anti-women or aggressively take up the banner of social conservatism (Swers and Larson 2005; Swers 2013, 2018)? Since 2010 as Republicans have gained more control over the levers of power in Washington, at various times holding the majority in the House and Senate and in 2016 winning the presidency,

US House of Representatives Republican Conference Chair Liz Cheney, Republican of Wyoming, speaks during a press conference after the conclusion of the House Republican Caucus leadership elections on Capitol Hill in Washington, DC, on November 14, 2018. *Source*: Alex Edelman/SIPA/Newscom.

they have focused more aggressively on limiting access to abortion. Rather than simply voting with their party, conservative Republican women are taking leadership roles in these efforts. For example, Representative Diane Black (R-TN) and Senator Joni Ernst (R-IA) both sponsored bills to defund Planned Parenthood. Black's bill passed the House, while Ernst's bill was considered on the Senate floor but fell to a Democratic filibuster. When House Republican leadership decided to create a special committee to investigate Planned Parenthood's sale of fetal tissue for research, they appointed Marsha Blackburn (R-TN) to chair the committee, and half of the committee's members were Republican women. Thus, it seems that the new generation of conservative women is more strongly engaged in women's issues, particularly abortion politics, but from a decidedly pro-life perspective (Swers 2016b, 2017, 2018).

Race, Ethnicity, and Social Class

Beyond party affiliations, women also differ from one another by race, ethnicity, and social class. Scholars are only beginning to examine the impact of intersectionality or overlapping social identities on the policy activities of legislators. Research demonstrates that women of color bring a different perspective to legislating, as they must confront both racism and sexism in their life experiences. In an in depth study of African American women in the Maryland legislature, Brown (2014) maintains that these legislators saw themselves as belonging to multiple identity groups whose interests are sometimes in conflict. As a result, their policy behavior differed from both black men and white women. Their stance on issues was further informed by their marital status, age, religion, and status as parents or caregivers. These life experiences and multiple identities uniquely impacted their legislative efforts concerning violence against women, elder care, and gay marriage.

With more women of color serving in the state legislatures since the 1990s, quantitative studies of policy priorities indicate that African American women are more likely to sponsor progressive legislation than other legislators. They are also more likely to sponsor both a women's interest bill and a black interest bill than other legislators, indicating that black women focus on serving multiple groups in their legislative activities (Barrett 1995; Bratton and Haynie 1999; Bratton, Haynie, and Reingold 2006; Orey et al. 2006; Brown 2014). Similarly, studying the policy priorities of Latinos, Fraga et al. (2006) find that compared to their male Latino colleagues, Latinas place more emphasis on representing the interests of multiple minority groups, particularly African Americans and Asians. While Latino men and women identify similar policy priorities including education, health care,

The 2016 elections brought three new women of color to the US Senate: former state attorney general Kamala Harris (D-CA); former US representative and veteran Tammy Duckworth (D-IL); and former state attorney general Catherine Cortez Masto (D-NV). Kamala Harris is running for the 2020 Democratic presidential nomination and Catherine Cortez Matso chairs the Democratic Senatorial Campaign Committee recruiting candidates and raising money for 2020. *Sources (from left to right):* ZUMA Press, Inc./Alamy Stock Photo; ZUMA Press, Inc./Alamy Stock Photo; dpa picture alliance/Alamy Stock Photo.

and economic development, Latinas are more likely than their male counterparts to propose and pass legislation reflecting their policy agenda (Fraga et al. 2008).

At the congressional level, case studies demonstrate that female legislators of color are aggressive advocates for the needs of women of color, particularly women in poverty. For example, Hawkesworth (2003) found that African American and Latina Democratic women were united in their opposition to welfare reform and used their floor time to speak against the stereotyping of welfare mothers as irresponsible, poor minority women. By contrast, neither men of color nor white women in the Democratic Party were unified on the welfare reform bill. Thus, women of color felt a greater responsibility to advocate for the interests of their poor minority women constituents than did men of color and white women (see also Barrett 1995; Reingold and Smith 2012; Garcia Bedolla, Tate, and Wong 2014). Similarly, Dodson (2006) finds that when Bill Clinton became president in 1992, abortion rights supporters hoped to achieve legislative victories after 12 years of Republican control of the presidency. She notes that white women focused their attention on the Freedom of Choice Act, a bill that would codify the right to abortion granted by *Roe v. Wade*. By contrast, women of color were more committed than white women to overturning the Hyde Amendment, which prevents federal Medicaid dollars from being used to fund abortions. These women placed a priority on facilitating access to abortion services for their poor and often racial minority constituents rather than codifying the abstract right. This advocacy for affordable reproductive health care for women of color continues. When Democrats took control of the House in the 2018 elections, Barbara Lee (D-CA) announced that she would be re-introducing a bill to guarantee coverage of abortion services in federal health insurance programs like Medicaid (Gomez 2018).

Interviewing women serving in the 114th Congress (2015–2017), Dittmar et al. (2018) found that women of color had agendas that were much broader than those of white women and their policy priorities were more focused on addressing the needs of women of color. For example, African American women pointed to the importance of criminal justice reform noting it is their children being killed and their sons and daughters being incarcerated, while Latina women expressed their deep anxiety about family separations and a desire to address the particular challenges faced by women and children in immigration policy debates (Dittmar et al. 2018). As more women from diverse backgrounds are elected to Congress and the state legislatures, researchers will continue to examine how the overlapping identities of race and gender influence members' policy priorities and the type of coalitions they build to support their initiatives.

Institutional Position

The ability of members to advocate for women's issues also depends on their position in the institution. Legislatures are hierarchical bodies in which an individual's power depends on his or her level of seniority, committee position, and status as a member of the majority or minority party. Regardless of the promises legislators make in campaigns, if they do not have a seat at the table where decisions are made, they cannot influence the content and shape of the legislation (Hall 1996; Swers 2002, 2013; Davidson et al. 2015).

Being a member of the majority party is one of the most important determinants of a member's influence. The majority party controls the agenda in Congress and the state legislatures. Majority party leaders determine what proposals will be included in bills and which bills will be considered on the floor. Majority party members chair the committees and determine what issues the committee will consider. In a study of women in the House of Representatives, Swers (2002) found that the legislative priorities of women were strongly affected by whether they were in the majority or the minority party. Thus, Republican women were more active on feminist issues when they were in the minority party. As minority party members, these women were only expected to vote in favor of the feminist bills that the Democratic majority brought to the floor. When they were in the majority, promoting feminist legislation meant going against the policy convictions of other majority party members and important interest groups that supported the party. In this situation, Republican women put more of their political capital at risk by supporting feminist causes as these causes were not likely to be taken up by the Republican majority.

Swers (2002) also found that congresswomen, both Democrats and Republicans, were more active on social welfare issues such as health care and education only when their party controlled the majority. This is because social welfare issues constitute a major fault line between the two parties. When their party controlled the majority, women had access to the legislative agenda and were more motivated to offer proposals on these issues because as majority party members they were now more likely to have an impact on the direction of policy in these areas (see also Dodson 2006).

In addition to majority party status, seniority and committee positions are important determinants of a legislator's influence within the institution. In the Congress and the state legislatures, members have the most influence over policies that fall under the jurisdiction of their committees. This is because most policies are first formulated in the committees. By holding hearings to draw attention to issues and drafting legislation, committee leaders and rank and file members decide what issues will be important and what policy ideas will get attention. (Hall 1996; Swers 2002, 2013).

With the election of more women to Congress and the state legislatures in the 1990s, women are now gaining the levels of seniority necessary to gain seats on the more prestigious committees such as those that control taxing and spending, and they are advancing to committee and subcommittee chairmanships. Women utilize their seats at these important policymaking tables to draw attention to how specific issues impact particular groups of women and to advocate for policies that address a variety of women's interests. After the 1992 election, when multiple women gained seats on the Appropriations Committee, these women banded together to advocate for more funding for women's health research and family planning services (Swers 2002; Norton 2002; Dodson 2006). When the Violence Against Women Act first passed Congress, female members on key committees made sure that the bill moved through the legislative process and did not get stalled at one of the many points in the process where bills are killed (Swers 2002; Dodson 2006).

In recent years, both Democratic and Republican women have leveraged their committee positions to bring attention to problems of sexual harassment and assault in schools, workplaces, and the military. For example, the presence of seven women on the Armed Services Committee and Kirsten Gillibrand's status as Personnel Subcommittee chair in the 113th Congress (2013–2014) gave these women the platform to aggressively pursue reforms of the military justice system (Henneberger 2014; Kaper 2014). The women pressed the committee chair to call a hearing with all of the heads of the branches of the military and pointedly questioned them about the prevalence of sexual assault within the military and the need for more proactive policies to deal with the issue and help victims. The activism of these women senators led to the adoption of policy changes and more active oversight of the military's reporting and enforcement practices (Whitlock 2013; Carlson 2013; Henneberger 2014; Kaper 2014)

In the wake of the #MeToo movement and with several prominent members of Congress facing accusations of sexual misconduct, female members from both parties called for action and helped draft legislation to overhaul the way Congress deals with incidents of sexual harassment in congressional offices. Female members with leadership posts on relevant committees, including Senate Rules Committee ranking member Amy Klobuchar (D-MN) and House Ethics Committee chair Susan Brooks (R-IN), played an active role in crafting new legislation along with other female members who had been congressional staffers including Barbara Comstock (R-VA) and Jackie Spier (D-CA). Spier even recounted her own experience being sexually harassed and assaulted when she was a staffer to bring more awareness and keep the pressure on colleagues to address the issue (Murphy 2018; Tully-McManus 2018).

As Democrats retake the House majority after the 2018 elections, Democratic women are set to take the gavel on multiple committees and subcommittees. Among the most influential will be Nita Lowey (D-NY) and Maxine Waters (D-CA). As chair of the Appropriations Committee, Lowey leads the panel that decides how much government money will be spent and for what priorities. With a polarized Congress and a divided government in which Republicans control the Senate and the presidency and Democrats control the House, most of the legislative action seen in Congress will revolve around the federal budget and government spending. Lowey is a longtime advocate of reproductive rights who will use her platform to push back on the Trump administration's efforts to roll back Obamacare's expansion of access to birth control and to defund Planned Parenthood and other family planning programs. Lowey has also worked very closely with the Republican ranking member Kay Granger (TX) on issues related to women and foreign policy. This is the first Congress that will feature two female leaders of the Appropriations Committee (Shutt 2018; Saint Louis 2018). Meanwhile, Maxine Waters will chair the Financial Services Committee, the committee that regulates the banking industry. Waters plans to focus on housing affordability and homelessness—issues that are especially important to communities of color that were hit particularly hard by the home mortgage crisis (Merle 2019).

Clearly, members who serve in the majority, hold seats on committees with jurisdiction over particular issues, and serve as chairs of committees and subcommittees hold important advantages in the legislative process. While Democratic women have steadily gained seniority since the early 1990s, the dearth of Republican women in Congress means that when Republicans hold the majority, which they have in a majority of congressional sessions since the late 1990s, women have very few seats at the policymaking table and a more limited influence on the policy agenda.

Gender, Race, and Institutional Norms

All institutions reflect the preferences and norms of the dominant group, and legislators who want to see their policy ideas enacted into law must understand and conform to the accepted rules and practices of the legislature. However, the standard operating procedures and accepted practices within legislatures are both raced and gendered (Acker 1992; Kenney 1996; Rosenthal 1998). The need to adapt to and negotiate these standards sets up additional hurdles for gaining acceptance within the institution (Duerst-Lahti 2002; Hawkesworth 2003). As a result of their underrepresentation and perceptions that it is more difficult for women to get elected, the women who win often feel they need to be more qualified and react to their minority status by trying to do more. Studies of legislative behavior indicate that in comparison to their male colleagues, female members of Congress secure more money in federal spending for their districts, they sponsor and cosponsor more bills, and they give more floor speeches to raise their visibility and draw attention to their policy priorities on a range of issues (Anzia and Berry 2011; Pearson and Dancey 2011b; Lazarus and Steigerwalt 2018). Lazarus and Steigerwalt (2018) argue that because women are more vulnerable electorally, in that they are more likely to draw challengers in their primaries and the general election and they are subject to more stereotyping about women's expertise, women members fashion legislative profiles that are more focused on reflecting constituent opinion. Looking to maximize their reelection chances, women devote more resources than male colleagues to communicating with constituents and being responsive to their needs by stationing more staff in the districts. They also seek out committee assignments that are most related to district needs and sponsor more bills related to constituent interests.

As in business, women legislators sometimes feel that despite having a seat at the table, they are marginalized, finding it more difficult to get their contributions and policy views heard. For example, Swers (2013) finds that staffers for female members felt that Democratic women senators had to work harder than ideologically similar male colleagues to prove themselves on defense issues and they believed that they were taken less seriously by Pentagon officials. Additionally, an analysis of senators' appearances on the major Sunday talk shows demonstrated that women needed to achieve leadership positions on defense-related committees and within the party before they were viewed as experts and invited to talk about defense issues on the Sunday shows. By contrast, credentials did not play as significant a role in the appearances by male senators. While male senators who led important committees dominated the Sunday talk shows, other male senators who had not achieved leadership positions on foreign policy were also invited to speak on defense issues (Swers 2007). Similarly, in their interviews with female members, Dittmar et al. (2018) report that many long serving women feel that the institution has changed for the better and women no longer face overt bias. However, these female members felt that women still have to work harder to prove themselves whereas male members are automatically considered experts and given deference.

Feelings of marginalization are particularly prevalent among women of color. Hawkesworth (2003) describes this experience as "race-gendering." Drawing on interviews with female members of Congress, she found that regardless of their level of seniority or committee leadership positions, women of color believed that their policy proposals were more likely to be ignored and their knowledge discounted by majority group members (both white men and women). In a case study of the passage of the welfare reform in the 1990s, Hawkesworth finds that despite the importance of the issue to their constituents, women of color were excluded from Democratic taskforces negotiating policy, and their efforts to combat negative views of welfare recipients as welfare queens were ignored (see Smooth 2008, for similar findings in state legislatures). Dittmar et al. (2018) demonstrate that feelings of marginalization persist among women of color as the women they interviewed in the 114th Congress (2015–2016) maintained that women of color are more likely to be challenged or face backlash from other members for speaking up. Uncovering the gender and race-based norms within a legislature is a very difficult task, but these norms have very real consequences for members' legislative power.

Critical Mass and Policy Influence

Given the gendered nature of institutions, it is possible that female legislators' desire to bring a distinctive point of view to policy deliberations and to advocate for legislation regarding women's interests depends on the number of other women in the legislature. To achieve their policy goals, legislators must build coalitions and find allies. Drawing on the theories of Rosabeth Moss Kanter (1977) concerning the impact of sex ratios on group behavior in corporate settings, scholars argue that when women constitute a small minority of legislators, they will be treated as tokens that represent their group, as symbols rather than as individuals. Feeling the pressure to conform to male norms, these women will not feel comfortable representing and advocating for the concerns of women. Once these women constitute a "critical mass," at least 20 to 30 percent, they will feel more comfortable pursuing policy preferences based on gender (see also chapter 8).

Research on state legislatures has found some evidence to support the idea that legislative activity on women's issues increases as the proportion of women in the legislature increases. However, there are no clear threshold effects. For example, in her study of bill sponsorship and passage in the Arizona legislature, Saint-Germain (1989) shows that women's activity on behalf of women's interests, such as health care and education, increased as the number of women in the legislature increased. Similarly, in a study of 12 state legislatures in the 1980s, Thomas (1994) found that in states where the proportion of women in the legislature reached 20 percent, women were more likely to give priority to bills concerning women, children, and families and were more successful in passing these bills into law. At the congressional level, MacDonald and O'Brien (2008) note that between 1973 and 2003, congresswomen sponsored more bills on feminist and social welfare issues as the proportion of women in the House increased.

The proportion of women in the legislature can also impact policy outcomes. In a study of abortion policy, Berkman and O'Connor (1993) found that committees that included greater numbers of Democratic women were most successful in blocking restrictive abortion laws such as requirements for parental consent. Reingold and Smith (2012) demonstrate that since the enactment of welfare reform, states with higher proportions of women of color in the legislature have developed less punitive welfare policies allowing more flexibility in eligibility and work requirements and providing more generous cash benefits.

Yet, other scholars have questioned the value of critical mass arguing that women behave more distinctively when they are few in number and feel the responsibility for representing their group. For example, Crowley (2004) found that in state legislatures with few women, the female members played a pivotal role in passing child support legislation. Bratton (2005) argues that legislators must build a policy niche. Women's issue bills provide a natural fit for women in heavily male-dominated legislatures and these women sponsored more women's issues legislation. However, when being a woman was not as distinctive and there were other women to share the burden, in some states sex differences in bill sponsorship diminished, as the legislature became more gender balanced. Examining sponsorship of black interest and women's interest bills, Bratton, Haynie, and Reingold (2006) note that women of color sponsored fewer women's interest bills as the overall number of women in the legislature increased. However, the proportion of racial minorities in the legislature did not impact their activism on black interest bills. This is likely due to the fact that both men and women are more likely to sponsor a women's interest bill than a black interest bill. Furthermore, across the ten state legislatures in their study, there were always more women's interest bills proposed than black interest bills.

Finally, focusing on critical mass ignores the legislator's position within the institution and the level of influence he or she wields. Therefore, Childs and Krook (2006) suggest that rather than looking at numbers of women, we should focus on the emergence of critical actors who build coalitions and mobilize support for policy change. These critical actors can be legislators with key committee or party leadership positions or individuals outside of the legislatures such as interest groups and social movement leaders (see also Dahlerup 2006; Grey 2006; Beckwith 2007).

Women in Leadership

Presence is only the first step to wielding power in the legislature. Members' length of service and their position in the institution impact their level of influence. Party leaders and committee chairs are the most powerful members of the legislature, wielding many formal and informal powers. Committee chairs craft the policy agenda for their committees, deciding which issues they want to highlight in hearings and drafting policy proposals (Hall 1996; Davidson et al. 2015). Party leaders set the legislative agenda for their chamber with an eye to expanding the electoral coalition of their party. They work to craft a message that will attract voters and serve as the major spokespersons for the party's platform in the media. The party leaders are also routinely involved in the final stages of negotiating policy with the president (or governor at the state level) (Rhode 1991; Davidson et al. 2015).

As women gain seniority and advance to leadership positions in their parties and on the committees, do they exhibit a different leadership style? Looking at committee chairs in state legislatures, male and female chairs exhibit different leadership styles, with women adopting more egalitarian leadership styles that value consensus and collaboration while men adopt more authoritative styles that emphasize competition and conflict (Kathlene 1994, 1995; Rosenthal 1997, 1998, 2000; Reingold 2000). However, Rosenthal (1998) notes that the female style of leadership is less prevalent in the legislatures that are more professionalized, meaning those that employ more staff, pay higher salaries, and meet over larger portions of the year. Thus, as more legislatures become professionalized, women may not continue expressing a different style of leadership. Rather than changing the institution, women may find that they need to adapt to the norms of the body to succeed.

In Congress, Volden et al. (2013) suggest that a consensus-oriented leadership style helps women build coalitions when they are in the minority party and these women are able to keep their bills alive through more stages of the legislative process. However, as Congress becomes more polarized, the ability to forge consensus is less valued and the parties work to sharpen the contrasts between them. As a result, Volden et al. (2013) find that in more recent years characterized by increased polarization, majority party women are less effective than men at pushing their bills through the legislative process and they compensate for this lack of success by introducing more legislation.

Indeed, the number of women in Congress increased most dramatically at the same time that Congress became more polarized, with Democrats becoming more uniformly liberal and Republicans more strongly conservative. It was in this atmosphere that Nancy Pelosi (D-CA) became the first woman to serve as Speaker of the House, a position she held from 2007 to 2010 and reclaimed when Democrats won the House majority in 2018. The election of Pelosi as Speaker of the House marks the first time a woman has become the leader of her party and the institution in either house of Congress (figure 7.9).

There is ample evidence that gender considerations influence Pelosi's leadership style. Pelosi speaks openly about the influence of her gender on her priorities. She often refers to herself as a mother of five and grandmother of nine. This mantra has a dual purpose, as she wants to send the message that the needs of women and children are a priority for her but she also wants to counteract efforts by her political opponents to paint her

When Nancy Pelosi (D-CA) became the first female Speaker of the House, she invited all the children in the audience to come up and touch the gavel. *Source*: Rich Lipski/The Washington Post/Getty Images.

as a San Francisco liberal whose policy views and values are outside the mainstream (Swers and Larson 2005; Rosenthal 2008; Sandalow 2008; Peters and Rosenthal 2010).

After the election of President Barack Obama, Pelosi renewed her commitment to issues related to women and children. She played a key role in the decision to pass the Lilly Ledbetter Fair Pay Act as the first piece of legislation passed into law in the 111th Congress (Halloran 2009). She also pushed through an expansion of the State Children's Health Insurance Program (SCHIP), which provides health insurance to low-income children whose family incomes are above the poverty threshold necessary to qualify for Medicaid (Pear 2009). Pelosi led the fight to pass President Obama's comprehensive health care reform bill. Many of the president's advisors and the Senate leader Harry Reid (D-NV) believed that the president should scale back his health plan in the face of fierce Republican opposition, but Pelosi pushed Obama to utilize his Democratic majority in Congress and pursue comprehensive reform. When abortion politics threatened to derail the final bill, Pelosi brokered a deal to resolve the concerns of pro-life Democrats while keeping the support of her pro-choice colleagues (Bzdek 2010).

While studies of women in leadership emphasize women's roles as consensus builders (Kathlene 1994; Rosenthal 1998), Pelosi clearly has a very partisan leadership style. She prefers to sharpen the Democratic Party's message and highlight its differences with the Republican Party (Swers and Larson 2005; Rosenthal 2008; Peters and Rosenthal 2010). Facing an even more polarized Washington with the election of President Trump, Pelosi began her second turn as Speaker of the House in the midst of the longest government shutdown in American history. Throughout the process Pelosi played hardball against the president refusing to give in to his demands to provide money to build a border wall and even disinviting him from giving the State of the Union address until after the government was reopened (Werner et al. 2019; McPherson 2019).

Pelosi is a prolific fundraiser and a favorite target of Republicans looking to highlight the wrongheaded policies of the Democrats. Her high negative ratings with the public, particularly Republican voters, and her long tenure as Democratic leader led some Democrats to try to derail her efforts to reclaim the Speaker's gavel after the 2018 election. Yet, through individual dealmaking, Pelosi managed to garner the necessary support to win the Speakership (Bade et al. 2018).

While reviled by Republicans, within the Democratic caucus, Pelosi is viewed as a consensus builder who tries to take care of the needs of the various factions of the Democratic caucus. Even as Pelosi's own ideological views are in line with the progressive wing of the caucus, she carefully consults with the more moderate and conservative Democrats, placing these members on key committees and as advisors within the leadership ranks (Swers and Larson 2005; Rosenthal 2008; Sandalow 2008; Peters and Rosenthal 2010). As one staffer noted, "Pelosi is a consensus builder; on liberal things she acts as a facilitator organizing and working behind the scenes but she does not act as the public face because she knows she has to take care of the whole caucus" (Swers and Larson 2005). With a large new freshman class and a much more racially and ethnically diverse caucus after the 2018 elections, Pelosi has had to find more ways to make room for new members at the leadership table and within committees. For example, when Barbara Lee (D-CA) lost her race to become conference chair her supporters complained that there would be no women of color at the leadership table after an election where women of color were key to the voting coalition that put Democrats back in the majority. In response, Pelosi created a new leadership position as a cochair of the party's Steering and Policy Committee which makes committee assignments (Caygle 2018).

Finally, Pelosi also uses her power as Speaker and party leader to elevate more women within committee leadership. Female Democrats were an important part of the coalition that helped elect Pelosi to leadership and she counts women, particularly members of the delegation of her home state of California, as some of her strongest supporters and advisors. She has worked to expand gender and racial diversity across the committees, appointing more women and minorities to serve on prestigious committees such as Appropriations and Ways and Means and expanding the number of committee and subcommittee chairs held by women and people of color (Swers and Larson 2005; Peters and Rosenthal 2010).

Despite Pelosi's success, few women have advanced to the highest ranks of leadership within the parties. Among House Republicans, women have not advanced beyond Conference Chair; three women, Deborah Pryce (OH), Cathy McMorris Rodgers (WA), and currently Liz Cheney (WY), have held this post which focuses on developing party messaging strategies. While women have chaired important committees in the Senate including Appropriations, Homeland Security and Government Affairs, Budget, and the Select Committee on Intelligence, no women have advanced to majority/minority leader or majority/minority whip, the highest ranks of party leadership in the Senate (Center for American Women and Politics 2018).

CONCLUSION

The halls of power in the nation's legislatures remain overwhelmingly male. Yet, women continue to increase their presence in state legislatures and Congress. Research on the impact of electing women to office supports many of the expectations regarding descriptive representation. Women do bring a different perspective to legislating that focuses more attention in the deliberative process on the needs of women, children, and families. The presence of women yields more policy proposals related to women's interests and shapes the nature of policy outcomes. Still, the policy decisions of an individual legislator are shaped by the political context in which he or she serves. In addition to reflecting the interests of their constituency, today's female legislators serve in a more partisan and polarized environment in which more women elected to office are Democrats. These Democratic women consider women's rights a priority and are eager to help their party reach out to women voters. Meanwhile, moderate Republicans are disappearing and a new generation of conservative women is slowly entering the field. Recent Republican activism to restrict abortion demonstrates that conservative women are taking leadership roles on that issue. However, it remains to be seen whether these conservative women will prioritize other women's issues from a socially conservative viewpoint or eschew these policies in favor of more traditional Republican priorities such as lowering taxes and cutting government spending.

Congress and the state legislatures are also becoming more diverse with more women of color entering the legislative arena. Even the US Senate, which had seen only two women of color elected in its history, became more diverse after the 2016 elections. Research on women of color indicates that they govern differently than white women and minority men as their multiple group memberships drive their legislative agenda.

Looking to the future, women are increasingly gaining seniority and advancing to leadership positions in their committees. Will these women wield their power differently exhibiting a more consensus-oriented leadership style and/or advancing more policy priorities based on their interpretation of women's interests? While Nancy Pelosi's advancement to Speaker of the House marked a historic crack in what Pelosi called "the marble ceiling" (Marcus 2007), it remains to be seen how having more women in the highest echelons of party leadership will impact the direction of policy and the tone of politics.

8

Women in the Executive Branch

As the Pentagon and Congress grapple with how to reduce sexual assault in the military, here's an idea that would transform and improve military culture: Recruit, retain and promote far more women to the upper ranks. (Anu Bhagwati, former Marine Corps Captain and Executive Director of Service Women's Action Network, 2013)

Sexual assault has been a serious problem in the US military for decades. In the spring of 2013, a few short months after Defense Secretary Leon Panetta opened most military combat positions to women, the Senate Armed Forces Committee dedicated high-profile hearings to the subject. At issue was a bill proposed by Senator Kirsten Gillibrand (D-NY) aimed at reforming the way the military investigates and prosecutes allegations of military sexual assault. Senator Gillibrand cited statistics from the Department of Defense that only one percent of alleged perpetrators were ever held accountable for their crimes. Witnesses before the committee offered numerous recommendations for fixing a broken system, such as supplying victims with lawyers and other advocates, using civilian courts to prosecute members of the military, and redirecting prevention efforts toward stopping perpetrators rather than counseling potential victims to avoid assault.

Yet, Captain Bhagwati offered a much more profound solution: change the culture of the military by adding more women. In her testimony before the committee, Ms. Bhagwati stressed the additional importance of having a critical mass of women, noting that a sea change in military culture was necessary and would only emerge when women constituted about 20 percent of military personnel, offering that only then could we expect to see "climates start to shift when it comes to discrimination, harassment, and assault" (United States. Congress. Senate. Committee on Armed Services 2013). Women today hold more than 16 percent of all military positions, but their share has remained virtually unchanged for the last 10 years, suggesting that reaching critical mass will take many years (Reynolds and Shendruk 2018; Women's Research and Education Institute 2013).

Captain Bhagwati offered very similar solutions four years earlier when lamenting the quality of health care provided to female veterans seeking care in VA medical facilities. Testifying before a House Veterans Affairs Committee, Bhagwati argued that VA facilities would need to undergo "an enormous cultural shift" to recognize the specific medical needs of its female patients and to make strides in treating female patients with greater dignity and respect (United States. Congress. House. Committee on Veterans' Affairs 2009). In a similar fashion, she emphasized how increasing the number of women in key health-care positions would improve the quality of care provided to female veterans.

Captain Bhagwati's faith in the promise of increasing women's descriptive representation reflects three themes that we draw upon in this chapter. First, many feminist scholars argue that the executive branch of government is the most masculine of the three branches of government and that this masculinity privileges men and disadvantages women (Brown 1998; Chappell and Waylen 2013; Duerst-Lahti and Kelly 1995; Stivers 2002). Executive leaders are expected to demonstrate masculine traits such as assertiveness, decisiveness, and command. Feminist scholars argue that combined with gender role expectations about proper behavior for men and women, a preference for masculine leadership, or masculinism, creates significant barriers for women seeking to fit into and mold executive environments.

Second, and related to the first, women in the executive branch of government are particularly noticeable as "the other." Their small numbers, combined with individuals' greater visibility in hierarchical structures such as the executive, guarantee that they are outsiders in a man's world and must navigate multiple pressures associated with being perceived as tokens by dominants in the organization. For women of color, these pressures are often even greater: their status as racial and gender outsiders makes them especially visible. As Bhagwati and Rosabeth Moss Kanter (1977) contend, such pressures diminish only when groups in the minority reach critical mass status within an organization and when they are no longer such a visible minority among leadership.

Finally, despite these gendered challenges, female executives and public servants can and often do make a difference for women in their organizations and the larger population. Indeed, Bhagwati's belief that increasing the numbers of women in leadership positions will make the military and veterans' medical facilities more responsive to female service members is borne out by much contemporary research in the field of representative bureaucracy.

This chapter examines women's contributions to governance within the executive branch of government. After sketching out women's descriptive representation in executive positions, we frame our discussion of substantive representation around the three themes highlighted above: Does policy look different, or is it more likely to consider the multitude of women's perspectives, when women wield executive branch positions? Do masculinism and tokenism work against women's inclinations to speak out or even recognize the ways in which policy differentially impacts women, constraining efforts to provide true responsiveness to the female citizenry? Will women at the helm of the executive branch lead differently than men, or has history created cultural norms and expectations that demand a particularly masculine type of leadership in these types of positions?

WOMEN'S ACCESS TO THE EXECUTIVE BRANCH

Masculinity, Power, and the Executive Branch

Captain Bhagwati's faith in the power of greater numbers of women in leadership ranks reminds us that the actions of public servants can make a real difference in the lives of the citizenry. These people rarely appear in the spotlight, but nonetheless play important roles in shaping government responsiveness to reflect public desires. Often referred to as the fourth branch of government, the executive branch is staffed by a multitude of individuals who serve alongside the president and state governors. Who are these executive branch individuals? How well have women fared in breaking into the ranks of the executive branch? What can we learn about women's symbolic and descriptive representation by focusing on the executive branch?

As discussed in chapter 4, women lag far behind men in terms of putting themselves forward as candidates for elected office, with the effect that women are underrepresented in the vast majority of elected offices. But in the executive branch, typically it is only those at the very top of the hierarchy, such as presidents and governors, who achieve their positions through elections. The majority of executive branch officials receive their positions through presidential or gubernatorial appointment or civil service merit-based systems. Even so, women remain underrepresented in most high-ranking executive branch positions. Why?

Many feminist scholars point to *gender power* or *masculinism* to explain the paucity of women at the top (Duerst-Lahti and Kelly 1995; King 1995; Stivers 2002). Masculinism is a system of formal and informal power arrangements that privilege masculine character traits, customs, and operating procedures above feminine ones. The presidency is a particularly good example of gender power at work. Since only men have been presidents in the United States, they have essentially defined what it means to be president. Donald Trump not so subtly invoked masculinism in his presidential campaign, criticizing Hillary Clinton for not having that "presidential look" and attacking Republican candidate Carly Fiorina's appearance, asking "Can you imagine that, the face of our next president?" (Heldman, Conroy, and Ackerman 2018). He could do so because women seeking the presidency will always be "the other" and judged by the masculine standards established by their male predecessors. Women entering such masculine domains do not have the liberty to change the rules of the game, but rather must go along to get along. The American populace expects the president to be assertive, commanding, and tough and will likely judge all future presidents, male and female, by these standards.

Most feminist writers have further argued that masculinism is especially prevalent in hierarchical organizations, with the consequence that females working in hierarchical organizations such as the executive branch have to manage their femaleness to succeed, whereas men face no comparable challenge. Because their femaleness sets them apart, they risk being punished if they do not abide by the gendered standards and norms of their organizations. For example, the Department of Defense has an environment particularly imbued with the masculine values of discipline, order, and hierarchy. Cynthia Enloe (1983) argues that women entering masculine domains such as the military are constantly reminded of their outsider status such that "women may serve the military, but they can never be permitted to *be* the military" (15). The military has relied on women for years, as nurses, military wives, civilian workers, soldiers, and prostitutes but has kept them on the periphery to preserve the essentially masculine nature of the military. According to Enloe, such a sexual division of labor is a mechanism for keeping women marginal to the core masculine identity of the military. Sexual harassment and assault of female members serve a similar purpose, reminding women that they are interlopers into a masculine environment where men have always set the standards for behavior and have no interest in relinquishing this power. Sharon Mastracci and Lauren Bowman (2015), in their analysis of gendered public organizations, argue that such behavior is typical, that "organizational norms and practices are rooted in those of their founders, who in older public organizations were almost exclusively male, and those structures are resistant to change" (866).

Women's difficulties in reaching the high-ranking and influential positions in the executive branch have been studied extensively by public administration scholars, who employ two metaphors to illustrate women's career advancement struggles: glass ceilings and glass walls. As the name glass ceiling suggests, the higher up the hierarchy one goes, the fewer women one finds. Popularized in the 1990s to explain why few women were serving as CEOs in corporate boardrooms and in top government positions, the glass ceiling metaphor suggests that women can rise only so high in organizations before an invisible barrier precludes further advancement. Glass walls, on the other hand, keep women segregated in particularly feminine occupations or within agencies whose functions are most consistent with feminine gender stereotypes such as health care and education and underrepresented in agencies with masculine foci such as defense, foreign affairs, and law enforcement (Duerst-Lahti and Kelly 1995). If all agencies and positions were equally powerful, such occupational sorting would cause little concern. But according to Meredith Newman (1995), these patterns result in female administrators being placed in relatively less powerful positions that afford less influence and discretion on the job than afforded to their male colleagues.

Hillary Clinton famously drew on the glass ceiling metaphor in her 2008 bid for the Democratic nomination, quipping that "although we weren't able to shatter that highest, hardest glass ceiling this time . . . it's got about 18 million cracks in it" (Milbank 2008). She was speaking as the most formidable female presidential candidate in the history of the United States, coming closer to the office of the presidency than had any woman before her (see also chapter 5). Eight years later, Barack Obama heaped high praise on Clinton during his convention speech, arguing "there has never been a man or a woman . . . more qualified than Hillary Clinton to serve as president of the United States of America." Yet despite winning the popular vote, she suffered defeat at the hands of a man with zero political experience who regularly claimed that he alone could solve America's problems. For all of the women who have ever been skipped over for a promotion only to see a less qualified man rise to the position, the glass ceiling metaphor rang all too true. Clinton's status as one of the most experienced politicians in America, however, did not protect her from the obstacles faced by many other women banging up against the glass ceiling, such as subtle discrimination as well as gendered stereotypes about her capacity to lead (see also chapter 5).

Despite women's historic omission from the US presidency, a growing number of women are building executive experience in other venues, including governors' mansions, presidential and gubernatorial administrations, and state and local governments. We turn now to women's descriptive representation in these domains.

Descriptive Representation
Governors
Female descriptive representation in the governor's mansions has never exceeded 18 percent, or nine out of 50 governorships. Despite women's historic gains in 2018, the number of female governors has essentially plateaued at nine, a number reached in 2004, 2007, and then again in 2019. In the history of the United States, a total of 44 women have served as their states'

governors, with Democratic women enjoying a slight historic advantage. Yet, only 60 percent of the states have ever elected a female head of state (see figure 8.1). Women of color were entirely absent from governors' mansions until 2010, when two Republican women made history by becoming the first female governors in their respective states as well as the first two women of color to win governors' seats in the history of the United States. Susana Martinez became the first Latina governor in the country when New Mexico overwhelmingly chose her over her male opponent and Nikki Haley became the first Asian American woman to lead a state when elected in the same year by the voters of South Carolina. In 2018, Michelle Lujan Grisham succeeded Martinez to become the nation's second Latina governor and first Democratic woman to hold the position (Center for American Women and Politics 2019b).

Ten different states have sent more than one woman to the governor's mansion. A girl born in Arizona in 1997 might erroneously conclude that female governors were the norm as three different female governors ruled

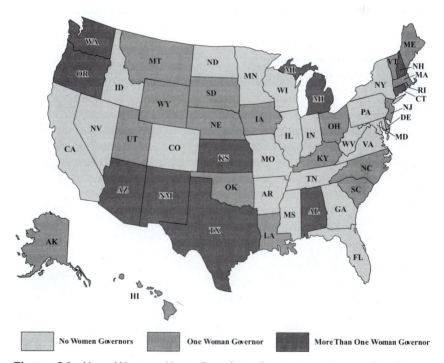

No Women Governors **One Woman Governor** **More Than One Woman Governor**

Figure 8.1 How Women Have Fared as Governors Across the States, 1925–2019

Source: Data accessed from Center for American Women and Politics, State Fact Sheets. Accessed online at http://www.cawp.rutgers.edu/fast_facts/resources/state_fact_sheet.php.

the state of Arizona for 18 consecutive years from 1997 to 2015. And until Grisham's victory in New Mexico in 2018, no other state had ever elected sequential female governors (Center for American Women and Politics 2019c).

Women are clearly faring better in reaching top political positions in the states compared to their failed attempts at the US presidency, yet still lag behind their sisters in the legislative and judicial branches of government, where women constitute closer to 25 percent of positions (see chapters 7 and 9). What accounts for this difference? Consistent with masculinism discussed earlier, some scholarship suggests that women seeking executive positions have greater difficulty convincing the public they are cut out for the job. The general public typically assumes that women's stereotypical strengths are better suited for legislative arenas than executive positions (Rosenwasser and Dean 1989). When the public thinks of a successful executive, it typically lists qualities such as strength, aggression, decisiveness, and the ability to get things done. But the same public typically gives women credit for being compassionate, sensitive, and cooperative (Huddy and Terkildsen 1993; Kahn 1996).

New Mexico Gov. Susana Martinez and US Rep. Michelle Lujan during a meeting at the State Capitol in Santa Fe, N.M., on Friday, November 9, 2018. Martinez, a Republican and the state's first female governor, served two consecutive terms. Lujan Grisham, a Democrat, took office January 1, 2019. *Source*: Associated Press / Craig Fritz.

Consistent with this explanation, the first three female governors in the United States were not originally elected to their posts but gained their positions when their husbands could no longer serve. The very first woman to hold this position was Nellie Tayloe Ross, a Democrat from Wyoming. Her husband fell ill and died while serving as governor, prompting the Wyoming Democratic Party to ask Ross to run in his stead. She was their unanimous choice and agreed to run to continue her husband's work. She won a special election to fill his seat by a margin of over 8,000 votes, no small feat for a state that was then, and continues to be, strongly Republican (Scharff 1995). Two years later, she lost her reelection bid to serve a second term. In retrospect, she lamented that she should have done more to court the women's vote. Wyoming became the first territory in the country to grant full female suffrage (in 1869), but Ross explained that she was wary of making her gender a focus of the campaign and did little to reach out to women's organizations (Scharff 1995). As we discuss later in the chapter, executive women are often reluctant to place too great an emphasis on gender, worrying that doing so will only remind others of their status as outsiders playing a man's game.

Texas elected Miriam "Ma" Ferguson in the same electoral cycle in 1924, but Nellie Ross enjoys the distinction of being the very first female governor in the United States because she was inaugurated some 15 days before Mrs. Ferguson. Ferguson succeeded her husband Governor Jim Ferguson when he was prohibited from running for his old seat because he had been impeached, convicted, and removed from office for corruption. Ironically, the Fergusons were opposed to female suffrage on the grounds that women's greatest contributions to society were in the home. Accordingly, the candidacy of "Ma" Ferguson emphasized her virtues as a feminine, traditional woman, as someone who would largely serve as a stand-in while Jim Ferguson ran the show behind the scenes (Sallee 1996).

Lurleen Burns Wallace became the third female governor almost 40 years later. Again, her husband preceded her in office and she ran to take his place because Alabama state law prohibited him from serving two consecutive terms as governor. In a strange twist of fate, Lurleen Wallace was hospitalized with a cancerous tumor while in office and her husband effectively took over all her official responsibilities during and after the hospitalization (Stineman 1980).

What can we glean about women's representation in governors' offices, offices that often serve as a stepping-stone to the US presidency? These first three female governors were largely symbolic placeholders, not true power brokers who demonstrated women's rightful place in presiding over the states. Women have come a long way since they were expected to be stand-ins for their husbands. But the fact that so few females serve as governor at

THE FIRST WOMAN GOVERNOR
Wyoming's Governor
THE WOMAN WHO MADE GOOD

NELLIE TAYLOE ROSS

Businesslike—Able—Courageous. She Has Earned Re-election

Nellie Tayloe Ross became the first female governor in the United States in 1925 when she won a special election to succeed her deceased husband in office. *Source*: Nellie Tayloe Ross Collection, American Heritage Center, University of Wyoming.

any given time ensures that they remain highly visible and held up as symbols for all to see. When elected in 2010, South Carolina governor Nikki Haley was hailed as the "new face of the south" and many pundits suggested that her election symbolized a new Republican Party, more open and inclusive to women and racial minorities than ever before (Campo-Flores 2010). Across the country in New Mexico, Susana Martinez became the first Latina governor in the United States, and the Republican Party soon thereafter appointed her to cochair its "Future Majority Project" to recruit, train, and support more diverse candidates, focusing especially on Latinos and women (Republican State Leadership Committee n.d.; Sanbonmatsu 2013).

Presidential Cabinets
Soon after election day, one of the first orders of business for the president-elect is to begin assembling his or her administration. Each president has responsibility for appointing thousands of individuals to work in the executive branch assisting him or her in fulfilling the constitutional responsibility to "faithfully execute the laws of the Nation." According to the latest version of the Plum Book, the federal government's listing of the top policy-making positions in the federal government, approximately 9,000 federal

Appointed by Barack Obama in 2015, Loretta Lynch is the first African American woman to serve at US attorney general. *Source*: The U.S. Department of Justice.

appointments were available to President Trump after he was elected in 2016 (Committe on Homeland Security and Governmental Affairs 2016). Many of these positions are fairly routine: only about 1,000 of them actually require Senate confirmation (Garcia 1997) and most receive very little public attention.

The most highly publicized and scrutinized executive branch appointments go to the members of the president's cabinet, at minimum composed of the vice president and the heads of the 15 executive departments. Most presidents also bestow cabinet rank on a few additional positions, such as the White House chief of staff, the administrator of the Environmental Protection Agency, the director of the Office of Management and Budget, the chair of the Council of Economic Advisers, the US Trade Representative, and the US Ambassador to the United Nations.

Most presidents seek to improve upon the record of their predecessor when it comes to appointing women and minorities, if not by increasing their sheer numbers, then by making appointment "firsts" that increase the diversity of the federal service. These appointees often symbolize the president's responsiveness to all the people, showing that his administration will "look like America." In her analysis of presidential cabinets going back to Franklin Delano Roosevelt, MaryAnne Borrelli (2002) argues that presidents historically tapped women to serve in positions distant from the president's agenda with few opportunities to influence policy, more valuable for their symbolic than substantive impact.

Yet women's fortunes began improving under the Clinton administration. President Bill Clinton became the first president to appoint a woman to the inner cabinet, the most prestigious positions that consist of the heads of Treasury, State, Defense, and Justice. He selected Janet Reno as his attorney general, and his two successors, George W. Bush and Barack Obama, followed suit by appointing Condoleezza Rice and Hillary Clinton as their Secretaries of State. In addition, all three of these presidents appointed women of color to posts they had never held before, selected women for positions central to their policy agendas, and chose women with substantial backgrounds in their designated areas so that they would be able to hit the ground running (MaryAnne Borrelli 2010; Dolan 2012). For example, Barack Obama appointed Janet Yellen as the very first female head of the Federal Reserve System, arguably one of the most influential positions in the world, let alone in Washington. She came to the position with extensive experience in the financial sector, including previous stints as the chair of the Council of Economic Advisers and a board member of the Federal Reserve System (Mui 2014).

In contrast, Donald Trump appears willing to break ranks with his predecessors, nominating mostly white men to serve in his inner cabinet and placing women in positions relatively distant from his agenda. Despite his promises to serve as a president for all the people, Donald Trump's initial cabinet looked a lot more like himself than America. Especially noteworthy are the number of millionaires and billionaires with no government experience he has called to serve. One of these individuals is Secretary of Education, billionaire philanthropist Betsy DeVos. A strong proponent of private school vouchers who has no government experience, DeVos's nomination met with scathing opposition from the largest teachers' union in the country, who objected to her corporate approach and "cookie-cutter solutions" for improving public education (Markon, Costa, and Brown 2016; Berman 2018). Similarly, Wilbur Ross, the multi-millionaire Commerce Secretary appointed by Trump, was widely derided for his comments during the 2018–19 government shutdown. After some 800,000 federal workers went two weeks without pay, Ross expressed surprise that some of these individuals visited food banks and suggested that they should secure small loans to make ends meet. For federal workers living paycheck to paycheck, the idea that they would have access to the same financial tools as someone like himself was widely mocked as quintessentially out of touch (Miller 2019).

At this juncture, Donald Trump's record in terms of appointing women is a mixed bag. Although he has nominated fewer women to cabinet-level positions than did Barack Obama in either of his two terms, his selection of women for 26 percent of these positions is similar to the records of his three Republican presidential predecessors (see figure 8.2). Nor is Trump breaking new ground by appointing important "firsts" to his cabinet or by creating a particularly racially diverse cabinet. His selection of two women of color, Nikki Haley as Ambassador to the United Nations and Elaine Chao as Secretary of Transportation, places him on par with both Democratic and Republican presidents going back to Bill Clinton, at least in terms of numbers (see figure 8.2). Yet Chao made history as the first Asian American woman to serve in a presidential cabinet when George W. Bush tapped her to be his Secretary of Labor in 2001. The Department of Transportation has never been led by a woman of color, so Chao's appointment is an historic first in that sense. Nikki Haley, the first female governor of South Carolina and Trump's Ambassador to the UN from 2017 to 2019 follows in the footsteps of a number of other women in her role. Although she

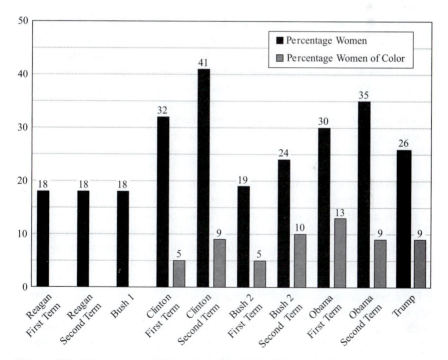

Figure 8.2   Women Appointed to Presidential Cabinets
Sources: Center for American Women and Politics. Accessed online at http://www.cawp.rutgers.edu/fast_facts/levels_of_office/documents/prescabinet.pdf. "PowerPost: Here Are the People Donald Trump Has Chosen for His Cabinet." 2017. Washington Post. Available at https://www.washingtonpost.com/graphics/politics/trump-administration-appointee-tracker/.

became the first Asian American woman in the position, President Obama made history by appointing Susan Rice, an African American woman, to the role during his first administration (Center for American Women and Politics 2018).

While glass ceilings do not appear to be keeping women out of the cabinet, at least in most recent presidential administrations, there is some evidence that glass walls remain. As of this writing, three cabinet departments have never been led by a woman: Defense, Treasury, and Veterans Affairs. Each is a highly masculine domain, supporting feminist scholars' contention that these types of departments are the least amenable to women's leadership. Women have cracked into the ranks below cabinet secretary, however. Barack Obama appointed Army veteran Tammy Duckworth to the position of Assistant Secretary for Veterans Affairs shortly after he assumed office in 2009 and appointed women to roughly one-third of the other available slots in the Department of Veterans' Affairs (data collected by authors).

Because most cabinet positions have now been held by women, perhaps gender power will be less problematic as presidential administrations become more and more gender integrated. As women prove their mettle in executive branch positions, they may begin to reshape dominant gender norms, shed the mantle of outsiders, and wield the levers of power like their male colleagues. Yet the masculinism inherent in Trump's key nominations should give us a pause; it reflects what many critics predicted during his campaign: that his vision for "making America great again" relies disproportionately on rich, white men holding the reins of power.

Career Civil Service/State and Local Bureaucracies

High-ranking positions such as presidential appointees receive a great deal of media attention but represent only the tip of the iceberg in terms of the sheer numbers of individuals working in the executive branch of government. The federal and state governments employ thousands more individuals through their civil service systems. These individuals, often referred to as bureaucrats or public administrators, are responsible for implementing government programs and delivering public services to American citizens. Michael Lipsky (2010) calls public-service workers who interact directly with citizens "street-level bureaucrats" and argues that they are important policy actors because "the discretionary actions of public employees are the benefits and sanctions of government programs and determine access to government rights and benefits."

At lower levels of the bureaucracy where jobs are much more plentiful, women tend to be very well represented. For example, women constitute 82 percent of the nurses working for Veterans' Affairs medical facilities and 81 percent of elementary and middle school teachers (Bureau of Labor

Statistics 2017; US OPM 2018). Yet, consistent with theories about gender power and patterns discussed earlier, women's access to state and local government positions remains uneven and shaped by glass ceilings and glass walls: women are least well represented at the highest rungs of these organizations and tend to have the greatest career success in agencies and departments focusing on women's issue areas.

To illustrate, we highlight two particularly gendered areas of public service in state and local bureaucracies: teaching and policing. Women are greatly overrepresented among the ranks of teachers, while men constitute a disproportionate share of the nation's police and firefighting forces. Consistent with gender stereotypes about the strengths of the sexes, men are called on to protect and serve, while women caretake and teach.

Kenneth Meier and Vicky Wilkins (2002) describe school districts as "classic glass ceiling organizations," noting that while women predominate at the lower levels, they have trouble reaching higher administrative posts. At the highest ranks, women constitute about 23 percent of school superintendents (Schmitz 2017), but their numbers are noticeably higher at lower levels of the hierarchy. Women recently achieved parity in principal positions, making up 52 percent of school principals in 2011 (Bitterman, Goldring, and Gray 2013), and they have always dominated the ranks of teachers by nearly a three-to-one margin over their male colleagues. But even so, gendered patterns of leadership persist. Male teachers are found disproportionately at the high school level while female teachers are disproportionately represented in elementary and middle schools (Bureau of Labor Statistics 2017).

Why are women not better represented at the top of this ostensibly feminine field? One national study of school superintendents found that women are not typically well positioned to become high-level education administrators, as few administrators come from the ranks of elementary school teachers, nor do they have as much experience in fiscal management as men—a stereotypically masculine criterion that boards of education increasingly consider when hiring superintendents (Glass 2000). Consistent with our previous discussion of glass walls, female superintendents also face discrimination in their fields as they are more likely to be assigned to work in less desirable locations and for lower pay than male superintendents (Wolverton 1999). One result of having so few women superintendents is that some often feel the need to distance themselves from their gender, as they must overcome perceptions from coworkers that they are somehow different or more emotional than male superintendents (Gardiner, Enomoto, and Grogan 2000). For these women, even in a female-dominated field, managing their femaleness in high-ranking positions remains a necessity.

Tammy Duckworth, assistant secretary of the US Department of Veterans Affairs arrives at the World War II Memorial in Washington for a ceremony honoring World War II veterans who fought in the Pacific. Duckworth lost her legs after her Blackhawk helicopter was shot down during a mission in Iraq and was awarded a purple heart for her service. President Obama appointed her assistant secretary in 2009, where she served until 2011. She was elected to the US House in 2012 and US Senate in 2016. *Source*: Associated Press / Cliff Owen.

Although the field of education is in many ways dominated by women, the same cannot be said for policing, where in 2017, women constitute less than 20 percent of all sworn law enforcement personnel in the United States (Weddell 2017). According to a 2010 study by the Department of Justice, women fared best in the largest police departments with more than 500 sworn personnel, of which 21 percent were female. By contrast, women comprised just 10 percent of personnel in small and rural police departments (Langton 2010).

At higher organizational levels, some argue that a "brass ceiling" exists that keeps women out of the top job of police chief. Of the 18,000 police departments across the United States, the Bureau of Justice Statistics reveals that less than 3 percent had female chiefs (Weddell 2017). Although progress is slow, women are breaking into the top law enforcement positions across the country. In 2018, female police commissioners, the majority of them women of color, led 12 different cities in the United States (Mirfendereksi et al. 2018).

The National Center for Women and Policing (NCWP) argues that the lack of female representation among police officers is due to a widespread gender bias in police hiring, which keeps the number of women officers artificially low. They believe that too much emphasis is placed on masculine characteristics such as physical prowess, keeping otherwise qualified women from serving (Lonsway et al. 2002). Yet, some changes underway offer a more welcoming environment for female recruits than in previous years. According to many, the policing field has begun to shift its emphasis away from a paramilitary structure in the wake of police brutality scandals to one that more prominently emphasizes more stereotypically feminine skills such as communication and community relations—a structure in which women officers can potentially excel ("Women Rise to Top Police Ranks in U.S. Cities" 2004). Studies show that women officers rely on a less physical style of policing and are better at de-escalating violent confrontations with citizens; they are particularly effective in dealing with domestic violence issues (Lonsway 2000).

Whether as presidential appointees, police officers, school teachers, or a myriad of other positions in public administration, women have the potential to influence public policy in many ways. Women have made great strides in terms of their overall representation in elected executive branch positions throughout American government, but still lag behind in many areas, particularly in leadership roles. Can they still make a substantive difference? We turn next to this question.

LINKING DESCRIPTIVE AND SUBSTANTIVE REPRESENTATION: DO WOMEN MAKE A DIFFERENCE?

The executive branch provides many pathways for enacting substantive representation. Executive branch officials shape policy outputs through agenda setting that enables them to place certain items on the agenda while keeping others off, as well as through their ability to decide how best to implement and enforce existing laws, rules, and regulations. But because most of these individuals are not elected, their responsiveness to the public is cause for concern.

Representative bureaucracy theorists offer a solution for keeping unelected bureaucrats accountable and responsive to the public: make the bureaucracy descriptively representative of the public. If the government is a true microcosm of the people it serves, the theory is that those in charge of making decisions will better reflect the wishes and demands of an increasingly diverse citizenry. The theory stresses that individuals' life experiences differ according to race, gender, sexual orientation, and, potentially, other characteristics. Such life experiences, in turn, shape their political attitudes and perspectives (Dolan and Rosenbloom 2003).

As chapter 3 discussed, women and men do have slightly different political attitudes, arguably shaped by their different life experiences in a gendered world. As bureaucrats exercising discretion to implement public policy, for example, making decisions about which motorists should be pulled over for traffic violations, which students should be assigned to gifted or remedial classes, and which small businesses should qualify for government loans, these life experiences and attitudes are thought to come to bear. If women's experiences differ from men's, the theory posits that women will bring different perspectives to the table and ultimately shape government outcomes to better reflect the experiences of women in their organizations as well as in the larger population. Captain Bhagwati's conviction that adding more women to the leadership ranks of the military would reduce sexual assaults nicely illustrates the logic of the theory: not only would women better understand the effects of sexual assault on women but would more likely devote time and energy toward fixing the problem.

Many executive women agree that women's presence in government changes policy processes and outcomes. When asked if they think women's presence in the federal government significantly changes the way policy is made, almost two-thirds of the female members of the Senior Executive Service (SES), the highest ranking members of the federal career service, agreed that it does. They were nearly three times more likely than their male colleagues to voice such sentiments (SOFE 1997). Former Vermont governor Madeline Kunin stresses that women bring something different to governing and that democracy is more legitimate with greater numbers of women sitting at the table:

> More women in public life may not immediately turn swords into plowshares, but women do bring a different and diverse set of life experiences to the process—and for democracy to be truly representative, it is only just that we [women] be equally represented. (Kunin 1987, 212)

Former Texas governor Ann Richards voiced a similar sentiment, noting that women tend to better understand the concerns and experiences of other women:

> The most sympathetic and sensitive of our men friends, no matter how hard he tries, cannot hear with a woman's ear or process information through a woman's experience. (quoted in Dow and Tonn 1993, 294)

As these examples suggest, women's presence brings new understandings and perspectives to bear on policy conversations and government actions. For men who have never experienced or been threatened by military sexual assault, it is unlikely that they will truly understand and appreciate the devastating effects it has on victims. Few male health-care providers will understand how the masculine environment of a VA medical facility affects women's comfort levels and their willingness to seek care as a woman might. As one female veteran apprehensive about seeking care in the VA explained, the VA "is a very, very anti-woman organization . . . the whole Veterans' Administration is geared to men, period" (Heikkila 2011, 127).

But understanding is only the first step. Does any evidence suggest that such attitudes and perspectives shape women's behavior in the executive branch? Do they ultimately serve as advocates or spokespersons for women? On these questions, the scholarship is mixed. In contrast with the wealth of studies on women's impact in the legislative and judicial branches, scholarship on executive women is more limited. A great deal of this literature focuses on the conditions that facilitate greater descriptive representation for women, but only a few demonstrate a link between descriptive and substantive representation. Much anecdotal evidence confirms that many executive women advocate on behalf of their female clientele, however.

Perhaps the most visible way in which female executives have left a unique impact on policy is through challenging some of the dominant values of public organizations, especially by making their organizations more attentive and responsive to women's often overlooked needs and perspectives. Former Reagan appointee Amoretta Hoeber reminded her male army colleagues that women and men in the military are not interchangeable. When the US Army was planning to purchase new combat boots for the troops, Hoeber noticed that the test group assembled to try out the new boots was composed entirely of men. She argued for including women in the group, emphasizing that women's feet are different than men's, and believes that including women in the group ultimately made a difference in the choice of boots (McGlen and Sarkees 1993). SES women are also significantly more likely than their male colleagues to consider the differential impact of policy decisions on women and men in their own work (SOFE 1997).

Pioneering women working for the Veterans Health Administration illustrate these perspectives at work. Two Florida VA hospitals, one in Bay Pines and another in Tampa, are often held up as exemplars in providing quality care to female veterans. According to VA official Connie LaRosa, female veterans deserve the credit for instigating significant changes at each. As she explains, change occurred in these facilities because "strong women Veterans . . . saw the need for other women Veterans to get the health care they themselves wanted from the VA" (Department of Veterans Affairs 2012). Three female nurses who served in the Vietnam War returned to work at the Bay Pines facility and were instrumental in reshaping the facility to better serve women: Joan Furey, the first Director of the Center for Women Veterans, Mary "Toni" Lawrie, a frequent witness at congressional hearings on women veterans health care, and Sara McVicker, a member of the Advisory Committee on Veterans Affairs. In the Tampa facility, Peggy Mikelonis spearheaded the opening of one of the nation's first Women's Health Centers in the VA. Despite her success, Mikelonis acknowledged the obstacles along the way, offering, "It's not easy building a women's program in a male-dominated system." As female veterans themselves, these women were acutely aware of the unique challenges women face in a male-dominated system and brought meaningful change to their facilities. In addition, both Lawrie and Mikelonis began hosting week-long training programs for other women working across the VA, providing guidance for establishing a women's program and getting their male colleagues to buy in to the changes (Department of Veterans Affairs 2012).

Additional evidence suggests that female executives use their positions to alter public policy to include previously excluded or marginalized women. Appointed as the first woman to head the National Institutes of Health (NIH), Director Bernadine Healy advocated women's health issues from the beginning of her tenure and launched a $625 million project to study breast cancer, osteoporosis, and heart disease in 160,000 women shortly after taking office. NIH funds clinical research studies to assess the efficacy of various medical treatments, but for years routinely excluded female patients from clinical trials. Consistent with the theory of masculinism, middle-aged men were considered the "normal" patient despite the obvious biological and physiological differences between the sexes, women's longer life expectancies, and their dissimilar responses to medical treatments. Healy presided over a shift in NIH policy, championing the importance of including the previously excluded half of the population in such important research studies (Glazer 1994).

From their seats in the inner cabinet, both Secretaries of State Hillary Clinton and Madeleine Albright prioritized women's rights during their tenure. Two months after taking office as the first female Secretary of State, Madeleine Albright instructed US diplomats to make women's rights central to American foreign policy (Lippman 1997). In her very first meeting with leaders from the Persian Gulf states, Albright led the charge herself, suggesting that women's rights be on the agenda for their next meeting (Gross 2003). Secretary of State Hillary Clinton similarly prioritized the needs of women and funded 67 programs across the globe to further the rights of women. She also appointed Melanne Verveer as special ambassador to shepherd efforts promoting the welfare of women (Calabresi 2011; The Economist 2012). In her 2016 presidential campaign, Clinton again stressed her commitment to women's rights and vowed to be a champion for those marginalized by the current economy, advocating, among other things, family-friendly policies that facilitate women's participation in the workforce (Gearan and Rucker 2015).

At lower levels of the hierarchy, additional findings corroborate that greater descriptive representation of women leads to substantive representation for women. In the female-dominated area of teaching, greater percentages of female school teachers and administrators are positively related to positive educational outcomes for female students (Keiser et al. 2002), suggesting that female staff use their discretion to improve the quality of the learning environment for their female students. Drawing from another feminine domain, the higher the percentage of female supervisors in child support enforcement offices, the greater the amount of child support dollars collected for female-headed families (Wilkins and Keiser 2006).

In a more masculine policy domain, Meier and Nicholson-Crotty (2006) find a positive relationship between the number of policewomen in a department and the number of rape reports and arrests for rape offenders. Using data from the 1990s, the authors estimate that increasing the numbers of women in police departments by around 5 percent would result in an almost 12 percent increase in the number of reported sexual assaults. But in another masculine domain, female farmers are no more likely to have their federal farm loans approved by Farmers Home Administration offices employing higher percentages of female loan officers than those with fewer female staff (Selden 1997).

In sum, the evidence suggests that having women in bureaucratic positions of power is oftentimes helpful to women in the population but is no guarantee that the diversity of women's voices will be heard or acted upon. Although representative bureaucracy scholars have made good faith efforts to untangle the ways in which female bureaucrats provide substantive representation for women in the population, the ways in which executive women do or do not provide substantive representation to American women remains unsettled. The masculinism of the executive branch often creates real obstacles for those who bring feminine viewpoints or values to the table, prompting many questions for future scholars: Is women's substantive representation more common in departments that are more heavily skewed toward "women's issues"? In departments that have a larger female clientele than others? Where there is an office dedicated to women's concerns? We are just beginning to tackle these questions to better understand whether descriptive and substantive representations are linked in the executive branch.

Challenges to Providing Substantive Representation

Over forty years ago, Rosabeth Moss Kanter (1977) highlighted the difficulties faced by demographic groups who are vastly outnumbered in an organization. She argues that when women or racial minorities are few and far between in an organization, or when they comprise 15 percent or less of the whole, they are regarded as tokens and face all sorts of performance pressures not experienced by dominants in the organization. These women are highly visible, their differences from men are exaggerated, and their behavior is often perceived as typical for all women. These performance pressures make it more difficult for them to carry out their jobs without having every action highly scrutinized for how well it fits the dominant values of the organization.

For executive women, the pressures of being a token are especially acute. For one, executive positions are often more highly visible than are legislative or judicial positions. Political executives usually sit at the apex of some hierarchy as the top official in charge of their respective organizations: head of the state, head of a large government department or agency, and so on. Such positioning is likely to invite increased attention and publicity for both men and women. But being a woman in such a position further heightens this attention. Positions such as governor, attorney general, and cabinet secretary tend to conjure up images of male politicians. When women achieve these positions, the public often has difficulties in reconciling their images of power with a female face. As Madeleine Kunin explains it,

> In conversation, when I was introduced, I noticed that people didn't hear the word "Governor" before my name. They smiled and nodded, as they would to anyone who had just joined the circle, and promptly resumed their conversation. They had not heard the word "Governor" because their eyes had not prepared them for it . . . men were governors and women were not. (1994, 349–50)

For women of color, these pressures are often even more acute. When Nikki Haley was running for the Republican Party nomination for South Carolina's open gubernatorial seat in 2010, a disgruntled fellow party member took a racist swipe at her Indian family's Sikh religious background by referring to her as a "raghead" and lamented that "people going into politics today are different than the people I always served with," not so subtly hinting that an outsider like Haley, a woman of color, was unqualified for the job. In a state with the lowest percentage of women serving in the state legislature and few elected officials of color, Haley clearly stood apart (Green 2011).

Like Haley, most high-ranking executive women are so visible that everything they do is subjected to heightened scrutiny. Because female politicians are anomalies, they cannot simply blend into the woodwork. Others are constantly watching their behavior to see if they behave as expected or contrary to stereotypical presumptions. Many political women attest to the increased attention their status as women in a man's world brings.

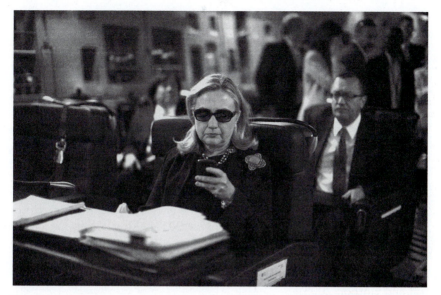

Then-Secretary of State Hillary Rodham Clinton checks her BlackBerry from a desk inside a C-17 military plane upon her departure from Malta, bound for Tripoli, Libya. It's a photo that became an Internet meme: Hillary Rodham Clinton, wearing sunglasses, staring at her BlackBerry. *Source*: Associated Press / Kevin Lamarque, Reuters Pool.

When Carla Anderson was undergoing Senate confirmation hearings after being nominated by President Ford as only the third woman ever to serve as a US cabinet secretary, Senator William Proxmire (D-WI) indirectly challenged her qualifications for the job, suggesting that gender sealed her nomination (Stineman 1980).

Such treatment is par for the course, according to MaryAnne Borrelli (2002), who argues that women nominees are often presumed less competent during Senate confirmation hearings than are men, a consequence of being judged by a "heroic man" standard. While male secretaries are routinely portrayed as heroic men who arrive ready to save the day, women are depicted as considerably less heroic and, consequently, as less capable of fulfilling their executive duties. Female cabinet nominees are often portrayed as possessing the same character traits as men do, but as exhibiting them only passively or failing to use them in a powerful fashion. Even though both male and female secretary nominees are described in newspaper coverage as "confident," only women are tagged as "unnervingly confident." While both male and female cabinet nominees often have families, only female nominees are faulted for "abandoning" them, while male nominees are praised for their sacrifice (Borrelli 2002). When the standard for success is so infused with masculinity, women have a difficult time proving their capacity to measure up.

In practice, heightened visibility often means that token women are presumed to speak and stand for all women. Many executive women have explained that they were cognizant of the fact that they would be held up as a standard by which all future executive women would be judged. The very first female governor, Nellie Tayloe Ross, remarked that if elected, she would conduct her administration so "that it might never be said that women were unfitted [sic] for executive office" (Scharff 1995, 93). Over 80 years later, Susana Martinez acknowledged the same pressures, adding that her status as a Latina invited additional scrutiny. "I'm often introduced as the first Latina governor. With that comes an enormous responsibility," she says. "Those little girls watching me have to see me deliver my promises" (*The Economist* 2011). After losing her bid to be the first female vice president in the United States, Geraldine Ferraro voiced a similar sentiment: "It is a sorry fact in this country that the defeat of one woman is often read as a judgment on all women" (quoted in Watson and Gordon 2003).

According to Kanter (1977), token individuals sometimes take special pains to demonstrate they have adopted the dominant values of the organization, and one way of exhibiting such loyalty is by avoiding any actions that appear to benefit their own social group. As Kanter explains, sometimes "the price of being 'one of the boys' is a willingness to occasionally turn against the girls" (79). In their analysis of high-ranking women working for the Department of Defense, Nancy McGlen and Meredith Reid Sarkees (1993) find evidence of such behavior. Women who have risen above the glass ceiling at defense differ very little from their male colleagues when asked about their policy attitudes, but they do evince more conservative ideology than their male colleagues. McGlen and Sarkees (1993) surmise that Defense women are highly conscious of their minority status within the organization and adjust their attitudes to better align with the strongly conservative culture of the department. Dolan (2002) finds corroborating evidence among senior executive women at Defense, showing that they align quite closely with their male colleagues when it comes to attitudes about gendered policy issues such as sexual harassment. Although the majority of male and female senior executives in the Defense Department agree that more should be done to combat sexual harassment in the federal government, greater numbers of *men* than women hold such opinions. In addition, women at Defense are somewhat *less* likely to consider how their own decisions might differentially impact women than their male colleagues, which suggests that advocating for women in a highly masculine environment is fraught with difficulty (SOFE 1997).

Yet, when women achieve a critical mass within an organization, token pressures typically dissipate—dominants can no longer assume that any one woman stands for all women, and women consequently feel less constrained in their own actions. As Captain Bhagwati's comments at the beginning of this chapter suggest, the military culture will not likely change until women achieve a critical mass. Whether women will feel more comfortable looking out for other women or men will become more sensitized to female service members' needs is not entirely clear, but the evidence suggests that critical mass is important. For example, Dolan (2000) finds that senior executive women are more likely to show support for a variety of gendered policy initiatives when they work for agencies and departments where women wield a critical mass of leadership positions. Similarly, women working in these types of agencies are more likely to consider how their policy decisions affect women and to agree that women's presence in government changes policymaking. When men work with greater numbers of influential women, they also agree that policymaking changes. Yet, these men are no more likely than men working elsewhere in the federal government to consider how their own policymaking decisions differentially affects women and men (SOFE 1997). These findings suggest, at least provisionally, that women who rise above the glass ceiling in organizations such as the Department of Defense will bear a disproportionate burden in advocating for women.

Even though women continue to increase their numbers across all branches of government, simply having a seat at the table is no guarantee that their voices and perspectives will be heard. Perhaps recognizing their status as outsiders, some argue that women develop distinct and feminine leadership styles or even eschew adopting an advocacy role for other women. If women are greatly outnumbered and perceive that their minority status has negative implications concerning their ability to get the job done, do they try to open up the process for other outsiders? Take special pains to include others who might have previously been excluded? Employ power-to rather than power-over leadership?

Power and Leadership Style

Hillary Clinton's tenure as Secretary of State was evaluated in an article published in *Foreign Affairs*, a leading foreign policy magazine. In the article, author Michael Hirsh characterized Clinton's approach as one of "soft power." As Hirsh (2013) explained,

> Her most lasting legacy will likely be the way that she thrust soft diplomacy to the forefront of U.S. foreign policy. . . . She set out to create . . . a new kind of people-to-people diplomacy, one designed to extend Washington's influence in

an Internet-driven world in which popular uprisings, such as the Arab Spring, could quickly uproot the traditional relationships between governments.

A *Time* magazine article similarly highlighted Clinton's strengths in mending broken relationships with other countries, arguing that her efforts to build deeper relationships and boost cooperation with nongovernmental organizations had won praise from Democrats and Republicans alike (Calabresi 2011). A great deal of scholarship suggests that Clinton's approach is typical, that many female leaders employ feminine styles of leadership that emphasize consensus, collaboration, and empowerment rather than masculine or "power over" leadership that stresses competition, command, and control, an emphasis on individual accomplishment, and hierarchy (Eagly and Johnson 1990; Jalalzai 2013).

One study of male and female governors finds that women are more likely than men to express an empowerment motivation in their positions (Barth and Ferguson 2002). Similarly, various scholars studying the rhetoric of former governor Ann Richards conclude that her speaking style and rhetoric were very much geared toward empowering others, especially women (Dow and Tonn 1993; Kaml 2000). According to these scholars, Richards used public speaking occasions to draw connections with her audience, to encourage them to connect their experiences as average citizens with hers, and to draw on their own instincts in judging politicians and the political process. They characterize her rhetoric as particularly feminine because she focuses on empowering others rather than boosting her own profile.

Former Secretary of State Madeleine Albright similarly suggests that consensus comes more easily for women and that women have a more difficult time with confrontation, but she acknowledges that the job sometimes necessitates as much.

> Men are capable of having strong personal disagreements or arguments about a subject and then walk out of a room and go and play golf or have a drink or something. And I think women do take it more personally. And I don't think we like to have face-to-face confrontations, but I sure learned that it was essential to state my views very clearly and not care whether I was liked or not. And it took me a while to learn it. But I think others will testify to the fact that I did learn it. (Gross 2003)

Other evidence suggests that many female governors adopt a consensus style of leadership (Kunin 1994; Barbara Lee Family Foundation 2001). Former New Jersey governor Christine Todd Whitman's speeches are peppered with references to government decision-making being an open process, based on consensus (Sheeler 2000). She credits her style to growing up on a farm, where people need to work cooperatively to get things done and points out that others criticize her for too much consensus building (Beard

1996). Former Republican governor Jane Dee Hull agrees that consensus is part of women's repertoire more often than it is for men: "Women tend to want to put people around the table and talk. Men order things, like ordering dinner" (Clift and Brazaitis 2000, 283).

But not all executive women lead by consensus. Research on women and men in state government executive positions finds that women do not necessarily have any special claims to using consensus-based leadership styles (Duerst-Lahti and Kelly 1995). While serving as Secretary of State under George W. Bush, Condoleezza Rice explained that her approach was more hierarchical than consensus based:

> Nor do I believe you can do everything by consensus. At the Pentagon, I learned that if you seek consensus you get a third of a tank, a third of a plane, and a third of an aircraft carrier. If you don't drive the process from the top, you get across-the-board cuts and everyone gets weaker. (quoted in Dowd 2000, 102)

Perhaps Rice's position reflects a fundamental difference between the Democratic and Republican parties, with the Republican Party placing a higher value on hierarchy whereas Democrats lean more heavily toward a consensual approach (Freeman 1986). As many other chapters in the book confirm, we are just beginning to better understand the ways in which political party shapes political women's approaches to campaigning and legislating. Whether political party similarly shapes their overall leadership style is a question for future scholars.

CONCLUSION

As this chapter demonstrates, women have made great strides in terms of their overall representation in executive branch positions throughout American government. With the exception of the Trump administration, the numbers of women in presidential cabinets have generally increased with each successive president who takes office; women of color continue breaking new ground in cabinets and governors' positions; and women continue to make inroads into masculine positions such as police chiefs and Secretary of Homeland Security. The evidence suggests that glass ceilings and glass walls persist but are showing signs of weakening.

Yet, many contemporary stories suggest that although women are gaining seats at the executive table, they are not yet fully fledged members of the club. As outsiders breaking into new territory, women are often cognizant that they are playing by someone else's rules. Because men have always been in charge, they have developed the rules, customs, and mores of the place. When women arrive, they cannot help but be reminded of the masculinism of the place—the executive branch is imbued with male power, male values, and men at the helm.

The evidence presented in this chapter suggests that there is often a link between descriptive and substantive representation such that women are more attentive to the needs and perspectives of other women than are their male colleagues in executive roles. On this score, Captain Bhagwati is on solid ground in suggesting that greater numbers of women in leadership will facilitate a culture change that is more attentive to the needs of its female service members. Yet, the highly masculine nature of the executive branch and the military, in particular, reminds us that women seeking to exercise influence in these domains face considerable constraints. They may avoid championing women's interests to avoid being defined by their gender or wait until a critical mass of women hold leadership positions before pressing for change. With the passage of time and with additional research, scholars will hopefully develop a more comprehensive understanding of when executive women are most likely to advocate for other women and whether some circumstances make substantive representation more likely than others.

9

Women in the Judiciary

◆ ◆ ◆

IN MAY 2009, President Barack Obama announced Judge Sonia Sotomayor to fill the Supreme Court vacancy left by retiring Justice David Souter—the first opportunity Obama had to replace a sitting justice upon his election in 2008. Sotomayor, a judge with 17 years' experience on the US appellate court and a Yale Law School grad, is not only the third woman to be appointed to the Supreme Court, but she is also the first Hispanic and has a compelling life story, having been raised by a widowed mother in public housing in the Bronx. Sotomayor graduated from Princeton University (on a full scholarship) summa cum laude in 1976, and after law school she worked as a prosecutor in New York City and in private practice before receiving her first judicial appointment by President George H. W. Bush in 1991.

Her selection did not elicit overwhelming support from Republican senators, many of whom expressed alarm at a speech that Sotomayor gave in 2001, as a sitting federal appellate judge, at the University of California at Berkeley's School of Law. In that speech, addressing the role that her background played in her jurisprudence, she remarked, "I would hope that a wise Latina woman with the richness of her experiences would more often than not reach a better conclusion than a white male who hasn't lived that life" (quoted in Savage 2009, 29). Sotomayor's 2001 comments challenged a sentiment that was often invoked by former Supreme Court Justice Sandra Day O'Connor—the first woman to be appointed to the Supreme Court in 1981—that "a wise old woman and a wise old man will reach the same conclusion." In her Berkeley Law School address, Sotomayor stated that she was unsure whether O'Connor was right in her statement, saying, "Whether born from experience or inherent physiological or cultural differences . . . our gender and national origins may and will make a difference in our judging."

Sotomayor's comments sparked much debate on both sides of the political aisle. Former Republican United States House Speaker Newt Gingrich

253

stated that Sotomayor's speech indicated that she was a "Latina woman racist," although he later backtracked from such language. Most conservatives expressed concern that the statement, combined with her previous ties with left-leaning Hispanic advocacy groups that actively promote affirmative action policies,* indicated that she would let her personal bias influence her judicial decision-making. President Barack Obama defended his nominee, arguing that, while she may have used a poor choice of words, "she was simply saying that her life experiences will give her information about the struggles and hardships that people are going through—that will make her a good judge" (quoted in Kirkpatrick 2009, A1). Sotomayor sought to diffuse the controversy over those specific words, saying in her testimony at the hearings for her confirmation that the words were "a rhetorical flourish that fell flat" and that they had been misinterpreted (quoted in Baker and Lewis 2009, A1). She said, "It was bad because it left an impression that life experiences command a result in a case. But that's clearly not what I do as a judge" (ibid.). Ultimately, Sotomayor won the confirmation and has successfully launched her career as a Supreme Court justice, but her 2001 comments, along with Sandra Day O'Connor's famous words, raise a fascinating question: To what extent should a judge's gender and background impact his or her decision-making?

This issue for Sotomayor once again emerged publicly in the aftermath of a 2014 Supreme Court decision, *Schuette v. Coalition to Defend Affirmative Action*. In a 6–2 decision, the court upheld Michigan's ban on affirmative action, which voters passed in a 2006 ballot initiative.† In a stinging dissent, Sotomayor used very personal language to dismiss the majority's decision that racial-based preferences perpetuate racial discrimination, calling on the Supreme Court to consider the "simple truth that race does matter." She writes,

> Race matters, in part, because of the long history of racial minorities being denied access to the political process. Race also matters because of persistent racial inequality in society—inequality that cannot be ignored and that has produced stark socioeconomic disparities. And race matters for reasons that really are only skin deep, that cannot be discussed in any other way, and that cannot be wished away. . . . Race matters because of the slights, the snickers, the silent judgments that reinforce the most crippling of thoughts: "I do not belong here."

Legal analysts, such as *Slate's* Dahlia Lithwick (2014), noted that Sotomayor's dissent painted a picture "that looks a lot like her own

---

*Affirmative action policies are designed to give preferential treatment to racial minorities in issues such as college admissions as a way to overcome past discrimination.
†Michigan voters passed the ban, which barred any preferential treatment for racial minorities in terms of admission to public colleges, hiring of government personnel, or the awarding of government contracts, by 58 percent of the vote. Justice Elena Kagan recused herself from the case, having worked on the case while she was Solicitor General serving in the Obama administration.

life." For instance, Joan Biskupic's biography of Sonia Sotomayor recounts how she once lodged a complaint against a partner in the Washington law firm where she worked for telling colleagues and prospective hires that Sotomayor was only admitted to Yale Law School because she was Latina (Biskupic 2014). Storied liberal publications such as *The New Yorker* and *The New Republic* described her *Schuette* dissent as eloquent and courageous. It is precisely because of Sonia Sotomayor's passionate rebuttal of attacks on affirmative action, drawing from a unique perspective as a woman of color and employing "practical language"—dubbed by *New Republic*'s legal analyst David Fontana (2014) as the "Sotomayor Style"—that her supporters believe Sotomayor to be the ideal person to talk about fairness and equality under the law.

Yet, conservative critics used extremely pointed language to express their disapproval of Sotomayor's dissent in *Schuette*. The *National Review* wrote that Sotomayor's opinion was "illiterate and logically indefensible," adding "the still-young career of this self-described 'wise Latina' on the Supreme Court already offers a case study in the moral and legal corrosion that inevitably results from elevating ethnic-identity politics over the law" (*National Review* 2014). Steve Hayes of *The Weekly Standard* described Sotomayor's dissent on a Fox News panel as "a decision written by somebody who was writing about emotion," language that feminist critic Marcie Bianco argues is often used as code to discredit or marginalize women and minorities (Bianco 2014).

The fallout after the *Schuette* decision once again brings up fundamental questions about the nature of representation and politics. Recall Sandra Day O'Connor's statement that she believes that wise women and wise men serving as judges will make similar decisions. Sotomayor, however, has taken a different stance, arguing that her experiences, as both a woman and a Latina, while not totally dictating her jurisprudence, do play a part in her decision-making.

That two such prominent women who have reached the pinnacle of the legal profession hold differing perspectives on the role that one's sex or ethnicity should play in judicial decision-making reminds us that elite political women are far from monolithic on the question of substantive representation. Interestingly, however, O'Connor has been outspoken in her advocacy for having more women serve as judges, despite her belief that a judge's gender will not affect the quality of decisions, saying that "there are cases where our experience as women might bring some perspective to the situation before the court" (quoted in Blackburn 2010). Of course, this begs a fundamental question: Does the behavior of women jurists differ from that of male jurists? Do women judges make different decisions than their male counterparts in certain areas of the law that

In May 2009, President Barack Obama nominated Sonia Sotomayor, the third woman—and first Latina—to serve on the US Supreme Court. *Source*: Associated Press / Alex Brandon.

have particular relevance for women, such as sex discrimination? Does gender actually make a difference on the bench? Would we even want such personal qualities to impact decision-making on the bench, given that the American legal system, as many legal scholars maintain, is built upon precedent and objectivity?

Before examining the scholarly literature that considers how (or if) gender affects judicial decision-making, this chapter takes a look at the number of women currently serving as judges nationwide, with a nod to the history of women in the judiciary. Before discussing women's roles as judges, however, this chapter briefly examines the role of the courts in American politics, considering how gender may potentially impact this branch of government.

WHY THE COURTS ARE IMPORTANT

Although different than the legislative and executive branches, the courts hold an important place in our political system. The judiciary handles a variety of disputes between two parties—whether those parties are private citizens or the government, or the dispute under question is civil or criminal in nature. One result is that the courts play a significant role in the lives of everyday Americans, as they provide one of the most frequent contacts between people and their governments, particularly at the state and local levels.

Verdicts made by the courts, especially when one of the parties involved is the government, can also have important political and policy ramifications. Nowhere is this more evident than at the United States Supreme Court. The job of the Supreme Court is to maintain national supremacy in the law by ensuring uniformity in the interpretation of national laws. One way that it does so is by examining the constitutionality of acts of Congress or, more frequently, state legislation. For example, if a state legislature passes a law that places certain limits on a woman's ability to obtain an abortion, the United States Supreme Court may decide to hear challenges to the law to decide if it violates liberties or guarantees provided in the United States Constitution. However, few such challenges make it all of the way to the Supreme Court and, as a result, the lower federal courts and state supreme courts have also come to play an important role in determining public policy.

In recognition of the increasing role of courts in policymaking, interest groups and citizens often turn to the courts—both federal and state—when the legislative process is not accessible or does not produce desired results. In that vein, the courts are often viewed as the institutions that protect the rights of minorities. Women have turned to the courts to expand their rights (O'Connor 1980). For example, in the late 1960s and 1970s, Congress passed several pieces of legislation that banned sex discrimination in the workplace and in higher education. Given that determining what constitutes discriminatory behavior can be nebulous at times, various women (often with the backing of women's legal and political organizations) have brought their individual cases regarding discrimination before the courts. For example, in 2015, the Supreme Court expanded the rights of pregnant women facing employer discrimination in *Young v. United Postal Service*. Peggy Young, a former UPS truck driver, was placed on unpaid leave as a result of her high-risk pregnancy after doctors told her she could not lift packages of more than 20 pounds. Young had petitioned instead for lighter duty, which she argued had been given to other workers who became sick and required lighter job responsibilities (Liptak 2015). Young sued UPS under the 1978 Pregnancy Discrimination Act, which amended the Civil Rights Act to outlaw "discrimination on the basis of pregnancy, childbirth, or related medical conditions." Under the law, employers must treat women affected by pregnancy in the same manner as "employees who are similar in their ability or inability to work" (EEOC n.d.). While an appellate court had dismissed Young's lawsuit, claiming that UPS had also denied light duty requests from other temporarily disabled employees—in essence, claiming that their policy was "pregnancy-blind"—the Supreme Court disagreed, remanding Young's case back to the lower courts and giving her the chance to prove that UPS had, in fact, discriminated against her because of her pregnancy (Grossman and Brake 2015). Notably, UPS has since changed its policy to routinely allow lighter duty for pregnant workers (Liptak 2015).

While women and other minorities have often sought relief in the courts for their grievances, the judiciary is restricted in its ability to make policy compared with the legislative or executive branches. Unlike legislators or administrators, for example, judges cannot make decisions that will affect policy unless a case appears before them in their dockets. Judges are often circumscribed from such behavior by the norms of their profession because they are expected to be impartial and detached from the cases that they hear, relying on evidence in a case before making a decision. Judges are also constrained by the nature of law. As Martin and Pyle (2000) note: "The law itself, statutes and precedents, the facts of the case, the requirements of evidence, the possibility of being overturned on appeal, even the nature of the adversarial system, all restrict the freedom of judicial discretion" (1211).

Yet, many who study the courts also acknowledge that the act of adjudication is potentially influenced by the personal characteristics of judges. It is in this capacity that the gender of judges could potentially make a difference in judicial decision-making. As research in political science finds that women differ from men politically, both in terms of their activism and their attitudes, many political observers believe that women judges may also differ in important ways from men judges. Proponents of increasing the presence of women on the bench argue that it is only fair to have a judiciary that is made up of both men and women. They contend that recruiting representatives with more diverse backgrounds and experiences to the bench would result in a judiciary that would be a fairer institution—one that would more effectively use the talents of all citizens (Bratton and Spill 2002; Kenney 2013).

WOMEN IN THE JUDICIARY

In the early twentieth century, a few women were appointed to specialized courts with limited jurisdictions (Morrison 2002).* For example, Georgia Bullock served on the Los Angeles Women's Court, which began in 1914

---

*History records indicate that Esther Morris was the first woman to serve as a jurist, who in 1869 became a part-time justice of the peace in Wyoming at the South Pass Mining Camp (Hermann and Kelly 1988). In 1886, Carrie Burnham Kilgore (the first female graduate of the University of Pennsylvania Law School) was appointed a master in chancery (essentially, the administrative head of the court), making her the first woman to serve in a state judiciary (O'Connor 2000). The first elected woman judge was Catherine McCullough, who became a justice of the peace in Evanston, Illinois, in 1907 (Hermann and Kelly 1988).

(Cook 1993). The court was developed during the Progressive Era, with the idea being that such a specialized court would help "fallen" women to learn and conform to the cultural gender role norms of the day if they were given special and separate treatment from male defendants. Judge Bullock believed that it was her duty as a judge on this court to help rather than merely punish women for small offenses, in the hope of reclaiming such women to society. Moreover, it was a duty that she believed was specially required of women at the time, remarking at the end of her first session: "The salvation of women must be through women" (Cook 1993, 146). Bullock later parlayed her experience on the women's court, along with the many connections she had made with various women's organizations of the day, to an appointment as a municipal judge in California in 1926 and then won the election to the superior court in Los Angeles in 1932—a seat that she held for 25 years (Cook 1993).

The first woman appointed to the federal court was Florence Allen. After serving more than a decade on the Ohio State Supreme Court, Franklin Delano Roosevelt appointed her in 1934 to the Sixth Circuit court of appeals. Allen wrote in her memoirs that after her appointment was announced one of her male colleagues went to bed for two days (Ginsburg and Brill 1995). She quickly won her colleagues' admiration, however, with her conscientious work. The first woman to serve as a federal trial court judge was Burnita Shelton Matthews, appointed to the District Court for the District of Columbia by President Truman in 1949 (Green 1994). An active suffragist, Matthews attended classes at National University (now George Washington University) while working in the Veterans' Administration. Upon her graduation in 1920, she could not find work in any law firm, so she began her own practice in Washington, DC (Ginsburg and Brill 1995). She also worked as counsel to the National Woman's Party, the suffragist organization founded by Alice Paul that later introduced the original text for the ERA. Upon announcement of her selection to the federal bench, one fellow judge was reported to have said, "Mrs. Matthews would make a good judge, [but there's] just one thing wrong; she's a woman" (ibid., 285). To show her faith in her fellow women, Matthews would only hire women as her law clerks (ibid.).

It was not until the 1960s that President John F. Kennedy appointed additional women to the federal bench, including Sarah Hughes in 1961 (Mezey 2000). Hughes later became famous as the federal judge who swore in Lyndon Baines Johnson after Kennedy's assassination in 1963. In 1968, President Johnson appointed Shirley Mount Hufstedler to the United States Court of Appeals for the Ninth Circuit. She is perhaps best known, however, as being the first Secretary of Education, after President Carter enlisted her to be the head of this newly created cabinet-level department in 1979 (Ginsburg and Brill 1995). Upon Carter's defeat in 1980, Hufstedler returned to private practice.

Under President Jimmy Carter's administration in the late 1970s, women began to have more than a token presence in the federal judiciary. Presidents Nixon and Ford only managed to appoint two additional women to the federal bench. But under Carter's watch, 40 women were nominated and approved. Carter also actively sought out qualified people of color. Carter was willing to reach deeper into the qualified pool of potential judges to ensure that more women were selected, in part because his deputy White House counsel, Margaret McKenna, prioritized this outcome by having the White House take control over judicial nominations from the Justice Department (Kenney 2014). McKenna and the White House encouraged Carter to forgo the traditional route of judicial selection: senatorial courtesy, in which senators of the president's party from states with openings in the judiciary make recommendations to the president. Instead, Carter established merit commissions to select potential nominees that included not just senators but also state bar association members, practicing attorneys, non-lawyers, women's and minority's organizations, sitting judges, and the American Bar Association (ABA) (Martin 1987). The result was that Carter's nontraditional nominees (both females and nonwhite males) were younger and less likely to be partners in traditional law firms. Carter was also helped in this endeavor by the creation of 152 new judgeships by Congress under the Omnibus Judgeship Act (Mezey 2000) (see figure 9.1).

President Ronald Reagan did not continue Carter's affirmative action policy toward women or minorities. Compared with Carter, for whom 15.5 percent of judicial appointees were women, Reagan appointed just 7.6 percent of women as federal judges (ibid.). The reasons for this were varied, but many believed it was due to Reagan's emphasis on ideology in selecting judges. Because Reagan made conservatism an important factor in his decision to appoint judges, there were likely fewer potential women nominees to select. Also, Reagan abandoned the merit system put in place by Carter, reverting to the more traditional system of senatorial courtesy (Martin 1987).

Reagan's successor, George H. W. Bush, did a much better job of appointing women to the federal bench, in part because he relied less on ideological purity as a factor for appointments. Bush was also aided, as Carter had been, by the establishment of more judicial positions nationwide. Bush appointed women to more than 19 percent of federal judgeships during his one term in office (Mezey 2000). President Bill Clinton further increased the judicial appointments in terms of women in the judiciary. Making it a top priority to diversify the bench, and also aided by the establishment of new judgeships by Congress, Clinton more than doubled the number of women serving in the federal judiciary in his time in office (Palmer 2001). For his first term, 52.1 percent of his appointments were nontraditional (either female or nonwhite). Clinton named 87 women (28.5 percent) as district court appointees. The percentage of female appointees under Clinton to

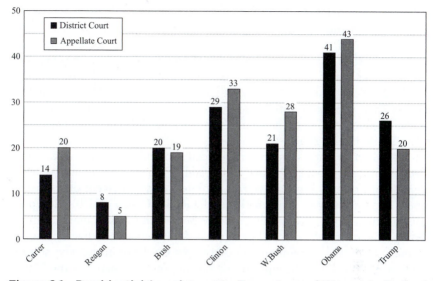

Figure 9.1 Presidential Appointments: Percentage of Women to Federal Courts
Source: Goldman, Federal Judicial Center.

the circuit court or court of appeals was even higher—32.8 percent. When Clinton began office, approximately 1 in 10 federal judges was female; when he left, the number was 1 in 5 (Goldman et al. 2001). Unlike Reagan, Clinton cared less about the ideology of judges and concentrated more on diversity. One result is that Clinton's nontraditional appointees (including minority men) were more likely to come from diverse backgrounds than the traditional ones. For example, they were more likely to have backgrounds in government or the state judiciary or to have prosecutorial experience than white males (ibid.). One study found, however, that despite having impeccable credentials, Clinton's female judicial nominees, under divided government, were delayed longer in their processing under the GOP Senate than were his male nominees (Hartley 2001).

President George W. Bush also had a good track record of appointing women to the bench—coming close to, but not quite matching, Clinton's numbers in terms of women. During his two terms in office, out of 327 judicial appointments, 77 (23.5 percent) were women (Federal Judicial Center 2017). Turning to the Obama presidency, Obama had the strongest record of judicial appointment of women by far. In addition to the appointment of two women to the United States Supreme Court, 42 percent of Obama's appointments to the district court level were women and a slight majority—53 percent—of his appointments to the appellate courts were women. Of those appointments, a significant number were women of color:

Obama appointed 46 nonwhite women (23 percent of all appointees) to the district courts and 5 nonwhite women (11 percent of all appointees) to the appellate courts. Among other notable appointments, Obama tapped the first Asian American woman, Jacqueline Nguyen, to serve on the US appellate courts. Obama also holds the distinction of nominating more openly LGBTQ federal judges than any other president: 11 of Obama's federal judges that were successfully confirmed identify as LGBTQ, compared with just one openly gay judge confirmed during Bill Clinton's presidency (The White House 2016).

However, women's progress as judicial appointees has taken a dramatic decline under the first two years' of Donald J. Trump's presidency—just 20 percent of Trump's appellate court appointees and 26 percent of his district court appointees were women (Federal Judicial Center 2019). Moreover, the vast majority of his appointees have been white, which makes him the first president in 24 years to leave the federal bench less diverse than he found it (Solberg and Waltenburg 2018). As we detail in the next section, Trump also declined the opportunity to appoint a female to the United States Supreme Court. As of January 2019, women make up approximately

Jacqueline Nguyen, appointed to the US court of appeals for the Ninth Circuit by Barack Obama in 2012, is the first Asian American woman to serve on any American appellate court. She is also the first Vietnamese-American federal judge. *Source*: United States Courts for the Ninth Circuit 2012 Annual Report, p. 10.

34 percent of all active federal judges at all levels of the federal judiciary (Federal Judicial Center 2017). Trump has appointed just one openly gay nominee, Mary Rowland, who was confirmed to serve as a judge on the US District Court for the Northern District of Illinois, although Trump's nominees have generally gotten more attention because they have tended to have bad records on LGBTQ equality issues (Allen 2018).

Women on the Supreme Court

Presidents Reagan, Clinton, and Obama share the distinction of appointing the only four women to serve on the United States Supreme Court. In 1981, keeping a promise he made while campaigning for president (in part to appeal to women voters), Reagan appointed Sandra Day O'Connor as the first female justice of the Supreme Court. Born in 1930, Sandra Day O'Connor grew up on the Lazy B cattle ranch on the Arizona–New Mexico border (Lane 2004). During the school year, she lived with her grandparents and attended private school in El Paso, Texas, but she returned to the ranch during the summers—where she grew up learning to ride horses and spent time with her father and his cowboys during their work, which no doubt made her comfortable working and competing with men (Lane 2004). Upon graduating high school at age 16, O'Connor attended Stanford University in 1946, earning a joint B.S. degree in economics and law in a six-year program. It was at Stanford Law that she met her husband, and she was a classmate of former Chief Justice William Rehnquist. Despite graduating magna cum laude, the only job offer she received upon completing law school was as a legal secretary.

Instead of private practice, O'Connor sought work in the public sector upon returning with her husband to Arizona. She found work as a deputy county attorney—but only because she volunteered to work for free until a paid position opened (Lane 2004). Later, she took leave from practicing law to raise her three small sons from 1960 to 1965. While raising her family, O'Connor was active in state Republican Party politics and in community service organizations such as the Junior League. In 1965, she returned to work full-time as a state assistant attorney general—a position she gained from her political contacts—and was later appointed to a vacant seat in the State Senate in 1969. Her time in the Senate was successful, as she won reelection twice and was the first woman to be elected nationally as majority leader in a State Senate (Maveety 1996). In 1975, she was elected as a county judge and was elevated to Arizona's highest court—the state court of appeals—in 1979.

Reagan tapped O'Connor to be the first woman on the Supreme Court because despite her short time as a state supreme court justice in Arizona, O'Connor had developed a reputation as a solid conservative on many issues that were important to the Reagan administration, especially federalism. Yet, she was a moderate on issues such as abortion, which led women's organizations to support her nomination while pro-life groups opposed her (Palmer 1991). The National Association of Women Judges, which was formed in 1979 in part to advocate for the appointment of a woman to the United States Supreme Court, was also pleased with O'Connor's nomination. After her confirmation hearings, the United States Senate confirmed O'Connor unanimously.

In 1993, President Bill Clinton appointed Ruth Bader Ginsburg as his first nominee to the Supreme Court. At the time, Ginsburg was serving her twelfth year as an appellate judge on the federal Court of Appeals for the District of Columbia Circuit. Ginsburg was brought to Clinton's attention as a possible nominee, in part because of the efforts of her husband Martin Ginsburg, a prominent tax attorney and law professor at Georgetown University. To help publicize his wife as a possible candidate, Martin Ginsburg began a letter-writing campaign, contacting various dignitaries and legal scholars to call or write to the White House in support of Ginsburg's candidacy as a Supreme Court justice. Upon his wife's nomination, Martin Ginsburg told the *Washington Post:* "If there was something that I could have done to be helpful, I would have done it, because I think my wife is super, and the President couldn't have made a better appointment than the one he just made" (O'Connor and Palmer 2001, 264).

In some ways, Ruth Bader Ginsburg's personal story differs dramatically from O'Connor's—but in other ways, it is very similar. Ginsburg was born in Brooklyn in 1933, and was taught by her mother to be independent and scholarly despite the gender norms that pervaded their ethnic neighborhood (Campbell 2002). Ginsburg's academic success in New York's public schools earned her a scholarship to Cornell University, where she met her husband Martin Ginsburg, whom she married in 1954 after graduating first in her class. Ginsburg followed her husband to Harvard Law School—he had just completed his first year there—where she was one of just nine women in a law class of 500 (Ginsburg 1997).

Ginsburg excelled at Harvard, and she earned a coveted spot on the *Harvard Law Review.* Her academic performance was all the more remarkable because not only was she the mother of a young child at the time, but also her husband developed testicular cancer while she was in her second year. She maintained her high level of work while also taking notes for him when he missed classes and typing his papers. When Martin Ginsburg accepted a job at a New York law firm, she transferred to Columbia Law School for her final year, graduating at the top of her class.

Similar to the situation faced by Sandra Day O'Connor, not a single law firm would hire Ginsburg upon her graduation and, despite recommendations from her Columbia professors, she was denied a chance to clerk with Supreme Court Justice Felix Frankfurter. She accepted a position as a clerk with a federal district court judge in New York and then went into academia, becoming a law professor at Rutgers University. She later became the first tenured woman faculty member at Columbia Law School (Ginsburg 1997).

Unlike Sandra Day O'Connor, Ginsburg did not work in the public sector nor was she involved in electoral politics. Instead, in addition to becoming a notable law professor, she also was founder and general counsel to the American Civil Liberties Union's (ACLU) Women's Rights Project (Campbell 2002). While still teaching at Rutgers, and realizing that women faculty members were paid less than men, Ginsburg took part in a class action lawsuit that brought women's salaries on par with men (Ginsburg 1997). At the same time, the ACLU was beginning to hear similar complaints about discriminatory behavior from other women in different fields, and they recruited Ginsburg to help with these sex discrimination cases under the auspices of the Women's Rights Project. As part of the ACLU, Ginsburg helped in 34 cases at the Supreme Court level (Campbell 2002).

Moreover, she successfully argued five out of six such cases in front of the Supreme Court, including the pivotal 1971 *Reed v. Reed* case, which was the first decision to establish that laws that segregated on sex-based differences were "entitled to some sort of scrutiny under the Fourteenth Amendment" (O'Connor and Clark 1999, 273). In other words, this case called into question the constitutionality of statutes that allowed for gender discrimination. Given Ginsburg's successful and prodigious record as a litigator, professor, and legal scholar, she was appointed to the United States court of appeals for the District of Columbia Circuit in 1980 by Jimmy Carter.

Upon joining the Supreme Court as the second female justice, Ginsburg quickly became a close friend of O'Connor, despite their ideological and partisan differences. Ginsburg was solidly in the liberal camp of the court, whereas O'Connor leaned more to the conservative side, although she was typically the key deciding vote on a number of issues on the court. Both women, however, shared a similar voting record when it came to issues that affected women disproportionately, such as abortion and sex discrimination. In 2006, O'Connor retired from the bench to spend time with her ailing husband, who was suffering from Alzheimer's disease and who passed away in 2009 (Brust 2008). At 86, and despite three bouts with cancer, Ginsburg shows no signs of slowing down. If anything, her popularity is at an all-time high, particularly with the younger generation of millennial women who are discovering Ginsburg's pioneering role as a crusader for women's legal rights and who respect her outspoken dissents championing women's legal rights. Ginsburg's popularity has spawned a Tumblr meme as

After starting the popular Tumblr meme, Notorious RBG, former law student Shana Knizhnik wrote a biography of the same name with Irin Carmon to celebrate Ginsburg's life. *Source:* Cover Image from *NOTORIOUS RBG: The Life and Times of Ruth Bader Ginsburg*, by Irin Carmon and Shana Knizhnik. Reprinted with permission from the authors.

well as a biography—with the tagline "The Notorious R.B.G"* (Schwartz 2015) and two popular films about her life were released in 2018.

O'Connor, Ginsburg, and Beyond: Gender and the Supreme Court

When Sandra Day O'Connor announced her retirement in July 2005, it set off a frenzy of speculation about who should replace the first female Supreme Court justice. Female senators, women's groups, and even First Lady Laura Bush pressured President George W. Bush to appoint another female justice. Instead, President Bush first nominated John Roberts but elevated him to nomination for Chief Justice after Chief Justice William Rehnquist died around the same time. Bush then tried to nominate a woman, his White House counsel, Harriet Miers, but a revolt within the Republican Party over her qualifications led Miers to withdraw her nomination and Bush ultimately nominated current Supreme Court justice

---

* The Notorious R.B.G. is a tweak of the moniker used by the late rapper Christopher "Notorious B.I.G" Wallace. In 2014, a student at NYU Law School launched the notoriousrbg.tumblr. com, a website where fans of Ginsburg post doctored art work inspired by her legacy, famous Ginsburg quotes, links to interviews of Ginsburg, and photos of Ginsburg with famous political leaders and celebrities.

Samuel Alito. O'Connor herself expressed disappointment that President Bush did not select a woman to replace her (Greenburg 2007).

In the years since Ronald Reagan appointed O'Connor to the court, the nature of Supreme Court nomination politics has drastically changed. Once the president selects a nominee, a majority of senators must vote to confirm the nomination. The polarization of the Democratic and Republican parties has made the ideology of the president and the presumed ideological leanings of the nominee more central to confirmation (Epstein and Segal 2005; Binder and Maltzman 2009). Speculation about the ideological views of a justice is even more intense on critical nominations where, as in the case of the O'Connor replacement, the new justice could swing the balance of opinion in a more liberal or conservative direction (Ruckman 1993).

Moreover, issues of race and gender now permeate the debate over nominees. While presidents and senators maintain that there is no litmus test for a potential justice, a nominee's position on *Roe v. Wade* is heavily scrutinized. The court plays an important role in determining the scope of women's rights, from reproductive rights to employment discrimination (Scherer 2005). The confirmation battle over Clarence Thomas's elevation to the Supreme Court in 1991, which included accusations of sexual harassment by his former work colleague Anita Hill, focused even more attention on gender and jurisprudence. As the country has become more diverse and more women and minorities have achieved the educational and employment credentials that qualify them for a seat on the federal bench, the parties compete to claim credit for increasing diversity on the courts or appointing the first member of a particular group to the Supreme Court or one of the federal appellate or district courts (Goldman 1997; Scherer 2005). This partisan conflict often exacerbates the controversy surrounding a particular female or minority nominee (Bell 2002; Soloweij, Martinek, and Brunell 2005).

Finally, there has been a change in the makeup of the Senate since O'Connor was first nominated to the court. Demonstrating the importance of descriptive representation, there are now more female senators who have a seat at the table and are able to weigh the records of nominees and cast confirmation votes. When O'Connor was nominated in 1981, there were only two women in the Senate. When the Senate considered O'Connor's replacement, 14 women senators weighed in on the nomination. Analyzing the floor debate and the votes senators cast on the nominations of John Roberts and Samuel Alito, Michele Swers (2013) found that in this polarized era, partisanship dominated confirmation votes. Members of the president's party, in this case Republicans, almost always supported the president's nominees. For the opposition party Democrats, a senator's ideological distance from the president and the nominee strongly impacted the vote as the most liberal senators were the most likely to oppose Roberts and Alito. Still, even after accounting for ideology, Swers found that among the more moderate senators, female Democrats were more likely to oppose the nominees than their moderate male counterparts. The most striking impact of the presence of women in the Senate, however, was their influence on the deliberative process. Analyzing senators' floor speeches explaining their votes on the nominations, Swers found that Democratic women were much more likely than their male Democratic colleagues to prioritize Roberts's and Alito's positions on women's rights when making their vote decisions. Furthermore, the female senators were also more likely to consider the nominees' positions on a range of women's rights issues beyond abortion including equal pay, employment discrimination, and family leave (Swers 2013).

In the years following O'Connor's departure from the court, Ruth Bader Ginsburg lamented the fact that she was the only woman on the Supreme Court. In high-profile decisions on partial birth abortion and employment discrimination, Ginsburg took the unusual step of reading her dissents from the bench and criticizing her colleagues for not understanding the social position of women. Thus, following the Lilly Ledbetter pay discrimination case, Ginsburg stated, "The court does not comprehend, or is indifferent to, the insidious way in which women can be victims of pay discrimination" (quoted in Barnes 2007).

Hence, when Barack Obama was elected president, there was a great deal of focus on whether he would appoint a woman or even the first Hispanic woman to the next Supreme Court vacancy. That moment arrived fairly soon in his presidency, when Justice David Souter announced in April 2009 his intention to step down from the Supreme Court. In May 2009, Obama announced Judge Sonia Sotomayor, a US appellate court judge with 17 years' experience, to be his pick for the Supreme Court. Her Supreme Court appointment was met (largely) with enthusiasm from both women's rights organizations and Latino groups (less so from conservative organizations). She was confirmed in August 2009, although she did not receive overwhelming support from Republican senators, many of whom stated their objections over her past support of affirmative action (see earlier discussion in this chapter). Former Justice Sandra Day O'Connor also lauded Sotomayor's appointment to the Supreme Court:

> I am very happy that another woman is being appointed. I think that's very important. I was terribly disappointed when I retired in 2006 not to be replaced by a woman. We have to remember that slightly more than 50 percent of us in this country have two X chromosomes and I think it doesn't hurt to look at our national institutions and see women represented. I don't think two females on the Supreme Court is enough, but it is certainly better than one. (Quoted in Lodge 2009)

In April 2010, Justice John Paul Stevens, who had served on the nation's highest court since his appointment by President Gerald Ford in 1975, again gave President Barack Obama the chance to make another appointment to the Supreme Court. The following month, Obama selected a second woman nominee, Elena Kagan, whom he had appointed US Solicitor General in his early months in office. The US Solicitor General is considered the government's top lawyer, tasked with the job of representing the United States in cases that appear before the United States Supreme Court, and hence is often referred to as the "10th Justice" given the frequency with which he or she interacts with the nation's highest court.

Elena Kagan grew up in a middle-class Jewish family in New York City to an educator mother and lawyer father. Like Sotomayor, Kagan attended Princeton University, graduating summa cum laude in 1981, attended Oxford to earn a master's degree, and then completed law school at Harvard, graduating in 1986, where she served on the law review. Unlike other Supreme Court justices, Kagan's early career encompassed both politics and law. For instance, she clerked with former Justice Thurgood Marshall in 1988 and also served as an advisor for the 1988 presidential campaign for Democratic nominee and former Massachusetts Governor Michael Dukakis. After a brief time in private practice, Kagan became a law professor at the University of Chicago law school but left this position to serve as a domestic policy assistant to Bill Clinton (Goldstein, Leonning, and Slevin 2010). Obama was not the first president to appoint Kagan to the federal bench—Clinton nominated her to the DC Circuit court of appeals in 1999, but her nomination got mired in judicial politics in the Senate Judiciary Committee, so she opted to return to academia, becoming a full law professor at Harvard and ultimately the first woman Dean of Harvard Law School in 2003 (Dillon 2003). Upon Obama's election as president, she was confirmed to be the first female Solicitor General.

Unlike Sotomayor's appointment, Obama's selection of Kagan was met with less overt drama that followed Sotomayor after her "wise Latina" comment became more widely known. Of course, some conservatives pointed to her previous political background in a Democratic White House as a potential problem while others were concerned that she had never served as a judge—although up until the 1970s, it was not unusual for many Supreme Court justices to come to the bench from outside of the judiciary. However, some proponents of Judge Kagan believed her lack of judicial experience was helpful to her prospects, given that she had no "judicial paper trail" to defend during her confirmation hearings (Baker and Zeleny 2010). Kagan was easily confirmed, mainly because the Democrats had a filibuster-proof 60-vote majority. She managed to obtain the votes of 5 Republicans as well as 2 Independents and all but one of the Democratic Senators, resulting in a 63-to-37 vote. However, Kagan received fewer votes than did Sotomayor at her confirmation, when she was confirmed 68-to-31. By contrast, Sandra Day O'Connor was confirmed unanimously, and Ruth Bader Ginsburg had only 3 votes cast against her. Of course, Samuel Alito, who had been

The first woman to serve on the Supreme Court, retired Justice Sandra Day O'Connor (left), visits the three current female justices residing on the Court: Justice Sonia Sotomayor, Justice Ruth Bader Ginsburg, and Justice Elena Kagan. *Source*: Steve Petteway, Collection of the Supreme Court of the United States.

nominated to replace O'Connor in 2005, was only confirmed by a majority of 58-to-42 votes, which reflects the growing political polarization of fights over nominees to the judicial branch.

On January 31, 2017, President Donald Trump appointed Neil Gorsuch to fill the seat of former Justice Antonin Scalia, who unexpectedly passed away in February 2016. Senate Republican Majority Leader Mitch McConnell opted to deny President Obama the opportunity to replace Scalia during the last year of his presidency, insisting that a new nominee should be appointed only after the results of the presidential election. Such a move was met with scorn among Democrats but generally applauded by many Republicans. One result is that the open seat on the Supreme Court played a prominent role in the 2016 presidential election, with Trump pledging to appoint only conservative justices if he were elected president. As of this writing, Trump has gotten two opportunities to nominate justices to the Supreme Court.

Trump's first appointee, Neil Gorsuch, was a Bush-appointed appellate court judge for the Tenth Circuit and was confirmed largely along partisan lines, 54–45 (Carlsen and Andrews 2017). Three Democratic senators from conservative states—Heidi Heitkamp from North Dakota, Joe Manchin from West Virginia, and Joe Donnelly from Illinois—joined Republicans in confirming Gorsuch. While Democrats were not thrilled with Gorsuch's appointment, he was replacing the most conservative member of the court, which would not alter the ideological balance of the court. He also had a sterling personal reputation.

Trump once again had the opportunity to shape the makeup of the High Court with the retirement of Anthony Kennedy at the end of the Supreme Court's 2017–2018 term in June 2018. Unlike the Gorsuch appointment, the political stakes of the nomination were much higher, given that Kennedy was long considered a moderate, swing-vote on the High Court. Trump and his fellow Republicans finally had the chance to replace Kennedy with a more consistent conservative jurist, which would bring the conservative bloc of the court to five members. Rather than selecting a female nominee, however, Trump chose Brett Kavanaugh, a long-standing judge on the DC Circuit Court of Appeals. Kavanaugh's nomination, however, soon became embroiled in controversy as a woman he once knew in high school, Christine Blasey Ford, publicly alleged that Kavanaugh tried to sexually assault her at a summer party during their high school days—an allegation that he vehemently denied. Several weeks of intensive fighting about Kavanaugh's nomination ensued, with Democrats demanding that Christine Blasey Ford, now a respected professor of psychology at Palo Alto University, be allowed to share her story publicly. The result was a day-long hearing that had Ford recounting her memory of the interaction with Kavanaugh from the 1980s, with Kavanaugh passionately disputing those allegations later in the day. In some respects, the emotionally charged hearings were reminiscent of the hearings of alleged sexual harassment brought by law professor Anita Hill during the Clarence Thomas hearing almost 25 years earlier that also gripped the nation. One important difference, however, was the makeup of the Judiciary Committee, which in 2018 included a number of women senators in this Congress, all of whom were Democrats. Although Democrats did successfully convince the Justice Department to delay the vote on Kavanaugh so that the FBI could extend its background check of Kavanaugh, the Senate eventually confirmed him by a vote of 50–48, again largely on party lines. Notably, both Heidi Heitkamp and Joe Donnelly sided with their fellow Democrats—and both lost reelection bids in November 2018, running in solidly conservatives states that broke overwhelmingly for Trump in 2016. The only Republican to vote against Brett Kavanaugh was Alaska Senator Lisa Murkowski, who said of her decision that "we need to have institutions that are viewed as fair and

In October 2018, psychology professor Christine Blasey Ford (top) testified to the Senate Judiciary Committee, claiming that Brett Kavanaugh, Donald Trump's nominee to Supreme Court, had tried to sexually assault her while both were in their teens. Twenty-five years earlier, law professor Anita Hill (bottom) also testified before the same committee at the Supreme Court confirmation hearings of Clarence Thomas. Hill alleged that while she worked for Clarence Thomas at the Equal Employment Opportunity Commission years before, Thomas sexually harassed her while she was his employee. Both men denied the claims, and both were ultimately confirmed by the Senate. *Sources*: (top) JIM BOURG/REUTERS/Newscom; (bottom) Rob Crandall Stock Connection Worldwide/Newscom.

if people who are victims, people who feel that there is no fairness in our system of government, particularly in our courts, then you've gone down a path that is not good and right for this country" (New York Times 2018).

Women in the State Judiciary

Most Americans will never have a case heard in front of the Supreme Court. Any personal interaction that Americans may have with the judiciary is most likely to occur at the state level, which, similar to the federal judicial system, is composed of state courts of last resort, intermediate appellate courts, and trial courts, where there are approximately 11,800 judges, and some (but not all) states have nonattorney courts, or state limited and special jurisdiction courts, which have approximately 4,900 judges (National Association of Women Judges [NAWJ] 2019). As political scientist Sally J. Kenny (2013) notes, women remain somewhat underrepresented as judges compared to their composition in the qualified labor pool—that is, the percentage of women as state judges is consistently lower than the proportion of women lawyers who have the requisite backgrounds to be eligible to serve. Data compiled by the NAWJ from the *2018 American Bench*, the annual biographical references on America's judges and courts, show that women make up 33 percent of America's judiciary. Breaking down the data by type of court, NAWJ reports that women constitute 33 percent of judges on state courts of last resort, 37 percent of judges on state intermediate appellate courts, 32 percent of judges on state general jurisdiction courts, and 35 percent of judges on state limited and special jurisdiction courts (NAWJ 2019; see figure 9.2).

The American Constitution Society for Law and Policy released a study called "The Gavel Gap" in 2016 that analyzed both the gender and racial breakdown of judges in each state. In addition to reporting about women's underrepresentation as judges nationally, they also found that the racial composition of states' judiciaries was also far less reflective of the populations and communities in which judges serve (George and Yoon 2016). They report that nationally, just 1 in 5 state court judges are people of color, although people of color make up 38 percent of the population nationally. Moreover, among state court judges, men of color are disproportionately more likely to be appointed or elected to state judgeships: nationally, 12 percent of state court judges are men of color and 8 percent of state court judges are women of color (ibid.). Moreover, in 16 states, they find that judges of color represent fewer than one in ten state judges. Given that more than 90 percent of the judicial business of America is handled at the state court level, George and Yoon argue that the general public's faith in the legitimacy of the court is predicated on "the idea that our courts will be staffed by judges who can understand the circumstances of the communities which they serve" (3). They call for greater attention to diversifying the court.

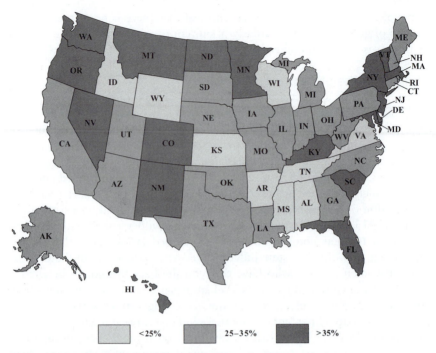

Figure 9.2 Women Appointed to State Courts
Source: https://www.nawj.org/statistics/2018-us-state-court-women-judges.

Unlike at the federal level, where judges are appointed by the president and approved by the Senate, selection of judges varies by state—although selection generally boils down to two major methods: election and appointment.* In 26 states, all or most judgeships are decided by either partisan (9 states) or nonpartisan (17 states) elections. In reality, many of these elections are noncontested, with incumbents carrying an extraordinary advantage. Moreover, in many cases, the governor often appoints incumbent judges, as vacancies on the bench frequently occur prior to elections. Thus, even in states with no appointive system, governors have a large hand in shaping the judiciary. The other states use some sort of appointment selection process. In four states, all or most judgeships are done by gubernatorial appointment, whereas two others use legislative appointment. The most popular method of judicial selection at the state level, however, is the merit selection or Missouri Plan used by 18 states. This plan involves a merit panel that makes suggestions to the governor for nominees for state judicial

---

* See the National Center for State Courts for information about how states select their judges. http://www.judicialselection.us/judicial_selection/methods/selection_of_judges.cfm?state=.

vacancies. Once appointed, these judges serve a trial one-year term and then face a retention election asking voters whether they should be retained in office (they face no opposition). Rarely do these appointed judges lose such retention elections.

Political scientists have examined whether the method of judicial selection at the state level—appointment or election—is related to the number of women serving on the bench. One theory is that appointive systems in general tend to depress diversity in state courts, because such systems tend to "favor the status quo by perpetuating the dominance of elites in the judiciary, thus decreasing judicial opportunities for political minorities who may not have the conventional legal backgrounds or experience" (Hurwitz and Lanier 2001, 86). Alternatively, others argue that appointive systems could be more beneficial to women because elite decision makers might be more cognizant of the need for greater diversity than voters, leading to an increase in the number of women in the judiciary (Alozie 1996; Hurwitz and Lanier 2003).

A study by scholars from the American Judicature Society examined all women and minority appellate court judges serving in 2008 to determine which method of judicial selection resulted in the most diverse bench and their findings are mixed. The most common selection method for both minority members and women members of state supreme courts was merit or appointive selection: roughly half of minority judges (54.3 percent) and women judges (48.5 percent) serving in 2008 were chosen through some sort of merit plan (Reddick, Nelson, and Caulfield 2009). However, at the intermediate appellate courts, partisan elections placed slightly more women on such courts than other selection processes, although merit selection remained the more typical avenue for minority judges. Their analysis also finds that party plays a factor when it comes to gender diversity on the state bench: women are more likely to be appointed by Democratic governors than Republican governors for appellate courts and are more likely to be elected to both types of courts in majority-Democratic states than in majority-Republican states (ibid.).

The American Judicature Society study, while thorough, does not consider how other factors, such as state characteristics, the size of the court, and pools of potential candidates, may work in conjunction with the style of selection to either promote or inhibit women's ascension to state courts. For example, research by Margaret Williams (2007) suggests that the merit system actually depresses women's representation on the bench when controlling for other factors, at least at the appellate court level. Williams writes that "states using merit selection to fill the appellate judiciary, on average, see three fewer women on the appellate bench relative to similar states using partisan elections to fill the appellate bench" (1199). However, the appointment system does appear to boost gender diversity on state supreme courts in one case: when such courts are all male. Yet, once women have been appointed to a vacancy in an all-male state supreme court, and their appearance as token women is solidified, "the chance that a woman will be appointed to the bench drops significantly once the court achieves any degree of gender diversity" (Bratton and Spill 2002, 516). Kenney and Windett's 2012 study finds further that women are more likely to be appointed to state supreme courts when the sitting governor is a woman rather than a man. Moreover, their work finds that state culture matters—states that have higher indices of gender equality are more likely to have women serving on their state's courts of last resort. What appears to count more than selection method when it comes to the presence of women on state courts of last resort is the number of judges on the bench, as scholars have noted a positive relationship between the size of the court and female presence on it (Alozie 1996; Bratton and Spill 2002; Hurwitz and Lanier 2003). The more seats that are available to be filled, the more opportunities women have to serve on the bench.

Women have not only increased their presence in the eligibility pool from which judges are considered, but the criteria for their eligibility have also expanded in recent years. For instance, women and men state supreme court justices often take a different path to the bench, with women being more likely to serve in the public sector, and men more likely to come from a private law practice. Moreover, women justices are less likely than their male counterparts to have served in elected political office (Martin and Pyle 2002). These findings suggest that the traditional eligibility pool has shifted to allow for people with more diverse backgrounds, especially women and minorities, to be considered for service on the high court. Many proponents of increasing the number of women are optimistic that women's increased presence in law school—as of 2016, women made up more than half (51 percent) of law school students (ABA 2018)—will eventually result in more qualified women to be tapped to serve as judges or in their taking the plunge and running for judicial office in states that have an elected judiciary. Yet, despite women's higher presence in law schools, women continue to make up far less of the percentage of practicing attorneys—approximately 35 percent (ABA 2018). Moreover, women's representation as leaders within the legal profession is also disproportionately low. For example, women make up only 23 percent of partners in law firms nationwide (ibid.). Political scientist Sally Kenney (2013) warns that the tendency of women to "trickle up" from the labor pool of qualified potential judges has not materialized as quickly as many proponents of women judges had hoped, suggesting that something other than simply the number of qualified women has kept women from serving as judges. As of 2016, however, the national data as indicated in figure 9.3 show that at least one woman serves on every state's court of last resort, with the exception of Iowa. In most cases, at least two women serve on their state's most prestigious courts and in nine states—California, Minnesota, New Mexico, New York, Tennessee, Vermont, Washington, West Virginia, and Wisconsin—women make up 50 percent or more of the bench.

The impact of the type of the judicial selection system on women's representation in state courts is also dependent on the level of the court under consideration and whether the election was partisan or nonpartisan. For instance, Margaret Williams's (2007) analysis finds that more women sit on state trial courts chosen by nonpartisan elections than on courts chosen by partisan elections. State ideology and the presence of female attorneys in a state is also linked to women's representation on state trial courts—women fare better in more liberal states and where more women practice law. For general jurisdiction courts, scholars from the American Judicature Society found the following breakdown of women's pathway to trial courts in their random sample of trial court judges: 30 percent came through merit selection, 28 percent came from judicial appointment, 24 percent came from partisan elections, 12 percent from nonpartisan elections, and the remaining 5 percent came from legislative or court appointment. However, given that

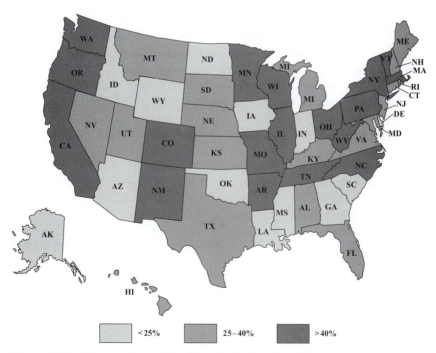

Figure 9.3   Women Appointed to State Courts of Last Resort
Source: https://www.nawj.org/statistics/2018-us-state-court-women-judges.

these data are derived from a random sample of courts, when the authors conducted tests to determine if such selection methods were significantly different, they found that they were not. In other words, at this level, it appears that women are just as likely to be appointed or elected to serve on the trial court bench (Reddick, Melson, and Caufield 2009).

Turning more specifically to judicial elections, several studies that analyze the impact of sex on such elections find in multivariate analyses that there is no systematic bias against women candidates (Hall 2001; Reid 2010). Indeed, Frederick and Streb's (2008) study of the success of female and male candidates running in state intermediate appellate court elections from 2000 to 2006 suggest that women candidates had a slight *advantage* over men candidates, as their regression models suggest that women are more likely to win their races than men. However, Traciel Reid (2010), a leading scholar of gender and judicial elections, notes that success in raising campaign funds is a better predictor of success than gender, although such spending has less impact on women's vote shares than men's. But scholars of judicial elections caution that we should not assume that gender has no impact in these races. Reid's assessment of general elections for state Supreme Court judgeships held between 1996 and 2006 suggests that women face specific challenges that their male counterparts do not. For example, male judicial candidates who are incumbents enjoy a significant fundraising advantage compared with female judicial candidates who are incumbents. Moreover, Reid's research finds that while a higher percentage of women who ran in state judicial elections had judicial experience, this indicator of quality did not boost the electoral chances of women. She writes, "Even having stronger credentials and more money, women [judicial candidates] were unable to parlay electoral assets into sizable electoral gains" (469). In other words, Reid contends that comparable to the work on women who run for other political offices (Lawless and Fox 2005), women who run for judgeships have to be *better* candidates in order to achieve similar electoral results.

Given the increasing prominence of judicial elections in American politics, and the fact that slightly more judges in the American states will be elected rather than appointed, political scientist Sally Kenney (2010) calls on scholars of women and politics to consider how gender intersects with such election results and also the initial decision to run for judgeships. One study, which draws on the work of Richard Fox and Jennifer Lawless on political ambition, analyzed a pool of "potential judges" (attorneys) in Texas to consider whether similar gender differences emerged in terms of ambition for seats on the state judiciary (Williams 2008). Fascinatingly, while controlling for other factors, women attorneys actually express *more* ambition for judicial office than men. This study suggests that women may appear more ambitious than men with respect to judicial elections because many of them believe that women actually face more barriers than men in legal careers as opposed to becoming a judge. Yet, while women express somewhat greater ambition to run for judicial office in Texas than men, the opportunity structure may still prevent women from taking the additional step of running for judgeships. Still, these results—while limited to just one state—suggest that scholars of women and politics should consider that there is variation in the ambition of women to run for office across political offices including the judiciary.

THE DIFFERENCE WOMEN JUDGES MAKE

Scholars focus on two primary questions when it comes to comparing men and women judges (Palmer 2001). First, do women judges use a different style or "voice" when it comes to legal reasoning? Second, do women judges make different decisions than men, especially when it comes to policy issues that are potentially of greater interest to women? For example, are they more sensitive to issues of sex and race discrimination?

Do Women Judges Use A "Different Voice"?

Few books in recent years have had as much of an impact on various fields in the social sciences as Carol Gilligan's *In a Different Voice: Psychological Theory and Women's Development* (1982). Gilligan's theory grapples with moral development among men and women, and how men and women often differ when it comes to speaking and thinking about moral problems and the relationship between oneself and the larger community. Through interviews about conceptions of self and morality, Gilligan found that women often thought about such problems differently than men, regardless of their age or social status. For most men, morality is viewed in terms of fairness, with a concern rooted in individual rights. For most women, care-taking rather than fairness is more important, and they tend to place greater emphasis not on the formal rules of society in deciding what is moral but more on an understanding of responsibilities that they have toward the larger community.

Gilligan argues that these conceptions of morality are rooted in childhood, as studies that focus on how girls and boys play show that when quarrels arise during games, boys are preoccupied—in a legal sense—with the rules of games, whereas girls are more tolerant in their attitudes toward the rules (Gilligan 1982). Boys care more about competition, and girls care more about cooperation. Over time, Gilligan argues that men and women begin to see larger moral problems differently. For women, she writes:

> The moral problem arises from conflicting responsibilities rather than from competing rights and requires for its resolution a mode of thinking that is

contextual and narrative rather than formal and abstract. This conception of morality as concerned with the activity of care centers moral development around the understanding of responsibility and relationships, just as the conception of morality as fairness ties moral development to the understanding of rights and rules. (19)

In essence, to solve problems men seek an answer available in existing rules, whereas women seek solutions that maintain their relationships. While Gilligan notes that most people use both "moral" voices at one time or another, women and men tend to emphasize one voice much more often.

Given its emphasis on reason and decision-making, legal scholars interested in the impact of gender on decision-making have analyzed whether Gilligan's theory has any applicability to jurisprudence. If Gilligan is correct, then we may find that women judges reach their decisions in a different manner than do men, bringing to the bench a different perspective. For example, Suzanna Sherry (1986) has argued that women could bring to the bench a "feminine" (*not* feminist) perspective, closely linked to what in political philosophy is known as the classical republican tradition. Unlike the modern, liberal philosophy that supports the current legal system, with its emphasis on individual rights and liberties, this classical tradition is communitarian and contextual. A feminine legal paradigm, according to Sherry, would be one that emphasizes connectedness, context, and responsibility rather than autonomy or rights.

A virtual cottage industry developed around whether this "different voice" was evident in the jurisprudence of the Supreme Court's first female justice, Sandra Day O'Connor. While O'Connor generally sided with her fellow conservatives on the High Court, her tendency to write concurring and separate opinions that rejected the reasoning of her colleagues led some scholars to speculate that she worked from a "feminine" perspective (Sherry 1986; Behuniak-Long 1992; Palmer 2001). Sherry (1986) writes that in many of her decisions, especially those regarding freedom of religion, "O'Connor often rejects bright-line rules and occasionally makes explicit her preference for contextual determinations" (ibid., 605). Sherry's legal analysis of several of O'Connor's decisions shows that, in some cases, O'Connor favored the concerns of the community over the rights of the individual. Other scholars point to her decisions in abortion cases as more evidence of O'Connor's unique feminine voice. Rather than asserting a woman's clear right to have an abortion—as feminist scholars would have hoped—O'Connor upheld some state restrictions on abortion, but only if they did not present an undue burden on a woman's fundamental right to seek an abortion (Sullivan and Goldzwig 1996). This "balancing-of-interests" approach to abortion is an attempt, according to some, to "circumvent the divisive polarity of her colleagues' ideologically driven tests" on the controversial issue (Maveety 1996, 33). Those who maintain that O'Connor spoke with this accommodationist, feminine voice criticized her from both sides of the spectrum: some on the right believe she inhibited the court's ability to form a solid conservative majority, whereas others on the left believe she undermined any potential for a more feminist jurisprudence on the court (Behuniak-Long 1992).

Still others question whether O'Connor's voice on the High Court was truly distinct, and, if so, if it was colored mainly by her gender. On 40 different equal protection cases, for example, Aliota (1995) finds that O'Connor's voice or voting pattern was not unique from that of fellow justices—in direct contrast to Sherry's work on O'Connor that focused on far fewer cases. O'Connor's proclivity to disagree with her fellow conservatives, some argue, may not have stemmed from any feminine voice but could have been because she was simply less conservative in these areas (Davis 1993; Maveety 1996). Moreover, others argue that her centrist or accommodationist tendencies in some cases may have stemmed more from her political experiences as a former majority leader in the Arizona State Senate than from her gender (Maveety 1996; Palmer 2001; Lane 2004).

Extending the "different voices" theory to other judges has also yielded few corroborating findings. Sue Davis (1992–1993) compared the legal reasoning of a group of women and men appellate judges from the Ninth Circuit court of appeals. For example, in discrimination cases, she looked for evidence that women judges, embodying a female voice according to Gilligan's theory, would be more likely to emphasize the importance of full membership in the community in their decisions, with the notion that exclusion (through discrimination) is unacceptable. Alternatively, a "male" voice in discrimination cases would show up in the decisions of judges when discrimination was discussed in terms of the "denial of personal autonomy of the victims," treating equality not in terms of connection but in terms of independence. Yet, while Davis found that sometimes women do speak in a different voice in their decisions, so do men. Therefore, she found little evidence to suggest that "the presence of women judges will transform the very nature of law" (171). David Allen and Diane Wall (1993) also looked for, but failed to find, evidence of a different voice among women judges at the state supreme court level by examining whether women justices were more likely to pen dissenting decisions, which would indicate that there was a lack of common ground between women and men on the bench. Although women were somewhat more likely to write dissents than men, particularly in criminal rights and economic liberty cases, there was no pattern that suggested that women state supreme court justices consistently used different legal reasoning to decide cases—although they did find that women justices were uniformly more supportive of expanding women's rights, regardless of party.

Generally speaking, empirical studies have not gathered much evidence to verify that women judges have a different voice when it comes to legal reasoning. Why not? Gilligan's theory itself might be flawed, or may not be appropriate for application to jurisprudence. Palmer (2001) argues that failure to find a unique, different voice among women judges could be linked to socialization experiences women face in law school: law school is structured to teach students to think about law in similar ways, and women who might otherwise wish to use any alternative approach to legal reasoning—one that is more contextual than abstract—may abandon it to become successful in their field. Moreover, once women become judges, the nature of the legal process, whereby judges "examine the facts of a legal dispute, identify the features of those facts, determine what legal principles should apply, and apply those principles to the facts" may subvert any sex-based differences (Davis 1992–1993, 151).

Notably, both retired Supreme Court justices Sandra Day O'Connor and Ruth Bader Ginsburg put little stock in the theory that women judges decide cases differently than do male judges merely because they are women. As political scientist Sally Kenney points out in her book, *Gender & Justice* (2013), O'Connor believes there is little evidence to suggest that "gender differences lead to discernible differences in rendering judgment" (5). Moreover, Kenney cites the following quote from Ruth Bader Ginsburg, who has said of such studies that try to isolate sex as a variable in analyzing jurisprudence: "I certainly know that there are women in federal courts with whom I disagree just as strongly as I disagree with any man" (ibid., 5). Yet, both women have argued for having more women serve as judges and, at least in certain areas of the law such as sex discrimination or women's rights, they have discussed why a woman's perspective is useful on the courts. As we shall see, for Ruth Bader Ginsburg, in particular, women judges may be essential for protecting the unique legal rights of women. It is to the question of whether having women judges advances women's legal rights that we now turn.

Empirical Studies: The Impact of Sex on Jurisprudence

One argument in support of having more women appointed or elected to the judiciary is that it would enhance women's representation in government. This argument, though, is predicated on the assumption that women judges will do a better job of "acting for" or representing other women's interests than men judges. Although some empirical evidence suggests that female legislators are more inclined to initiate or support policies that disproportionately affect women or children (see chapter 7 on Women in Congress and the State Legislatures), can the same be said for female judges? This question has less to do with the reasoning of cases—unlike those empirical studies reviewed earlier that analyzed whether Gilligan's "different voice" theory was applicable to judicial decision-making—and more to do with whether the actual outcomes of cases favor the interests or rights of women. For instance, do women jurists make judgments that can be interpreted as more liberal or more conservative? Do women judges decide cases in such a way that women's rights or other minority rights are expanded? Given that women are most frequently the victims of harassment, for example, women judges may be more sympathetic to victims of discrimination than men judges.

Early studies found few differences among men and women judges—or found that women judges were *less* likely to make decisions that disproportionately affected the interests of women in the ways that feminists had hoped. For example, one study of local trial judges in a large northeastern city who served from 1971 through 1979 found that men and women judges did not differ with respect to conviction or sentencing behavior—with one exception (Gruhl, Spohn, and Welch 1981). Male judges were much less likely than women trial court judges to sentence women to prison, causing the authors to label their behavior as "paternalistic" (ibid.). Another study focused on men and women on the federal bench, examining 12 matched sets of judges appointed by President Carter (Walker and Barrow 1985). These judges served in the same district and were of the same race. The idea behind the study was that if differences were found between the matched pairs of judges, the likely explanation for such differences would be their gender since they were similar in most other respects. Walker and Barrow found no real evidence that these female district court judges were more likely to "act for" other women when it came to cases involving sexual harassment, gender discrimination, maternity rights, or affirmative action. Although female district judges were more likely to be liberal on economic regulation cases, in that they deferred more often to the government's position in such cases, they were actually less supportive than male district judges of personal rights claims (at least in some cases).

Why did early studies find that women judges were not more likely than men judges to represent the interests of women in their decision-making? On the one hand, given their minority status within the judiciary—both at the state and federal levels—there is some concern that women judges would not want to stand out or appear too different from their male counterparts. As "tokens" on the court, women judges may feel pressured to conform to a more male model of judicial behavior, causing them to act more conservatively in such cases (Martin 1993). On the other hand, the early findings that show a lack of support among women judges for female litigants could simply be a result of having too few female judges to examine.

Later studies of women judges, which have come about as their numbers have greatly increased, have shown mixed results when it comes to gender differences among judges. One study of state supreme court justices found that women judges vote more liberally than male judges on two types of cases not necessarily associated with women's issues: obscenity and death penalty sentencing. However, those gender differences appeared only among Democratic judges, as Republican men and women of the bench tended to vote the same (Songer and Crews-Meyer 2000). The preponderance of evidence from empirical studies that isolate the impact of sex on decision-making on cases not directly germane to women's rights shows that gender is not significant (Segal 2002; Songer, Davis, and Haire 1994; Walker and Barrow 1985).

Studies of justices on the Michigan Supreme Court, one of the few state high courts to have had a majority of women serve on its bench, find that although women justices generally do make more liberal decisions than men on "feminist" issue cases, party matters more than gender. One exception is for cases concerning divorce, in which women justices are more likely than men to support a woman's claim (Martin and Pyle 2000). Segal (2000) used the same research design employed by Walker and Barrow in their study of Carter appointees. In this case, Segal selected 13 matched gender pairs of Clinton appointees, and found, like Walker and Barrow, few gender differences among Clinton appointees. If anything, Clinton's female appointees were more likely to rule against women's claims than were his male appointees in those districts, leading Segal to conclude that Clinton's female appointees "are not inclined to support a judicial role that is particularly sensitive to the claims of various out-groups in American society" (149). Finally, one study of trial judges found that although younger judges and Democratic judges were more likely to rule in favor of plaintiffs in sexual discrimination cases, gender was not a significant predictor in statistical models that examined such cases (Kulik, Perry, and Pepper 2003).

Yet, turning to studies that specifically isolate analyses to discrimination cases, most—but not all—show that women judges have been found to be more supportive of plaintiffs in employment discrimination cases (even after controlling for party) whether at the United States Court of Appeals (Davis, Haire, and Songer 1993; Songer, Davis, and Haire 1994; Boyd, Epstein, and Martin 2010; Haire and Moyer 2015) or on state supreme courts (Gryski, Main, and Dixon 1986; Allen and Wall 1993). For instance, in Boyd, Epstein, and Martin's (2010) comprehensive study of the effects of sex on judging in all sex discrimination cases in the US appellate courts from 1995 to 2002, they find that the probability of a male judge deciding favorably for a female plaintiff in a sex discrimination case is 10 percent less than a female judge, even controlling for ideology.

The presence of at least one female judge on courts can also influence the behavior of the male judges on the bench, resulting in the court being more likely to find the presence of sex discrimination in noncriminal cases at the state supreme court level (Gryski, Main, and Dixon 1986). At the US appellate court level, in which a three-judge panel typically hears appeals, having a woman on the panel significantly increases the likelihood that a male judge will rule in favor of a female plaintiff (Peresie 2005; Boyd, Epstein, and Martin 2010). Although difficult to isolate exactly why this effect occurs, some scholars believe that having a woman on a panel sensitizes her male colleagues to issues of gender equality through the deliberation process, in which judges have to come to a consensus on a decision.

There is also is evidence that race and gender can have an intersectional impact on the bench. Law Professor Kimberlé Crenwshaw (1992, 1998) has written extensively about the need to consider racial dimensions to legal issues such as sexual harassment and sex discrimination in employment. Initially writing in response to the Anita Hill hearings, Crenshaw argues (1992) that black women's treatment in courtrooms by juries and judges has often historically been different from that of white women's treatment:

> Pervasive stereotypes about Black women not only shape the kind of harassment that Black women experience but also influence whether Black women's stories are likely to be believed. Historically Black women's words were not taken as true. In our own legal system, a connection was once drawn between chastity and lack of veracity. In other words, a woman who was likely to have sex was not likely to tell the truth. Because Black women were not expected to be chaste, similarly, they were unlikely to tell the truth. Judges were known to instruct juries to take a Black woman's word with a grain of salt. (1467)

Moreover, black women have often been put in a dilemma regarding whether or not to come forward with charges against men of color, sometimes forcing them to "to choose between specifically articulating the intersectional aspects of their subordination, thereby risking their ability to represent Black men, or ignoring intersectionality in order to state a claim that would not lead to the exclusion of Black men" (Crenshaw 2005, 365). These experiences faced by black women can be extended to the ways that political institutions such as courts can be "race-gendered," which is why studies that consider intersectionality are warranted (Haire and Moyer 2015).

Although there have been relatively few studies that emphasize intersectionality in terms of judicial decision-making, several have focused on the US court of appeals. Analyzing criminal cases decided between 1977 and 2001, Collins and Moyer (2008) find that just considering race or gender does not reveal any significant differences with respect to whether judges voted in a liberal, as opposed to a conservative, manner. However, they find that black appellate court female judges were "6 to 10 percent more likely to support a liberal outcome than males or Caucasian females" (224). Haire and Moyer (2015) examine the impact of sex and race on judicial decision-making at the appellate court by looking at positions taken in gender and race salient cases from 1995 to 2008. They find that African American female judges are significantly more likely than African American male judges to find in favor of the plaintiff in sex discrimination cases but that no sex differences appear in cases dealing with racial discrimination. Instead, black male judges hold the most distinctly liberal voting records on racial discrimination cases. Haire and Moyer argue that these findings perhaps "underscore arguments made by intersectionality theorists that representation by minority women is not necessarily the sum of racism plus sexism, but rather a more nuanced and contextual process" (77). However, in looking at overall liberalism scores of appellate judges in the United States, they find that Latina judges on the courts of appeals had the most consistently liberal voting record of any racial-gendered group; black and white women and men appellate judges had similar averages in terms of voting records, but the range of liberalism scores were much wider for white women compared with white men. In other words, black women on the appellate courts were more uniformly liberal. Both studies suggest the need for more research as to how race and gender impacts decision-making on the courts, particularly at the lower federal and state level.

Gender and the Supreme Court: Why Gender Matters

At the Supreme Court level, the appointment of both Sandra Day O'Connor and Ruth Bader Ginsburg led to increased support among male justices for sex discrimination cases (Palmer 2002; O'Connor and Yanus 2010). Further analysis of the impact of O'Connor and Ginsburg on sex discrimination cases shows that both justices wrote a disproportionate number of majority opinions in the areas of women's rights: between 1993 and 2000, they wrote on half of the 12 cases in this area (Palmer 2002). Even though O'Connor and Ginsburg differed with respect to many of their decisions—in their 12 years (1993–2005) of serving together, they agreed only 52 percent of the time with respect to decisions handed down from the bench (O'Connor and Yanus 2010)—on gender discrimination cases and abortion cases, they agreed 90 percent of the time.

While O'Connor and Ginsburg were serving together, the Supreme Court heard 14 sex discrimination cases, and the women justices were on the same side of the decision-making in 12 of those cases. One of the most well-known sex discrimination cases was *United States v. Virginia et al.*, the 1996 decision that required the Virginia Military Institute (VMI)—an all-male military academic funded by the state—to open its doors to women cadets as the court ruled that all categorical exclusion of women from state-funded colleges was unconstitutional. In a 7–1 decision penned by Justice Ginsburg, the court held that "Virginia's categorical exclusion of women from the educational opportunities VMI provides denies equal protection to women."

After O'Connor's departure, the court headed in a more conservative direction with respect to women's rights, leaving Ginsburg as the sole female voice until Obama's appointment of Sotomayor in 2009. In 2007, the Supreme Court, in *Ledbetter v. Goodyear*, narrowly upheld a lower court decision that prevented women from seeking back pay over pay discrimination alleged to have occurred years earlier. In a stinging dissent, Justice Ginsburg argued that the majority was either indifferent to or failed to recognize the "insidious" way that women can be subject to pay discrimination and she called on Congress to pass legislation that would allow victims of past pay discrimination to be able to seek justice under Title VII of the Civil Rights Act (Barnes 2007). (Congress did, in fact, pass such legislation, and the Lilly Ledbetter Fair Pay Act—named after the plaintiff of the Supreme Court case—was the first piece of legislation President Barack Obama signed in January 2009.) Moreover, in the heated arena of abortion politics, the Supreme Court upheld a federal abortion statute, the Partial Birth Abortion Ban Act, that banned a certain abortion procedure to be used in late-term abortions in *Gonzalez v. Carhart* (2007). Seven years earlier, with Justice O'Connor still serving, the Supreme Court had struck down a similar Nebraska statute, so the court took the rare path of essentially overturning a similar decision (O'Connor and Yanus 2010).

The addition of two other women to the Supreme Court, however, has not stemmed the more conservative trend of decision-making when it comes to women's rights. In the court's *Burwell v. Hobby Lobby* (2014) decision, which challenged a provision in the Affordable Care Act (ACA) that requires employers' insurance plans to provide free contraception as part of its comprehensive health-care guidelines, the court sided with the owners of the craft shop Hobby Lobby, who objected to the provision on religious grounds. In a contentious 5–4 decision, the court's majority held that the ACA provision violated the religious rights of a privately held corporation under the federal Religious Freedom Restoration Act. For the first time, the Supreme Court recognized that for-profit businesses are "persons" capable of exercising religion. As the National Women's Law Center notes about the majority decision, there was no discussion of the "important role that birth control plays in women's lives" (NWLC 2014).

In a sharply worded dissenting decision, Justice Ginsburg expressed alarm at the implications the case may have for women's rights. In the dissent, she wrote, "In a decision of startling breadth, the Court holds that commercial enterprises, including corporations, along with partnerships and sole proprietorships, can opt out of any law (saving only tax laws) they judge incompatible with their sincerely held religious beliefs" (1).

She later added that the exemption sought by Hobby Lobby and other privately held corporations whose owners had religious objections to providing certain forms of birth control would "deny legions of women who do not hold their employers' beliefs access to contraceptive coverage that the ACA would otherwise ensure" (*Burwell v. Hobby Lobby* 2014). Moreover, Ginsburg took the relatively unusual step of publicly speaking out about the *Hobby Lobby* decision in ways that highlight the unique perspective that women judges can bring to jurisprudence. In an interview with the Associated Press (2014) following the end of the 2013–2014 term, Ginsburg said, "I have no doubt that if the court had been composed of nine women the result would have been different in *Hobby Lobby*."

On *Hobby Lobby* and on most other cases, the Supreme Court's three female justices Ginsburg, Sotomayor, and Kagan have typically voted together. For instance, a recent analysis of decisions made since Neil Gorsuch joined the court in 2017 through the end of the 2018 term shows that Ginsburg and Sotomayer agreed with each other 94 percent of the time; only Clarence Thomas and Samuel Alito, the two most conservative justices, had a similar matched voting record (Roeder 2018). In those same two years, Kagan has agreed with Ginsburg and Sotomayor 88 and 87 percent of the time, respectively; Stephen Breyer, Clinton's other Supreme Court appointee, in fact, has a slightly higher agreement rate with Ginsburg (91 percent) and Sotomayor (90 percent) than Kagan.

In the past two years, Elena Kagan has shown more of a willingness to craft some moderate compromises on high-profile cases with the conservative justices, such as the *Masterpiece Cakeshop* 7–2 decision that sided with a conservative Christian baker from Colorado, Jack Phillips, who refused to sell a wedding cake to a same-sex couple. Rather than ruling that businesses could legitimately discriminate against LGBTQ Americans as a function of their owner's religious beliefs more broadly, the Supreme Court focused on how Phillips was treated by the Colorado Civil Rights Commission, which the court's majority claimed showed anti-religious bias (Lopez 2018). Ginsburg and Sotomayor, however, pointedly disagreed with this decision in their dissent. Some legal scholars, especially, point to Sotomayor as having emerged as the most effective minority voice on the court who is willing to advance more liberal jurisprudence (Fontana 2018). It is worth pointing out, however, that despite the deep ideological differences among many of the Supreme Court justices, they are very likely to agree on many cases. For example, in the 2017–2018 term the Supreme Court was far more likely to issue a 9–0 decision (36 percent of case outcomes) compared with 5–4 decisions (19 percent of case outcomes) (Turberville and Marcum 2018).

Nonetheless, as the Supreme Court is poised to hear more cases that involve the rights of women, racial minorities, and LGBTQ Americans in the future, and given that political scientists have found that the gender and/

or racial composition of the federal judiciary can impact the outcomes in gender and race salient cases in the lower courts, considering who presides on the bench at all levels of the federal judiciary is important and warrants more analysis.

Beyond the Essentialist Argument: Why Gender Still Matters

Do women, then, make a difference when it comes to serving as judges? Yes and no. Clearly, many female judges themselves believe that it is important to have women serving in the judiciary because women bring a unique view and much-needed qualities to the bench—including raising awareness about issues such as gender discrimination to their male brethren. Some studies find, in addition, that women judges are more liberal in their decision-making when it comes to some issues of greater relevance to women, such as sexual harassment. Yet, other studies find little evidence that women judges decide cases differently from men. For example, there is not much indication that women judges have a unique decision-making style, or "different voice," compared with men when it comes to their jurisprudence. Although women can potentially make distinctive contributions in some limited areas of the law while serving on the bench, they are limited in the changes they can pursue by the constraints of the judiciary itself. More often than not, women decide cases in similar ways to men because they are socialized in law school and later in the profession to think like lawyers and judges. Judges are also constrained in their decision-making by their needs to consider precedent, the rule of law, and fact patterns in their cases. Some scholars, in fact, believe it may not be a bad thing that there are few consistent data to show that women judges routinely act differently than their male counterparts—even in sexual harassment cases. Studies that find few differences between men and women judges are an indication that most judges apply consistent standards in their decisions, regardless of gender (Kulik, Perry, and Pepper 2003). That one's personal characteristics such as gender take a back seat to the more relevant situational or behavioral factors in court cases can raise our confidence about judges—regardless of their gender or personal background—and about the judiciary more generally.

But some feminist scholars believe that having more women serve on the judiciary, even if women and men make similar decisions, is important for other reasons. In her work *Gender & Justice,* political scientist Sally J. Kenney (2013) makes what she calls the "nonessentialist case" for having more women in the judiciary. Noting that women make up a "far cry from half" of sitting judges on the federal and state courts, she argues that making the bench more gender diverse should not be based on the fact that women and men have essential differences—an argument, notably, that feminism emerged to challenge, which often kept women and men in separate spheres and justified women's exclusion from public life. Instead, she writes that the most persuasive arguments to increase gender diversity on the bench appeal to democracy and legitimacy. The argument for having more women serve as judges—and more minorities, as well—goes beyond mere window dressing or symbolism. Sally Kenney writes:

> The presence of women [in the judiciary] disrupts the normal assumption that heterosexual white men are the only citizens capable of performing the core ritual of rendering objective judgment, that only privileged men are naturally suited to assume authority on behalf of the state and to exercise their parochial care on behalf of society. (176)

To return to the controversy surrounding Supreme Court Justice Sonia Sotomayor's confirmation hearings, Kenney writes that they "clearly triggered anxiety about expanding the deciders to include women of color. Privilege and authority are joined in ways that seem natural and proper, and appointments such as Sotomayor's disrupt those naturalized links and enable us to see exclusion" (176–77). Sotomayor's comments about a "wise Latina" making better judgments than a "white man who hasn't lived that life" struck a nerve and challenged the notion that judging can be entirely objective and neutral, made in a vacuum without reference to life's experiences. Her passionate dissent in the *Schuette* decision, which upheld a state ban on affirmative action, further illustrates that a judge's life history, rooted in his or her racial, gender, or social class identities, perhaps brings something valuable to rendering judgment. Simply put, there are many reasons why a bench that looks more like America is important, just, and fair.

CONCLUSION

From the pioneering days of early female judges such as Florence Allen, the first woman appointed to the federal judiciary, women have made huge strides in the legal profession. Women now make up about 34 percent of all federal judges and 33 percent of all state judges. At the upper pinnacle, women make up one-third of the United States Supreme Court and 33 percent of state supreme court justices. With more than half of all law students currently being female, it is likely that more women will make their impact felt both as attorneys and as judges in this crucial third branch of government. Having more women represented as judges is important, for in the words of Ruth Bader Ginsburg, "A system of justice will be richer for diversity of background and experience. It will be poorer, in terms of appreciating what is at stake and the impact of its judgments, if all its members are cast from the same mold" (quoted in Martin 1993, 126).

Although the representation of more women in the judiciary is important with respect to democratic norms, and may also inspire future generations of girls and boys by providing more diverse judges as role models, whether the inclusion of more women on the bench actually leads to the enhanced representation of women or women's interests is more debatable. For instance, although some studies show that female judges are somewhat more sympathetic to the victims of sexual or racial discrimination (who tend to be female or minority), most studies show that women and men judges largely decide cases in the same manner. Moreover, the hypothesis that women would potentially use a different, "feminine" voice in terms of their jurisprudence has not been borne out. On the bench, women largely decide cases in the same way as men—which likely reflects their common legal training and the conservative nature of law itself. Some believe that the finding that gender has little effect on the way that judges make decisions actually boosts our confidence in women's ability to perform this demanding job—and supports the notion that more women should be selected to serve in the judiciary.

Appendix A

"Declaration of Sentiments" and "Resolutions" Adopted by the Seneca Falls Convention of 1848

WHEN, IN THE COURSE OF HUMAN EVENTS, it becomes necessary for one portion of the family of man to assume among the people of the earth a position different from that which they have hitherto occupied, but one to which the laws of nature and of nature's God entitle them, a decent respect to the opinions of mankind requires that they should declare the causes that impel them to such a course.

We hold these truths to be self-evident: that all men and women are created equal; that they are endowed by their Creator with certain inalienable rights; that among these are life, liberty, and the pursuit of happiness; that to secure these rights governments are instituted, deriving their just powers from the consent of the governed. Whenever any form of government becomes destructive of these ends, it is the right of those who suffer from it to refuse allegiance to it, and to insist upon the institution of a new government, laying its foundation on such principles, and organizing its powers in such form, as to them shall seem most likely to effect their safety and happiness. Prudence indeed will dictate that governments long established should not be changed for light and transient causes; and accordingly all experience hath shown that mankind are more disposed to suffer, while evils are sufferable, than to right themselves by abolishing the forms to which they were accustomed. But when a long train of abuses and usurpations, pursuing invariably the same object evinces a design to reduce them under absolute despotism, it is their duty to throw off such government, and to provide new guards for their future security. Such has been the patient sufferance of the women under this government, and such is now the necessity which constrains them to demand the equal station to which they are entitled.

The history of mankind is a history of repeated injuries and usurpations on the part of man toward woman, having in direct object the establishment of an absolute tyranny over her. To prove this, let facts be submitted to a candid world.

He has never permitted her to exercise her inalienable right to the elective franchise.

He has compelled her to submit to laws, in the formation of which she had no voice.

He has withheld from her rights which are given to the most ignorant and degraded men—both natives and foreigners. Having deprived her of this first right of a citizen, the elective franchise, thereby leaving her without representation in the halls of legislation, he has oppressed her on all sides.

He has made her, if married, in the eye of the law, civilly dead.

He has taken from her all right in property, even to the wages she earns. He has made her, morally, an irresponsible being, as she can commit many crimes with impunity, provided they be done in the presence of her husband. In the covenant of marriage, she is compelled to promise obedience to her husband, he becoming, to all intents and purposes, her master—the law giving him power to deprive her of her liberty, and to administer chastisement.

He has so framed the laws of divorce, as to what shall be the proper causes, and in case of separation, to whom the guardianship of the children shall be given, as to be wholly regardless of the happiness of women—the law, in all cases, going upon a false supposition of the supremacy of man, and giving all power into his hands.

After depriving her of all rights as a married woman, if single, and the owner of property, he has taxed her to support a government which recognizes her only when her property can be made profitable to it.

He has monopolized nearly all the profitable employments, and from those she is permitted to follow, she receives but a scanty remuneration. He closes against her all the avenues to wealth and distinction which he considers most honorable to himself. As a teacher of theology, medicine, or law, she is not known.

He has denied her the facilities for obtaining a thorough education, all colleges being closed against her.

He allows her in Church, as well as State, but a subordinate position, claiming Apostolic authority for her exclusion from the ministry, and, with some exceptions, from any public participation in the affairs of the Church.

He has created a false public sentiment by giving to the world a different code of morals for men and women, by which moral delinquencies which exclude women from society are not only tolerated, but deemed of little account in man.

He has usurped the prerogative of Jehovah himself, claiming it as his right to assign for her a sphere of action, when that belongs to her conscience and to her God.

He has endeavored, in every way that he could, to destroy her confidence in her own powers, to lessen her self-respect, and to make her willing to lead a dependent and abject life.

Now in view of this entire disfranchisement of one-half the people of this country, their social and religious degradation—in view of the unjust laws above mentioned, pressed, and fraudulently deprived of their most sacred rights, we insist that they have immediate admission to all the rights and privileges which belong to them as citizens of the United States.

In entering upon the great work before us, we anticipate no small amount of misconception, misrepresentation, and ridicule; but we shall use every instrumentality within our power to effect our object. We shall employ agents, circulate tracts, petition the State and National legislatures, and endeavor to enlist the pulpit and the press on our behalf. We hope this convention will be followed by a series of conventions embracing every part of the country.

The following resolutions were discussed by Lucretia Mott, Thomas and Mary Ann McClintock, Amy Post, Catharine A. F. Stebbins, and others, and were adopted.

WHEREAS, The great precept of nature is conceded to be, that "man shall pursue his own true and substantial happiness." Blackstone in his Commentaries remarks, that this law of Nature being coeval with mankind, and dictated by God himself, is of course superior in obligation to any other. It is binding over all the globe, in all countries and at all times; no human laws are of any validity if contrary to this, and such of them as are valid, derive all their force, and all their validity, and all their authority, mediately, and immediately, from this original; therefore,

Resolved, That such laws as conflict, in any way, with the true and substantial happiness of woman, are contrary to the great precept of nature and of no validity, for this is "superior in obligation to any other."

Resolved, That all laws which prevent woman from occupying such a station in society as her conscience shall dictate, or which place her in a position inferior to that of man, are contrary to the great precept of nature, and therefore of no force or authority.

Resolved, That woman is man's equal—was intended to be so by the Creator, and the highest good of the race demands that she should be recognized as such.

Resolved, That the women of this country ought to be enlightened in regard to the laws under which they live, that they may no longer publish their degradation by declaring themselves satisfied with their present position, nor their ignorance, by asserting that they have all the rights they want.

Resolved, That inasmuch as man, while claiming for himself intellectual superiority, does accord to woman moral superiority, it is pre-eminently his duty to encourage her to speak and teach, as she has an opportunity, in all religious assemblies.

Resolved, That the same amount of virtue, delicacy, and refinement of behavior that is required of woman in the social state, should also be required of man, and the same transgressions should be visited with equal severity on both man and woman.

Resolved, That the objection of indelicacy and impropriety, which is so often brought against woman when she addresses a public audience, comes with a very ill-grace from those who encourage, by their attendance, her appearance on stage, in the concert, or in feats of the circus.

Resolved, That woman has too long rested satisfied in the circumscribed limits which corrupt customs and a perverted application of the Scriptures have marked out for her, and that it is time she should move in the enlarged sphere which her great Creator has assigned her.

Resolved, That it is the duty of the women of this country to secure themselves their sacred right to the elective franchise.

Resolved, That the equality of human rights results necessarily from the fact of the identity of the race in capabilities and responsibilities.

Resolved, therefore, That, being invested by the Creator with the same capabilities, and the same consciousness of responsibility for their exercise, it is demonstrably the right and duty of woman, equally with man, to promote every righteous cause by every righteous means; and especially in regard to the great subjects of morals and religion, it is self-evidently her right to participate with her brother in teaching them, both in private and in public, by writing and by speaking, by any instrumentalities proper to be used, and in any assemblies proper to be held; and this being a self-evident truth growing out of the divinely implanted principles of human nature, any custom or authority adverse to it, whether modern or wearing the hoary sanction of antiquity, is to be regarded as a self-evident falsehood, and at war with mankind.

At the last session Lucretia Mott offered and spoke to the following resolution:

Resolved, That the speedy success of our cause depends upon the zealous and untiring efforts of both men and women, for the overthrow of the monopoly of the pulpit, and for the securing to women an equal participation with men in the various trades, professions, and commerce.

Source: Shanley, Mary Lyndon. 1988. *Women's Rights, Feminism, and Politics in the United States.* Washington, DC: American Political Science Association.

National Organization for Women's Bill of Rights and Redstockings Manifesto

BILL OF RIGHTS

Adopted at NOW's first national conference, Washington, DC, 1967.

I. Equal Rights Constitutional Amendment.
II. Enforce Law Banning Sex Discrimination in Employment.
III. Maternity Leave Rights in Employment and in Social Security Benefits.
IV. Tax Deduction for Home and Child Care Expenses for Working Parents.
V. Child Day Care Centers.
VI. Equal and Unsegregated Education.
VII. Equal Job Training Opportunities and Allowances for Women in Poverty.
VIII. The Right of Women to Control Their Reproductive Lives.

WE DEMAND

I. That the US Congress immediately pass the Equal Rights Amendment to the Constitution to provide that "quality of rights under the law shall not be denied or abridged by the United States or by any State on account of sex," and that such then be immediately ratified by several states.
II. That equal employment opportunities be guaranteed to all women, as well as men, by insisting that the Equal Employment Opportunity Commission enforces the prohibitions against sex discrimination in employment under Title VII of the Civil Rights Act of 1964 with the same vigor as it enforces the prohibitions against racial discrimination.

III. That women be protected by law to ensure their rights to return to their jobs within a reasonable time after childbirth without loss of seniority or other accrued benefits, and be paid maternity leave as a form of social security and/or employee benefit.

IV. Immediate revision of tax laws to permit the deduction of home and child-care expenses for working parents.

V. That child-care facilities be established by law on the same basis as parks, libraries, and public schools, adequate to the needs of children from the preschool years through adolescence, as a community resource to be used by all citizens from all income levels.

VI. That the right of women to be educated to their full potential equality with men be secured by federal and state legislation, eliminating all discrimination and segregation by sex, written and unwritten, at all levels of education, including colleges, graduate and professional schools, loans and fellowships, and federal and state training programs such as the Job Corps.

VII. The right of women in poverty to secure job training, housing, and family allowances on equal terms with men, but without prejudice to a parent's right to remain at home to care for his or her children; revision of welfare legislation and poverty programs which deny women dignity, privacy, and self-respect.

VIII. The right of women to control their own reproductive lives by removing from the penal code laws limiting access to contraceptive information and devices, and by repealing penal laws governing abortion.

Source: Shanley, Mary Lyndon. 1988. *Women's Rights, Feminism, and Politics in the United States.* Washington, DC: American Political Science Association. Also available in the Early Documents section of the Feminist Chronicles online at www.feminist.org/research/chronicles/early4.html.

REDSTOCKINGS MANIFESTO

I. After centuries of individual and preliminary political struggle, women are uniting to achieve their final liberation from male supremacy. Redstockings is dedicated to building this unity and winning our freedom.

II. Women are an oppressed class. Our oppression is total, affecting every facet of our lives. We are exploited as sex objects, breeders, domestic servants, and cheap labor. We are considered inferior beings, whose only purpose is to enhance men's lives. Our humanity is denied. Our prescribed behavior is enforced by the threat of physical violence.

Because we have lived so intimately with our oppressors, in isolation from each other, we have been kept from seeing our personal suffering as a political condition. This creates the illusion that a woman's relationship with her man is a matter of interplay between two unique personalities and can be worked out individually. In reality, every such relationship is a *class* relationship, and the conflicts between individual men and women are *political* conflicts that can only be solved collectively.

III. We identify the agents of our oppression as men. Male supremacy is the oldest, most basic form of domination. All other forms of exploitation and oppression (racism, capitalism, imperialism, etc.) are extensions of male supremacy: men dominate women, a few men dominate the rest. All power structures throughout history have been male-dominated and male-oriented. Men have controlled all political, economic, and cultural institutions and backed up this control with physical force. They have used their power to keep women in an inferior position. *All men* receive economic, sexual, and psychological benefits from male supremacy. *All men* have oppressed women.

IV. Attempts have been made to shift the burden of responsibility from men to institutions or to women themselves. We condemn these arguments as evasions. Institutions alone do not oppress; they are merely tools of the oppressor. To blame institutions implies that men and women are equally victimized, obscures the fact that men benefit from the subordination of women, and gives men the excuse that they are forced to be oppressors. On the contrary, any man is free to renounce his superior position provided that he is willing to be treated like a woman by other men.

We also reject the idea that women consent to or are to blame for their own oppression. Women's submission is not the result of brainwashing, stupidity, or mental illness but of continual, daily pressure from men. We do not need to change ourselves, but to change men.

The most slanderous evasion of all is that women can oppress men. The basis for this illusion is the isolation of individual relationships from their political context and the tendency of men to see any legitimate challenge to their privileges as persecution.

V. We regard our personal experience, and our feelings about that experience, as the basis for an analysis of our common situation. We cannot rely on existing ideologies as they are all products of male supremacist culture. We question every generalization and accept none that are not confirmed by our experience.

Our chief task at present is to develop female class consciousness through sharing experience and publicly exposing the sexist foundation of all our institutions. Consciousness-raising is not "therapy," which implies the existence of individual solutions and falsely assumes that the male-female relationship is purely personal, but the only method by which we can ensure that our program for liberation is based on the concrete realities of our lives.

The first requirement for raising class consciousness is honesty, in private and in public, with ourselves and other women.

VI. We identify with all women. We define our best interest as that of the poorest, most brutally exploited woman.

We repudiate all economic, racial, educational, or status privileges that divide us from other women. We are determined to recognize and eliminate any prejudices we may hold against other women.

We are committed to achieving internal democracy. We will do whatever is necessary to ensure that every woman in our movement has an equal chance to participate, assume responsibility, and develop her political potential.

VII. We call on all our sisters to unite with us in struggle.

We call on men to give up their male privileges and support women's liberation in the interest of our humanity and their own.

In fighting for our liberation we will always take the side of women against their oppressors. We will not ask what is "revolutionary" or "reformist," only what is good for women.

The time for individual skirmishes has passed. This time we are going all the way.

July 7, 1969

Source: Shanley, Mary Lyndon. 1988. *Women's Rights, Feminism, and Politics in the United States*. Washington, DC: American Political Science Association.

References

CHAPTER 1

Bacon, Jr. Perry. 2018. "Why the Republican Party Elects So Few Women." *Five Thirty Eight*. June 25. https://fivethirtyeight.com/features/why-the-republican -party-isnt-electing-more-women/. Accessed February 1, 2019.

Borrelli, MaryAnne. 2002. *The President's Cabinet: Gender, Power, and Representation*. Boulder, CO: L. Rienner Publishers.

Bittner, Amanda and Elizabeth Goodyear-Grant. 2017. "Sex Isn't Gender: Reforming Concepts and Measurements in the Story of Public Opinion." *Political Behavior* 39(4): 1019–41.

Caygle, Heather. 2018. "Female Candidates Take on Taboos in New Campaign Ads." *Politico*. April 3. https://www.politico.com/story/2018/04/03/women-ru le-campaign-ads-495799. Accessed December 13, 2018.

CAWP (Center for American Women and Politics). 2018. "Women in State Legislatures 2018." http://cawp.rutgers.edu/women-state-legislature-2018. Accessed December 10, 2018.

Chappell, Carmin. 2018. "In Historic Election for Female Candidates, Republican Women Lose Ground in the House." *CNBC*. November 21. https://www.cnb c.com/2018/11/21/democratic-women-make-big-gains-in-house-as-gop-women -lose-ground-in-historic-election.html. Accessed December 14, 2018.

Cillizza, Chris. 2018. "Amy Klobuchar's Moment in the Kavanaugh Hearings." *CNN*. October 1. https://www.cnn.com/2018/10/01/politics/amy-klobuchar- brett-kavanaugh-supreme-court/index.html. Accessed February 5, 2019.

Collins, Patricia Hill. 2008. *Black Feminist Thought: Knowledge, Consciousness, and the Politics of Empowerment*. New York: Routledge.

Cope, Edward D. 1888. "The Relation of the Two Sexes to Government." In *Women's Rights in the United States: A Documentary History*, edited by Winston Langley and Vivian C. Fox, 166–69. Westport, CT: Praeger Publishers.

Cottle, Michelle. 2018. "The G.O.P Is a Boys' Club. This Woman is Trying to Change That." *New York Times*. December 12. https://www.nytimes.com/ 2018/12/12/opinion/gop-women-republican-stefanik.html. Accessed December 14, 2018.

Cox, Daniel and Melissa Deckman. 2018. "Young Women Could Redefine the Women's Vote." *FiveThirtyEight*. July 5. https://fivethirtyeight.com/features/why -young-women-might-get-more-women-elected/. Accessed December 17, 2018.

——. 2018. "Young Women Could Redefine the Women's Vote." *FiveThirtyEight*. July 5. https://fivethirtyeight.com/features/why-young-women-might-get-mo re-women-elected/. Accessed December 13, 2018.

Deckman, Melissa. 2017. "How the Resist Trump Movement Could Transform into the Tea Party of the Left." *London School of Economics Blog on American Politics and Policy*. March 3. http://bit.ly/2mT6cd6. Accessed December 10, 2018.

——. 2018a. "A New Poll Shows How Younger Women Could Help Drive A Democratic Wave in 2018." *Washington Post*. March 5. https://www.was hingtonpost.com/news/monkey-cage/wp/2018/03/05/a-new-poll-shows-how-younger-women-could-help-drive-a-democratic-wave-in-2018/?noredirec t=on&utm_term=.2a0686d306a1. Accessed December 13, 2018.

——. 2018b. "This Poll Shows Why There's Never Been a Better Time for Women to Run for Office." *Washington Post*. August 27. https://www.washingtonpos t.com/news/monkey-cage/wp/2018/08/27/this-survey-shows-why-theres-neve r-been-a-better-time-for-women-to-run-for-office/?utm_term=.78037f25a287. Accessed December 13, 2018.

Deckman, Melissa and Shauna Shames. 2018. "Will Young Women of Color Shape the Democratic Party?" *Vox*. August 23. https://www.vox.com/mischiefs-of-fa ction/2018/8/23/17765414/women-of-color-democratic-party. Accessed February 1, 2019.

Diamond, Jeremy. 2018. "Trump Says 'It's a Very Scary Time for Young Men in America." *CNN*. October 2. https://www.cnn.com/2018/10/02/politics/trump -scary-time-for-young-men-metoo/index.html. Accessed December 17, 2018.

Dittmar, Kelly. 2018a. "By the Numbers: Women Congressional Candidates in 2018." *Center for American Women and Politics*. September 12. http://cawp. rutgers.edu/congressional-candidates-summary-2018. Accessed December 13, 2018.

——. 2018b. "By the Numbers: Women Candidates for State Executive and State Legislative Office in 2018." *Center for American Women and Politics*. September 14. http://cawp.rutgers.edu/state-candidates-summary-2018. Accessed December 13, 2018.

——. 2018c. "Running as Women or Men? Candidates Use of Gender in 2018." *GenderWatch 2018*. May 31. https://www.genderwatch2018.org/running-women-men/. Accessed December 17, 2018.

——. 2015. *Navigating Gendered Terrain: Stereotypes and Strategies in Political Campaigns*. Philadelphia, PA: Temple University Press.

Dittmar, Kelly, Kira Sanbonmatsu, Susan J. Carrol, Debbie Walsh, and Catherine Wineinger. 2017. *Representation Matters: Women in the U.S. Congress*. http: //www.cawp.rutgers.edu/sites/default/files/resources/representationmatters.pdf. Accessed December 17, 2018.

Edmonson, Catie and Jasmine C. Lee. 2018. "Meet the New Freshmen in Congress: More Democrats, Diversity and Women." *The New York Times*. November 30. https://www.nytimes.com/interactive/2018/11/28/us/politics/congress-fr eshman-class.html. Accessed December 14, 2018.

Frederick, Angela. 2014. "'Who Better to Do It Than Me!': Race, Gender & the Deciding to Run Accounts of Political Women in Texas." *Qualitative Sociology* 37(3): 301–21.

Green, Emma. 2013. "A Lot Has Changed in Congress Since 1992, the 'Year of the Woman.'" *The Atlantic*. http://www.theatlantic.com/politics/archive/2013/ 09/ a-lot-has-changed-in-congress-since-1992-the-year-of-the-woman/280046. Accessed June 24, 2015.

Godfrey, Elaine, Lena Felton, and Taylor Hosking. 2018. "The 25 Candidates for 2018 Sunk by the #MeToo Movement." *The Atlantic*. July 26. https://www.the atlantic.com/politics/archive/2018/07/the-25-candidates-for-2018-sunk-by-me too-allegations/565457. Accessed December 13, 2018.

Hardy-Fanta, Carol, Pei-te Lien, Dianne M. Pinderhughes, and Christine Marie Sierra. 2006. "Gender, Race, and Descriptive Representation in the United States: Findings from the Gender and Multicultural Leadership Project." *Journal of Women, Politics & Policy* 28(3–4): 7–41.

Hawkesworth, Mary. 2003. "Congressional Enactments of Race-Gender: Toward a Theory of Raced-Gendered Institutions." *American Political Science Review* 97(4): 529–50.

hooks, Bell. 1981. *Ain't I a Woman: Black Women and Feminism*. Boston, MA: South End Press.

Jones, Jacqueline. 1986. *Labor of Love, Labor of Sorrow: Black Women, Work, and the Family from Slavery to the Present*. New York: Vintage Books.

Katz, Jackson. 2016. *Man Enough? Donald Trump, Hillary Clinton, and the Politics of Presidential Masculinity*. Northampton, MA: Interlink Books.

King, Cheryl Simrell. 1995. "Sex-Role Identity and Decision Styles: How Gender Helps Explain the Paucity of Women at the Top." In *Gender Power, Leadership and Governance*, edited by Georgia Duerst-Lahti and Rita Mae Kelly, 67–92. Ann Arbor: University of Michigan Press.

Kurtzleben, Danielle. 2018. "A Record 309 Women are Running for Seats in the House (and 1,103 Men)." *NPR*. April 13. https://www.npr.org/2018/04/13/601866062/there-are-a-record-breaking-309-women-house-candidates-and-1-103-men. Accessed December 17, 2018.

Langley, Winston and Vivian C. Fox. 1994. *Women's Rights in the United States: A Documentary History*. Westport, CT: Greenwood Press.

Lessenberry, Jack. 2017. "That Dana Nessel Ad about Sexual Harassment is Shocking, but Effective." Michigan Radio. December 11. http://www.michiganradio.org/post/dana-nessel-ad-about-sexual-harassment-shocking-effective. Accessed December 13, 2018.

Malloy, Allie, Kate Sullivan, and Jeff Zeleny. 2018. "Trump Mocks Christine Blasey Ford's Testimony, Tells People 'Think of Your Son.'" *CNN*. October 3. https://www.cnn.com/2018/10/02/politics/trump-mocks-christine-blasey-ford-kavanaugh-supreme-court/index.html. Accessed December 17, 2018.

Mansbridge, Jane. 1999. "Should Blacks Represent Blacks and Women Represent Women? A Contingent 'Yes.'" *The Journal of Politics* 61(3): 628–57.

McDermott, Monica L. 2016. *Masculinity, Femininity, and American Political Behavior*. New York: Oxford University Press.

Mitchell, Eileen. 2018. "Record Number of Female Veterans to serve in Next Congress." *The Hill*. November 11. https://thehill.com/homenews/house/416343-record-number-of-female-veterans-to-serve-in-next-congress. Accessed December 13, 2018.

National Conference of State Legislators. 2018. "Women in State Legislatures." http://www.ncsl.org/legislators-staff/legislators/womens-legislative-network/women-in-state-legislatures-for-2018.aspx. Accessed December 14, 2018.

North, Anna. 2018. "The Midterm Election Shows White Women are Finally Starting to Abandon Trump." *Vox*. November 7. https://www.vox.com/policy-and-politics/2018/11/7/18064260/midterm-elections-turnout-women-trump-exit-polls. Accessed December 14, 2018.

Olheiser, Abby. 2017. "The Woman Behind MeToo Knew the Power of the Phrase when she Created it—10 years ago." *Washington Post*. October 19. https://ww

w.washingtonpost.com/news/the-intersect/wp/2017/10/19/the-woman-behind
-me-too-knew-the-power-of-the-phrase-when-she-created-it-10-years-ago/
?utm_term=.8516aac95a8c. Accessed December 10, 2018.

Pitkin, Hanna Fenichel. 1967. *The Concept of Representation.* Berkeley: University
of California Press.

Political Parity. n.d. "Why Women." http://www.politicalparity.org/why-women

Putnam, Lara and Theda Skocpol. 2018. "Middle America Reboots Democracy."
Democracy: A Journal of Ideas. February 20. https://democracyjournal.org/a
rguments/middle-america-reboots-democracy. Accessed December 10, 2018.

Reflective Democracy Campaign. 2018. "A Rising Tide? The Changing Demographics on Our Ballots." https://whioleleads.us/2018-report. October. Accessed
February 1, 2019.

Sandberg, Sheryl. 2013. *Lean In: Women, Work, and the Will to Lead.* New York:
Knopf.

Sapiro, Virginia. 1981. "Research Frontier Essay: When Are Interests Interesting?
The Problem of Political Representation of Women." *The American Political
Science Review* 75(3): 701–16.

Schaeffer, Sabrina. 2018. "Identity Politics Aren't Necessary to See That Republicans Need to Recruit Women." *The Federalist.* December 10. http://thefeder
alist.com/2018/12/10/identity-politics-arent-necessary-see-republicans-need
-recruit-women/?fbclid=IwAR06OVba6IreLrrqIdlwoPh5SqZ0yUzJslG2saoB
drdQhbdT4ayn0ft-SZ8. Accessed December 14.

Silver, Nate. 2017. "The Long March Ahead for Democrats." *FiveThirtyEight.*
January 23. https://fivethirtyeight.com/features/the-long-march-ahead-for-dem
ocrats. Accessed December 10.

Smooth, Wendy. 2011. "Standing for Women? Which Women? The Substantive Representation of Women's Interests and the Research Imperative of Intersectionality." *Politics & Gender* 7(3): 436–41.

Stern, Mark Joseph and Sofie Werthan. 2018. "Boys on the Bench." *Slate.* July 26.
https://slate.com/news-and-politics/2018/07/trump-female-judges-all-the-lam
e-excuses-conservatives-are-making-to-explain-the-presidents-overwhelmingly
-male-nominees.html. Accessed December 14, 2018.

Strolovitch, Dara Z. 2007. *Affirmative Advocacy: Race, Class, and Gender in Interest Group Politics.* Chicago, IL: University of Chicago Press.

Tyson, Alex. 2018. "The 2018 Midterm Vote: Divisions by Race, Gender, Education." *Pew Research Center.* November 8. http://www.pewresearch.org/fac
t-tank/2018/11/08/the-2018-midterm-vote-divisions-by-race-gender-education.
Accessed December 14, 2018.

Valencia, Janie. 2018. "The Gender Gap Was Huge. And it Helped Democrats Win
the House." *FiveThirtyEight.* November 9. https://fivethirtyeight.com/features/
the-2018-gender-gap-was-huge. Accessed December 10.

Valencia, Janie and Dhrumil Mehta. 2018. "A Final Look at Where Voters Stand
On Kavanaugh Before the Senate Votes." *FiveThirtyEight.* October 5. https://
fivethirtyeight.com/features/a-final-look-at-where-voters-stand-on-kavanaugh-
before-the-senate-votes. Accessed December 17.

Vandermaas-Peeler, Alex, Daniel Cox, Maxine Najle, Molly Fisch-Friedman, Rob
Griffin, and Robert D. Jones. 2018. "Partisanship Trumps Gender: Sexual
Harassment, Women Candidates, Access to Contraception, and Key Issues
in 2018." *Public Religion Research Institute (PRRI).* October 3. https://ww
w.prri.org/research/abortion-reproductive-health-midterms-trump-kavanaugh.
Accessed December 13, 2018.

Victory Fund. 2018. "Historic Number of LGBTQ People Elected to U.S. House; LGBTQ Pickups Helped Strengthen New Democratic Majority." November 7. https://victoryfund.org/historic-number-of-lgbtq-people-elected-to-u-s-house-lgbtq-pickups-helped-strengthen-new-democratic-majority. Accessed February 1, 2019.

Women and Politics Institute, American University. 2018. "She Votes. She Leads. Women in the 2018 Midterm Elections." December 4. https://nmcdn.io/e18 6d21f8c7946a19faed23c3da2f0da/260d68d1128048ee975671be3636a5b6/fi les/Women-and-Politics-Institute.pdf. Accessed December 10, 2018.

Zhou, Li. 2018. "It's Official: A Record-Breaking Number of Women Have Won Seats in Congress." *Vox*. November 7. https://www.vox.com/policy-and -politics/2018/11/7/18024742/midterm-results-record-women-win. Accessed December 13, 2018.

CHAPTER 2

Altman, Alex. 2010. "Jenny Beth Martin." *Time*, April 29.

Andersen, Kristi. 1996. *After Suffrage: Women in Partisan and Electoral Politics before the New Deal*. Chicago: University of Chicago Press.

Baker, Paula. 1984. "The Domestication of Politics: Women and American Political Society, 1780–1920." *American Historical Review* 89(3): 620–47.

Barakso, Maryann. 2004. *Governing NOW: Grassroots Activism in the National Organization for Women*. Ithaca: Cornell University Press.

Barr, Cameron W., and Elizabeth Williamson. 2004. "Women's Rally Draws Vast Crowd: Marchers Champion Reproductive Rights, Opposition to Bush." *Washington Post*, April 26.

Bates, Karen Grigsby. 2017. "Race and Feminism: Women's March Recalls the Touchy History." *NPR*, January 21.

Berry, Jeffrey M. 1997. *The Interest Group Society*. New York: Longman.

Berry, Marie, and Erica Chenoweth. 2018. *The Resistance: The Dawn of the Anti-Trump Opposition Movement*. Eds. David S. Meyer and Sidney Tarrow. New York: Oxford University Press.

Blair, Karen. 1980. *The Clubwoman as Feminist*. New York: Holmes and Meier Publishers.

Bordin, Ruth. 1981. *Woman and Temperance*. Philadelphia: Temple University Press.

Brewer, Sierra, and Lauren Dundes. 2018. "Concerned Meet Terrified: Intersectional Feminism and the Women's March." *Women's Studies International Forum* 69: 49–55.

Boushey, Heather. 2014. "A Woman's Place Is in the Middle Class." From *The Shriver Report: A Woman's Nation Pushes Back From the Brink*. A Study by Maria Shriver and the Center for American Progress.

Buckley, Cara. 2018. "Powerful Hollywood Women Unveil Anti-Harassment Action Plan." *New York Times*, January 1.

Burke, Tamara. 2017. "#MeToo Was Started for Black and Brown Women and Girls: They're Still Being Ignored." *Washington Post*, November 9.

Calamur, Krishnadev. 2017. "What Trump's Executive Order on Immigration Does—And Doesn't Do." *The Atlantic*, January 29.

Cauterruci, Christina. 2017. "The Women's March on Washington Has Released an Unapologetically Progressive Platform." *Slate*, January 12.

Carabillo, Toni, Judith Meuli, and June Bundy Csida. 1993. *Feminist Chronicles 1953–1993*. Los Angeles: Women's Graphics.

Concerned Women for America. 2017a. "Our Mission." http://www.cwfa.org/about/vision-mission (accessed January 28, 2017).

———. 2017b. "Our History." http://www.cwfa.org/about/our-history (accessed January 28, 2017).

———. 2017c. "Issues." http://www.cwfa.org/about/issues (accessed January 28, 2017).

Chenoweth, Erica, and Maria J. Stephan. 2012. *Why Civil Resistance Works: The Strategic Logic of Nonviolent Conflict.* New York: Columbia University Press.

Conover, Pamela Johnston, and Virginia Gray. 1983. *Feminism and the New Right: Conflict Over the American Family.* New York: Praeger Publishers.

Conway, M. Margaret, David W. Ahern, and Gertrude Steuernagel. 1999. *Women and Public Policy: A Revolution in Progress,* 2nd ed. Washington, DC: Congressional Quarterly Press.

Corkey, Michael. 2018. "Low-Paid Women Get Hollywood Money to File Harassment Suits." *New York Times,* March 22.

Costain, Anne N. 1992. *Inviting Women's Rebellion.* Baltimore: Johns Hopkins University Press.

Cott, Nancy F. 1987. *The Grounding of Modern Feminism.* New Haven: Yale University Press.

Crenshaw, Kimberlé. 1989. "Demarginalizing the Intersection of Race and Sex: A Black Feminist Critique of Antidiscrimination Doctrine, Feminist Theory, and Antiracist Policies." *University of Chicago Legal Forum* 1989: 139–67.

Crockett, Emily. 2017a. "The 'Women's March on Washington' Explained." *Vox,* January 21.

———. 2017b. "The House Just Passed a Sweeping Abortion Funding Ban: Here's What It Does." *Vox,* January 24.

Cushman, Clare, ed. 2001. *Supreme Court Decisions and Women's Rights: Milestones to Equality.* Washington, DC: Congressional Quarterly, Inc.

Deckman, Melissa. 2016a. *Mama Grizzlies and Politics: Motherhood, Feminism, and the Tea Party in America.* New York: NYU Press.

———. 2016b. "Some Women Actually Do Support Donald Trump. Here's Why." *Washington Post,* April 7.

———. 2017. "Can Pro-Choice and Pro-Life Women Find Common Ground? It's Complicated." *Washington Post,* January 20.

Deckman, Melissa, and John McTague. 2015. "Did the 'War on Women' Work? Women, Men, and the Birth Control Mandate in the 2012 Presidential Election." *American Politics Research* 43(1): 3–26.

Desanctis, Alexandra. 2017. "Huge Diverse Crowd Marches for Life in the Nation's Capitol." *National Review,* January 27.

Desmond-Harris, Jennee. 2017. "To Understand the Women's March on Washington You Need to Understand Intersectional Feminism." *Vox,* January 21.

Dickerson, Caitlin. 2018. "Ida B. Wells: Took on Racism in the Deep South with Powerful Reporting on Lynchings" *New York Times,* March 9.

Dorr, Rheta Childe. 1910. *What Eight Million Women Want.* Boston: Small, Maynard & Company.

Edmondson, Catie, and Jasmine C. Lee. 2018. "Meet the New Freshmen in Congress: More Democrats, Diversity, and Women." *New York Times,* November 28.

Equalrightsamendment.org. 2019, "Ratification Info State by State." Equalrightsamendment.org (accessed January 30, 2019).

Ferree, Myra Marx, and Beth B. Hess. 1994. *Controversy and Coalition: The New Feminist Movement,* rev. ed. New York: Twayne Publishers.

Fiorina, Morris. 2017. *Unstable Majorities: Polarization, Party Sorting, & Political Stalemate*. Stanford: Hoover Institution Press.

Fisher, Dana R., Dawn M. Dow, and Rashawn Ray. 2017. "Intersectionality Takes it to the Streets: Mobilizing Across Diverse Interests for the Women's March." *Science Advance* 3: 1–8.

Flexner, Eleanor, and Ellen Fitzpatrick. 1996. *Century of Struggle: The Women's Rights Movement in the United States*. Cambridge, MA: Belknap Press of Harvard University.

Freeman, Jo. 1975. *The Politics of Women's Liberation*. New York: Longman Inc.

———. 2000. *A Room at a Time: How Women Entered Party Politics*. New York: Rowman & Littlefield Publishers, Inc.

Friedman, Estelle B. 2002. *No Turning Back: The History of Feminism and the Future of Women*. New York: Ballantine.

Frostenson, Sarah. 2017. "The Women's Marches May Have Been the Largest Demonstration in US History." *Vox*, January 22.

Gade, Emily Kalah. 2017. "Why the Women's March May be the Start of a Serious Social Movement." *Washington Post*, January 30.

Gelb, Joyce, and Marian Lief Palley. 1996. *Women and Public Policies: Reassessing Gender Politics*. Charlottesville, VA: University Press of Virginia.

Grady, Constance. 2018. "The Waves of Feminism, and Why People Keep Fighting Over Them, Explained." *Vox*, July 12.

Green, Emma. 2017. "Will the Pro-Life Movement Split with Trump on Issues Other Than Abortion." *The Atlantic*, January 27.

Grossman, Matt, and David A. Hopkins. 2016. *Assymetric Politics: Ideological Republicans and Group Interest Democrats*. New York: Oxford University Press.

Haberkorn, Jennifer. 2017. "Trump Revises Funding Ban to Groups Providing Abortion Overseas." *Politico*, January 23.

Hall, Richard, and Frank Wayman. 1990. "Buying Time: Moneyed Interests and the Mobilization of Bias in Congressional Committees." *American Political Science Review* 84: 797–820.

Harris, Duchess. 2001. "From the Kennedy Commission to the Combahee Collective: Black Feminist Organizing, 1960–80." In *Sisters in the struggle: African American Women in the Civil Rights-Black Power Movement*, edited by Bettye Collier-Thomas and V. P. Franklin, 280–305. New York: New York University Press.

———. 2009. *Black Feminist Politics From Kennedy to Clinton*. Palgrave Macmillan.

Hartmann, Susan M. 1989. *From Margin to Mainstream: American Women and Politics Since 1960*. Philadelphia: Temple University Press.

Harvey, Anna L. 1998. *Votes Without Leverage: Women in American Electoral Politics, 1920–1970*. New York: Cambridge University Press.

Heaney, Michael T. 2018. "Making Protest Great Again." *Contexts* 17: 42–47.

Hemmer, Nicole. 2017. :#MeToo's Roots in the Feminist Awakening of the 1960s." *Vox*, November 29.

Hooks, Bell. 1981. *Ain't I a Woman: Black Women and Feminism*. Boston: South End Press.

Institute for Women's Policy Research. n.d. *The Status of Women in the States*. Washington, DC: Institute for Women's Policy Research. http://statusofwomendata.org

Ireland, Patricia. 1996. *What Women Want*. New York: Dutton.

Klatch, Rebecca E. 1987. *Women of the New Right*. Philadelphia: Temple University Press.

Klein, Ethel. 1984. *Gender Politics: From Consciousness to Mass Politics*. Cambridge, MA: Harvard University Press.

Ko, Lisa. 2016. "Unwanted Sterilization and Eugenics Programs in the United States." *PBS Independent Lens*, January 29.

Kraditor, Aileen S. 1981. *The Ideas of the Woman Suffrage Movement: 1890–1920*. New York: W.W. Norton & Company.

LaHaye, Beverly. 1984. *Who but a Woman? Concerned Women Can Make a Difference*. Nashville: Thomas Nelson Publishers.

Langone, Alix. 2018. "#MeToo and Time's Up Founders Explain the Difference Between the 2 Movements-And How They're Alike." *Time*, March 22.

Lo, Clarence. 2012. "AstroTurf Versus Grass Roots: Scenes from Early Tea Party Mobilization." In *Steep: The Precipitous Rise of the Tea Party*, edited by Lawrence Rosenthal and Christine Trost, 98–129. Berkeley: University of California Press.

Lorber, Judith. 1994. *Paradoxes of Gender*. New Haven: Yale University Press.

Lourde, Audre. 1984. *Sister Outsider: Essays and Speeches*. New York: Crossing Press.

Lukas, Carrie. 2014. "The Family Act." *Policy Focus* Washington, DC: Independent Women's Forum, Vol. 4, No. 1, January. http://c1355372.cdn.cloudfiles.rack spacecloud.com/167e75a7-d65b-4c41-8b1a-14570e2268b1/PolicyFocus14_Jan_p1.pdf

Mansbridge, Jane. 1986. *Why We Lost the ERA*. Chicago: University of Chicago Press.

McAdam, Doug. 1982. *Political Process and the Development of Black Insurgency, 1930–1970*. Chicago: University of Chicago Press.

McConnaughy, Corrine. 2017. "4 Lessons for Today's Women's Marchers from the Suffrage Movement." *Washington Post*, January 26.

———. 2013. *The Woman Suffrage Movement in America: A Reassessment*. New York: Cambridge University Press.

Michals, Debra. 2017. "Mary Church Terrell." National Women's History Museum. https://www.womenshistory.org/education-resources/biographies/mary-church-terrell

Mott, Stacy. 2013. Personal Interview with Melissa Deckman. February 27.

National Organization for Women. 2007. "NOW Political Action Committee Proudly Endorses Senator Hillary Rodham Clinton for President of the United States in 2008." Accessed online at http://www.now.org/press/03-07/03-28.html

———. 2015a. "NOW Foundation Joins Amicus Briefs in Supreme Court Cases." Accessed online at http://now.org/update/now-foundation-joins-amicus-briefs-in-supreme-court-cases

———. 2015b. "NOW is a Proud Supporter of Women for Hillary." September 4. http://now.org/media-center/press-release/now-is-a-proud-supporter-of-women-for-hillary

———. 2017a. "Frequently Asked Questions." Accessed online at http://now.org/about/faqs

———. 2017b. "Issues." Accessed online at http://now.org/issues/

———. 2017c. "History of Marches and Mass Actions." Accessed online at http://now.org/about/history/history-of-marches-and-mass-actions

O'Leary, Ann, and Karen Kornbluh. 2009. "Family Friendly for All Families." From *The Shriver Report: A Woman's Nation Changes Everything*, edited by Heather Boushey and Ann O'Leary, 75–109. A Study by Maria Shriver and the Center for American Progress. Washington, D.C.

Omolade, Barbara. 2004. "Ella's Daughters." In *Women's Lives: Multicultural Perspectives*, 3rd ed., edited by Gwyn Kirk and Margo Okazawa-Rey, 536–45. New York: McGraw-Hill.

Paquette, Danielle. 2016. "The Enormous Ambition of Hillary Clinton's Child-Care Plan." *Washington Post*, May 12.

Phillips, Erica E. 2014. "Sex Equality Backers Seek Impetus in Oregon Measure." *Wall Street Journal*, October 29.

Putnam, Laura and Theda Skocpol. 2018. "Middle America Reboots Democracy." *Democracy: A Journal of Ideas*, February 20.

Quarshire, Mabinty. 2018. "Is The Women's March More Inclusive This Year?" *USA Today*, January 20.

Robnett, Belinda. 2000. *How Long? How Long? African-American Women in the Struggle for Civil Rights*. Oxford: Oxford University Press.

Ryan, Barbara. 1992. *Feminism and the Women's Movement: Dynamics of Change in Social Movement Ideology and Activism*. New York: Routledge.

Sanbonmatsu, Kira. 2002. *Gender Equality, Political Parties, and the Politics of Women's Place*. Ann Arbor: University of Michigan Press.

Schreiber, Ronnee. 2002a. "Injecting a Woman's Voice: Conservative Women's Organizations, Gender Consciousness, and the Expression of Women's Policy Preferences." *Sex Roles* 47: 331–42.

———. 2002b. "Playing 'Femball': Conservative Women's Organizations and Political Representation in the United States." In *Right-Wing Women: From Conservatives to Extremists Around the World*, edited by Paola Bacchetta and Margaret Power, 211–224. New York: Routledge.

———. 2008. *Righting Feminism: Conservative Women and American Politics*. New York: Oxford University Press.

Shanley, Mary Lyndon. 1988. *Women's Rights, Feminism, and Politics in the United States*. Washington, DC: American Political Science Association.

Shulevitz, Judith. 2017. "Year One: Resistance Research." *New York Review of Books*, November 9.

Silver, Nate. 2017. "The Long March Ahead for Democrats." *FiveThirtyEight*, January 23.

Skocpol, Theda. 1992. *Protecting Soldiers and Mothers*. Cambridge, MA: The Belknap Press of Harvard University Press.

Sommers, Christina Hoff. 2014. "No, Women Don't Make Less Money Than Men." *Daily Beast*, February 1.

Stewart, Emily. 2018. "The Equal Rights Amendment's Surprise Comeback, Explained." *Vox*, May 31.

Stockman, Farah. 2018. "Women's March Roiled by Accusations of Anti-Semitism." *New York Times*, December 23.

Strolovitch, Dara. 2007. *Affirmative Advocacy: Race, Class, and Gender in Interest Group Politics*. Chicago: University of Chicago Press.

Sussman, Anna Louise, and Laura Meckler. 2016. "Clinton Offers New Details About Paid Family Leave Plan." *The Wall Street Journal*, January 7.

Swers, Michele L. 2013. *Women in the Club: Gender and Policy Making in the Senate*. Chicago: The University of Chicago Press.

———. 2018. "From the Republican Revolution to the Tea Party Wave: Republican Women and the Politics of Women's Issues." In *The Right Women: Republican*

Party Activists, Candidates, and Legislators, edited by Shauna Shames and Malliga Och, 199–228. Santa Barbara: Praeger Press.

Tyler, Helen. 1949. *Where Prayer and Purpose Meet: 1874–1949, The WCTU Story*. Evanston: The Signal Press National Woman's Christian Temperance Union Inc.

Walker, Alice. 1983. *In Search of Our Mother's Gardens: Womanist Prose*. San Diego: Harcourt Brace Jovanovich.

Wells, Mildred White. 1953. *The History of the General Federation of Women's Clubs*. Washington, DC: General Federation of Women's Clubs.

Wilcox, Clyde, and Barbara Norrander. 2005. "Change and Continuity in the Geography of Women Legislators." In *Women and Elective Office*, 2nd ed., edited by Sue Thomas and Clyde Wilcox, 176–96. New York: Oxford University Press.

Wolbrecht, Christina. 2000. *The Politics of Women's Rights: Parties, Positions, and Change*. Princeton: Princeton University Press.

Wood, Mary I. 1912. *The History of the General Federation of Women's Clubs for the First Twenty-Two Years of Its Organization*. New York: History Department, General Federation of Women's Clubs.

CHAPTER 3

Abramowitz, Alan I., and Kyle L. Saunders. 1998. "Ideological Realignment in the U.S. Electorate." *Journal of Politics* 60: 634–652.

Allen, Jonathan. 2015. "What Losing in 2008 Taught Hillary About How to Win in 2016." *Vox*, April 10.

Andersen, Kristi. 1996. *After Suffrage: Women in Partisan and Electoral Politics Before the New Deal*. Chicago: University of Chicago Press.

Anderson, L.V. 2016. "White Women Sold Out the Sisterhood and the World by Voting for Trump." *Slate*, November 9.

Badas, Alex and Katelyn E, Stauffer. 2019. "Voting for Women in Nonpartisan and Partisan Elections." *Electoral Studies* 57: 245–255.

Baird, Samira. 2016. "Hillary Clinton has been Fighting for Women, Children, and Families Since She Began Her Career." *hillaryclinton.com*, June 20. https://www.hillaryclinton.com/post/om-hillary-clinton-has-been-fighting-women-children-and-families-she-began-her-career.

Ball, Molly. 2016. "What Kind of Man Is Donald Trump." *The Atlantic*, October 8.

Banaszak, Lee Ann. 1996. *Why Movements Succeed or Fail: Opportunity, Culture, and the Struggle for Woman Suffrage*. Princeton: Princeton University Press.

Bellstrom, Kristen. 2016. "Hillary Clinton's Campaign Is Issuing Actual 'Woman Cards.'" *Fortune*, April 29.

Blake, Aaron. 2016. "Yes You Can Blame Millennials for Hillary Clinton's Loss." *Washington Post*, December 2.

Bonk, Kathy. 1988. "The Selling of the Gender Gap." In *Politics of the Gender Gap: The Social Construction of Political Influence*, ed. Carol Mueller, 82–101. Newbury Park, CA: Sage.

Box-Steffensmeier, Janet, Suzanna De Boef, and Tse-Min Lin. 2004. "The Dynamics of the Partisan Gender Gap." *American Political Science Review* 98: 515–528.

Bracic, Ana, Mackenzie Israel-Trummel, and Allyson F. Shortle. 2018. "Is Sexism for White People? Gender Stereotypes, Race, and the 2016 Presidential Election." *Political Behavior*. Published online February 24, 2018.

Bradley, Laura. 2016. "Samantha Bee Slams White Women After Trump's Win." *Vanity Fair*, November 10.

Brownstein, Ronald. 2008. "The Hidden History of the American Electorate." *National Journal*, October 18.

———. 2013. "Bad Bet: Why Republicans Can't Win With Whites Alone." *National Journal*, September 5.

———. 2016. "How the Rustbelt Paved Trump's Road to Victory." *The Atlantic*, November 10.

Bruenig, Elizabeth. 2016. "Why Are Millennial Women Gravitating to Bernie Sanders?" *New Republic*, February 9.

Bump, Phil. 2016. "Donald Trump Will Be President Thanks to 80,000 People in Three States." *Washington Post*, December 1.

———_. 2018. "The Demographic Surges That Spurred 2018's Heavy Turnout." *Washington Post* November 13.

Burns, Nancy, and Donald Kinder. 2011. "Categorical Politics: Gender, Race, and Public Opinion." In *New Directions in Public Opinion*, ed. Adam Berinsky, 139–167. New York: Routledge.

Burrell, Barbara C. 2005. "Gender, Presidential Elections and Public Policy: Making Women's Votes Matter." *Journal of Women, Politics, & Policy* 27: 31–50.

Carroll, Susan J. 1988. "Women's Autonomy and the Gender Gap: 1980 and 1982." In *The Politics of the Gender Gap: The Social Construction of Political Influence,* ed. Carol Mueller, 236–257. Newbury Park: Sage.

———. 1999. "The Disempowerment of the Gender Gap: Soccer Moms and the 1996 Elections." *PS: Political Science and Politics* 32: 7–11.

Cassese, Erin C. and Tiffany D. Barnes. 2018. "Reconciling Sexism and Women's Support for Republican Candidates: A Look at Gender, Class, and Whiteness in the 2012 and 2016 Presidential Races." *Political Behavior* 1-24.

Center for American Women and Politics. 2008. "Proportions of Men and Women Who Voted for Hillary Clinton in the Super Tuesday Races of February 5, 2008." New Brunswick: Center for American Women and Politics, Rutgers, State University of New Jersey.

———. 2012. "Women's Votes Decisive in 2012 Presidential Race." New Brunswick: Center for American Women and Politics, Rutgers, State University of New Jersey.

———. 2016. "Women Candidates 2016." New Brunswick: Center for American Women and Politics, Rutgers, State University of New Jersey.

———. 2017. "The Gender Gap: Voting Choices in Presidential Elections." New Brunswick: Center for American Women and Politics, Rutgers, State University of New Jersey.

———. 2017. "Fact Sheet: Gender Differences in Voter Turnout." New Brunswick: Center for American Women and Politics, Rutgers, State University of New Jersey.

———. 2018. "2018 Summary of Women Candidates" New Brunswick: Center for American Women and Politics, Rutgers, State University of New Jersey.

———. 2019. "History of Women in the U.S. Congress." New Brunswick: Center for American Women and Politics, Rutgers, State University of New Jersey.

Chaney, Carole K., R. Michael Alvarez, and Jonathan Nagler. 1998. "Explaining the Gender Gap in the U.S. Presidential Elections, 1980–1992." *Political Research Quarterly* 51: 311–340.

Chavez, Paola, and Veronica Stracqualursi. 2016. "From 'Crooked Hillary' to 'Little Marco,' Donald Trump's Many Nicknames." *ABC News*, May 11.

Cilliza, Chris, and Jon Cohen. 2012. "President Obama and the White Vote? No Problem." *Washington Post*, November 8.

CNN. 2004. "U.S. President/National/Exit Poll." http://www.cnn.com/ELECTION/ 2004/pages/results/states/US/P/00/epolls.0.html. Accessed January 10, 2017.

———. 2008a. "Election Center 2008 Exit Polls." www.cnn.com/ELECTION/2008/ results/polls/#USP00p1. Accessed March 25, 2009.

———. 2008b. "Election Center Primaries." http://www.cnn.com/ELEC-TION/2008/ primaries/results/candidates/#1746. Accessed January 10, 2017.

———. 2012. "Election Center President: Full Results." http://www.cnn.com/ election/2012/results/race/president/. Accessed January 10, 2017.

———. 2014. "House Full Results Exit Polls" http://www.cnn.com/election/2014/ results/race/house#exit-polls. Accessed May 7, 2015.

———. 2016a. "Exit Polls" http://edition.cnn.com/election/results/exit-polls/nati onal/president. Accessed January 10, 2017.

———. 2016b. "Democratic and Republican Exit Polls." http://www.cnn.com/e lection/primaries/polls. Accessed January 24, 2017.

———. 2016c. "Mississippi Exit Polls" http://www.cnn.com/election/primaries/ polls/MS/Dem. Accessed January 24, 2017.

———. 2018. "Exit Polls." https://www.cnn.com/election/2018/exit-polls. Accessed January 23, 2019.

Collingswood, Loren. 2016. "The County by County Data on Trump Voters Shows Why He Won." *Washington Post*, November 19.

Corder, J. Kevin, and Christinan Wolbrecht. 2016. *Counting Women's Ballots: Female Voters from Suffrage through the New Deal.* New York: Cambridge University Press.

Cramer, Katherine. 2016. "How Rural Resentment Helps Explain the Surprising Victory of Donald Trump." *Washington Post*, November 13.

Crockett, Emily. 2016. "Hillary Clinton Plans to Fill Half Her Cabinet with Women, Here's Why That Matters." *Vox*, July 6.

Deckman, Melissa. 2012. ""The GOP's Marriage Problem." *Public Religion Research Institute*, November 16. http://publicreligion.org/2012/11/the-go ps-marriage-problem/#.VYhVjqaPqUd.

———. 2016. "Some Women Actually Do Support Donald Trump. Here's Why." *Washington Post*, April 7.

Deckman, Melissa, and John McTague. 2015. "Did the 'War on Women' Work? Women, Men, and the Birth Control Mandate in the 2012 Presidential Election." *American Politics Research* 43: 3–26.

Dittmar, Kelly. 2016a. "No, Women Didn't Abandon Clinton, Nor Did She Fail to Win Their Support." *Presidential Gender Watch*, November 11.

———. 2016b. "Gender Matters: A Status Check on the Gender Gap in Presidential Primaries." *Presidential Gender Watch*, March 17.

Dolan, Kathleen. 2004. *Voting for Women: How the Public Evaluates Women Candidates.* Boulder: Westview Press.

———. 2008a. "Women Voters, Women Candidates: Is There a Gender Gap in Support for Women Candidates?" In *Voting the Gender Gap*, ed. Lois Duke Whitaker, 91–107. Urbana and Chicago: University of Illinois Press.

———. 2008b. "Is There a 'Gender Affinity Effect' in American Politics? Infor-mation, Affect, and Candidate Sex in U.S. House Elections." *Political Research Quarterly* 61: 79–89.

———. 2014. *When Does Gender Matter? Women Candidates & Gender Ste-reotypes in American Elections.* New York: Oxford University Press.

Drabold, Will. 2016. "Read Ivanka Trump's Speech at the Republican Con-vention." *Time*, July 21.

Ehrenfreund, Max, and Jim Tankersley. 2016. "What Hillary Clinton Would Do to America." *Washington Post*, June 7.

Eilperin, Juliet. 2014. "Obama Takes Executive Action to Lift the Veil of Pay Secrecy." *Washington Post*, April 8.

Elder, Laurel. 2008. "Whither Republican Women: The Growing Partisan Gap Among Women in Congress." *The Forum* 6: Issue 1, Article 13.

Enten, Harry. 2016. "'Demographics Aren't Destiny' and Four Other Things This Election Taught Me." *FiveThirtyEight*, November 14.

Estepa. Jessica. 2015. "Donald Trump on Carly Fiorina: 'Look at that Face!'" *USA Today*, September 10.

Fang, Marina. 2016. "Watch Hillary Clinton Break the Glass Ceiling." *Huffington Post*, July 27.

Fiorina, Morris P., with Samuel J. Abrams and Jeremy C. Pope. 2011. *Culture War? The Myth of a Polarized America*, 3rd ed. New York: Longman.

Flexner, Eleanor, and Ellen Fitzpatrick. 1996. *Century of Struggle: The Woman's Rights Movement in the United States*. Cambridge: The Belknap Press of Harvard University Press.

Flores, Reena. 2016. "Republican Debate: Donald Trump Defends the Size of His Hands, and More." *CBS News*, March 3.

Fraga, Bernard, Sean McElwee, Jesse Rhodes, and Brian Schaffner. 2017. "Why Did Trump Win? More Whites-and Fewer Blacks-Actually Voted." *Washington Post* May 8.

Frankovic, Kathleen. 1988. "The Ferraro Factor, the Women's Movement, the Polls, and the Press." In *Politics of the Gender Gap: The Social Construction of Political Influence*, ed. Carol Mueller, 102–123. Newbury Park: Sage.

Frasure-Yokley, Lorrie. 2018. "Choosing the Velvet Glove: Women Voters, Ambivalent Sexism and Vote Choice in 2016." *Journal of Race, Ethnicity and Politics* 3: 3–25.

Freeman, Jo. 1986. "The Political Culture of the Democratic and Republican Parties." *Political Science Quarterly* 101: 327–356.

Frey, William H., Ruy Teixeira and Robert Griffin. 2016. "America's Electoral Future: How Changing Demographics Could Impact Presidential Elections from 2016 to 2032." *Center for American Progress*, February.

Fry, Richard. 2016. "This May Be the Last Election Dominated by Boomers and Prior Generations." *Pew Research Center*, August 29.

Fulton, Sarah A. 2014. "When Gender Matters: Macro-Dynamics and Micro-Mechanisms." *Political Behavior* 36: 605–630.

Gass, Nick. 2016. "Michelle Obama, Warrant to Campaign for Clinton." *Politico*, September 6.

Gilens, Martin. 1988. "Gender and Support for Ronald Reagan: A Comprehensive Model of Presidential Approval." *American Journal of Political Science* 32: 19–49.

Glueck, Katie. 2016. "Trump Takes Aim at Clinton's Lead Among Women." *Politico*, September 10.

Gontchorova, Natalie. 2018. "The Verdict is In: The Youth Vote Shaped the Midterm Results." *Refinery29*. November 8. Accessed January 24, 2019.

Green, Emma. 2016. "The Weaponization of Heidi Cruz and Melania Trump." *The Atlantic*, March 24.

Grossmann, Matt, and David A. Hopkins. 2015. "Ideological Republicans and Group Interest Democrats: The Asymmetry of American Party Politics." *Perspectives on Politics* 13: 119–139.

Guo, Jeff. 2016. "Yes, Working Class Whites Really Did Make Trump Win. No, It Wasn't Simply Economic Anxiety." *Washington Post*, November 11.

Haider-Markel, Donald P., and Andrea Vieux. 2008. "Gender and Conditional Support for Torture in the War on Terror." *Politics & Gender* 4: 5–33.

Hains, Tim. 2016. "Hillary Clinton Campaigns with Beyoncé, Jay-Z, Bon Jovi, LeBron James, Katy Perry." *Real Clear Politics*, November 6.

Hayes, Danny. 2011. "When Gender and Party Collide: Stereotyping in Canddidate Trait Attributions." *Politics & Gender* 7: 133–165.

Healy, Patrick. 2008. "With Elbows in Check, Making a Pitch to Women." *New York Times*, September 21.

Herrnson, Paul. 2012. *Congressional Elections: Campaigning at Home and in Washington*, 6th ed. Washington, DC: CQ Press.

Huddy, Leonie, Erin Cassese, and Mary-Kate Lizotte. 2008. "Sources of Political Unity and Disunity Among Women: Placing the Gender Gap in Perspective?" In *Voting the Gender Gap*, ed. Lois Duke Whitaker. Urbana and Chicago: University of Illinois Press.

Huddy, Leonie, and Tony E. Carey, Jr. 2009. "Group Politics Redux: Race and Gender in the 2008 Democratic Presidential Primaries?" *Politics & Gender* 5: 81–95.

Inter-Parliamentary Union. 2005. "Women's Suffrage: A World Chronology of the Recognition of Women's Rights to Vote and to Stand for Election." www.ipu.org/wmn-e/suffrage.htm. Accessed May 28, 2009.

Jackson, Natalie. 2016. "Trump's Win Isn't All About White People: Clinton Lost Black and Brown Votes in Key States." *Huffington Post*, November 15.

Jacobson, Gary. 2013. *The Politics of Congressional Elections*, 8th ed. Boston: Pearson. Jamieson, Amber. 2016. "Why She Wore White: Deconstructing Hillary Clinton's Convention Pantsuit." *The Guardian*, July 29.

Jelen, Ted G., and Clyde Wilcox. 2005. "Attitudes Toward Abortion in Poland and the U.S." *Politics & Gender* 1: 297–317.

Junn, Jane, and Lisa Garcia Bedolla. 2013. "Redefining the Gender Gap: An Intersectional Analysis of Vote Choice." Prepared for Presentation at the Annual Meeting of the Midwest Political Science Association, Chicago.

Kanthak, Kristin, and Barbara Norrander. 2004. "The Enduring Gender Gap?" In *Models of Voting in Presidential Elections: The 2000 Election*, ed. Herbert Weisberg and Clyde Wilcox, 141–160. Stanford: Stanford University Press.

Kantor, Jodi. 2008a. "Clintons Bloc Becomes the Prize for Election Day." *New York Times*, June 7.

———. 2008b. "Gender Issue Lives on as Clinton's Bid Wanes." *New York Times*, May 19.

Kaufman, Jonathan. 2008. "Crossing Over: As the U.S. Economy Sputters, Working- Class Women Shift to Obama." *Wall Street Journal*, October 11.

Kaufmann, Karen M. 2002. "Culture Wars, Secular Realignment, and the Gender Gap in Party Identification." *Political Behavior* 24: 283–307.

Kaufmann, Karen M., and John R. Petrocik. 1999. "The Changing Politics of American Men: Understanding the Sources of the Gender Gap." *American Journal of Political Science* 43: 864–887.

Kernell, Samuel, Gary C. Jacobson, Thad Kousser, and Lynn Vavreck. 2014. *The Logic of American Politics*, 6 ed. Washington, DC: CQ Press.

Klein, Ethel. 1984. *Gender Politics*. Cambridge: Harvard University Press.

Ladd, Everett Carll. 1997. "Media Framing of the Gender Gap." In *Women, Media, and Politics,* ed. Pippa Norris, 113–128. New York: Oxford University Press.

Lawrence, Regina G., and Melody Rose. 2010. *Hillary Clinton's Race for the White House: Gender Politics & The Media on the Campaign Trail*. Colorado: Lynne Rienner.

Levey, Noam M. 2008. "Obama Courts Female Vote with His Family Stories." *Los Angeles*, September 4.

Lewis, Carolyn. 1999. "Are Women for Women? Feminist and Traditional Values in the Female Electorate." *Women and Politics* 20: 1–28.

Luhby, Tami. 2016. "How Hillary Clinton Lost." *CNN*, November 9.

Lynch, Timothy R., and Kathleen Dolan. 2014. "Voter Attitudes, Behaviors, and Women Candidates." In *Women and Elective Office: Past, Present, and Future*, eds. Sue Thomas and Clyde Wilcox. New York: Oxford University Press, pp. 46–66.

Malone, Clare. 2016. "Clinton Couldn't Win Over White Women." *Fivethirtyeight*, November 9.

Mansbridge, Jane. 1986. *Why We Lost the ERA*. Chicago: University of Chicago Press.

Martinez, Gebe, and Mary Agnes Carey. 2004. "Erasing the Gender Gap Tops Republican Playbook." *CQ Weekly* (March 6): 564–570.

McDermott, Monika L. 1997. "Voting Cues in Low-Information Elections: Candidate Gender as a Social Information Variable in Contemporary U.S. Elections." *American Journal of Political Science* 41: 270–283.

Merica, Dan. 2016. "New Clinton Ad Shows Girls Looking in Mirror as Trump Insults Women." *CNN*, September 23.

Murphy, Patricia. 2018. "Women Played a Key Role in Harassment Bill." *Roll Call* January 23.

Murray, Shailagh. 2009. "Fair-Wage Bill Clears the Senate." *Washington Post*, January 23.

National Election Study. Guide to Public Opinion and Behavior. www.umich.edu/~nes/nesguide/nesguide.htm. Accessed May 1, 2015.

Newport, Frank. 2008. "Hillary Maintains Loyalty of Democratic Women Up to End." Gallup, June 3.

Newton-Small, Jay. 2015. "Inside Hillary Clinton's Beijing Speech." *Time*, November 23.

———. 2016. "Why So Many Women Abandoned Hillary Clinton." *Time*, November 10.

Norrander, Barbara. 1999. "Is the Gender Gap Growing?" In *Reelection 1996: How Americans Voted*, ed. Herbert F. Weisberg and Janet M. Box-Steffensmeier, 145–161. New York: Chatham House Publishers.

———. 2003. "The Intraparty Gender Gap: Differences Between Male and Female Voters in the 1980–2000 Presidential Primaries." *PS: Political Science and Politics* 36: 181–186.

———. 2008. "The History of the Gender Gaps." In *Voting the Gender Gap*, ed. Lois Duke Whitaker, 9–32. Urbana and Chicago: University of Illinois Press.

———. 2016a. "Women Vote at Higher Rates Than Men. That Might Help Clinton in November." *Washington Post*, June 27.

———. 2016b. "Is Hillary Losing the Women's Vote? Nope. Here's How the Gender Gap Really Works." *Washington Post*, February 26.

Norton, Mary Beth, David M. Katzman, Paul D. Escott, Howard P. Chudacoff, Thomas G. Paterson, and William M. Tuttle, Jr. 1986. *A People and a Nation: A History of the United States*. 2nd ed., Volume II: Since 1865. Boston: Houghton Mifflin Company.

O'Leary, Ann, and Karen Kornbluh. 2009. "Family Friendly for All Families." In *The Shriver Report: A Woman's Nation Changes Everything*, eds. Heather Boushey and Ann O'Leary, 75–109. A Study by Maria Shriver and the Center for American Progress. Washington, D.C.

Palmer, Barbara, and Dennis Simon. 2012. *Women & Congressional Elections: A Century of Change*. Boulder: Lynne Rienner Publishers.

Paolino, Phillip. 1995. "Group-Salient Issues and Group Representation: Support for Women Candidates in the 1992 Senate Elections." *American Journal of Political Science* 39: 294–313.

Paquette, Danielle. 2016a. "The Enormous Ambition of Hillary Clinton's Child-Care Plan." *Washington Post*, May.

———. 2016b. "The Unexpected Voters Behind the Widest Gender Gap in Recorded Election History." *Washington Post*, November 9.

PBS Newshour. 2014. "Election 2014 Briefing Book."

Phillip, Abby. 2016. "Clinton Pitches to Minority Millennials with the Help of Beyoncé, Jay Z." *Washington Post*, November 4.

Phillips, Amber. 2016. "Is Split-Ticket Voting Officially Dead?" *Washington Post*, November 17.

Poloni-Staudinger, Lori, J. Cherie Strachan, and Brian Schaffner. 2016. "In 6 Graphs, Here's Why Young Women Don't Support Hillary Clinton as Much as Older Women Do." *Washington Post*, April 11.

Ramakrishnan, Karthick. 2016. "Trump Got More Votes from People of Color than Romney Did. Here's the Data." *Washington Post*, November 11.

Reily, Katie. 2016. "Donald Trump Again Dismissed His Lewd Comments as 'Locker Room Talk.'" *Fortune*, October 9.

Reinhard, Beth. 2012. "Caught in the Cross Fire: The So-Called War on Women is More About Playing to Their Fears." *National Journal*, August 30.

Reston, Maeve, and Gabe Ramirez. 2016. "Hillary Clinton Splits Younger, Older Democratic Women." *CNN*, June 10.

Rinehart, Sue Tolleson. 1992. *Gender Consciousness and Politics*. New York: Routledge.

Roarty, Alex. 2012. "Debate Triggers War Over Women on TV, Twitter, Trail and Phone." *National Journal*, October 17.

Rosenthal, Cindy Simon. 1995. "The Role of Gender in Descriptive Representation." *Political Research Quarterly* 48: 599–611.

Rubin, Jennifer. 2016. "Conway Loses Her Integrity and Eviscerates GOP's Appeal to Women." *Washington Post*, October 11.

Rucker, Philip. 2016. "Ivanka Trump Stars in New Campaign Ad to Help Her Father Appeal to Women." *Washington Post*, September 30.

Sanbonmatsu, Kira. 2002. "Gender Stereotypes and Vote Choice." *American Journal of Political Science* 46(1): 20–34.

Sapiro, Virginia, and Pamela Johnston Conover. 1997. "The Variable Gender Basis of Electoral Politics: Gender and Context in the 1992 U.S. Election." *British Journal of Political Science* 27: 523.

Schaffner, Brian, Matthew McWilliams, and Tatishe Nteta. 2018. "Understanding White Polarization in the 2016 Election: The Sobering Role of Racism and Sexism" *Political Studies Quarterly* 133: 9–34.

Seelye, Katherine Q. 2008. "In Clinton vs. Obama, Age Is One of the Greatest Predictors." *New York Times*, April 22.

Seltzer, Richard, Jody Newman, and Melissa Voorhees Leighton. 1997. *Sex as a Political Variable: Women as Candidates and Voters in American Elections.* Boulder: Lynne Rienner Publishers.

Shapiro, Robert, and Harpreet Mahajan. 1986. "Gender Differences in Policy Preferences: A Summary of Trends from the 1960s to the 1980s." *Public Opinion Quarterly* 50: 42–61.

Sherman, Jake, and John Bresnahan. 2013. "GOP Pollster: Stop Talking About Rape." *Politico*, January 17.

Siddiqui, Sabrina, and Lauren Gambino. 2016. "How Women Could Vote Hillary Clinton into the White House." *The Guardian*, November 3.

Skocpol, Theda. 1992. *Protecting Soldiers and Mothers.* Cambridge: The Belknap Press of Harvard University Press.

Smith, Eric R. A. N., and Richard Fox. 2001. "The Electoral Fortunes of Women Candidates for Congress." *Political Research Quarterly* 54: 205–221.

Smith, Tom. 1984. "The Polls: Gender and Attitudes Toward Violence." *Public Opinion Quarterly* 48: 384–396.

Steiger, Kay. 2016. "Why Younger Women Love Bernie Sanders and Why It Drives Older Women Crazy." *Vox*, February 11.

Stewart, Emily. 2018. "2018's Record Setting Voter Turnout, in One Chart." *Vox* November 19.

Sullivan, Sean, and Robert Costa. 2016. "Donald Trump Unveils Child-Care Policy Influenced by Ivanka Trump." *Washington Post*, September 13.

Sussman, Anna Louise, and Laura Meckler. 2016. "Clinton Offers New Details About Paid Family Leave Plan." *The Wall Street Journal*, January 7.

Swers, Michele L. 2002. *The Difference Women Make: The Policy Impact of Women in Congress.* Chicago: University of Chicago Press.

———. 2013. *Women in the Club: Gender and Policy Making in the Senate.* Chicago: University of Chicago Press.

Tesler, Michael. 2016. "Why the Gender Gap Doomed Hillary Clinton." *Washington Post*, November 9.

Thompson, Krissah. 2012. "Obama Campaign Steps Up Appeals to Women Voters." *Washington Post*, August 24.

Traister, Rebecca. 2016. "Hillary Clinton vs. Herself." *New York Magazine*, May 30.

Trotta, Daniel. 2012. "Who's the Undecided Voter? It May be the 'Walmart Mom.'" *Reuters*, October 3.

Tully-McManus, Katherine. 2018. "Lawmakers Reach Deal to Tackle Sexual Harassment on Capitol Hill." *Roll Call* December 12.

Tumulty, Karen. 2012. "To Claim Virginia, Obama's Hopes Rest on Women." *Washington Post*, September 19.

Tyler, Helen. 1949. *Where Prayer and Purpose Meet 1874–1949: The WCTU Story.* Evanston: The Signal Press National Woman's Christian Temperance Union Inc.

Tyson, Alec, and Shiva Maniam. 2016. "Behind Trump's Victory: Divisions by Race, Gender, and Education." *Pew Research*, November 9.

U.S. Elections Project. 2018. "2018 November General Election Turnout Rates." http://www.electproject.org/2018g December 4 (Accessed January 30, 2019)

Vedantam, Shankar. 2008. "The Oprah Effect." *Washington Post*, September 1.

Walsh, Kenneth. 2016. "Clinton Wins Popular Vote by Nearly 3 Million Ballots." *US News and World Report*, December 21.

Wheeler, Lydia. 2015. "Obama to Push for Mandatory Paid Leave." *The Hill*, January 14.

Winter, Nicholas J. G. 2010. "Masculine Republicans and Feminine Democrats: Gender and Americans' Explicit and Implicit Images of the Political Parties." *Political Behavior* 32: 587–618.

Zernike, Kate. 2008. "Both Sides Seeking to Be What Women Want." *New York Times*, September 15.

Zhou, Li. 2018. "12 Charts that Explain the Record-Breaking Year Women Have Had in Politics." *Vox*. November 6.

CHAPTER 4

Alter, Charlotte. 2018. "A Year Ago, They Marched." *Time*, January 18, 2018. http://time.com/magazine/us/5107476/january-29th-2018-vol-191-no-3-u-s/.

American National Election Studies. n.d. "The ANES Guide to Public Opinion and Electoral Behavior: General Interest in Public Affairs 1960–2008." https://electionstudies.org/resources/anes-guide/second-tables/?id=336.

Andersen, Kristi. 1996. *After Suffrage: Women in Partisan and Electoral Politics before the New Deal*. Chicago: University of Chicago.

Atkeson, Lonna Rae. 2003. "Not All Cues Are Created Equal: The Conditional Impact of Female Candidates on Political Engagement." *Journal of Politics* 65 (4): 1040–61. https://doi.org/10.1111/1468-2508.t01-1-00124.

Baker, Paula. 1984. "The Domestication of Politics: Women and American Political Society, 1780–1920." *The American Historical Review* 89 (3): 620–47.

Bennett, Freeholder Ashley. 2018. "Thank You to @WhoopiGoldberg and @TheView! It's Been Great Speaking about the Change Coming to Atlantic County, NJ! Representation Matters, and If You Don't See Yourself Reflected in Your Elected Officials, Maybe You Should Run to Be an Elected Official.Https://Youtu.Be/KNuMq41DAk4." Tweet. *@AshleyBennettNJ* (blog), January 22, 2018. https://twitter.com/AshleyBennettNJ/status/955518635413594112?ref_src=twsrc%5Etfw%7Ctwcamp%5Etweetembed%7Ctwterm%5E955518635413594112&ref_url=http%3A%2F%2Fwww.philly.com%2Fphilly%2Fnews%2Fnew_jersey%2Fshore%2Fashley-bennett-womens-march-whoopi-goldberg-kirstin-gillibrand-new-jersey-20180129.html.

Burrell, Barbara. 1988. "The Political Opportunity of Women Candidates for the U.S. House of Representatives in 1984." *Women & Politics Women & Politics* 8 (1): 51–68.

———. 2014. *Gender in Campaigns for the U.S. House of Representatives*. Ann Arbor: University of Michigan Press.

———. 2018. "Political Parties and Women's Organizations: Bringing Women into the Electoral Arena." In *Gender & Elections: Shaping the Future of American Politics*, edited by Susan J. Carroll and Richard L. Fox, 4th ed., 220–49. New York: Cambridge University Press.

Campbell, David E., and Christina Wolbrecht. 2006. "See Jane Run: Women Politicians as Role Models for Adolescents." *Journal of Politics* 68 (2): 233–47. https://doi.org/10.1111/j.1468-2508.2006.00402.x.

Carroll, Susan J., and Kira Sanbonmatsu. 2013. *More Women Can Run: Gender and Pathways to the State Legislatures*. New York: Oxford University Press.

Center for American Women and Politics. 2017. *Gender Differences in Voter Turnout*. New Brunswick, NJ: Center for American Women and Politics, Rutgers University. http://cawp.rutgers.edu/sites/default/files/resources/genderdiff.pdf.

———. 2018a. *Results: Women Candidates in the 2018 Elections*. Eagleton Institute of Politics: Center for American Women and Politics.

———. 2018b. *Women Candidates for Congress, 1974–2018*. Eagleton Institute of Politics: Rutgers University.

Collins, Gail. 1998. "Why the Women Are Fading Away." *New York Times Magazine*, October 25, 1998.

Cox, Christopher. 2012. "Governor Nikki Haley: New Horizons." *Vogue*, April 18, 2012. http://www.vogue.com/865354/governor-nikki-haley-new-horizons/.

Crowder-Meyer, Melody, and Rosalyn Cooperman. 2018. "Can't Buy Them Love: How Party Culture among Donors Contributes to the Party Gap in Women's Representation." *The Journal of Politics* 80 (4): 1211–24. https://doi.org/10.1086/698848.

Crowder-Meyer, Melody, and Benjamin E. Lauderdale. 2014. "A Partisan Gap in the Supply of Female Potential Candidates in the United States." *Research & Politics* 1 (1): 1–7. https://doi.org/10.1177/2053168014537230.

Darcy, R., and Charles D. Hadley. 1988. "Black Women in Politics: The Puzzle of Success." *Social Science Quarterly* 69 (3): 629–45.

Darcy, R., Susan Welch, and Janet Clark. 1994. *Women, Elections & Representation*. Lincoln: University of Nebraska Press.

Deckman, Melissa. 2018. "Analysis | A New Poll Shows How Younger Women Could Help Drive a Democratic Wave in 2018." *Washington Post*, March 5, 2018, sec. Monkey Cage Analysis Analysis Interpretation of the news based on evidence, including data, as well as anticipating how events might unfold based on past events. https://www.washingtonpost.com/news/monkey-cage/wp/2018/03/05/a-new-poll-shows-how-younger-women-could-help-drive-a-democratic-wave-in-2018/.

Dittmar, Kelly. 2018a. "'Pink Wave': A Note of Caution | CAWP." *Footnotes* (blog), January 26, 2018. http://cawp.rutgers.edu/footnotes/pink-wave-note-caution.

———. 2018b. *By the Numbers: Women Congressional Candidates in 2018*. Eagleton Institute of Politics: Center for American Women and Politics. http://cawp.rutgers.edu/congressional-candidates-summary-2018.

Doan, Alesha E., and Donald P. Haider-Markel. 2010. "The Role of Intersectional Stereotypes on Evaluations of Gay and Lesbian Political Candidates." *Politics & Gender* 6 (1): 63. https://doi.org/10.1017/S1743923X09990511.

Dolan, Julie and Paru Shah. 2019. Confidential telephone interviews conducted with female congressional candidates. August 2018–February 2019.

Dolan, Julie, Paru Shah, and Semilla Stripp. 2019. "Missing the Wave? Women Congressional Candidates Who Lost in the 2018 Election." Paper presented at the Annual Conference of the Midwest Political Science Association. Chicago, IL. April 4–7.

Edmondson, Catie, and Jasmine C. Lee. 2018. "Meet the New Freshmen in Congress." *The New York Times*, November 28, 2018, sec. U.S. https://www.nytimes.com/interactive/2018/11/28/us/politics/congress-freshman-class.html, https://www.nytimes.com/interactive/2018/11/28/us/politics/congress-freshman-class.html.

Emily's List. 2018. "Over 34,000 Women Want to Run for Office." https://www.emilyslist.org/news/entry/over-34000-women-want-to-run-for-office.

Fox, Richard L., and Jennifer L. Lawless. 2004. "Entering the Arena? Gender and the Decision to Run for Office." *American Journal of Political Science* 48 (2): 264–80. https://doi.org/10.1111/j.0092-5853.2004.00069.x.

———. 2011. "Gendered Perceptions and Political Candidacies: A Central Barrier to Women's Equality in Electoral Politics." *American Journal of Political Science* 55 (1): 59–73. https://doi.org/10.1111/j.1540-5907.2010.00484.x.

Frederick, Angela. 2013. "Bringing Narrative In: Race–Gender Storytelling, Political Ambition, and Women's Paths to Public Office." *Journal of Women, Politics & Policy* 34 (2): 113–37. https://doi.org/10.1080/1554477X.2013.776379.

———. 2014. "'Who Better to Do It Than Me!:' Race, Gender & the Deciding to Run Accounts of Political Women in Texas." *Qualitative Sociology* 37 (3): 301–21. https://doi.org/10.1007/s11133-014-9282-z.

Freeman, Jo. 1993. "Feminism vs. Family Values: Women at the 1992 Democratic and Republican Conventions." *Pspolisciepoli PS: Political Science and Politics* 26 (1): 21–28.

———. 2002. *A Room at a Time: How Women Entered Party Politics*. Lanham, MD: Rowman & Littlefield.

Garcia, Sonia R., and Marisela Marquez. 2001. "Motivational and Attitudinal Factors Amongst Latinas in U.S. Electoral Politics." *NWSA Journal* 13 (2): 112–22. https://doi.org/10.1353/nwsa.2001.0038.

Hardy-Fanta, Carol, Pei-te Lien, Dianne M. Pinderhughes, and Christine Marie Sierra. 2016. *Contested Transformation: Race, Gender, and Political Leadership in 21st Century America*.

Holman, Mirya R., and Monica C. Schneider. 2018. "Gender, Race, and Political Ambition: How Intersectionality and Frames Influence Interest in Political Office." *Politics, Groups, and Identities* 6 (2): 264–80. https://doi.org/10.1080/21565503.2016.1208105.

Imse, Elliot. 2018. *2018 Rainbow Wave by the Numbers: Historic Number of Gubernatorial, Congressional Nominees*. Washington, DC: LGBTQ Victory Fund.

Jacobson, Gary C. 2013. *The Politics of Congressional Elections*. Boston: Pearson.

Karpowitz, Christopher F., J. Quin Monson, and Jessica Robinson Preece. 2017. "How to Elect More Women: Gender and Candidate Success in a Field Experiment." *American Journal of Political Science* 61 (4): 927–43.

Kay, Katty, and Claire Shipman. 2014. "The Confidence Gap." *The Atlantic*, April 14, 2014. http://www.theatlantic.com/features/archive/2014/04/the-confidence-gap/359815/.

Kirby, Jen. 2018. "No Senator Has Ever given Birth While Holding Office. Sen. Tammy Duckworth Just Changed That." *Vox*, April 10, 2018. https://www.vox.com/2018/4/10/17219416/tammy-duckworth-first-senator-birth-baby.

Kliff, Sarah. 2018. "The Tantrum over Babies on the Senate Floor, Explained." *Vox*, April 19, 2018. https://www.vox.com/policy-and-politics/2018/4/19/17256390/tammy-duckworth-baby-senate-orrin-hatch.

Kluttz, Billy. 2014. "Outness and Identity in Context: Negotiating Sexual Disclosure in LGBT Campaigns." *Sexuality & Culture* 18 (4): 789–803. https://doi.org/10.1007/s12119-014-9221-x.

Lai, K. K. Rebecca, Denise Lu, Lisa Lerer, and Troy Griggs. 2018. "The Faces of Change in the Midterm Elections." *The New York Times*, October 31, 2018, sec. U.S. https://www.nytimes.com/interactive/2018/10/31/us/politics/midterm-election-candidates-diversity.html.

Lawless, Jennifer L., and Richard L. Fox. 2017. *The Trump Effect*. American University, School of Public Affairs: American University.

Magni, Gabriele, and Andrew Reynolds. 2018. "Analysis | The 2018 Blue Wave Included Quite a Few LGBT Wins — Even Though Voters Are Still Wary of Gay and Trans Candidates." *Washington Post* (blog), November 25, 2018. https://www.washingtonpost.com/news/monkey-cage/wp/2018/11/25/the-2018-blue-wave-included-quite-a-few-lgbt-wins-even-though-voters-are-still-wary-of-gay-and-trans-candidates/.

MAKERS. n.d. *Rashida Tlaib*. Accessed January 14, 2019. https://www.makers.com/profiles/5bbdfbf833132d0d110d3b32.

Mandel, Ruth B. 1981. *In the Running: The New Woman Candidate*. New Haven: Ticknor & Fields.

Mansbridge, Jane. 1999. "Should Blacks Represent Blacks and Women Represent Women? A Contingent 'Yes.'" *The Journal of Politics* 61 (3): 628–57. https://doi.org/10.2307/2647821.

Mariani, Mack, Bryan W. Marshall, and A. Lanethea Mathews-Schultz. 2015. "See Hillary Clinton, Nancy Pelosi, and Sarah Palin Run? Party, Ideology, and the Influence of Female Role Models on Young Women." *Political Research Quarterly* 68 (4): 716–31. https://doi.org/10.1177/1065912915605904.

Matthews, Morgan C. 2016. "When Women Roar: Women's Political Participation in the 2016 General Election – Feminist Reflections." *The Society Pages* (blog), November 2, 2016. https://thesocietypages.org/feminist/2016/11/02/when-wo men-roar-womens-political-participation-in-the-2016-general-election/.

Mattise, Jonathan. 2018. "Campaign: Only 'Sexist Pig' Would Think Blackburn Can't Win." *US News & World Report*, February 13, 2018. https://www.usn ews.com/news/best-states/tennessee/articles/2018-02-13/campaign-only-sexist -pig-would-think-blackburn-cant-win.

Nilsen, Ella. 2018. "This Democrat Thinks She Can Win in 'Trump Country' Kentucky." *Vox*, January 17, 2018. https://www.vox.com/policy-and-politics/ 2018/1/17/16849262/amy-mcgrath-kentucky-house-andy-barr.

Niven, David. 1998. "Party Elites and Women Candidates: The Shape of Bias." *Women & Politics* 19 (2): 57–80.

"No Limits for Women: The Official Word." 2002. *In These Times*, July, 12.

North, Anna. 2018. "This Mom Just Won the Right to Use Campaign Funds to Pay for Child Care." *Vox*, May 11, 2018. https://www.vox.com/2018/5/11/ 17340698/mom-mothers-congress-child-care-liuba-grechen-shirley-campaig n-funds-babysitting.

Pager, Tyler. 2018. "After Big Losses, a N.Y. House Republican Clashes With Her Party." *The New York Times*, December 21, 2018, sec. New York. https://ww w.nytimes.com/2018/12/20/nyregion/elise-stefanik-republican-women.html.

Pathé, Simone. 2019. "Stefanik Launches PAC to Boost Female Candidates, Now with GOP Leadership Support." January 18, 2019, sec. campaigns. https://ww w.rollcall.com/news/campaigns/stefanik-launches-pac-leadership-support.

Piscopo, Jennifer M. 2018. "The Limits of Leaning in: Ambition, Recruitment, and Candidate Training in Comparative Perspective." *Politics, Groups, and Identities*: 1–12. https://doi.org/10.1080/21565503.2018.1532917.

Reingold, Beth, and Jessica Harrell. 2010. "The Impact of Descriptive Rep-resentation on Women's Political Engagement: Does Party Matter?" *Political Research Quarterly* 63 (2): 280–94. https://doi.org/10.1177/10659129083 30346.

Remnick, David. 2018. "Alexandria Ocasio-Cortez's Historic Win and the Future of the Democratic Party | The New Yorker." *New Yorker*, July 23, 2018. https ://www.newyorker.com/magazine/2018/07/23/alexandria-ocasio-cortezs-his toric-win-and-the-future-of-the-democratic-party.

Rose, Melody. 2012. *Women and Executive Office: Pathways and Performance*. Boulder: Lynne Rienner Publishers.

Sanbonmatsu, Kira. 2006. "Do Parties Know That 'Women Win'? Party Leader Beliefs about Women's Electoral Chances." *Politics & Gender* 2 (4): 431–50.

———. 2010. "Life's a Party." *Harvard International Review* 32 (1): 36–39.

Schmidt, Samantha. 2017. "A Politician Cracked That Women Belong in the Kitchen. A 'furious' Woman Just Took His Job." *Washington Post*, November 9, 2017, sec. Morning Mix. https://www.washingtonpost.com/news/morn

ing-mix/wp/2017/11/09/a-politician-cracked-that-women-belong-in-the-ki
tchen-a-furious-woman-just-took-his-job/.

Schneider, Monica C., Mirya R. Holman, Amanda B. Diekman, and Thomas
McAndrew. 2016. "Power, Conflict, and Community: How Gendered Views
of Political Power Influence Women's Political Ambition." *Political Psychology*
37 (4): 515–31. https://doi.org/10.1111/pops.12268.

Schultz, Marisa. 2019. "Elise Stefanik Launches PAC in Bid to Elect GOP Women
to Congress." *New York Post* (blog), January 19, 2019. https://nypost.com/2
019/01/18/elise-stefanik-launches-pac-in-bid-to-elect-gop-women-to-congress/.

Shames, Shauna. 2015. *3:1 Republican Women Are Outnumbered in Congress:
Right the Ratio.* Cambridge, MA: Political Parity. Hunt Alternatives.

Silbermann, Rachel. 2014. "Gender Roles, Work-Life Balance, and Running for
Office." http://csap.yale.edu/sites/default/files/files/silbermann.pdf.

Silva, Andrea, and Carrie Skulley. 2018. "Always Running: Candidate Emergence
among Women of Color over Time." *Political Research Quarterly*, July. https
://doi.org/10.1177/1065912918789289.

Stokes-Brown, Atiya Kai, and Kathleen Dolan. 2010. "Race, Gender, and Symbolic
Representation: African American Female Candidates as Mobilizing Agents."
Journal of Elections, Public Opinion and Parties 20 (4): 473–94. https://doi.org
/10.1080/17457289.2010.511806.

Stout, Christopher, and Katherine Tate. 2013. "The 2008 Presidential Election,
Political Efficacy, and Group Empowerment." *Politics, Groups and Identities*
1 (2): 143–63. https://doi.org/10.1080/21565503.2013.785960.

Takash, Paule Cruz. 1993. "Breaking Barriers To Representation: Chicana/Latina
Elected Officials In California." *Urban Anthropology and Studies of Cultural
Systems and World Economic Development* 22 (3/4): 325–60.

""This Is Our Time": Women of Color Break Barriers in 2018 Midterms." n.d.
Washington Post. Accessed August 31, 2018. http://www.washingtonpost
.com/video/politics/this-is-our-time-women-of-color-break-barriers-in-2018-
midterms/2018/08/23/209fb1a6-a64d-11e8-ad6f-080770dcddc2_video.html.

Thomsen, Danielle M., and Michele L. Swers. 2017. "Which Women Can Run?
Gender, Partisanship, and Candidate Donor Networks." *Political Research
Quarterly* 70 (2): 449–63. https://doi.org/10.1177/1065912917698044.

Williams, Vanessa. 2018. "Analysis | 'Unbought and Unbossed': Shirley Chisholm's
Feminist Mantra Is Still Relevant 50 Years Later." *Washington Post*, January
26, 2018. https://www.washingtonpost.com/news/post-nation/wp/2018/01/2
6/unbought-and-unbossed-shirley-chisholms-feminist-mantra-is-as-relevant-to
day-as-it-was-50-years-ago/.

CHAPTER 5

"About Lucy." n.d. Lucia McBath for Congress. Accessed January 26, 2019. https://
lucyforcongress.com.

Aday, Sean, James Devitt, White House Project Education Fund, and Women's
Leadership Fund. 2000. *Style over Substance: Newspaper Coverage of
Female Candidates: Spotlight on Elizabeth Dole.* New York: Women's Lead-
ership Fund.

Alexander, Deborah, and Kristi Andersen. 1993. "Gender as a Factor in the Attri-
bution of Leadership Traits." *Political Research Quarterly* 46 (3): 527–45.

Ball, Molly. 2016. "What Kind of Man Is Donald Trump?" *The Atlantic*, October
8, 2016. http://www.theatlantic.com/politics/archive/2016/10/donald-trump-
and-the-women/503402/?wpisrc=nl_daily202&wpmm=1#about-the-authors.

———. 2018. "Stacey Abrams Could Become America's First Black Female Governor—If She Can Turn Georgia Blue." *Time.Com*, July, 1–1.

Bauer, Nichole M. 2015. "Emotional, Sensitive, and Unfit for Office? Gender Stereotype Activation and Support Female Candidates." *Political Psychology* 36 (6): 691–708. https://doi.org/10.1111/pops.12186.

Beal, Frances M. 2008. "Double Jeopardy: To Be Black and Female." *Meridians: Feminism, Race, Transnationalism* 8 (2): 166–76.

Bejarano, Christina E. 2013. *The Latina Advantage: Gender, Race, and Political Success*. Austin, TX: University of Texas Press.

Blake, Aaron. 2016. "About 1 in 5 Voters Think Trump Made Unwanted Sexual Advances, but Are Still Voting for Him." *Washington Post*, October 17, 2016. https://www.washingtonpost.com/news/the-fix/wp/2016/10/17/roughly-1-in-5-voters-think-trump-has-made-unwanted-sexual-advances-but-are-still-voting-for-him.

Boggioni, Tom. 2015. "Not Even a Room Full of Puppies Can Make Carly Fiorina Likable." December 15, 2015. https://www.rawstory.com/2015/12/not-even-a-room-full-of-puppies-can-make-carly-fiorina-likable.

Borrelli, MaryAnne. 2002. *The President's Cabinet: Gender, Power, and Representation*. Boulder: L. Rienner Publishers.

Brooks, Deborah Jordan. 2013. *He Runs, She Runs: Why Gender Stereotypes Do Not Harm Women Candidates*. Princeton: Princeton University Press.

"Brown: Tucker Bounds Interview Becomes Lightning Rod." 2008. CNN. http://www.cnn.com/2008/POLITICS/09/05/brown.bounds/#cnnSTCText.

Burrell, Barbara. 2014. *Gender in Campaigns for the U.S. House of Representatives*. Ann Arbor: University of Michigan Press.

Buzzfeed News. 2015. "What If Women Talked Like Men In The Workplace?" BuzzFeed News. July 16, 2015. https://www.buzzfeednews.com/article/sajp/if-men-were-treated-like-women-in-the-workplace.

Carew, Jessica D. Johnson. 2016. "How Do You See Me? Stereotyping of Black Women and How It Affects Them in an Electoral Conte." In *Distinct Identities: Minority Women in US Politics*, edited by Nadia E. Brown and Sarah Allen Gershon, 95–115. Routledge Series on Identity Politics. New York: Routledge.

Cargile, Ivy A.M. 2016. "Latina Issues: An Analysis of the Policy Issue Competence of Latina Candidates." In *Distinct Identities: Minority Women in US Politics*, edited by Nadia E. Brown and Sarah Allen Gershon, 134–50. Routledge.

Carlin, Diana B., and Kelly L. Winfrey. 2009. "Have You Come a Long Way, Baby? Hillary Clinton, Sarah Palin, and Sexism in 2008 Campaign Coverage." *Communication Studies* 60 (4): 326–43. https://doi.org/10.1080/10510970903109904.

Casca, Mike. 2016. "If You Support @berniesanders, Please Follow the Senator's Lead and Be Respectful When People Disagree with You." Tweet. @cascamike (blog). January 25, 2016. https://twitter.com/cascamike/status/691844891652001792.

Cassese, Erin C., and Mirya R. Holman. 2017. "Party and Gender Stereotypes in Campaign Attacks." *Political Behavior*, July.

Center for American Women and Politics. 2016. "Women Presidential and Vice Presidential Candidates." *Presidential Gender Watch* (blog). 2016. http://presidentialgenderwatch.org/research/facts.

———. 2019a. "Women in State Legislatures 2019." Eagleton Institute of Politics: Center for American Women and Politics. http://www.cawp.rutgers.edu/women-state-legislature-2019.

———. 2019b. "Women in the U.S. Congress 2019." Eagleton Institute of Politics: Center for American Women and Politics. http://www.cawp.rutgers.edu/wo men-us-congress-2019.

———. 2019c. "Majority Party Women Presidential Candidates in 2020." New Brunswick: Center for American Women and Politics, Rutgers, The State University of New Jersey.

Chira, Susan. 2018. "Mom Is Running for Office." *The New York Times*, April 16, 2018, sec. Sunday Review. https://www.nytimes.com/2018/04/14/sunday-rev iew/mom-is-running-for-office.html.

Chozick, Amy. 2015. "Hillary Clinton Announces 2016 Presidential Bid." *The New York Times*, April 12, 2015. https://www.nytimes.com/2015/04/13/us/politics/ hillary-clinton-2016-presidential-campaign.html.

Cillizza, Chris. 2011. "Michele Bachmann Wins the Ames Straw Poll." *The Washington Post*, August 13, 2011. http://www.washingtonpost.com/blogs/the-fix/post/michel e-bachmann-wins-the-ames-straw-poll/2011/08/13/gIQApgnoDJ_blog.html.

Clift, Eleanor, and Tom Brazaitis. 2000. *Madam President: Shattering the Last Glass Ceiling*. New York: Scribner.

CNN. 2016. "2016 Election Results: Exit Polls." http://www.cnn.com/election/20 16/results/exit-polls.

———. 2018. "2018 Midterms: EXIT POLLING | CNN." https://www.cnn.com/ election/2018/exit-polls.

Collins, Patricia Hill. 2008. *Black Feminist Thought: Knowledge, Consciousness, and the Politics of Empowerment*. 1st ed. New York: Routledge.

Darcy, R. Susan Welch, and Janet Clark. 1994. *Women, Elections & Representation*. Lincoln: University of Nebraska Press.

Deckman, Melissa. 2016a. *Tea Party Women: Mama Grizzlies, Grassroots Leaders, and the Changing Face of the American Right*. New York: New York University Press.

———. 2016b. "Why Is Anyone Sticking with Trump? His 'alpha Male' Appeal." *Washington Post*, October 14, 2016. https://www.washingtonpost.com/post everything/wp/2016/10/14/why-is-anyone-sticking-with-trump-his-alpha-m ale-appeal.

———. 2018. "This Survey Shows Why There's Never Been a Better Time for Women to Run for Office—The Washington Post." *Monkey Cage, Washington Post* (blog). August 27, 2018. https://www.washingtonpost.com/news/monk ey-cage/wp/2018/08/27/this-survey-shows-why-theres-never-been-a-better-time -for-women-to-run-for-office/?utm_term=.406c7803970c.

Des Moines Register. 2015. "Clinton Hears 'eagerness' for Talk of Female Presidency." Des Moines Register. June 14, 2015. https://www.desmoinesregister. com/story/news/elections/presidential/caucus/2015/06/14/hillary-clinton-ext ra-burden-president-jennifer-jacobs-des-moines-register-interview-iowa-stat e-fairgrounds/71224966.

Dittmar, Kelly. 2015a. *Navigating Gendered Terrain: Stereotypes and Strategy in Political Campaigns*. Philadelphia: Temple University Press.

———. 2015b. "Everyone's Playing the Gender Card: The Question Is How." *Presidential Gender Watch* (blog). August 2, 2015. http://presidentialgender watch.org/everyones-playing-the-gender-card-the-question-is-how.

———. 2016. "Why Is Bernie Yelling at Me? - Ms. Magazine Blog." *Ms. Magazine* (blog). January 19, 2016. http://msmagazine.com/blog/2016/01/19/why-is- bernie-yelling-at-me.

———. 2018. "By the Numbers: Women Congressional Candidates in 2018." Eagleton Institute of Politics: Center for American Women and Politics. http://cawp.rutgers.edu/congressional-candidates-summary-2018.

Dolan, Kathleen. 2014. *When Does Gender Matter? Women Candidates and Gender Stereotypes in American Elections*. OUP USA.

Dolan, Kathleen, and Timothy Lynch. 2014. "It Takes a Survey: Understanding Gender Stereotypes, Abstract Attitudes, and Voting for Women Candidates." *American Politics Research* 42 (4): 656–76. https://doi.org/10.1177/153267 3X13503034.

Duerst-Lahti, Georgia, and Madison Oakley. 2018. "Presidential Elections, Gendered Space, and the Case of 2016." In *Gender and Elections: Shaping the Future of American Politics*, edited by Susan J. Carroll and Richard L. Fox, 15–47. Cambridge, MA: Cambridge University Press.

Dutton, Sarah, Jennifer De Pinto, Fred Backus, and Anthony Salvanto. 2016. "Clinton Maintains Lead after Claiming Nomination - CBS News Poll." *CBS News*. http://www.cbsnews.com/news/clinton-maintains-lead-after-claiming-nomination-cbs-news-poll.

Edmondson, Catie, and Jasmine C. Lee. 2018. "Meet the New Freshmen in Congress." *The New York Times*, November 28, 2018, sec. U.S. https://www.nytimes.com/interactive/2018/11/28/us/politics/congress-freshman-class.html, https://www.nytimes.com/interactive/2018/11/28/us/politics/congress-freshman-class.html.

Estepa, Jessica. 2015. "Donald Trump on Carly Fiorina: 'Look at That Face!'" *USA Today*, September 10, 2015. https://www.usatoday.com/story/news/nation-now/2015/09/10/trump-fiorina-look-face/71992454.

Farhi, Paul. 2016. "Trump Revokes Post Press Credentials, Calling the Paper 'Dishonest' and 'Phony.'" *The Washington Post*, June 13, 2016. https://www.washingtonpost.com/lifestyle/style/trump-revokes-post-press-credentials-calling-the-paper-dishonest-and-phony/2016/06/13/f9a61a72-31aa-11e6-95c0-2a6873031302_story.html?utm_term=.422f0b24423d.

Fiorina, Carly. 2015. "Redefining Feminism." *Carly Fiorina* (blog). June 24, 2015. https://medium.com/@CarlyFiorina/redefining-feminism-19d25d8d8dfc.

Frizell, Sam. 2016. "Bernie Sanders Does Not Concede Democratic Nomination to Hillary Clinton." *Time.Com*, June, 1.

Fulton, Sarah A., and Sarah Allen Gershon. 2018. "Too Liberal to Win? Race and Voter Perceptions of Candidate Ideology." *American Politics Research*, February, 1532673X18759642. https://doi.org/10.1177/1532673X18759642.

Gambino, Lauren. 2015. "Carly Fiorina Expertly Defuses Trump on 'Beautiful Face' Retort and Foreign Policy." *The Guardian*, September 17, 2015, sec. US news. https://www.theguardian.com/us-news/2015/sep/17/carly-fiorina-republican-debate-donald-trump-sexism-foreign-policy-women.

Gates, Henry Louis. 1996. "Hating Hillary." *The New Yorker*, February 26, 1996. http://www.newyorker.com/magazine/1996/02/26/hating-hillary.

Gershon, Sarah. 2012. "When Race, Gender, and the Media Intersect: Campaign News Coverage of Minority Congresswomen." *Journal of Women, Politics & Policy* 33 (2): 105–25. https://doi.org/10.1080/1554477X.2012.667743.

Gershon, Sarah Allen. 2013. "Media Coverage of Minority Congresswomen and Voter Evaluations: Evidence from an Online Experimental Study." *Political Research Quarterly* 66 (3): 702–14.

Gillespie, Andra. 2016. "Race, Perceptions of Femininity, and the Power of the First Lady: A Comparative Analysis." In *Distinct Identities: Minority Women in US Politics*, edited by Nadia E. Brown and Sarah Allen Gershon, 234–51. Routledge.

Gilmartin, Patricia. 2001. "Still the Angel in the Household." *Women & Politics* 22 (4): 51–67.

Gina Ortiz Jones for Congress—I Run Towards. n.d. Accessed January 26, 2019. https://www.youtube.com/channel/UC6e6dzam49qUp3fDH_G3Tlw.

Glueck, Katie. 2015. "Fiorina Finds Her Fans." POLITICO. September 13, 2015. https://www.politico.com/story/2015/09/carly-fiorina-2016-straw-poll-213580.

Gordon, Ann, and Jerry L. Miller. 2005. *When Stereotypes Collide: Race/Ethnicity, Gender, and Videostyle in Congressional Campaigns*. New York: Peter Lang Inc., International Academic Publishers.

Graham, David A. 2015. "Carly Fiorina Makes Planned Parenthood a National Story Again." *The Atlantic*, September 18, 2015. https://www.theatlantic.com/politics/archive/2015/09/fiorina-abortion-planned-parenthood-video-debate/406168.

Hayes, Danny, and Jennifer L. Lawless. 2015. "A Non-Gendered Lens? Media, Voters, and Female Candidates in Contemporary Congressional Elections." *Perspectives on Politics* 13 (1): 95–118. https://doi.org/10.1017/S1537592714003156.

Healy, Patrick, and Erica Berenstein. 2015. "How Bernie Sanders Connects With His Audience." *The New York Times*, October 12, 2015, sec. U.S. https://www.nytimes.com/interactive/2015/10/12/us/politics/bernie-sanders-campaign-video-analysis.html, https://www.nytimes.com/interactive/2015/10/12/politics/bernie-sanders-campaign-video-analysis.html.

Heim, Joe. 2018. "Native American Women Candidates Seek Historic Wins in November." *Washington Post*, October 12, 2018. https://www.washingtonpost.com/politics/native-american-women-candidates-seek-historic-wins-in-november/2018/10/12/7df3064c-c10e-11e8-9005-5104e9616c21_story.html.

Heldman, Caroline, Meredith Conroy, and Alissa R. Ackerman. 2018. *Sex and Gender in the 2016 Presidential Election*. ABC-CLIO. https://www.abc-clio.com/ABC-CLIOCorporate/product.aspx?pc=A5566C.

Hodges, Lauren. 2016. "Did FBI Director James Comey's Email Announcement Break The Law?" *NPR.Org*. October 31, 2016. http://www.npr.org/2016/10/31/500071704/did-fbi-director-james-comeys-email-announcement-break-the-law.

Huddy, Leonie, and Nayda Terkildsen. 1993. "The Consequences of Gender Stereotypes for Women Candidates at Different Levels and Types of Office." *Political Research Quarterly* 46 (3): 503–25.

Jacobson, Gary C. 2013. *The Politics of Congressional Elections*. Boston: Pearson.

Jahnke, Christine K. 1992. "Beauty Pageant: How to Avoid Gender Issues in Your Campaign." *Campaigns & Elections* 12 (5).

Jamieson, Kathleen Hall. 1995. *Beyond the Double Bind: Women and Leadership*. New York: Oxford University Press.

Jordan, Mary. 2018. "After Iraq and Afghanistan, Pioneering Women in the Military Set Sights on Congress—The Washington Post." *Washington Post*, February 7, 2018. https://www.washingtonpost.com/politics/2018/02/07/237865a2-fad7-11e7-8f66-2df0b94bb98a_story.html?utm_term=.3ed7b269a7d2.

Kahn, Kim Fridkin. 1996. *The Political Consequences of Being a Woman: How Stereotypes Influence the Conduct and Consequences of Political Campaigns*. New York: Columbia University Press.

Kantor, Jodi, and Rachel L. Swarns. 2008. "A New Twist in the Debate on Mothers." *The New York Times*, September 2, 2008, sec. U.S. / Politics. http://www .nytimes.com/2008/09/02/us/politics/02mother.html.

Karni, Annie. 2015. "Hillary's Hair: She's in on the Joke." POLITICO. May 28, 2015. https://www.politico.com/story/2015/05/hillary-clinton-hair-11838 1.html.

King, David C., and Richard E. Matland. 2003. "Sex and the Grand Old Party An Experimental Investigation of the Effect of Candidate Sex on Support for a Republican Candidate." *American Politics Research* 31 (6): 595–612. https:// doi.org/10.1177/1532673X03255286.

Koch, Jeffrey W. 2000. "Do Citizens Apply Gender Stereotypes to Infer Candidates' Ideological Orientations?" *The Journal of Politics* 62 (2): 414–29.

Korecki, Natasha. 2018. "Warren Battles the Ghosts of Hillary." POLITICO. December 31, 2018. https://politi.co/2EZAHv1.

Kreig, Gregory. 2016. "Donald Trump Defends Size of His Penis." *CNN*. March 16, 2016. https://www.cnn.com/2016/03/03/politics/donald-trump-small-h ands-marco-rubio/index.html.

Lavery, Lesley. 2013. "Gender Bias in the Media? An Examination of Local Television News Coverage of Male and Female House Candidates." *Politics & Policy* 41 (6): 877–910. https://doi.org/10.1111/polp.12051.

Lawless, Jennifer L., and Kathryn Pearson. 2008. "The Primary Reason for Women's Underrepresentation? Reevaluating the Conventional Wisdom." *The Journal of Politics* 70 (1): 67–82. https://doi.org/10.1017/S002238160708005X.

Lawrence, Regina G., and Melody Rose. 2011. "Bringing Out the Hook Exit Talk in Media Coverage of Hillary Clinton and Past Presidential Campaigns." *Political Research Quarterly* 64 (4): 870–83. https://doi.org/10.1177/10659129103 76390.

———. 2012. "The Real '08 Fight: Clinton vs. Palin." In *Women and Executive Office: Pathways and Performance*, edited by Melody Rose, 11–31. Boulder: Lynne Rienner Publishers.

———. 2014. "The Race for the Presidency: Hillary Rodham Clinton." In *Women and Elective Office: Past, Present and Future*, edited by Sue Thomas and Clyde Wilcox, 3rd ed., 67–79. New York: Oxford University Press.

Lemieux, Jamilah. 2016. "Sen. Bernie Sanders Speaks to the Issues." EBONY. July 22, 2016. https://www.ebony.com/news/sen-bernie-sanders-interview-jamilah-l emieux.

Limbaugh, Rush. 2008. "Feminism and Sarah Palin—The Rush Limbaugh Show." Rush Limbaugh. 2008. http://www.rushlimbaugh.com/daily/2008/09/05/femin ism_and_sarah_palin.

Lucy McBath for Congress. n.d. *Lucy McBath for Congress: "Jordan."* Accessed January 23, 2019. https://www.youtube.com/watch?time_continue=202&v= xiZQ-JU9zbw.

Marcotte, Amanda. 2015. "Hillary Baits Bernie Beautifully: 'Shouting,' Sexism— and the Simple Sorry That Would Make Sanders Look Less Jerky." *Salon* (blog). 2015. https://www.salon.com/2015/10/27/hillary_baits_bernie_beauti fully_shouting_sexism_and_the_simple_sorry_that_would_make_sanders_loo k_less_jerky.

Matson, Marsha, and Terri Susan Fine. 2006. "Gender, Ethnicity, and Ballot Information: Ballot Cues in Low-Information Elections." *State Politics & Policy Quarterly; Springfield* 6 (1): 49–72,112–13.

McDermott, Monika L. 1997. "Voting Cues in Low-Information Elections: Candidate Gender as a Social Information Variable in Contemporary United States Elections." *American Journal of Political Science* 41 (1): 270–83. https://doi.org/10.2307/2111716.

———. 1998. "Race and Gender Cues in Low-Information Elections." *Political Research Quarterly* 51 (4): 895–918. https://doi.org/10.2307/449110.

McElrath, Leah. 2019. "There Are Countless Photos of Stacey Abrams and Her Glorious Smile. Axios Must Have Had to Search to Find an Image to Fit the 'Angry Black Woman' Trope.Pic.Twitter.Com/NvH5HrVOlV." Tweet. @*leahmcelrath* (blog). January 29, 2019. https://twitter.com/leahmcelrath/status/1090344894051348482.

McElwee, Sean, Matt McDermott, and Will Jordan. 2017. "4 Pieces of Evidence Showing FBI Director James Comey Cost Clinton the Election." *Vox.* January 11, 2017. http://www.vox.com/the-big-idea/2017/1/11/14215930/comey-email-election-clinton-campaign.

Merida, Kevin. 2008. "She's the Star the GOP Hitched Its Bandwagon To." *The Washington Post*, September 11, 2008, sec. Arts & Living.

Meyer, Robinson. 2015. "Here Comes the Berniebro." *The Atlantic.* October 17, 2015. https://www.theatlantic.com/politics/archive/2015/10/here-comes-the-berniebro-bernie-sanders/411070.

Michel, Casey. 2019. "GOP Moves to Block Anyone from Running a 2020 Primary Challenge against Trump." *ThinkProgress* (blog). January 27, 2019. https://thinkprogress.org/gop-moves-to-block-anyone-from-running-a-2020-primary-challenge-against-trump-ddaecd967c7a.

"Michele Bachmann Plays Gender Card as Iowa GOP Vote Nears." 2012. *Iowa Caucuses* (blog). January 1, 2012. http://caucuses.desmoinesregister.com/2012/01/01/bachmann-plays-gender-card-as-iowa-gop-vote-nears.

Newport, Frank. 2016. "Eight Things We Learned in This Election." *Gallup.Com.* November 10, 2016. http://www.gallup.com/opinion/polling-matters/197357/eight-things-learned-election.aspx.

"No One Had to Ask"—Gina Ortiz Jones for Congress. n.d. Accessed January 26, 2019. https://www.youtube.com/channel/UC6e6dzam49qUp3fDH_G3Tlw.

Norris, Pippa. 1997. *Women, Media, and Politics.* New York: Oxford University Press.

Page, Susan. 2016. "'Why Are You Yelling': Women Still Face a Political Double Standard: Clinton at Cusp of History, but Obstacles Remain on Landscape." *USA TODAY*, June 6, 2016, sec. NEWS.

Page, Susan, and Paulina Firozi. 2015. "Poll: By 2-1, Funding for Planned Parenthood Supported." *USA TODAY.* September 29, 2015. https://www.usatoday.com/story/news/politics/2015/09/29/poll-2-1-funding-planned-parenthood-supported/73016440.

Palmer, Barbara, and Dennis Simon. 2001. "The Political Glass Ceiling: Gender, Strategy, and Incumbency in U.S. House Elections, 1978–1998." *Women & Politics* 23: 59–78.

Palmer, Barbara, and Dennis Michael Simon. 2012. *Women and Congressional Elections: A Century of Change.* Boulder: Lynne Rienner Publishers.

Paquette, Danielle. 2015. "Carly Fiorina and the Problem of Smiling While Woman." *Washington Post.* October 29, 2015. https://www.washingtonpost.com/news/wonk/wp/2015/10/29/carly-fiorina-and-the-problem-of-smiling-while-woman.

Parlapiano, Alicia, and Karen Yourish. 2016. "If You Think the Democratic Primary Race Is Close, the 2008 One Was Even Tighter." *The New York Times.* June 7, 2016. http://www.nytimes.com/interactive/2016/06/07/us/elections/clinton-sanders-delegate-fight.html.

Petri, Alexandra. 2016. "The Hideous, Diabolical Truth about Hillary Clinton." *The Washington Post.* October 14, 2016. https://www.washingtonpost.com/blogs/compost/wp/2016/10/14/the-hideous-diabolical-truth-about-hillary-clinton/?utm_term=.4ef9d6c77515&wpisrc=nl_p1wemost-partner-1&wpmm=1.

Pew Research Center. 2015. "Chapter 2: What Makes a Good Leader, and Does Gender Matter?" http://www.pewsocialtrends.org/2015/01/14/chapter-2-what-makes-a-good-leader-and-does-gender-matter.

Pew Research Center's Project for Excellence in Journalism. 2007. "The Invisible Primary: Invisible No More." Pew Research Center.

Politico. 2016. "Hillary Clinton's Major Endorsements." POLITICO. March 7, 2016. https://www.politico.com/story/2016/03/hillary-clinton-endorsement-list-219796.

Public Religion Research Institute. 2018. "Partisan Polarization Dominates Trump Era: Findings from the 2018 American Values Survey." *PRRI* (blog). October 29, 2018. https://www.prri.org/research/partisan-polarization-dominates-trump-era-findings-from-the-2018-american-values-survey.

RealClearPolitics. 2016. "RealClearPolitics—Election 2016 Democratic Delegate Count." https://www.realclearpolitics.com/epolls/2016/president/democratic_delegate_count.html.

Richardson, Bradford. 2015. "Fiorina Slams 'The View.'" Text. TheHill. November 1, 2015. https://thehill.com/blogs/ballot-box/gop-primaries/258775-fiorina-slams-the-view-for-remarks-about-her-face.

Ring, Wilson. 2018. "Democrat Christine Hallquist Becomes First Major Party Transgender Candidate for Governor." *Time.Com.* August, 1–1.

Roberts, Dan. 2015. "Bernie Sanders' Democratic Debate Challenge: Turning down the Volume." *The Guardian.* October 12, 2015, sec. US news. https://www.theguardian.com/us-news/2015/oct/12/bernie-sanders-hillary-clinton-democratic-debate-preview.

Rosenwasser, Shirley Miller, and Norma G. Dean. 1989. "Gender Role and Political Office." *Psychology of Women Quarterly* 13 (1): 77.

Rosenwasser, Shirley Miller, and Jana Seale. 1988. "Attitudes Toward a Hypothetical Male or Female Presidential Candidate—A Research Note." *Political Psychology* 9 (4): 591–98. http://dx.doi.org/10.2307/3791529.

Rothkopf, Joanna. 2016. "Bernie Sanders' Campaign Is Concerned About the 'Berniebro,' As They Maybe Should Be." *The Slot.* January 29, 2016. https://theslot.jezebel.com/bernie-sanders-campaign-is-concerned-about-the-berniebr-1755911898.

Sanbonmatsu, Kira. 2002. "Gender Stereotypes and Vote Choice." *American Journal of Political Science* 46 (1).

Sanbonmatsu, Kira, and Kathleen Dolan. 2009. "Do Gender Stereotypes Transcend Party?" *Political Research Quarterly* 62 (3): 485–94. https://doi.org/10.1177/1065912908322416.

Schneider, Monica C., and Angela L. Bos. 2011. "An Exploration of the Content of Stereotypes of Black Politicians." *Political Psychology* 32 (2): 205–33. https://doi.org/10.1111/j.1467-9221.2010.00809.x.

Shane, Leo, III. 2018. "Here Are the 173 Veterans Running for Congress in November." *Military Times.* November 6, 2018. https://www.militarytimes.com/

news/pentagon-congress/2018/10/19/here-are-the-172-veterans-running-fo
r-congress-in-november.

Shannon, Joel. 2018. "Election Results 2018: These Women, Minority Candidates Made History." *USA Today*. November 6, 2018. https://www.usatoday.com/ story/news/politics/elections/2018/11/06/election-results-2018-women-minori ty-candidates-history-firsts/1912048002.

Sharockman, Aaron. 2016. "The Truth about the 2016 Presidential Campaign." *PolitiFact*. September 26, 2016. http://www.politifact.com/truth-o-meter/artic le/2016/sep/26/trump-clinton-fact-check-2016-president.

Shorenstein Center on Media, Politcs and Public Policy. 2016a. "Pre-Primary News Coverage of the 2016 Presidential Race: Trump's Rise, Sanders' Emergence, Clinton's Struggle." Boston, MA: Harvard Kennedy School. http://shorenst eincenter.org/pre-primary-news-coverage-2016-trump-clinton-sanders.

———. 2016b. "News Coverage of the 2016 General Election: How the Press Failed the Voters." Boston: Harvard Kennedy School. https://shorensteincenter .org/news-coverage-2016-general-election.

Sigelman, Carol K., Lee Sigelman, Barbara J. Walkosz, and Michael Nitz. 1995. "Black Candidates, White Voters: Understanding Racial Bias in Political Per-ceptions." *American Journal of Political Science* 39 (1): 243–65. https://doi. org/10.2307/2111765.

Smith, Anne. 2008. "Limbaugh Returned to 'Testicle Lockbox'; Claimed Clinton 'Reminds Men of the Worst Characteristics of Women.'" Media Matters for America. 2008. http://mediamatters.org/research/2008/02/15/limbaugh-returne d-to-testicle-lockbox-claimed-c/142573.

Smooth, Wendy. 2006. "Intersectionality in Electoral Politics: A Mess Worth Mak-ing." *Politics & Gender* 2 (3): 400–14.

Stolberg, Sheryl Gay. 2014. "Joni Ernst's Playbook, for Women to Win Men's Vote." *The New York Times*. October 28, 2014. http://www.nytimes.com/20 14/10/29/us/iowans-playbook-for-women-to-win-mens-vote.html.

Tani, Maxwell. 2016. "Donald Trump Mocks Jeb Bush for Asking His 'mommy' to Campaign with Him." *Business Insider*. February 7, 2016. https://www.bus inessinsider.com/donald-trump-jeb-barbara-bush-mommy-2016-2.

The New York Times. n.d. "Texas Election Results: 23rd House District," sec. U.S. Accessed January 26, 2019. https://www.nytimes.com/elections/results/tex as-house-district-23.

The Washington Post. 2012. "Michele Bachmann Drops out of GOP Race after Iowa Caucuses," January 4, 2012. http://www.washingtonpost.com/politics/ michele-bachmann-drops-out-of-gop-race-after-iowa-caucuses/2012/01/04/g IQAP6L9aP_story.html.

Tromble, Rebekah, and Dirk Hovy. 2016. "These 6 Charts Show How Much Sex-ism Hillary Clinton Faces on Twitter." *Washington Post—Blogs* (blog). Feb-ruary 24, 2016. http://search.proquest.com/newsstand/docview/1767832935/ citation/26E24FC4492A44F4PQ/1.

Villani, Chris. 2015. "Fiorina Blasts Gender Attacks from Cruz Camp." *Boston Herald* (blog). December 22, 2015. https://www.bostonherald.com/2015/1 2/22/fiorina-blasts-gender-attacks-from-cruz-camp.

Waldman, Paul. 2016. "Trump's History of Corruption Is Mind-Boggling. So Why Is Clinton Supposedly the Corrupt One?" *The Washington Post*. September 5, 2016. https://www.washingtonpost.com/blogs/plum-line/wp/2016/09/05/trum ps-history-of-corruption-is-mind-boggling-so-why-is-clinton-supposedly-the-corrupt-one/?utm_term=.495a6cc7a327.

Walsh, Joan. 2016. "Why I'm Supporting Hillary Clinton, With Joy and Without Apologies," January 27, 2016. https://www.thenation.com/article/why-im -supporting-hillary-clinton-with-joy-and-without-apologies.

Ward, Orlanda. 2016a. "Media Framing of Black Women's Campaigns for the US House of Representatives." In *Distinct Identities: Minority Women in US Politics*, edited by Nadia E. Brown and Sarah Allen Gershon. Routledge Series on Identity Politics, 153–70. New York: Routledge.

———. 2016b. "Seeing Double: Race, Gender, and Coverage of Minority Women's Campaigns for the U.S. House of Representatives." *Politics & Gender; Cambridge* 12 (2): 317–43. http://dx.doi.org.ezproxy.macalester.edu/10.1017/S1743 923X16000222.

Watkins, Bonnie, and Nina Rothchild. 1996. *In the Company of Women: Voices from the Women's Movement*. St. Paul: Minnesota Historical Society Press.

Watson, Robert P., and Ann Gordon. 2003. *Anticipating Madam President*. Boulder: Lynne Rienner.

West, Carolyn M. 2008. "Mammy, Jezebel, Sapphire, and Their Homegirls: Developing an 'Oppositional Gaze' toward the Images of Black Women." In *Lectures on the Psychology of Women*, edited by J. Chrisler, C. Golden, and P. Rozee, 4th ed., 286–99. New York: McGraw-Hill.

Young, Lauren. 2018. "Gina Ortiz Jones Is Running for Texas's 23rd District in March 6 Texas Primary—Teen Vogue," March 5, 2018. https://www.tee nvogue.com/story/gina-ortiz-jones-is-running-for-texass-23rd-district-in-ma rch-6-texas-primary.

CHAPTER 6

Akers, Roy. 2019. "Women for Trump Hold 'Build the Wall' Rally in Bloomfield Hills, in Photos." *New Herald.com*. January 26. http://www.thenewsherald. com/multimedia/women-for-trump-hold-build-the-wall-rally-in-bloomfield/ collection_a8f8e11a-969a-5afe-9619-ffa91b0ac9bf.html#4. Accessed January 31, 2019.

Alozie, Nicholas O., and Lynne L. Manganaro. 1993. "Women's Council Representation: Measurement Implications for Public Policy." *Political Research Quarterly* 46(2): 383–98.

Antolini, Denise. 1984. "Women in Local Government: An Overview." In *Political Women: Current Roles in State and Local Government*, edited by Janet A. Flammang, 23–40. Beverly Hills: Sage Publications.

Beck, Susan Abrams. 2001. "Acting as Women: The Effects and Limitations of Gender in Local Governance." In *The Impact of Women in Public Office*, edited by Susan J. Carroll, 49–67. Bloomington: Indiana University Press.

Bernick, Ethan M., and Brianne Heidbreder. 2018. "Disproportionately Overrepresented: Women in Local Elected Offices." *State and Local Government Review*. DOI: 10.1177/0160323X18813641 1-12. Accessed December 26, 2018.

Black Lives Matter. N.d. "Herstory," https://blacklivesmatter.com/about/herstory. Accessed January 12, 2019.

Blair, Karen J. 1980. *The Clubwoman as Feminist: True Womanhood Redefined, 1868–1914*. New York: Holmes and Meier.

Bookman, Ann, and Sandra Morgen. 1988. *Women and the Politics of Empowerment*. Philadelphia: Temple University Press.

Boles, Janet. 2001. "Local Elected Women and Policy-Making: Movement Delegates or Feminist Trustees?" In *The Impact of Women in Public Office*, edited by Susan J. Carroll, 68–86. Bloomington: Indiana University Press.

Boris, Eileen. 2002. "On Grassroots Organizing, Poor Women's Movements, and the Intellectual as Activist." *Journal of Women's History* 14(2): 140–42.

Brown, Clyde, Neil R. Heighberger, and Peter A. Shocket. 1993. "Gender-Based Differences in Perceptions of Male and Female City Council Candidates." *Women & Politics* 13(1): 1–17.

Browning, Rufus P., Dale Rogers Marshall, and David H. Tabb. 1984. *Protest Is Not Enough: The Struggle of Blacks and Hispanics for Equality in Urban Politics*. Berkeley: University of California Press.

Brownstone, Sydney. 2018. "Mayor Durkan Says She's Getting Rid of Sexual Harassment Settlements Inside City Departments." *The Stranger*. January 25. https://www.thestranger.com/slog/2018/01/25/25751858/mayor-durkan-says-shes-getting-rid-of-sexual-harassment-settlements-inside-city-departments. Accessed January 3, 2019.

Budd, Darlene, Angelique Myers, and Thomas Longoria. 2015. "The Role of A Gendered Policy in Closing the Mayoral Ambition Gap: the Case of Texas Female City Council Members." *Journal of Research on Women and Gender* 6: 81–93.

Bullock, Charles S. III, and Susan A. MacManus. 1991. "Municipal Electoral Structure and the Election of Councilwomen." *Journal of Politics* 53(1): 75–89.

Butler, Daniel, and Jessica Robinson Preece. 2016. "Recruitment and Perceptions of Gender Bias in Party Leader Support." *Political Research Quarterly* 69(4): 842–51.

Byers, Jacqueline J. 2008. "Role of the County Clerk (Research Brief)." National Association of Counties. http://www.naco.org/sites/default/files/documents/Role%20of%20the%20County%20Clerk.pdf. Accessed December 26, 2018.

California Women Lead. 2017. "The Status of Women in California Government: 2017." July. https://cdn.ymaws.com/www.cawomenlead.org/resource/resmgr/files/7.26.2017_Status_of_Women_in.pdf. Accessed December 27, 2018.

Cannon, Austin. 2018. "Iowa's Gender-Balance Law is Nearly a Decade Old, but Progress is Slow." *Des Moines Register*. November 21. https://www.desmoinesregister.com/story/news/2018/11/21/iowas-gender-balance-law-nearly-progress-slow-parity-waukee-des-moines-pocahontas-government/1992344002. Accessed December 29, 2018.

Carroll, Susan J., and Kira Sanbonmatsu. 2010. "Entering the Mayor's Office: Women's Decision to Run for Municipal Office." http://www.cawp.rutgers.edu/research/research_by_cawp_scholars/documents/Carroll_and_Sanbonmatsu_2010_MPSA-mayors.pdf

Center for American Women and Politics. 2019. Fast Facts. "Women Mayors in U.S. Cities 2018." January. www.cawp.rutgers.edu/fast_facts/levels_of_office/Local-WomenMayors/php

Cohen, Cathy J. 2003. "A Portrait of Continuing Marginality: The Study of Women of Color in American Politics." In *Women and American Politics: New Questions, New Directions*, edited by Susan J. Carroll, 190–213. New York: Oxford University Press.

Crow, Barbara A. 1997. "Relative Privilege? Reconsidering White Women's Participation in Municipal Politics." In *Women Transforming Politics: An Alternative Reader*, edited by Cathy J. Cohen, Kathleen B. Jones, and Joan C. Tronto, 435–46. New York: New York University Press.

Crowder-Meyer, Melody. 2013. "Gendered Recruitment without Trying: How Local Party Recruiters Affect Women's Representation." *Politics & Gender* 9: 390–413.

Crowder-Meyer, Melody, Shana Kushner Gadarian, and Jessica Trounstine. 2015. "Electoral Institutions, Gender Stereotypes, and Women's Local Representation, Politics, Groups, and Identities." 3(2): 318–334, DOI: 10.1080/21565503.2015.1031803.

Crowder-Meyer, Melody, and Adrienne R. Smith. 2015. "How the Strategic Context Affects Women's Emergence and Success in Local Legislative Elections." *Politics, Groups, and Identities* 3(2): 295–317.

Czubaj, Camilla Anne. 2002. "An Analysis of School Board Members." *Education* 122(3): 615–18.

Darcy, Robert, Susan Welch, and Janet Clark. 1994. *Women, Elections & Representation*. 2nd ed. Lincoln: University of Nebraska Press.

Davis, Carolyn, and Molly Fisch-Friedman. 2018. "Young Americans Increasingly Flexible about Gender Expression, See Connections between Gender and Violence." January 19. https://www.prri.org/spotlight/young-americans-inc reasingly-flexible-gender-expression-see-connections-gender-violence. Accessed December 26, 2018.

Deckman, Melissa. 2004. *School Board Battles: The Christian Right in Local Politics*. Washington, DC: Georgetown University Press.

———. 2007. "Gender Differences in the Decision to Run for School Board." *American Politics Research* 35(4): 541–63.

———. 2016. *Tea Party Women: Mama Grizzlies, Grassroots Activists, and the Changing Face of the American Right*. New York: New York University Press.

———. 2018. "A New Poll Shows How Younger Women Could Help Drive a Democratic Wave." *Washington Post*. March 5.

DeSena, Judith N, ed. 2008. *Gender in an Urban World*. Research in Urban Sociology. 9(1). Bingley, UK: JAI Press, Emerald Group Publishing.

Donahue, Jesse. 1997. "It Doesn't Matter: Some Cautionary Findings about Sex and Representation from School Committee Conversations." *Policy Studies Journal* 25(4): 630–48.

———. 1999. "The Non-Representation of Gender: School Committee Members and Gender Equity." *Women & Politics* 20(3): 65–81.

Farmer, Liz. 2018. "Women Mayors and #MeToo: 'We Have a Responsibility.'" *Governing*. January 26. http://www.governing.com/topics/mgmt/gov-wome n-mayors-metoo-uscm-harassment.html. Accessed January 3, 2019.

Flammang, Janet. 1985. "Female Officials in the Feminist Capital: The Case of Santa Clara County." *Western Political Quarterly* 38(1): 94–118.

———. 1987. *Women's Political Voice: How Women Are Transforming the Practice and Study of Politics*. Philadelphia: Temple University Press.

Gonzalez, Emma. 2018. "A Young Activist's Advice: Vote, Shave Your Head and Cry Whenever You Need To." *New York Times*. October 5. https://ww w.nytimes.com/2018/10/05/opinion/sunday/emma-gonzalez-parkland.html. Accessed January 12, 2019.

Gordon, Michael, Mark S. Price, and Katie Peralta. 2016. "Understanding HB 2: North Carolina's Newest Law Solidifies State's Role in Defining Discrimination." *Charlotte Observer*. March 26. https://www.charlotteobserver. com/news/politics-government/article68401147.html. Accessed December 23, 2018.

Graham, David A. 2017. "Red State, Blue City." *The Atlantic*. March. https://www.theatlantic.com/magazine/archive/2017/03/red-state-blue-city/513857. Accessed December 26, 2018.

Hardy-Fanta, Carol. 1993. *Latina Politics, Latino Politics: Gender, Culture, and Political Participation in Boston*. Philadelphia: Temple University Press.

———. 1997. "Latina Women and Political Consciousness: La Chispa Que Prende." In *Women Transforming Politics: An Alternative Reader*, edited by Cathy J. Cohen, Kathleen B. Jones, and Joan C. Tronto, 223–37. New York: New York University Press.

Hardy-Fanta, Carol, Pei-te Lien, Dianne M. Pinderhughes, and Christine Marie Sierra. 2016. *Contested Transformation: Race, Gender, and Political Leadership in 21ˢᵗ Century America*. Cambridge: Cambridge University Press.

Herrick, Rebekah, and Susan Welch. 1992. "The Impact of At-Large Elections on the Representation of Black and White Women." *National Political Science Review* 3: 62–77.

Holman, Mirya R. 2014. *Women in Politics in the American City*. Philadephia: Temple University Press.

Human Rights Campaign. 2016. "Years of Progress and Change: Municipal Equality Index: A Nationwide Evaluation of Municipal Law." http://assets2.hrc.org/files/assets/resources/MEI-2016-Final-Online.pdf. Accessed December 26, 2018.

Kansas Historical Society. n.d. "Susanna Madora Salter." https://www.kshs.org/kansapedia/susanna-madora-salter/12191

Karpowitz, Christopher, and Tali Mendelberg. 2014. *The Silent Sex: Gender, Deliberation, and Institutions*. Princeton: Princeton University Press.

Kellogg, Leander D., Al G. Gourrier, E. Lee Bernick, and Kathereyn Brekken. 2017. "County Government Boards: Where are all the Women?" *Politics, Groups, and Identities*. DOI: 10.1080/21565503.2017.1304223.

Kominiak, Todd. 2016. "There are too Few Women Superintendents—and What We Can Do About it." *Trusted:K-12 Insight*. November 4. https://www.k12 insight.com/trusted/women-superintendents-can. Accessed January 4, 2–19.

Lacour, Greg. 2017. "HB2: How North Carolina Got Here (Updated)." *Charlotte Magazine*. March 30. http://www.charlottemagazine.com/Charlotte-Magazine/April-2016/HB2-How-North-Carolina-Got-Here. Accessed December 22, 2018.

———. 2016. "The Education of Jennifer Roberts." *Charlotte Magazine*. June 26. http://www.charlottemagazine.com/Charlotte-Magazine/July-2016/The-Education-of-Jennifer-Roberts. Accessed December 26, 2018.

Lien, Pei-te. 2014. "Reassessing Descriptive Representation by Women and Men of Color: New Evidence at the Subnational Level." *Urban Affairs Review* 51(2): 239–62.

Lopez, German. 2018. "Myth#3: Letting Trans People Use their Bathroom or Locker Room Matching their Gender Identity is Dangerous." *Vox*. November 14. https://www.vox.com/identities/2016/5/13/17938102/transgender-people-bathrooms-locker-rooms-schools. Accessed December 26, 2018.

———. 2017a. "Anti-transgender Bathroom Hysteria, Explained." *Vox*. February 22.

———. 2017b. "HB2, North Carolina's Sweeping Anti-LGBTQ Law, Explained." *Vox*. March 30. https://www.vox.com/2016/2/23/11100552/charlotte-north-carolina-lgbtq-pat-mccrory. Accessed December 26, 2018. https://www.vox.com/2016/5/5/11592908/transgender-bathroom-laws-rights. Accessed December 26, 2018.

Lublin, David, and Sarah Brewer. 2003. "The Continuing Dominance of Traditional Gender Roles in Southern Elections." *Social Science Quarterly* 84(2): 379–96.

MacManus, Susan A. 1999. "The Resurgent City Councils." In *American State and Local Politics*, edited by Ronald E. Weber and Paul Brace, 166–93. New York: Chatham House.

MacManus, Susan A., and Charles S. Bullock. 1993. "Women and Racial/Ethnic Minorities in Mayoral and Council Positions." *The Municipal Yearbook*, 70–84. Washington, DC: International City/County Management Association.

Maharaj, Nicole. 2004. U.S. Conference of Mayors Press Release. "Women Mayors Chair Mayor Shelia Young Brings More Structure to Group." www.usmayors.org. Accessed February 9.

Manning, Richard D. 1988. "How Three Women Took Over Missoula County and the Gender Factor Became an Edge." *Governing* (May): 1–7.

Mansbridge, Jane. 1999. "Should Blacks Represent Blacks and Women Represent Women? A Contingent 'Yes.'" *The Journal of Politics* 61(3): 628–57.

Marschall, Melissa J. 2002. "Organizing across the Divide: Local Feminism, Everyday Life, and the Election of Women to Office." *Social Science Quarterly* 83: 707–25.

Mazzei, Patricia. 2018. "Florida Governor Signs Gun Limits Into Law, Breaking with the NRA." *New York Times*. March 9. https://www.nytimes.com/2018/03/09/us/florida-governor-gun-limits.html. Accessed January 12, 2019.

McFarland, Christiana. 2017. "When Cities and State Clash, Women and Families Suffer." National League of Cities. March 8. https://www.nlc.org/article/when-cities-and-states-clash-women-and-families-suffer. Accessed December 26, 2018.

Merritt, Sharyne. 1980. "Sex Differences in Role Behavior and Policy Orientations of Suburban Officeholders: The Effect of Women's Employment." In *Women in Local Politics*, edited by Debra W. Stewart, 115–29. Metuchen: Scarecrow Press.

Mezey, Susan Gluck. 1978. "Support for Women's Rights Policy: An Analysis of Local Politicians." *American Politics Quarterly* 6(4): 485–97.

Moreau, Julie. 2018. "No Link between Trans-Inclusive Policies and Bathroom Safety." *NBC News*. September 19. https://www.nbcnews.com/feature/nbc-out/no-link-between-trans-inclusive-policies-bathroom-safety-study-finds-n911106. Accessed December 22, 2018.

National Association of Counties. 2003. "A Brief Overview of County Government." Washington, DC: National Association of Counties.

National League of Cities. 2018. "City Rights in an Era of Preemption: A State-by-State Analysis." April 2. https://www.nlc.org/resource/city-rights-in-an-era-of-preemption-a-state-by-state-analysis. Accessed December 26, 2018.

National School Boards Association. 2015. "Frequently Asked Questions: What Do We Know About School Board Members?" https://www.nsba.org/about-us/frequently-asked-questions.

Oliver, Sarah, and Meredith Conroy. 2018. "Tough Enough for the Job? How Masculinity Predicts Recruitment of City Council Members." *American Politics Research* 46(6): 1094–22.

Our Children's Trust. 2018. "Press Release: Florida Youth Sue Gov. Rick Scott, Adam Putnam for Endangering Their Future." April 16. https://static1.squarespace.com/static/571d109b04426270152febe0/t/5ad4a848f950b77bff95192e/1523886152974/2018.04.16+Florida+Youth+File+Constitutional+Climate+Lawsuit+-+Press+Release.pdf. Accessed January 4, 2019.

Oztekin-Gunaydin, Berna. Senior Analyst, Research and Data, International City/County Managament Association. 2018. Personal Correspondence with Author. December 31, 2018.

Palley, Marian Lief. 2001. "Women's Policy Leadership in the United States." *PS: Political Science & Politics* 34(2): 247–50.

Pearson, Kathryn, and Eric McGee. 2013. "What It Takes to Win: Questioning 'Gender Neutral' Outcomes in U.S. House Elections." *Politics & Gender* 9(4): 439–62.

Peterson, Paul. 1981. *City Limits.* Chicago: University of Chicago Press.

Piven, Frances Fox, and Richard A. Cloward. 1997. *The Breaking of the American Social Compact.* New York: The New Press.

Preece, Jessica Robinson, Olga Bogach Stoddard, and Rachel Fisher. 2016. "Run, Jane, Run! Gendered Responses to Political Party Recruitment." *Political Behavior* 38(30): 561–77.

Prindeville, Diane-Michele, and John G. Bretting. 1998. "Indigenous Women Activists and Political Participation: The Case of Environmental Justice." *Women & Politics* 19(1): 39–58.

Rainey, Shirley A., and Glenn S. Johnson. 2009. "Grassroots Activism: An Exploration of Women of Color's Role in the Environmental Justice Movement." *Race, Gender & Class* 16(3/4): 144–73.

Rentz, Catherine. 2017. "Few Women Hold Top Elected Offices in Maryland." *Baltimore Sun.* August 5. https://www.baltimoresun.com/news/maryland/investigations/bs-md-sun-investigates-women-in-office-20170726-story.html. Accessed December 26, 2018.

Ross, Bernard H., and Myron A. Levine. 2001. *Urban Power: Politics in Metropolitan America.* 6th ed. Itasca: F. E. Peacock Publishers, Inc.

Schlozman, Kay Lehman, Nancy Burns, Sidney Verba, and Jesse Donahue. 1995. "Gender and Citizen Participation: Is There a Different Voice?" *American Journal of Political Science* 39(2): 267–93.

Schumaker, Paul, and Nancy Elizabeth Burns. 1988. "Gender Cleavages and the Resolution of Local Policy Issues." *American Journal of Political Science* 32(4): 1070–95.

Seeding Sovereignty. 2019. "About Us." https://seedingsovereignty.org/who-we-are/. Accessed January 4, 2019.

Silbermann, Rachel. 2014. "Gender Roles, Work-Life Balance, and Running for Office." Working Paper. https://dl.dropboxusercontent.com/u/9802842/Silbermann_WLB_Paper.pdf

Smith, Adrienne R., Beth Reingold, and Michael Leo Owens. 2012. "The Political Determinants of Women's Descriptive Representation in Cities." *Political Research Quarterly* 65(2): 315–29.

Smith, Kevin B., and Alan Greenblatt. *Governing States and Localities.* 6th ed. Los Angeles: Sage.

Sweet-Cushman, Jennie. 2018. "Where does the Pipeline get Leaky? The Progressive Ambition of School Board Members and Personal and Political Network Recruitment." *Politics Groups, and Identities*, 1–24. https://doi.org/10.1080/21565503.2018.1541417.

Thomas, Sue. 1998. "Introduction." In *Women and Elective Office: Past, Present, and Future*, edited by Sue Thomas and Clyde Wilcox, 1–14. New York: Oxford University Press.

Tolleson-Rinehart, Sue. 2001. "Do Women Leaders Make a Difference?" In *The Impact of Women in Public Office*, edited by Susan J. Carroll, 149–65. Bloomington: Indiana University Press.

Trounstine, Jessica, and Melody E. Valdini. 2008. "The Context Matters: The Effect of Single-Member versus At-Large Districts on City Council Diversity." *American Journal of Political Science* 52(3): 554–69.

U. S. Census Bureau. 2018. "Government Units in 2012." *US Census of Governments*, July. Washington: Department of Commerce. https://factfinder.c ensus.gov/faces/tableservices/jsf/pages/productview.xhtml?src=bkmk. Accessed December 26, 2018.

Van Assendelft, Laura. 2014. "Entry Level Politics? Women as Candidates and Elected Officials at the Local Level." In *Women and Elective Office: Past, Present, and Future*. 3rd ed., edited by Sue Thomas and Clyde Wilcox, 199–215. New York: Oxford University Press.

Vassolo, Martin. 2018. "Parkland Students Who Became Activists After Massacre Just Won a Prestigious Global Prize." *Miami Herald*. November 20. https://ww w.miamiherald.com/news/politics-government/state-politics/article221949190. html. Accessed January 12, 2019.

The Victory Institute. 2019. "Out for America" Database. https://outforamerica.org /?office-level=Mayor. Accessed January 2, 2019.

Voorhies, Heidi, and Rachel Lange-Skaggs. 2015. "Women Leading Government: Why So Little Progress in 30 Years?" *PM Magazine*, January/February. http://icma.org/en/Article/105323/Women_Leading_Government.

Wang, Shirley, Katelyn Harrop, and Ben Kieffer. 2018. "Iowa is the Only State Requiring a Gender Balance on County and State Boards." *Iowa Public Radio*. August 2. http://www.iowapublicradio.org/post/iowa-only-state-requiring-gen der-balance-county-and-state-boards-has-it-helped#stream/0. Accessed December 29, 2018.

Weber, Ronald E., and Paul Brace. 1999. "States and Localities Transformed." In *American State and Local Politics: Directions for the 20th Century*, edited by Ronald E. Weber and Paul Brace, 1–20. New York: Chatham House Press.

Weikart, Lynne A., Greg Chen, Daniel W. Williams, and Haris Hromic. 2006. "The Democratic Sex: Gender Differences and the Exercise of Power." *Journal of Women, Politics & Policy* 28(1): 119–39.

Witt, Emily. 2018. "How the Survivors of Parkland Began the Never Again Movement." *New Yorker*. February 19. https://www.newyorker.com/news /news-desk/how-the-survivors-of-parkland-began-the-never-again-movement. Accessed January 12, 2019.

Wrigley, Julia. 1998. "From Housewives to Activists: Women and the Division of Political Labor in the Boston Antibusing Movement." In *No Middle Group: Women and Radical Protest*, edited by Kathleen Bree, 251–88. New York: New York University Press.

CHAPTER 7

Acker, Joan. 1992. "Gendered Institution: From Sex Roles to Gendered Institutions." *Contemporary Sociology* 21: 565–69.

Andersen, Kristi, 1996. *After Suffrage: Women in Partisan and Electoral Politics Before the New Deal*. Chicago: University of Chicago Press.

Anzia, Sarah, and Christopher R. Berry. 2011. "The Jackie (and Jill) Robinson Effect: Why Do Congresswomen Outperform Congressmen?" *American Journal of Political Science* 55: 478–93.

Arietta-Kenna, Ruairi. 2019. "'We Call Ourselves the Badasses': Meet the New Women of Congress." *Politico* January 18.

Bade, Rachel, Heather Caygle, and John Bresnahan. 2018. "'We Were Shocked as Sh—': How Pelosi Crushed the Dem Rebels." *Politico* December 13.

Barrett, Edith. 1995. "The Policy Priorities of African-American Women in State Legislatures." *Legislative Studies Quarterly* 20: 223–47.

Beckwith, Karen. 2007. "Numbers and Newness: The Descriptive and Substantive Representation of Women." *Canadian Journal of Political Science* 40: 27–49.

Benenson, Bob. 2005. "Former Rep. Shirley Chisholm Remembered for Opening Doors for Minorities and Women." *CQ Weekly* (January 10): 81.

Berkman, Michael B., and Robert E. O'Connor. 1993. "Do Women Legislators Matter? Female Legislators and State Abortion Policy." *American Politics Quarterly* 21: 102–24.

Bratton, Kathleen A. 2005. "Critical Mass Theory Revisited: The Behavior and Success of Token Women in State Legislatures." *Politics & Gender* 1: 97–125.

Bratton, Kathleen A., and Kerry L. Haynie. 1999. "Agenda Setting and Legislative Success in State Legislatures: The Effects of Gender and Race." *The Journal of Politics* 61: 658–79.

Bratton, Kathleen A., Kerry L. Haynie, and Beth Reingold. 2006. "Agenda Setting and African American Women in State Legislatures." *Journal of Women, Politics & Policy* 28: 71–96.

Brown, Nadia E. 2014. *Sisters in the Statehouse: Black Women and Legislative Decision Making.* New York: Oxford University Press.

Burrell, Barbara. 1994 *A Woman's Place Is in the House: Campaigning for Congress in the Feminist Era.* Ann Arbor: University of Michigan Press.

———. 2014. *Gender in Campaigns for the U.S. House of Representatives.* Ann Arbor: University of Michigan Press.

Bzdek, Vince. 2010. "Why Did Health-Care Reform Pass? Nancy Pelosi Was in Charge." *Washington Post* (March 28): B1.

Carlson, Margaret. 2013. "Female Senators Battle Over Military Sex Assaults." *Bloom- berg View*, November 20.

Carroll Susan J. 2002. "Representing Women: Congresswomen's Perception of Their Representational Roles." In *Women Transforming Congress*, edited by Cindy Simon Rosenthal, 50–68. Norman: University of Oklahoma Press.

Carroll Susan J., and Krista Jenkins. 2001. "Unrealized Opportunity? Term Limits and the Representation of Women in State Legislatures." *Women and Politics* 23(4): 1–30.

Carroll, Susan J., and Kira Sanbonmatsu. 2013. *More Women Can Run: Gender and Pathways to the State Legislatures.* New York: Oxford University Press.

Caygle, Heather. 2018. "Pelosi Creates Leadership Position for Barbara Lee." *Politico* November 30.

Center for American Women and Politics. (CAWP). 2004. "Firsts for Women in U.S. Politics." New Brunswick: Center for American Women and Politics, Rutgers, The State University of New Jersey.

———. 2019a. "Fact Sheet: Women in the U.S. Congress 2019." New Brunswick: Center for American Women and Politics, Rutgers, The State University of New Jersey.

———. 2019b. "Fact Sheet: Women in State Legislatures 2019." New Brunswick: Center for American Women and Politics, Rutgers, The State University of New Jersey.

———. 2019c. "Fact Sheet: Women of Color in Elective Office 2019." New Brunswick: Center for American Women and Politics, Rutgers, The State University of New Jersey.

———. 2018. "Fact Sheet: Women in Congress: Leadership Roles and Committee Chairs." New Brunswick: Center for American Women and Politics, Rutgers, The State University of New Jersey.

Childs, Sarah, and Mona Lena Krook. 2006. "Should Feminists Give Up on Critical Mass? A Contingent 'Yes.'" *Politics & Gender* 2(4): 522–30.

Chinoy, Sahil and Jessia Ma. 2019. "How Every Member Got to Congress." *New York Times* January 26.

Cooperman, Rosalyn. 2013. "The Elephant in the Room: Conservative Women's PACs and Republican Women Candidates in U.S. House Elections, 2008–2012." Prepared for Presentation at the ECPR General Conference. Sciences Po Bordeaux, Domaine Universitaire.

Cooperman, Rosalyn and Melody Crowder-Meyer. 2018. "A Run for Their Money: Republican Women's Hard Road to Campaign Funding." In *The Right Women: Republican Party Activists, Candidates, and Legislators*, edited by Shauna Shames and Malliga Och, 199–228. Santa Barbara: Praeger Press.

Cox, Elizabeth M. 1996. *Women State and Territorial Legislators, 1895–1995: A State-by-State Analysis with Rosters of 6,000 Women.* Jefferson, NC: McFarland.

Coy, Peter and Katia Dmitrieva. 2019. "Alexandria Ocasio-Cortez is the Darling of the Left, Nightmare of the Right." *Bloomberg Businessweek* January 17.

Cramer Walsh, Katherine. 2002. "Resonating to Be Heard: Gendered Debate on the Floor of the House." In *Women Transforming Congress*, edited by Cindy Simon Rosenthal, 370–96. Norman: University of Oklahoma Press.

Crespin, Michael H., and Janna L. Dietz. 2010. "If You Can't Join 'Em, Beat 'Em: The Gender Gap in Individual Donations to Congressional Candidates." *Political Research Quarterly* 63: 581–593.

Crowder-Meyer, Melody and Rosalyn Cooperman 2018. "Can't Buy Them Love: How Party Culture Among Donors Contributes to the Party Gap in Women's Representation." *Journal of Politics* 80: 1211–1224.

Crowley, Jocelyn Elise. 2004. "When Tokens Matter." *Legislative Studies Quarterly* 29: 109–36.

Dahlerup, Drude. 2006. "The Story of the Theory of Critical Mass." *Politics & Gender* (2): 511–22.

Davidson, Roger H., Walter J. Oleszek, Frances E. Lee, and Eric Schickler. 2015. *Congress and Its Members*, 15th ed. Washington, DC: CQ Press.

Deckman, Melissa, and John McTague. 2014. "Did the 'War on Women' Work? Women, Men, and the Birth Control Mandate in the 2012 Presidential Election." *American Politics Research* 43: 3–26.

Dittmar, Kelly, Kira Sanbonmatsu, and Susan J. Carroll. 2018. *A Seat at the Table: Congresswomen's Perspectives on Why Their Presence Matters*. New York: Oxford University Press.

Dodson, Debra L. 2006. *The Impact of Women in Congress*. New York: Oxford University Press.

Dodson, Debra L., and Susan Carroll. 1991. *Reshaping the Agenda: Women in State Legislatures*. New Brunswick: Center for American Women and Politics, Rutgers, State University of New Jersey.

Dolan, Julie. 1997. "Support for Women's Interests in the 103rd Congress: The Distinct Impact of Congressional Women." *Women & Politics* 18: 81–94.

Dolan, Kathleen. 2001. "Electoral Context, Issues, and Voting for Women in the 1990s." *Women & Politics* 23(1–2): 21–36.

———. 2004. *Voting for Women: How the Public Evaluates Women Candidates.* Boulder: Westview Press.

Dovi, Suzanne. 2002. "Preferable Descriptive Representatives: Or Will Just Any Woman, Black, or Latino Do?" *American Political Science Review* 96: 745–54.

Duerst-Lahti, Georgia. 2002. "Knowing Congress as a Gendered Institution: Manliness and the Implications of Women in Congress." In *Women Transforming Congress*, edited by Cindy Simon Rosenthal, 20–49. Norman: University of Oklahoma Press.

Elder, Laurel. 2008. "Whither Republican Women: The Growing Partisan Gap Among Women in Congress." *The Forum* 6: Issue 1, Article 13.

———. 2012. "The Partisan Gap Among Women State Legislators." *Journal of Women, Politics & Policy* 33: 65–85.

———. 2014. "Women and the Parties: An Analysis of Republican and Democratic Strategists for Recruiting Women Candidates." Presented at American Political Science Association Conference, Washington, DC, August 28–31.

Epstein, Kayla. 2019. "For Ayanna Pressley, the Beauty of Unexpected Wins Lead to Congress and a Historic Office." *Washington Post* January 16.

Etoniru, Nneka. 2014. "2014 Election Blog: A Look at Gender Quotas Ahead of Latin America's 2014 Legislative Votes." January 6. http://www.as-coa.org/blogs/2014-election-blog-look-gender-quotas-ahead-latin-americas-2014-legislative-votes (accessed June 23, 2015).

Feinstein, Dianne. 2006. "Women in Politics and Business." http://www.feinstein.senate.gov/public/index.cfm/speeches?ID=5aceabe1-7e9c-9af9-7152-0a03ca4a9fe6 (accessed June 3, 2015).

Fraga, Luis Ricardo, Linda Lopez, Valerie Martinez-Ebers, and Ricardo Ramirez. 2006. "Gender and Ethnicity: Patterns of Electoral Success and Legislative Advocacy Among Latina and Latino State Officials in Four States." *Journal of Women, Politics, & Policy* 28: 121–45.

———. 2008. "Representing Gender and Ethnicity: Strategic Intersectionality." In *Legislative Women: Getting Elected, Getting Ahead*, edited by Beth Reingold, 157–74. Boulder: Lynne Rienner Publishers.

Frederick, Brian. 2009. "Are Female House Members Still More Liberal in a Polarized Era? The Conditional Nature of the Relationship Between Descriptive and Substantive Representation." *Congress and the Presidency* 36: 181–202.

———. 2010. "Gender and Patterns of Roll Call Voting in the US Senate." *Congress and the Presidency* 37: 103–24.

Garcia Bedolla, Lisa, Katherine Tate, and Janelle Wong. 2014. "Indelible Effects: The Impact of Women of Color in the U.S. Congress." In *Women and Elective Office*, 3rd ed., edited by Sue Thomas and Clyde Wilcox, 235–52. New York: Oxford University Press.

Gelb, Joyce, and Marian Lief Palley. 1996. *Women and Public Policies: Reassessing Gen- der Politics.* Charlottesville, VA: University Press of Virginia.

Gertzog, Irwin. 1995. *Congressional Women: Their Recruitment, Integration, and Behavior.* 2nd ed. Westport, CT: Praeger Publishers.

Gomez, Amanda Michelle. 2018. "The New House Will Have an Unprecedented Number of Members Who Support Repealing Hyde." *ThinkProgress.* November 27.

Grey, Sandra. 2006. "Numbers and Beyond: The Relevance of Critical Mass in Gen- der Research." *Politics & Gender* 2(4): 492–502.

Haberkorn, Jennifer. 2018. "Senate Votes to Allow Duckworth's Baby on the Floor." *Politico* April 18.

Hagen, Lisa. 2019. "Elise Stefanik Seeks to Tackle GOP's Women 'Crisis' Ahead of 2020." *Roll Call* January 21.

Hall, Richard. 1996. *Participation in Congress*. New Haven: Yale University Press.

Halloran, Liz. 2009. "House Approves Bills to Fight Gender Wage Gap." *NPR. org*, January 9, 2009.

Hawkesworth, Mary. 2003. "Congressional Enactments of Race-Gender: Toward a Theory of Raced-Gendered Institutions." *American Political Science Review* 97: 529–50.

Henneberger, Melinda. 2014. "Sen. McCaskill's Military Sexual-Assault Bill Is Meatier Than Advertised." *Washington Post*, March 9.

Herman, Elizabeth D. and Celeste Soman. 2019. "Redefining Representation: The Women of the 116th Congress." *New York Times* January 14.

Herrnson, Paul S. 2012. *Congressional Elections: Campaigning at Home and in Washington*, 6th ed. Washington, DC: CQ Press.

Inglehart, Ronald, and Pippa Norris. 2003. *Rising Tide: Gender Equality and Cultural Change*. New York: Cambridge University Press.

Jacobson, Gary. 2013. *The Politics of Congressional Elections*. 8th ed. New York: Pearson.

Johnson, Cathy Marie, Georgia Duerst-Lahti, and Noelle H. Norton. 2007. *Creating Gender: The Sexual Politics of Welfare Policy*. Boulder: Lynne Rienner.

Kanter, Rosabeth Moss. 1977. "Some Effects of Proportions on Group Life: Skewed Sex Ratios and Responses to Token Women." *American Journal of Sociology* 82: 965–90.

Kaper. Stacy. 2014. "Kirsten Gillibrand Blames White House in Failure of Military Sexual-Assault Bill." *National Journal*, March 7.

Kaptur, Marcy. 1996. *Women of Congress: A Twentieth-Century Odyssey*. Washington, DC: Congressional Quarterly.

Kathlene, Lynn. 1994. "Power and Influence of State Legislative Policymaking: The Interaction of Gender and Position in Committee Hearing Debates." *American Political Science Review* 88: 560–76.

———. 1995. "Alternative Views of Crime: Legislative Policymaking in Gendered Terms." *Journal of Politics* 57: 696–723.

Kelly, Jemima. 2017. "France Elects Record Number of Women to Parliament." *Reuters* June 18.

Kenney, Sally J. 1996. "New Research on Gendered Political Institutions." *Political Research Quarterly* 49: 445–66.

Kitchens, Karin E., and Michele L. Swers. 2016. "Why Aren't There More Republican Women in Congress? Gender, Partisanship, and Fundraising Support in the 2010 and 2012 Elections." *Politics & Gender* 12: 648–676.

Krook, Mona Lena. 2009. *Quotas for Women in Politics: Gender and Candidate Selection Reform Worldwide*. New York: Oxford University Press.

Lazarus, Jeffrey and Amy Steigerwalt. 2018. *Gendered Vulnerability: How Women Work Harder to Stay in Office*. Ann Arbor: University of Michigan Press.

Levy, Dena, Charles Tien, and Rachelle Aved. 2002. "Do Differences Matter? Women Members of Congress and the Hyde Amendment." *Women & Politics* 23(1/2): 105–27.

MacDonald, Jason A., and Erin E. O'Brien. 2011. "Quasi-Experimental Design, Constituency, and Advancing Women's Interests: 'Critically' Reexamining the Influence of Gender on Substantive Representation." *Political Research Quarterly* 64: 472–86.

Manning, Jennifer E., and Colleen J. Shogan. 2012. "African-American Members of the United States Congress: 1870–2012." *Congressional Research Service*, November 26.

Mansbridge, Jane. 1999. "Should Blacks Represent Blacks and Women Represent Women? A Contingent 'Yes.'" *Journal of Politics* 61: 628–57.

Marcos, Cristina. 2016. "115th Congress Will Be Most Racially Diverse in History." *The Hill*, November 17.

Marcus, Ruth. 2007. "Grandma with a Gavel." *Washington Post* (January 10): A13.

McPherson, Lindsey. 2019. "Trump Agrees to Initial Pelosi Request and Delays State of the Union." *Roll Call* January 23.

Merle, Renae. 2019. "Maxine Waters Takes the Reins of a Powerful House Committee. Wall Street is Nervous." *Washington Post* January 14.

Mikulski, Barbara, Kay Bailey Hutchison, Dianne Feinstein, Barbara Boxer, Patty Murray, Olympia Snowe, Susan Collins, Mary Landrieu, and Blanche L. Lincoln with Catherine Whitney. 2001. *Nine and Counting: The Women of the Senate*. New York: Harper Collins Publishers.

Mimms, Sarah. 2014. "A Ceiling of Her Making." *National Journal*, September 20.

Murphy, Patricia. 2018. "Women Played a Key Role in Harassment Bill." *Roll Call* January 23.

National Conference of State Legislatures. 2015. "The Term-Limited States." http://www.ncsl.org/research/about-state-legislatures/chart-of-term-limits-states.aspx (accessed June 1, 2015).

Norrander, Barbara, and Clyde Wilcox. 2014. "Trends in the Geography of Women in the United States State Legislatures." In *Women and Elective Office*, 3rd ed., edited by Sue Thomas and Clyde Wilcox, 273–87. New York: Oxford University Press.

Norris, Pippa, and Mona Lena Krook. 2014. "Women in Elective Office Worldwide: Barriers and Opportunities." In *Women and Elective Office*, 3rd ed., edited by Sue Thomas and Clyde Wilcox, 288–306. New York: Oxford University Press.

Norton, Noelle H. 1999. "Committee Influence Over Controversial Policy: The Reproductive Policy Case." *Policy Studies Journal* 27: 203–16.

———. 2002. "Transforming Congress from the Inside: Women in Committee." In *Women Transforming Congress*, edited by Cindy Simon Rosenthal, 316–40. Norman: University of Oklahoma Press.

Office of the Historian and Office of the Clerk of the House of Representatives. 2013. *Hispanic Americans in Congress 1822–2012*. Washington, DC: United States Government Printing Office.

Orey, Byron D'Andra, Wendy Smooth, Kimberly S. Adams, and Kisha Harris-Clark. 2006. "Race and Gender Matter; Refining Models of Legislative Policy Making in State Legislatures." *Journal of Women, Politics & Policy* 28: 97–119.

Osborn, Tracy L. 2012. *How Women Represent Women: Political Parties, Gender, and Representation in the State Legislatures*. New York: Oxford University Press.

Osborn, Tracy L., and Rebecca Kreitzer. 2014. "Women State Legislators: Women's Issues in Partisan Environments." In *Women and Elective Office: Past, Present and Future*, edited by Sue Thomas and Clyde Wilcox, 181–98. New York: Oxford University Press.

Osborn, Tracy, and Jeanette Morehouse Mendez. 2010. "Speaking as Women: Women and Floor Speeches in the Senate." *Journal of Women, Politics, & Policy* 31: 1–21.

Palmer, Barbara, and Dennis Simon. 2008. *Breaking the Political Glass Ceiling: Women and Congressional Elections*. 2nd ed. New York: Routledge.

Paxton, Pamela, and Melanie M. Hughes. 2007. *Women, Politics, and Power: A Global Perspective.* Thousand Oaks, CA: Pine Forge Press.

Pear, Robert. 2009. "House Votes to Expand Children's Health Care." *New York Times,* January 15.

Pearson, Kathryn, and Logan Dancey. 2011a. "Speaking for the Underrepresented in the House of Representatives: Voicing Women's Interests in a Partisan Era." *Politics & Gender* 7: 493–519.

———. 2011b. "Elevating Women's Voice in Congress: Speech Participation in the House of Representatives." *Political Research Quarterly* 64(4): 910–23.

Pearson, Kathryn, and Eric McGhee. 2013. "What It Takes to Win: Questioning 'Gender Neutral' Outcomes in United States House Elections." *Politics & Gender* 9: 439–62.

Peters, Jr., Ronald M., and Cindy Simon Rosenthal. 2010. *Speaker Nancy Pelosi and the New American Politics.* Oxford: Oxford University Press.

Peterson, Kristina. 2014. "Senate Clears Way for McCaskill's Military Sex-Assault Bill." *Wall Street Journal,* March 6.

Phillips, Anne. 1991. *Engendering Democracy.* University Park: The Pennsylvania State University Press.

———. 1995. *The Politics of Presence.* Oxford: Oxford University Press.

———. 1998. "Democracy and Representation: Or, Why Should It Matter Who Our Representatives Are?" In *Feminism and Politics,* edited by Anne Phillips, 224–240. New York: Oxford University Press.

Pitkin, Hanna Fenichel. 1967. *The Concept of Representation.* Berkeley: University of California Press.

Poggione, Sarah. 2004. "Exploring Gender Differences in State Legislators' Policy Preferences." *Political Research Quarterly* 57: 305–14.

Political Parity. 2015. Primary Hurdles Report. Available at https://www.political parity.org/wp-content/uploads/2015/01/primary-hurdles-full-report.pdf.

Poole, Keith T., and Howard Rosenthal. 1997. *Congress: A Political-Economic History of Roll Call Voting.* New York: Oxford University Press.

Reingold, Beth. 1992. "Concepts of Representation Among Female and Male State Legislators." *Legislative Studies Quarterly* 17: 509–37.

———. 2000. *Representing Women: Sex, Gender, and Legislative Behavior in Arizona and California.* Chapel Hill: University of North Carolina Press.

Reingold, Beth, and Adrienne R. Smith. 2012. "Welfare Policymaking and Intersections of Race, Ethnicity, and Gender in United States State Legislatures." *American Journal of Political Science* 56: 131–47.

Rhode, David W. 1991. *Parties and Leaders in the Post-reform House.* Chicago: University of Chicago Press.

Rosenthal, Cindy Simon. 1997. "A View of Their Own: Women's Committee Leadership Styles and State Legislatures." *Policy Studies Journal* 25: 585–600.

———. 1998. *When Women Lead: Integrative Leadership in State Legislatures.* New York: Oxford University Press.

———. 2000. "Gender Styles in State Legislative Committees: Raising Their Voices in Resolving Conflict." *Women & Politics* 21: 21–45.

———. 2008. "Climbing Higher: Opportunities and Obstacles within the Party System." In *Legislative Women: Getting Elected, Getting Ahead,* edited by Beth Reingold, 197–222. Boulder: Lynne Rienner Publishers.

Saint-Germain, Michelle A. 1989. "Does Their Difference Make a Difference? The Impact of Women on Public Policy in the Arizona Legislature." *Social Science Quarterly* 70: 956–68.

Saint Louis, Christina. 2018. "Lowey on Leveraging Leadership on the Appropriations Committee." *City & State New* York November 18.

Sanbonmatsu, Kira. 2002. "Political Parties and the Recruitment of Women to State Legislatures." *Journal of Politics* 64: 791–809.

———. 2006. *Where Women Run: Gender & Party in the American States*. Ann Arbor: University of Michigan Press.

———. 2018. "Women's Election to Office in the Fifty States: Opportunities and Challenges." In *Gender and Elections: Shaping the Future of American Politics*, Fourth Edition. Eds. Susan J. Carroll and Richard L. Fox, 280–302. New York: Cambridge University Press.

Sandalow, Marc. 2008. *Madam Speaker: Nancy Pelosi's Life, Times, and Rise to Power*. New York: Modern Times.

Scola, Becki. 2013. "Predicting Presence at the Intersections: Assessing the Variation in Women's Office Holding Across the States." *State Politics & Policy Quarterly* 13(3): 333–348.

———. 2006. "Women of Color in State Legislatures: Gender, Race, Ethnicity and Legislative Office Holding." *Journal of Women, Politics & Policy* 28(3–4): 43–70.

Shogan, Colleen J. 2001. "Speaking Out: An Analysis of Democratic and Republican Women-Invoked Rhetoric of the 105th Congress." *Women & Politics* 23: 129–46.

Shutt, Jennifer. 2018. "Women on the Verge of a Breakthrough on House Appropriations." *Roll Call* May 24.

Smooth, Wendy. 2008. "Gender, Race, and the Exercise of Power and Influence." In *Legislative Women: Getting Elected, Getting Ahead*, edited by Beth Reingold, 175–96. Boulder: Lynne Rienner Publishers.

Storing, Herbert J. 1981. *The Anti-Federalist: Writings by Opponents of the Constitution*. Chicago: University of Chicago Press.

Swenson, Kyle. 2019. "Kamala Harris is Among the Few Black Women to Run for President. Here is the Amazing Story of the First." *Washington Post* January 22.

Swers, Michele L. 1998. "Are Congresswomen More Likely to Vote for Women's Issue Bills Than Their Male Colleagues?" *Legislative Studies Quarterly* 23: 435–48.

———. 2002. *The Difference Women Make: The Policy Impact of Women in Congress*. Chicago: University of Chicago Press.

———. 2007. "Building a Reputation on National Security: The Impact of Stereotypes Related to Gender and Military Experience." *Legislative Studies Quarterly* 32: 559–96.

———. 2013. *Women in the Club: Gender and Policy Making in the Senate*. Chicago: University of Chicago Press.

———. 2016a. "Pursuing Women's Interests in Partisan Times: Explaining Gender Differences in Legislative Activity on Health, Education, and Women's Health Issues." *Journal of Women, Politics & Policy* 37: 249–273.

———. 2016b. "Women & Legislative Leadership in the U.S. Congress: Representing Women's Interests in Partisan Times." *Daedalus* 145: 44–56.

———. 2017. "Gender and Party Politics in a Polarized Era." In *Party and Procedure in the United States Congress*, 2nd ed., edited by Jacob R. Straus and Matthew E. Glassman, 279–99. Lanham, MD: Rowman & Littlefield.

———. 2018. "From the Republican Revolution to the Tea Party Wave: Republican Women and the Politics of Women's Issues" In *The Right Women: Republican*

Party Activists, Candidates, and Legislators, edited by Shauna Shames and Malliga Och, 199–228. Santa Barbara: Praeger Press.

Swers, Michele L., and Christine C. Kim. 2013. "Replacing Sandra Day O'Connor: Gender and the Politics of Supreme Court Nominations." *Journal of Women, Politics, & Policy* 34: 23–48.

Swers, Michele L., and Carin Larson. 2005. "Women and Congress: Do They Act as Advocates for Women's Issues?" In *Women and Elective Office: Past, Present, and Future*, 2nd ed., edited by Sue Thomas and Clyde Wilcox, 110–28. New York: Oxford University Press.

Tate, Katherine. 2003. *Black Faces in the Mirror: African Americans and Their Representatives in the U.S. Congress*. Princeton: Princeton University Press.

———. 2013. *Concordance: Black Lawmaking in the U.S. Congress from Carter to Obama*. Ann Arbor: University of Michigan Press.

Thomas, Sue. 1994. *How Women Legislate*. New York: Oxford University Press.

———. 1997. "Why Gender Matters: The Perceptions of Women Officeholders." *Women & Politics* 17: 27–53.

Thomsen, Danielle M. 2015. "Why So Few (Republican) Women? Explaining the Partisan Imbalance of Women in the United States Congress." *Legislative Studies Quarterly* 40: 295–323.

Tripp, Aili Mari. 2013. "Women and Politics in Africa Today." *Democracy in Africa*, December 9. http://democracyinafrica.org/women-politics-africa-today (accessed June 23, 2015).

———. 2015. *Women and Power in Post-conflict Africa*. New York: Cambridge University Press.

Tully-McManus, Katherine. 2018. "Lawmakers Reach Deal to Tackle Sexual Harassment on Capitol Hill." *Roll Call* December 12.

Volden, Craig, Alan E. Wiseman, and Dana E. Wittmer. 2013. "When Are Women More Effective Lawmakers Than Men?" *American Journal of Political Science* 57: 326–41.

Werner, Emmy E. 1968. "Women in the State Legislatures." *Western Political Quarterly* 21: 40–50.

Werner, Erica, Mike DeBonis, and John Wagner. 2019. "Trump Signs Bill to Open the Government, Ending the Longest Shutdown in History." *Washington Post* January 25.

Whitlock, Craig. 2013. "Military Chiefs Balk at Sexual-Assault Bill." *Washington Post*, June 4.

Winter, Nicholas J. G. 2010. "Masculine Republicans and Feminine Democrats: Gen- der and Americans' Explicit and Implicit Images of the Political Parties." *Political Behavior* 32: 587–618.

Wolbrecht, Christina. 2000. *The Politics of Women's Rights: Parties, Positions, and Change*. Princeton: Princeton University Press.

———. 2002. "Female Legislators and the Women's Rights Agenda." In *Women Transforming Congress*, edited by Cindy Simon Rosenthal, 170–97. Norman: University of Oklahoma Press.

CHAPTER 8

Barbara Lee Family Foundation. 2001. "Keys to the Governor's Office: Unlock the Door." Brookline, MA: Barbara Lee Family Foundation. http://www.barbaraleefoundation.org/wp-content/uploads/Keys-to-the-Governors-Office.pdf.

Barth, Jay, and Margaret R Ferguson. 2002. "Gender and Gubernatorial Personality." *Women & Politics* 24 (1): 63–82.

Beard, Patricia. 1996. *Growing up Republican: Christie Whitman, the Politics of Character*. New York: HarperCollins Publishers.

Berman, Russell. 2018. "The Donald Trump Cabinet Tracker." *The Atlantic*. November 7, 2018. https://www.theatlantic.com/politics/archive/2018/11/trump-cabinet-tracker/510527.

Bitterman, Amy, Rebecca Goldring, and Lucinda Gray. 2013. "Characteristics of Public and Private Elementary and Secondary School Principals in the United States: Results from the 2011-12 Schools and Staffing Survey. First Look. NCES 2013-313." *National Center for Education Statistics*. http://eric.ed.gov/?id=ED544176.

Borrelli, MaryAnne. 2002. *The President's Cabinet: Gender, Power, and Representation*. Boulder, Colo.: L. Rienner Publishers.

Borrelli, Maryanne. 2010. "The Contemporary Presidency: Gender Desegregation and Gender Integration in the President's Cabinet, 1933-2010." *Presidential Studies Quarterly* 40 (4): 734–49. https://doi.org/10.1111/j.1741-5705.2010.03809.x.

Brown, Wendy L. 1998. *Manhood and Politics: A Feminist Reading in Political Theory*. Rowman & Littlefield Publishers.

Bureau of Labor Statistics. 2017. "Women in the Labor Force: A Databook : BLS Reports: U.S. Bureau of Labor Statistics." 1065. https://www.bls.gov/opub/reports/womens-databook/2016/home.htm.

Calabresi, Massimo. 2011. "Head of State." *Time* 178 (18): 26.

Campo-Flores, Arian. 2010. "Woman on the Verge." *Newsweek*, July 12, 2010. Expanded Academic ASAP.

Center for American Women and Politics. 2018. "Women Appointed to Presidential Cabinets." Eagleton Institute of Politics: Rutgers University. http://www.cawp.rutgers.edu/fast_facts/levels_of_office/documents/prescabinet.pdf.

———. 2019. "History of Women Governors." Rutgers University, New Brunswick, NJ: Center for American Women and Politics. http://www.cawp.rutgers.edu/history-women-governors.

Chappell, Louise, and Georgina Waylen. 2013. "Gender and the Hidden Life of Institutions." *Public Administration* 91 (3): 599–615. https://doi.org/10.1111/j.1467-9299.2012.02104.x.

Clift, Eleanor, and Tom Brazaitis. 2000. *Madam President: Shattering the Last Glass Ceiling*. New York: Scribner.

Committe on Homeland Security and Governmental Affairs. 2016. "United States Government Policy and Supporting Positions." S. Rpt 114-26. Washington, DC: United States Senate. http://linkinghub.elsevier.com/retrieve/pii/027793909390042N.

Department of Veterans Affairs. 2012. "Pioneers of Women Veterans Health." *Vanguard*, April 2012.

Dolan, Julie. 2000. "The Senior Executive Service: Gender, Attitudes, and Representative Bureaucracy." *Journal of Public Administration Research and Theory* 10 (3): 513–29.

———. 2002. "Representative Bureaucracy in the Federal Executive: Gender and Spending Priorities." *Journal of Public Administration Research and Theory* 12 (3): 353–75.

———. 2012. "Women in the Obama Administration: Insiders or Outsiders Looking In?" In *Women and Executive Office: Pathways and Performance*, 75–87. Boulder, CO: Lynne Rienner Publishers.

Dolan, Julie, and David H. Rosenbloom. 2003. *Representative Bureaucracy: Classic Readings and Continuing Controversies*. Armonk, NY: M.E. Sharpe.

Dow, Bonnie J., and Mari Boor Tonn. 1993. "'Feminine Style' and Political Judgment in the Rhetoric of Ann Richards." *Quarterly Journal of Speech* 79 (3): 286–302. https://doi.org/10.1080/00335639309384036.

Dowd, Ann Reilly. 2000. "Is There Anything This Woman Can't Do?" *George* 5: 86–91+.

Duerst-Lahti, Georgia, and Rita Mae Kelly. 1995. *Gender Power, Leadership, and Governance*. Ann Arbor: University of Michigan Press.

Eagly, Alice H., and Blair T. Johnson. 1990. "Gender and Leadership Style: A Meta-Analysis." *Psychological Bulletin* 108 (2): 233–56. https://doi.org/10.1037/0033-2909.108.2.233.

Enloe, Cynthia. 1983. *Does Khaki Become You?* Pluto Press.

Garcia, Rogelio. 1997. *Women Appointed by President Clinton to Full-Time Positions Requiring Senate Confirmation, 1993-96*. Congressional Research Service, Library of Congress.

Gardiner, Mary E, Ernestine Enomoto, and Margaret Grogan. 2000. *Coloring Outside the Lines Mentoring Women into School Leadership*. Albany, NY: State University of New York Press. http://site.ebrary.com/id/10021842.

Gearan, Anne, and Philip Rucker. 2015. "Democracy Not 'Just for Billionaires,' Hillary Clinton Tells Crowd in N.Y." *The Washington Post*, June 13, 2015. http://www.washingtonpost.com/politics/democracy-not-just-for-billionaires-hillary-clinton-tells-crowd-in-ny/2015/06/13/346e3318-11fb-11e5-a0fe-dccfea4653ee_story.html.

Glass, Thomas E. 2000. "Where Are All the Women Superintendents?" *School Administrator* 57 (6): 28–32.

Glazer, Sarah. 1994. "Women's Health Issues: Will Women Benefit from Increased Research Funding?" *CQ Researcher by CQ Press* 4 (May): 409–32.

Green, J. 2011. "Good O'Girl: Does Nikki Haley, the New Governor of South Carolina, Signal a Fundamental Change in the GOP's Relationship with Women, and in the GOP Itself?" *Atlantic Monthly* 307 (1): 56–63.

Gross, Terry. 2003. "Former Secretary of State Madeleine Albright." *Fresh Air*. NPR News. http://www.npr.org/templates/story/story.php?storyId=1432866.

Heikkila, Kim. 2011. *Sisterhood of War: Minnesota Women in Vietnam*. St. Paul, MN: Minnesota Historical Society Press.

Heldman, Caroline, Meredith Conroy, and Alissa R. Ackerman. 2018. *Sex and Gender in the 2016 Presidential Election*. Santa Barbara, CA: Praeger Publishers.

Hirsh, Michael. 2013. "The Clinton Legacy: How Will History Judge the Soft-Power Secretary of State?" *Foreign Affairs*, 2013. Expanded Academic ASAP.

Huddy, Leonie, and Nayda Terkildsen. 1993. "The Consequences of Gender Stereotypes for Women Candidates at Different Levels and Types of Office." *Political Research Quarterly* 46 (3): 503–25.

Jalalzai, Farida. 2013. *Shattered, Cracked or Firmly Intact? Women and the Executive Glass Ceiling Worldwide*. Oxford; New York: Oxford University Press.

Kahn, Kim Fridkin. 1996. *The Political Consequences of Being a Woman: How Stereotypes Influence the Conduct and Consequences of Political Campaigns*. New York: Columbia University Press.

Kaml, Shannon Skarphol. "The Fusion of Populist and Feminine Styles in the Rhetoric of Ann Richards." In *Navigating Boundaries: The Rhetoric of Female Governors*, edited by Brenda DeVore Marshall and Molly A. Mayhead, 59–82. Westport, Conn: Praeger Publishers.

Kanter, Rosabeth Moss. 1977. "Some Effects of Proportions on Group Life: Skewed Sex Ratios and Responses to Token Women." *American Journal of Sociology* 82 (5): 965–90.

Keiser, Lael R., Vicky M. Wilkins, Kenneth J. Meier, and Catherine A. Holland. 2002. "Lipstick and Logarithms: Gender, Institutional Context, and Representative Bureaucracy." *The American Political Science Review* 96 (3): 553–64. https://doi.org/10.2307/3117929.

King, Cheryl Simrell. 1995. "Sex-Role Identity and Decision Styles: How Gender Helps Explain the Paucity of Women at the Top." In *Gender Power, Leadership and Governance*. Ann Arbor: University of Michigan Press.

Kunin, Madeleine. 1994. *Living a Political Life*. New York: Knopf : Distributed by Random House.

Kunin, Madeleine M. 1987. "Lessons From One Woman's Career. (Political Equality is Essential to True Equality)." *Journal of State Government* 60 (5): 209–13.

Langton, Lynn. 2010. *Women in Law Enforcement*. http://books.google.com/books?hl=en&lr=&id=nqW3BgAAQBAJ&oi=fnd&pg=PA355&dq=%22and+size+of+agency+(number+of+full-time+sworn%22+%22to+the+reorganization+of+several+large%22+%22Service+(USPIS)+and+the%22+%22Fish+and+Wildlife%22+%22Force+Protection+Agency+did+not+provide+1998+data+on+the+sex+of+officers%3B+these+four%22+&ots=CDhxQFEjw6&sig=nT_v2_qYke7jy_b_VD0bNisaQ_k.

Lippman, Thomas W. 1997. "State Dept. Seeks Gains for Women." *The Washington Post*, March 25, 1997. http://www.washingtonpost.com/archive/politics/1997/03/25/state-dept-seeks-gains-for-women/2bddd98e-6b79-45a9-8346-0a466e30de32/.

Lonsway, Kim, Susan Carrington, Patricia Aguirre, Michelle Wood, Margaret Moore, Penny Harrington, Eleanor Smeal, and Kathernine Spillar. 2002. "Equality Denied." http://womenandpolicing.org/PDF/2002_Status_Report.pdf.

Markon, Jerry, Robert Costa, and Emma Brown. 2016. "Trump Nominates Two Prominent GOP Women: DeVos as Education Secretary, Haley as U.N. Ambassador." *Washington Post*, November 23, 2016. https://www.washingtonpost.com/politics/trump-nominates-nikki-haley-to-be-un-ambassador/2016/11/23/401f4a7a-b183-11e6-be1c-8cec35b1ad25_story.html.

Mastracci, Sharon, and Lauren Bowman. 2015. "Public Agencies, Gendered Organizations: The Future of Gender Studies in Public Management." *Public Management Review* 17 (6): 857–75. https://doi.org/10.1080/14719037.2013.867067.

McGlen, Nancy E., and Meredith Reid Sarkees. 1993. *Women in Foreign Policy: The Insiders*. New York: Routledge.

Meier, Kenneth J., and Jill Nicholson-Crotty. 2006. "Gender, Representative Bureaucracy, and Law Enforcement: The Case of Sexual Assault." *Public Administration Review* 66 (6): 850–60. https://doi.org/10.1111/j.1540-6210.2006.00653.x.

Milbank, Dana. 2008. "A Thank-You for 18 Million Cracks in the Glass Ceiling." *The Washington Post*, June 8, 2008, sec. Opinions. http://www.washingtonpost.com/wp-dyn/content/article/2008/06/07/AR2008060701879.html.

Miller, Hayley. 2019. "Lawmakers, Twitter Users Shred Wilbur Ross Over 'Shameful' Shutdown Apathy." *Huffington Post*, January 24, 2019, sec. Politics. https://www.huffingtonpost.com/entry/twitter-wilbur-ross-federal-workers_us_5c49e502e4b06ba6d3bb2ba3.

Mirfendereksi, Taylor, Jake Whittenberg, Russ Walker, and Giuliana Viglione. 2018. "Female Police Chiefs Rare in Nation's Largest Cities." KING. July 18, 2018. https://www.king5.com/article/news/local/female-police-chiefs-rare-in-nations-largest-cities/281-574941123.

Mui, Ylan Q. 2014. "Janet Yellen Confirmed as Federal Reserve Chairman." *The Washington Post*, January 6, 2014. http://www.washingtonpost.com/business/economy/janet-yellen-confirmed-as-next-fed-chief/2014/01/06/14b38582-76f2-11e3-8963-b4b654bcc9b2_story.html.

Newman, Meredith Ann. 1995. "The Gendered Nature of Lowi's Typology; or Who Would Guess You Could Find Gender Here?" In *Gender Power, Leadership and Governance*, edited by Georgia Duerst-Lahti and Rita Mae Kelly, 141–66. Ann Arbor: University of Michigan Press.

Republican State Leadership Committee. n.d. "The Future Majority Project and 'Right Women, Right Now.'"

Reynolds, George M., and Amanda Shendruk. 2018. "Demographics of the U.S. Military." *Council on Foreign Relations*, April 24, 2018. https://www.cfr.org/article/demographics-us-military.

Rosenwasser, Shirley Miller, and Norma G. Dean. 1989. "Gender Role and Political Office." *Psychology of Women Quarterly* 13 (1): 77.

Sallee, Shelley. 1996. "'The Woman of It': Governor Miriam Ferguson's 1924 Election." *The Southwestern Historical Quarterly* 100 (1): 1–16.

Sanbonmatsu, Kira. 2013. "The Candidacies of U.S. Women of Color for Statewide Executive Office." Chicago, IL: Social Science Research Network. http://papers.ssrn.com/abstract=2300783.

Scharff, Virginia. 1995. "Feminism, Femininity, and Power: Nellie Tayloe Ross and the Woman Politician's Dilemma." *Frontiers: A Journal of Women Studies* 15 (3): 87–106. https://doi.org/10.2307/3346786.

Schmitz, Kirsten. 2017. "Where Are All The Female Superintendents?" *Ahead of the Heard* (blog). March 8, 2017. https://aheadoftheheard.org/where-are-all-the-female-superintendents.

Selden, Sally Coleman. 1997. *The Promise of Representative Bureaucracy: Diversity and Responsiveness in a Government Agency*. Armonk, NY: M.E. Sharpe.

Sheeler, Krista Horn. 2000. "Christine Todd Whitman and the Ideology of the New Jersey Governorship." In *Navigating Boundaries: The Rhetoric of Women Governors*, edited by Brenda DeVore Marshall and Molly Mayhead, 99–122. Westport, Conn: Praeger Publishers Inc.

Stineman, Esther. 1980. *American Political Women : Contemporary and Historical Profiles*. Littleton, Colo.: Libraries Unlimited,.

Stivers, Camilla. 2002. *Gender Images in Public Administration: Legitimacy and the Administrative State*. Thousand Oaks: Sage Publications.

The Economist. 2011. "How to Grab Them; New Mexico's Governor," December 17, 2011. Expanded Academic ASAP.

———. 2012. "What Hillary Did next; American Diplomacy," March 24, 2012. Educators Reference Complete.

United States. Congress. House. Committee on Veterans' Affairs. 2009. *Eliminating the Gaps: Examining Women Veterans' Issues*. Washington, DC: Government Printing Office. http://www.gpo.gov/fdsys/pkg/CHRG-111hhrg51873/pdf/CHRG-111hhrg51873.pdf.

———. Congress. Senate. Committee on Armed Services. 2013. *Sexual Assaults in the Military.* http://www.armed-services.senate.gov/hearings/oversight-sexu al-assaults-in-the-military.

U.S. Office of Personnel Management. 2018. Fedscope. Accessed at http://www. fedscope.opm/gov

Watson, Robert P, and Ann Gordon. 2003. *Anticipating Madam President.* Boulder, Colo.: Lynne Rienner.

Weddell, Angelica. 2017. "Women in Law Enforcement." *National Research Center* (blog). August 21, 2017. https://www.n-r-c.com/gender-balance-law -enforcement/.

Wilkins, Vicky M., and Lael R. Keiser. 2006. "Linking Passive and Active Representation by Gender: The Case of Child Support Agencies." *Journal of Public Administration Research and Theory* 16 (1): 87–102.

Wolverton, Mimi. 1999. "The School Superintendency: Male Bastion or Equal Opportunity?" *Advancing Women in Leadership Journal.* https://www.res earchgate.net/publication/234574164_The_School_Superintendency_Male_Ba stion_or_Equal_Opportunity.

"Women Rise to Top Police Ranks in U.S. Cities." 2004. *Msnbc.Com.* http://www .nbcnews.com/id/5076267/ns/us_news/t/women-rise-top-police-ranks-us-cities.

Women's Research and Education Institute. 2013. *Women in the Military: Where They Stand*, 8th ed. Washington, DC: Women's Research and Education Institute. http://www.wrei.org/WIM2013e.pdf.

CHAPTER 9

Aliota, Jilda M. 1995. "Justice O'Connor and the Equal Protection Clause: A Feminine Voice?" *Judicature* 78(5): 232–35.

Allen, David, and Diane Wall. 1993. "Role Orientations and Women State Supreme Court Justices." *Judicature* 7(3): 156–65.

Allen, Samantha. 2018. "Trump Nominates his first Out-LGBT Judge. Will He Match Obama's 11?" *Daily Beast.* August 24. https://www.thedailybeast.com/ trump-nominates-his-first-out-lgbt-judge-will-he-match-obamas-11. Accessed January 17, 2019.

Alozie, Nicholas. 1996. "Selection Methods and the Recruitment of Women to State Courts of Last Resort." *Social Science Quarterly* 77(1): 110–26.

American Bar Association (ABA). 2018. "A Current Glance at Women in the Law: January 2018." https://www.americanbar.org/content/dam/aba/administrative/ women/a-current-glance-at-women-in-the-law-jan-2018.pdf. Accessed January 22, 2019.

The Associated Press. 2014. "Ginsburg: Court Right to Void Buffer Zones." *New York Times.* August 1. http://mobile.nytimes.com/aponline/2014/08/01/us/p olitics/ap-us-supreme-court-ginsburg.html?ref=politics&_r=0&referrer

Baker, Peter, and Neil A. Lewis. 2009. "Republicans Press Judge About Bias and Activism." *New York Times* (July 15): A1.

Baker, Peter, and Jeff Zeleny. 2010. "Obama Picks Kagan as Justice Nominee." *New York Times* (May 9): A1.

Barnes, Robert. 2007. "Over Ginsburg's Dissent, Court Limits Bias Suits." *Washington Post* (May 30): A1.

Bazelon, Emily. 2009. "The Place of Women on the Court." *New York Times Magazine* (July 12): 22.

Behuniak-Long, Susan. 1992. "Justice Sandra Day O'Connor and the Power of Maternal Legal Thinking." *Review of Politics* 54(3): 417–44.

Bell, Lauren Cohen. 2002. "Senatorial Discourtesy: The Senate's Use of Delay to Shape the Federal Judiciary." *Political Research Quarterly* 55: 589–607.

Bianco, Marcie. 2014. "Sexist Critics Dismiss Justice Sotomayor's Impassioned Affirmative Action Dissent as 'Emotional.'" *Identities.Mic*, April 24. http://mic.com/articles/88297/sexist-critics-dismiss-justice-sotomayor-s-impassioned-affir mative-action-dissent-as-emotional

Binder, Sarah A., and Forrest Maltzman. 2009. *Advice and Dissent: The Struggle to Shape the Federal Judiciary.* Washington, DC: Brookings Institution.

Biskupic, Joan. 2014. *Breaking in: The Rise of Sonia Sotomayor and the Politics of Justice.* New York: Sarah Chricton Books.

Blackburn, Bradley. 2010. "Justices Ruth Bader Ginsburg and Sandra Day O'Connor on Life and the Supreme Court." abcnews.com. October 26. http://abcnews. go.com/WN/diane-sawyer-interviews-maria-shriver-sandra-day-o connor/story?id=11977195

Bowers, Jeremy, Adam Liptak, and Derek Willis. 2014. "Which Supreme Court Justices Vote Together Most and Least Often." *New York Times.* July 3. http://www.nytimes.com/interactive/2014/06/24/upshot/24up-scotus-agreement-rates.html?_r=0&abt=0002&abg=1

Boyd, Christina, Lee Epstein, and Andrew D. Martin. 2010. "Untangling the Causal Effects of Sex on Judging." *American Journal of Political Science* 54(2): 389–411.

Bratton, Kathleen A., and Rorie L. Spill. 2002. "Existing Diversity and Judicial Selection: The Role of the Appointment Method in Establishing Gender Diversity in State Supreme Courts." *Social Science Quarterly* 83(2): 504–19.

Brennan Center for Justice. 2014. "TV Ad Spending in Judicial Races Surpasses $9.1 Million." http://www.brennancenter.org/press-release/tv-ad-spending-ju dicial-elections-surpasses-91-million

Brust, Richard. 2008. "A Cowgirl Rides the Circuit." *ABA Journal* 94(4): 26–8.

Burwell v. Hobby Lobby. 2014. 573 U.S. 354 Dissent.

Campbell, Amy Leigh. 2002. "Raising the Bar: Ruth Bader Ginsburg and the ACLU Women's Rights Project." *Texas Journal of Women and the Law* 11(20): 157–244.

Cook, Beverly Blair. 1984. "Women on the State Bench: Correlates of Access." In *Political Women: Current Roles in State and Local Government*, edited by Janet A. Flammang, 191–218. Beverly Hills: Sage.

———. 1993. "Moral Authority and Gender Difference: Georgia Bullock and the Los Angeles Women's Court." *Judicature* 77(3): 144–55.

Crenshaw, Kimberlé. 1992. "Race, Gender, and Sexual Harassment." *Southern California Law Review* 65: 1467–76

———. 1998. "A Black Feminist Critique of Antidiscrimination Law and Politics." In *the Politics of Law*, rev. ed., edited by David Kaiyrs, 356–80. New York: Basic Books.

Davis, Sue. 1992–1993. "Do Women Speak in a Different Voice? Carol Gilligan, Feminist Legal Theory, and the Ninth Circuit." *Wisconsin Women's Law Journal* 81(1): 143–73.

———. 1993. "The Voice of Sandra Day O'Connor." *Judicature* 77(3): 134–39.

Davis, Sue, Susan Haire, and Donald R. Songer. 1993. "Voting Behavior and Gender on the United States Courts of Appeal." *Judicature* 77(3): 129–33.

Dillon, Sam. 2003. "First Woman Is Appointed as Dean of Harvard Law School." *New York Times*, April 4. http://www.nytimes.com/2003/04/04/us/first-wo man-is-appointed-as-dean-of-harvard-law.html

Egelko, Bob. 2012. "Jacqueline Nguyen Confirmed for 9th Circuit Court." *SF Gate*, May 8. http://www.sfgate.com/politics/article/Jacqueline-Nguyen-con firmed-for-9th-Circuit-court-3541241.php

Epstein, Lee, and Jeffrey A. Segal 2005. *Advice and Consent: The Politics of Judicial Appointments*. New York: Oxford University Press.

Equal Employment Opportunity Commission. n.d. "Facts about Pregnancy Discrimination." http://www.eeoc.gov/eeoc/publications/fs-preg.cfm

Federal Judicial Center. 2017. *Federal Judges Biographical Database*. www.fjc.gov/public/home.nsf/hisj

Fontana, David. 2014. "Sonia Sotomayor Is a National Treasure." *New Republic*, April 24. http://www.newrepublic.com/article/117501/sonia-sotomayor-sc huette-dissent-national-treasure

Frederick, Brian, and Matthew J. Streb. 2008. "Women Running for Judge: The Impact of Candidate Sex in State Intermediate Appellate Court Elections." *Social Science Quarterly* 89(4): 937–54.

George, Tracey E. and Albert H. Yoon. 2016. "The Gavel Gap? Who Sits in Judgment on State Courts?" http://gavelgap.org/pdf/gavel-gap-report.pdf. Accessed January 17, 2019.

Gilligan, Carol. 1982. *In a Different Voice: Psychological Theory and Women's Development*. Cambridge, MA: Harvard University Press.

Ginsburg, Ruth Bader. 1997. "Remarks on Women's Progress in the Legal Profession in the United States." *Tulsa Law Journal* 33: 13–21.

———. 2001. "The Supreme Court: A Place for Women." *Vital Speeches of the Day* 67(14): 420–25.

Ginsburg, Ruth Bader, and Laura W. Brill. 1995. "Address: Women in the Federal Judiciary: Three Way Pavers and the Exhilarating Change President Carter Wrought." *Fordham Law Review* 64: 281–90.

Goldman, Sheldon. 1997. *Picking Federal Judges: Lower Court Selection From Roosevelt Through Reagan*. New Haven: Yale University Press.

Goldman, Sheldon, Elliot Slotnick, Gerald Gryski, and Gary Zuk. 2001. "Clinton's Judges: Summing up the Legacy." *Judicature* 84(5): 220–54.

Goldstein, Amy, Carol D. Leonning, and Peter Slevin. 2010. "For Supreme Court Nominee Elena Kagan, a History of Pragmatism over Partisanship." *Washington Post*. May 11. http://www.washingtonpost.com/wp-dyn/content/artic le/2010/05/10/AR2010051002787.html?sid=ST2010080505264.

Green, Kathanne. 1994. "Torts Over Tempo: The Life and Career of Judge Burnita Shelton Matthews." *Journal of Mississippi History* 56(3): 181–210.

Greenburg, Jan Crawford. 2007. *Supreme Conflict: The Inside Story of the Struggle for Control of the United States Supreme Court*. New York: The Penguin Press.

Grossman, Joanna L., and Deborah L. Brake. 2015. "Forceps Delivery: The Supreme Court Narrowly Saves the Pregnancy Discrimination Act in *Young v. UPS*." *Verdict*. https://verdict.justia.com/2015/03/31/forceps-delivery-the-suprem e-court-narrowly-saves-the-pregnancy-discrimination-act-in-young-v-ups

Gruhl, John, Cassia Spohn, and Susan Welch. 1981. "Women as Policymakers: The Case of Trial Judges." *American Journal of Political Science* 25(2): 308–22.

Gryski, Gerald S., Eleanor C. Main, and William J. Dixon. 1986. "Models of State High Court Decision Making in Sex Discrimination Cases." *Journal of Politics* 48(1): 143–55.

Haire, Susan B., and Laura P. Moyer. 2015. *Diversity Matters: Judicial Policymaking in the U.S. Courts of Appeals*. Charlottesville: University of Virginia.

Hall, Melinda Gann. 2001. "State Supreme Courts in American Democracy: Probing the Myths of Judicial Reform." *American Political Science Review* 95: 315–30.

Hartley, Roger E. 2001. "A Look at Race, Gender, and Experience." *Judicature* 84(4): 191–97.

Hermann, Ria, and Rita Mae Kelly, with the assistance of Donna Langston and Julie Greenburg. 1988. "Women in the Judiciary." In *Women and the Arizona Political Process*, edited by Rita Mae Kelly, 84–108. Lanham, MD: University Press of America.

Hulse, Carl. 2010. "Senate Confirms Kagan in Partisan Vote." *The New York Times*, August 5. http://www.nytimes.com/2010/08/06/us/politics/06kagan.html

Hurwitz, Mark, and Drew Noble Lanier. 2001. "Women and Minorities on State and Federal Appellate Benches, 1985 and 1999." *Judicature* 85(2): 84–92.

———. 2003. "Explaining Judicial Diversity: The Differential Ability of Women and Minorities to Attain Seats on State Supreme and Appellate Courts." *State Politics & Policy Quarterly* 3(4): 329–52.

Kenney, Sally J. 2010. "Critical Perspectives on Gender and Judging." *Politics & Gender* 6: 433–95.

———. 2013. *Gender & Justice: Why Women in the Judiciary Really Matter*. New York: Routledge.

———. 2014. "Judicial Women." In *Women in Elective Office: Past, Present and Future*, 3rd ed., edited by Sue Thomas and Clyde Wilcox, 216–34. New York: Oxford University Press.

Kenney, Sally J., and Jason Windett. 2012. "Diffusion of Innovation or State Political Culture? Explaining the First Women State Supreme Court Justices." Paper prepared for 2012 State Politics and Policy Conference. http://2012sppconference. blogs.rice.edu/files/2012/02/Kenney_Windett_S PPC_Draft.pdf

Kirkpatrick, David D. 2009. "A Judge's Focus on Race Issues May Be Hurdle." *New York Times* (30 May): A1.

Kulik, Carol T., Elissa L. Perry, and Molly B. Pepper. 2003. "Here Comes the Judge: The Influence of Judge Personal Characteristics on Federal Sexual Harassment Case Outcomes." *Law and Human Behavior* 27(1): 69–86.

Lane, Charles. 2004. "Courting O'Connor: Why the Chief Justice Isn't the Chief Justice." *Washington Post Magazine* (July 4): W10.

Lawless, Jennifer L., and Richard L. Fox. 2005. *It Takes a Candidate: Why Women Don't Run for Office*. Cambridge: Cambridge University Press.

Liptak, Adam. 2015. "UPS Worker's Pregnancy Discrimination Suit Reinstated by Supreme Court." *New York Times*, March 25. http://www.nytimes.com/20 15/03/26/us/ups-workers-pregnancy-discrimination-suit-reinstated-by-supreme -court.html

Lithwick, Dahlia. 2014. "What We Talk About When We Talk About Talking About Race." April 24. http://www.slate.com/articles/news_and_politics/juris prudence/2014/04/race_and_the_supreme_court_what_the_schuette_decision _reveals_about_how.html

Lodge, Sally. 2009. "Q&A with Sandra Day O'Connor." *Publisher's Weekly*, May 28. www.publishersweekly.com/article/CA6660760.html

Lopez, German. 2018. "Why You Shouldn't Freak Out About the Masterpiece Cakeshop Ruling" *Vox*. June 4. https://www.vox.com/identities/2018/6/4/ 17425294/supreme-court-masterpiece-cakeshop-gay-wedding-cake-baker-rul ing. Accessed January 22, 2019.

Martin, Elaine. 1987. "Gender and the Judicial Selection: A Comparison of the Reagan and Carter Administrations." *Judicature* 71(3): 136–42.

———. 1993. "Women on the Bench: A Different Voice?" *Judicature* 77(3): 126–28.

Martin, Elaine, and Barry Pyle. 2000. "Gender, Race, and Partisanship on the Michigan Supreme Court." *Albany Law Review* 63: 1205–36.

———. 2002. "Gender and Racial Diversification of State Supreme Courts." *Women & Politics* 24(2): 35–52.

Maveety, Nancy. 1996. *Justice Sandra Day O'Connor: Strategist on the Supreme Court*. Lanham, MD: Rowman & Littlefield.

McCarthy, Megan. 2001. "Judicial Campaigns: What Can They Tell Us About Gender on the Bench?" *Wisconsin Women's Law Journal* 16: 87–112.

Mezey, Susan Gluck. 2000. "Gender and the Federal Judiciary." In *Gender and American Politics*, edited by Sue Tolleson-Rinehart and Jyl Josephson, 205–26. London: M.E. Sharpe.

Morrison, Linda. 2002. "The National Association of Women Judges: Agent of Change." *Wisconsin Women's Law Journal* 17: 291–93.

National Association of Women Judges. 2019. https://www.nawj.org/statistics/201 8-us-state-court-women-judges. Accessed January 17, 2019.

National Review. 2014. "Half a Win on Racial Discrimination." April 22. http:// www.nationalreview.com/article/376340/half-win-racial-discrimination-editors

National Women's Law Center. 2014. "Fact Sheet: *Burwell v. Hobby Lobby Stores, Inc. and Conestoga Wood Specialties v. Burwell*: Supreme Court Allows Some Closely Held Corporations to Use Religion to Undermine Women's Health and Equality." August.http://www.nwlc.org/sites/default/files/pdfs/hobby_lobby_s upreme_court_decision_factsheet.pdf.

The New York Times. 2018. "Senator Murkowski Voted Against Kavanaugh. Read Her Remarks Declaring Why." October 5. https://www.nytimes.com/2018/1 0/05/us/politics/lisa-murkowski-brett-kavanaugh-vote.html. Accessed January 16, 2019.

O'Connor, Karen. 1980. *Women's Organizations' Use of the Courts*. Lexington, MA: Lexington Books.

O'Connor, Karen, and Patricia Clark. 1999. "Women's Rights and Legal Wrongs: The United States Supreme Court and Sex Discrimination." In *Women in Politics: Outsiders or Insiders?* edited by Lois Duke Whitaker, 262–77. Upper Saddle River, NJ: Prentice Hall.

O'Connor, Karen, and John R. Hermann. 1995. "United States Supreme Court Law Clerk Participation before the Supreme Court." *Judicature* 78(5): 247–52.

O'Connor, Karen, and Barbara Palmer. 2001. "The Clinton Clones: Ginsburg, Breyer, and the Clinton Legacy." *Judicature* 84(5): 262–73.

O'Connor, Karen, and Alixandra Yanus. 2010. "Judging Alone: Reflections on the Importance of Women on the Court." *Politics & Gender* 6(3): 441–52.

O'Connor, Sandra Day. 2000. "Remarks Delivered by Sandra Day O'Connor." University of Pennsylvania School of Law. November 17. https://www.law .upenn.edu/alumni/alumnijournal/Spring2001/feature1/oconnorremarks.html.

Palmer, Barbara. 1991. "Feminist or Foe? Justice Sandra Day O'Connor, Title CVII Sex Discrimination, and Support for Women's Rights." *Women's Rights Law Reporter* 13(2 and 3): 159–70.

———. 2001. "Women in the American Judiciary." *Women & Politics* 23(3): 89–99.

———. 2002. "Justice Ruth Bader Ginsburg and the Supreme Court's Reaction to Its Second Member." *Women and Politics* 24(1): 1–23.

Parloff, Roger, 2007. "The War Over Unconscious Bias." *Fortune* 156(8): 90–102.

Peresie, Jennifer. 2005. "Female Judges Matter: Gender and Collegial Decision Mak-ing in the Federal Appellate Courts." *Yale Law Journal* 114: 1759–90.

Reddick, Malia, Michael J. Nelson, and Rachel Paine Caulfield. 2009. "Racial and Gender Diversity on State Courts." *The Judges' Journal* 48(3): Summer. American Bar Association. http://www.judicialselection.com/uploads/documents/ Racial_and_Gender_Diversity_on_Stat_8F60B84D96CC2.pdf

Reid, Traciel. 2010. "Women Candidates and Judicial Elections: Telling an Untold Story." *Women & Politics* 6(3): 465–74.

Roeder, Oliver. 2018. "Which Justices were BFFs This Supreme Court Term." *FiveThirtyEight.com*. June 27. https://fivethirtyeight.com/features/which-justices-were-bffs-this-scotus-term. Accessed January 22, 2019.

Ruckman Jr., P. S. 1993. "The Supreme Court Critical Nominations, and the Senate Confirmation Process." *Journal of Politics* 55: 793–805.

Savage, Charlie. 2009. "A Judge's View of Judging Is on the Record." *New York Times*. May 14.

Segal, Jennifer A. 2002. "Representative Decision Making on the Federal Bench: Clinton's District Court Appointees." *Political Research Quarterly* 53(137): 142–47.

Scherer, Nancy. 2005. *Scoring Points: Politicians, Activists, and the Lower Federal Court Appointment Process*. Stanford: Stanford University Press.

Schuette v. Coalition to Defend Affirmative Action, 134 S. Ct. 1623, 572 U.S., 188 L. Ed. 2d 613 (2014).

Schwartz, Hunter. 2015. "Ruth Bader Ginsburg Goes Full Notorious RBG." *Washington Post*. April 16. http://www.washingtonpost.com/blogs/the-fix/wp/2015/04/16/ruth-bader-ginsburg-goes-full-notorious-rbg/

Segal, Jennifer A. 2000. "Representative Decision Making on the Federal Bench: Clinton's District Court Appointees." *Political Research Quarterly* 53(1): 137–51.

Sherry, Suzanna. 1986. "Civic Virtue and the Feminine Voice in Constitutional Adjudication." *Virginia Law Review* 72: 543–615.

Solberg, Rorie L., and Kathleen A. Bratton. 2005. "Diversifying the Federal Bench: Presidential Patterns." *The Justice System Journal* 26(2): 119–33.

Soloweij, Lisa A., Wendy L. Martinek, and Thomas L. Brunell. 2005. "Partisan Politics: The Impact of Party in the Confirmation of Minority and Female Federal Court Nominees." *Party Politics* 11: 557–77.

Songer, Donald, Sue Davis, and Susan Haire. 1994. "A Reappraisal of Diversification in the Federal Courts: Gender Effects in the Courts of Appeals." *Journal of Politics* 56(2): 425–39.

Songer, Donald R., and Kelley A. Crews-Meyer. 2000. "Does Judge Gender Matter? Decision Making in State Supreme Courts." *Social Science Quarterly* 81(3): 750–62.

Spill, Rorie, and Kathleen A. Bratton. 2001. "Clinton and the Diversification of the Federal Judiciary." *Judicature* 84(5): 256–61.

Sullivan, Patricia A., and Steven R. Goldzwig. 1996. "Abortion and Undue Burdens: Justice Sandra Day O'Connor and Judicial Decision Making." *Women & Politics* 16(3): 27–54.

Swers, Michele L. 2013. *Women in the Club: Gender and Policy Making in the Senate*. Chicago: University of Chicago Press.

US Census Bureau. 2013. "How Do We Know: America's Changing Labor Force." https://www.census.gov/how/pdf/EEO_infographic.pdf

Walker, Thomas G., and Deborah J. Barrow. 1985. "The Diversification of the Federal Bench: Policy and Process Ramifications." *Journal of Politics* 47(2): 596–617.

The White House. 2016. "This is the First Time Our Judicial Pool has been this Diverse." June 8. https://obamawhitehouse.archives.gov/share/judicial-nominations. Accessed January 17, 2019.

Williams, Margaret. 2007. "Women's Representation on State Trial and Appellate Courts." *Social Science Quarterly* 88(5): 1192–1204.

———. 2008. "Ambition, Gender, and the Judiciary." *Political Research Quarterly* 61(1): 68–78.

Index

◆ ◆ ◆

Page references in italics refer to tables or illustrations.

355